Sand Rush

Sand Rush

The Revival of the Beach in Twentieth-Century Los Angeles

Elsa Devienne

Foreword by Jenny Price

Translated by Troy J. Tice

OXFORD

UNIVERSITY PRESS

OXFORD
UNIVERSITY PRESS

Oxford University Press is a department of the University of Oxford. It furthers the University's objective of excellence in research, scholarship, and education by publishing worldwide. Oxford is a registered trade mark of Oxford University Press in the UK and certain other countries.

Published in the United States of America by Oxford University Press
198 Madison Avenue, New York, NY 10016, United States of America.

This book is a translation of *La ruée vers le sable. Une histoire environnementale du littoral de Los Angeles au xxe siècle* © 2020, Éditions de la Sorbonne—Paris, France

English language edition © Oxford University Press 2024

This work received support for excellence in publication and translation from Albertine Translation, formerly French Voices, a program created by Villa Albertine.

Library of Congress Cataloging-in-Publication Data
Names: Devienne, Elsa, author.
Title: Sand Rush : The Revival of the Beach in Twentieth-Century
Los Angeles / Elsa Devienne ; foreword by Jenny Price ;
translated by Troy J. Tice. Other titles: Ruée vers le sable. English
Description: New York, NY : Oxford University Press, 2024. |
Translation and revision of: La ruée vers le sable : une histoire
environnementale des plages de Los Angeles (Sorbonne Editions, 2020). |
Includes bibliographical references and index. |
Identifiers: LCCN 2023053715 (print) | LCCN 2023053716 (ebook) |
ISBN 9780197539750 (hardback) | ISBN 9780197539774 (epub) | ISBN 9780197539781
Subjects: LCSH: Bathing beaches—Government policy—California—
Los Angeles—History—20th century. | Bathing beaches—Environmental
aspects—California—Los Angeles—History—20th century. |
Urban renewal—California—Los Angeles—History—20th century. |
City planning—California—Los Angeles—History—20th century. |
Los Angeles (Calif.)—Social life and customs—20th century. |
Los Angeles (Calif.)—History—20th century.
Classification: LCC F869.L857 D4813 2024 (print) | LCC F869.L857 (ebook)|
DDC 979.4/9405—dc23/eng/20231229
LC record available at https://lccn.loc.gov/2023053715LC ebook
record available at https://lccn.loc.gov/2023053716

DOI: 10.1093/oso/9780197539750.001.0001

Printed by Sheridan Books, Inc., United States of America

CONTENTS

FOREWORD

JENNY PRICE

Imagine you've set your towel down on a Santa Monica beach—a vast, five-hundred-foot-wide stretch of public sand that's a famously scenic natural spot—and Elsa Devienne hands you a viewfinder, with a slide of what it looked like almost one hundred years ago. The beach isn't vast— it's seventy-five to one hundred feet wide—and it's not public, and you're soaking up the rays in filthy water, and you can see the Venice oil derricks. A viewfinder for two hundred years ago? It's maybe a hundred feet wide, and you might be tanning on dunes or in a marsh, and there might be cattle. Three hundred years? The Gabrielino-Tongva used the coast very irregularly, but you might see grizzly bears.

There's little that's "natural" about the Los Angeles coast in 2023. As Devienne tells us, the LA region cleaned up and expanded these beaches from the 1930s to the 1960s. They remade the coastal environments. That's how you build a city, right? You have to remake your environments. Hugely—and the essential question isn't whether. It's *how*. And, as Devienne shows so vividly, as we remake nature, we remake ourselves.

That's what *Sand Rush* is about. Devienne recounts how Angelenos constantly remade Los Angeles—and its force-field influence nationally on the economy, mass leisure, and American ideals about beauty, bodies, youth, and the good life— by remaking one of LA's definitive natural features. She reminds us that the beach, like all "natural" places, has a history. Some of it is quite laudable, and some of it is wildly regrettable—or worse—but all of it is highly consequential. We forget it at our peril. It's complicated. We need viewfinders.

This story isn't *Gidget*, but it's not all *Chinatown* either. As a veteran myself of the endless battles in Malibu for public beach access, I confess that I began *Sand Rush* with an orca-size chip on my shoulder. And yes, as powerful Angelenos remade the coast, they banned African Americans and wiped out a gay district—often in the service of white middle-class ideals. And yes, wealthy beachfront homeowners in Malibu still deploy security guards and illegal signage to chase the "hordes" off public sands. And yet . . . since the 1940s, public entities in the LA region have bought up 60 percent of the coast, and the 1976 California Coastal Act protects both the coast itself and the right of public access—with a powerful legal framework that no other state possesses. In *Los Angeles*—a city that historians (and seemingly everyone else) have bashed for remaking nature badly, and for worshiping private property—the stunning seventy-five-mile public coast is largely accessible to all.

It's not the Beach Boys, but it's not *Blade Runner*. And it's all here—real-estate shenanigans, municipal boosters, Muscle Beach, Hollywood, class conflict, body cults, oil company lobbies, gendered notions of beauty, eminent domain and gentrification, gay culture, expulsion of communities of color, the Disneyland connection.

The climate crisis looms large, as does the strange gravitational pull that LA has exerted on the rest of the country and around the globe.

It's not sunshine, but it's not noir. It is, however, a great read.

Go to the beach. Set down a towel. Enjoy the scenery.

Open this book.

ACKNOWLEDGMENTS

When I tell people I wrote a book about LA and its beaches, they always joke that I must have spent a lot of time lying on a towel by the ocean. That's not how history works, which is probably all for the best considering I'm one of those people whose skin turns red at the first sign of sunshine. Writing *Sand Rush* meant spending a lot of time indoors in the archives and at my desk, but it would have never seen the light of day were it not for the many friends, relatives, colleagues, mentors, archivists, and beach lovers who helped me along the way. It is a great pleasure to thank them all here. I also benefited enormously from receiving a living wage throughout my PhD and later becoming a permanent member of the faculty at Université Paris Nanterre and Northumbria University. As academic jobs become rarer, more precarious, and less well-paid, the type of slow science that enabled the making of this book is at risk. I am grateful for the opportunities that made writing *Sand Rush* possible, and I will advocate for future scholars so that they receive the same support.

This book started as a French dissertation, which I defended at the Ecole des Hautes Etudes en Sciences Sociales. I am grateful to my PhD adviser, François Weil, who was the first to believe in this strange little project, thereby legitimizing it to others, but most importantly to myself. The Centre d'Etudes Nord-Américaines (CENA) made me the historian I am today. For our lively exchanges in the small seminar room on Boulevard Raspail, I am grateful to Virginie Adane, Camille Amat, Nicolas Barreyre, Sonia Birocheau, Alexia Blin, Thomas Grillot, Simon Grivet, Romain Huret, Peter Marquis, Nicolas Martin-Breteau, Pap Ndiaye, Emmanuelle Perez-Tisserant, Paul Schor, and Cécile Vidal. Manuel Covo deserves special mention for being the one who was always a step ahead of me. My colleagues at Université Paris Nanterre provided advice and support as I worked on the dissertation and, later, on the book. I want to thank Laurence Gervais, Caroline Rolland-Diamond, and Michaël Roy in particular. *Sand Rush* also benefited from the insights of the French community of environmental historians, which, just as I was writing my dissertation, was taking shape under the helm of le RUCHE, le Réseau universitaire de chercheurs en histoire environnementale. I would like to thank Geneviève Massard-Guilbaud for commenting on early versions of the book and for modeling the kind of generous, uncompromising, and deeply innovative scholar I hope one day to be. My thanks also go to Stéphane Frioux, Patrick Fournier, Charles-François Mathis, and all the members of RUCHE, with whom I have enjoyed working over the last decade to develop and promote environmental history in France and beyond.

This book owes a great deal to the American scholars who took the time to exchange ideas with me and comment on conference papers and early drafts. The team at the Princeton-Mellon Initiative in Architecture, Urbanism, and the Humanities deserves a special mention for opening me up to other ways of thinking and doing urban history, and for giving me so many opportunities. I would like to thank Aaron Shkuda and Alison Isenberg in particular. Steven Aron, Eric Avila, Lawrence Culver, Ronald Davidson, Sarah Elkind, Sara Fingal, Mike Fowley, Joseph Heathcott, Andrew W. Kahrl, Ayala Levin, Sarah Lopez, Mark Fathi Massoud, Adam Rome, Andrew Sandoval-Strausz, Perry Sherouse, and Arthur Verge have also enriched this book with their remarks and comments. Thomas Sugrue, the most Francophile of all American historians, played a key role in bringing this book to fruition, first as a member of my dissertation committee and, in the following years, as a great supporter of my work. *Merci beaucoup*, Tom!

I am infinitely grateful to Nasia Anam, who put me up so many times in her Orange Street apartment and let me borrow her car on several occasions, which, in Los Angeles, is not the least of favors. Annabelle Cone and Thea Sircar sent me dozens of articles and primary sources that they kindly downloaded or scanned from the United States, also making a crucial contribution to this book. Alexandre Pires, whom I met toward the end of this journey, deserves special recognition as well for taking a day out of his graduate research to look for a single (but well-hidden!) document at the Los Angeles City Archives, which I needed in a higher resolution for the publication. His enthusiasm for the study of Los Angeles was an important reminder of where it had all started. Many other Los Angeles friends looked after me and kept my spirits up while I was trying to make sense of this research. For continuing to make LA feel like home to me, thank you to Citlali Sosa-Riddell (and Jorge), Tri Tran, Mark Schulte, and Laurie Groh.

Because there is no such thing as a beach archive, finding traces of the past that involved historical actors as diverse as surfers, engineers, urban planners, beatniks, and bathing beauties involved the help of many archivists and librarians. I'd like to thank Michael Holland and Todd Gaydowski at the Los Angeles City Archives, Susan Lamb at the Santa Monica Public Library, Dace Taube at the University of Southern California, the staff at the Water Resources Collections & Archives, and the Santa Monica History Museum. I also would like to thank the beachgoers who shared their memories of afternoons spent on the sands: Clara Byrd, Michael Connelly, Steve Ford, Skip Gillett, Margo Jim, Merritt Johnson, Seymour Koenig, Ken Nagy, Sandra Odor, Jeanette Salter, Bruce Saylors, Lois Warner, and Ann Winfield. Merry Ovnick not only agreed to give me an interview, believing in the project from the moment we met, but also expertly shepherded an article I submitted on the history of Muscle Beach to *Southern California Quarterly* from submission to publication (and even helping me win my first award in the process!).

Sand Rush is the fruit of many years of research, writing, revising, translating, rewriting, and re-revising. I could not have completed it without the financial support of the institutions I wish to thank here (by order of appearance in my life): the doctoral school of EHESS, la Commission Franco-Américaine, the American Society for Environmental History, the European Society for Environmental History, the Southern California Historical Society, the Haynes Foundation, the CREA of Université Paris Nanterre, the Princeton-Mellon Initiative in Architecture, Urbanism, and the Humanities, and Northumbria University.

This book was first published in French under the title *La ruée vers le sable: Une histoire environnementale des plages de Los Angeles au XXe siècle* by the Éditions de la Sorbonne. I want to thank the staff at the Éditions de la Sorbonne, where my book was given full attention. Audrey Orillard, a dear friend of mine, was the best editor I could have hoped for. My gratitude goes out to the institutions that funded the translation into English: the Organization of American Historians (which awarded *La ruée vers le sable* the 2021 Willi Paul Adams Award), l'Association Française d'Etudes Américaines et la Société des Anglicistes de l'Enseignement supérieur (which granted *La ruée vers le sable* a finalist position in their 2021 joint book prize), the FACE Foundation and the French embassy in the United States (for the 2020 French Voices Award, which represented a critical financial contribution to the translation), the Department of Humanities at Northumbria University, and the Historical Society of Southern California and the Ahmanson Foundation (which awarded the project a joint publication grant in 2019). The book would not exist if it weren't for Troy Tice, who did a fantastic job on the translation of six out of my seven chapters and caught more than one mistake that I had left in the French version. I ended up completely rewriting entire parts of those chapters as they did not fit with what I had in mind for the US version. While the final product may look different from what he originally delivered, his translation represented a key step in the process toward making *Sand Rush* a reality.

As *La ruée vers le sable* made its way into the world, it found incredible champions in the United States who encouraged me to work toward its publication in English. The community of coastal historians gave the French book a warm welcome, with Isaac Land being no doubt its greatest cheerleader; he was not only the first American historian to review *La ruée vers le sable* for an English-speaking audience but he also sent me lengthy comments and asked me tough questions, which pushed my thinking further and ensured that *Sand Rush* would not just be a translated version of the French book, but a bolder, more ambitious intervention in the scholarship. I would like to thank Laura Portwood-Stacer, whose blog posts and advice on the book proposal helped me land a contract with my dream press. As I was revising the book into English, Sarah Shrank and Josh Sides made important comments and suggestions. The epilogue, which is an original addition to the English version, was written with both of them in mind. Glenna Matthews is another Francophile historian who cheered me on as I finished the revisions of *Sand Rush*. I am deeply grateful for her support. I would also like to thank Michael Adamson, Olivier Burtin, and Natalia Mehlman Petrzela who read early drafts of the project, in one form or another, and gave me supportive feedback. Jenny Price has been an inspiration, as a scholar, a writer, and an activist, ever since I went on one of her famous LA River tours. I am so thankful that she accepted to write this witty and perceptive foreword.

Susan Ferber was a superb editor of the English version of *Sand Rush*, and I am so grateful that someone of her stature and expertise saw potential in my book. She made it immeasurably better, sharper, and more pleasant to read. A few weeks after receiving my book contract from Susan, the world shut down as the COVID-19 pandemic unfolded. We lost all access to childcare for over six months. A year later, I gave birth to my second son. Throughout it all, my colleagues at Northumbria University supported this project, challenged my thinking, and never once doubted that spending time essentially rewriting my first book was worth it. I have been incredibly lucky to end up among such an incredible group of smart, interesting, and kind colleagues. I am especially grateful to Patrick Andelic, Matthew Kelly, Daniel Laqua, Joe Street, Brian Ward, and Rebecca Wright for their support.

Finally, I would like to thank my friends and family who have nurtured and sustained me in various ways as I wrote (and rewrote) this book, moved back and forth between France and the United States, and eventually settled, by a strange twist of fate, in England. Julie Deloupy, Olivia Devienne, Andrew Diamond, Augustin Jomier, and Léa-Catherine Szacka deserve special mention. So does Clémence Devienne, my sister, who designed all the maps in the book. And of course, I owe everything to my parents, Annie and Luc Devienne. As a parent myself, I am only too painfully aware of all that they have done to encourage my interests and support my life choices. A *merci* seems too little, but it is keenly felt. To Rob, my partner, thank you for crossing my path on that fateful night in Paris! You, more than any other person, made writing *Sand Rush* possible. I dedicate this book to our children, Aurel and Remi, and to their generation. May their children, and their children's children, know the simple joy of building sandcastles on the beach.

Sand Rush

The Greater Los Angeles region in 1925. © Clémence Devienne

BEACHES IN THE LOS ANGELES AREA (Late 1960s)

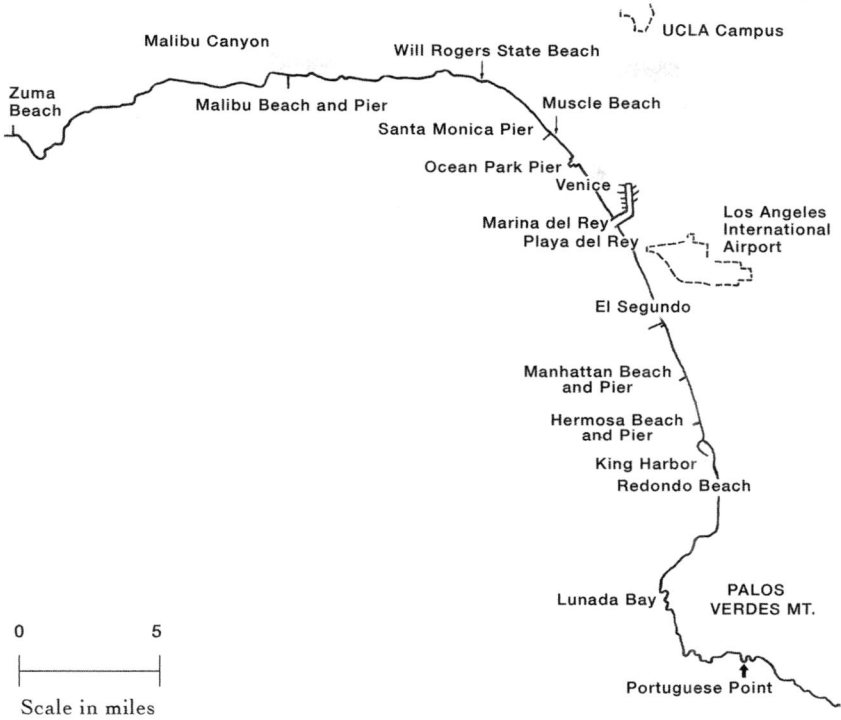

Malibu Canyon

Will Rogers State Beach

UCLA Campus

Zuma Beach

Malibu Beach and Pier

Muscle Beach

Santa Monica Pier

Ocean Park Pier

Venice

Marina del Rey

Playa del Rey

Los Angeles International Airport

El Segundo

Manhattan Beach and Pier

Hermosa Beach and Pier

King Harbor

Redondo Beach

Lunada Bay

PALOS VERDES MT.

Portuguese Point

0   5

Scale in miles

Beaches of the Los Angeles area in the late 1960s. Adapted from Reyner Banham, *Los Angeles and the Architecture of Four Ecologies* (Berkeley: University of California Press, 2001). © Clémence Devienne

Introduction

"The Greatest City-on-the-Shore in the World"

The Los Angeles shoreline is one of the most iconic landscapes in the United States, if not the world. Despite news stories about epic traffic on beach-bound freeways, sewage pollution, smelly bathrooms, and conflicts between the public and privacy-obsessed coastal homeowners, the Los Angeles beaches have had far-reaching influence not just on the city but also on the metropolitan area's international prestige, economic vitality, and quality of life.

Featured in countless movies and TV shows—from Charlie Chaplin's *The Circus*, filmed in early twentieth-century Venice, to the immensely successful 1990s *Baywatch* TV series, aired in over 145 countries—Los Angeles beaches are familiar sights to audiences worldwide. Their pristine sand, carefree fun, and glamorous bodies have influenced the ways in which people globally enjoy the sea and shore. From Malibu's blonde and bronzed-skin surfers to the well-oiled Venice Muscle Beach bodybuilders, the city has been fertile ground for popular fashion trends and body cultures. Since the promotion of the region as a paradise in the early twentieth century, but especially since the postwar period—when the Beach Boys made Southern California synonymous with the beach and surf lifestyle—the region has stood as a powerful reference in seaside imaginaries. For anyone who sets foot on the sand, from Cannes to Sydney, Durban to Rio, Southern California beach culture looms large.

As urban public parks, the beaches are impressive both in quantity and scale. The seventy-five-mile Los Angeles County coastline represents almost twice the area of New York's Central Park; 60 percent is in public hands (compared to as little as 7 percent in some eastern states). Over fifty million people visit the beach each year.[1] While Los Angeles is often portrayed, in popular culture and scholarship alike, as an antidemocratic city characterized by "spatial apartheid" between the rich and the poor, it is also home to this vast public space, free and open to all.[2] Some beaches, either because they are private or de facto inaccessible due to lack of parking and public transport options, remain off limits to ordinary Angelenos. There is also a long history of segregation and racial exclusion at the beach, which continues to affect who feels welcome on the sands. Nonetheless, vast swathes of the coastline are prized public playgrounds for locals and tourists alike. Since the Expo Line subway extension connected the ocean to Downtown in 2016, it has become easier for Angelenos and visitors without cars to spend an afternoon at the beach. Far from being reserved for an elite, the beaches are accessible to most residents in the metropolitan region.

But the beaches are not just a place where Angelenos come for leisure. The coastline has played a major role in the region's economy in the twentieth century. Many businesses have opened up on or near the sands, notably 1950s surfboard-makers that set up shops in dusty Malibu garages. More recently, Snapchat and Google's headquarters in Venice have sped up the conversion of the legendary bohemian hangout into the epicenter of "Silicon Beach," Silicon Valley's latest rival in startup density.

On a par with the national parks of the West, the beaches of Los Angeles are considered among the country's premier tourist destinations. In the early twentieth century, wealthy businessmen looking to profit from new ventures opened up beach resorts along the coastline, luring millions of visitors to the ocean with surfing exhibitions and Coney Island–style attractions. Today, the coastline is the second most popular tourist destination in Southern California, just behind Disneyland.[3] Tourists from around the world rent pricey Airbnb apartments in the trendy parts of Venice and Santa Monica to temporarily enjoy life as a Westside Angeleno/a. This recent development explains why coastal neighborhoods are among the most expensive parts of the metropolis, with some areas even outpricing Beverly Hills.[4]

The popularity of LA's coastal neighborhoods is, in part, related to the recent interest in waterfront urban areas, which has transformed riverine and coastal cities worldwide and reenergized many derelict industrial districts. But Los Angeles's coastal appeal is the product of a much longer history. In the postwar period, an ambitious beach planning and development program established the city as a leading national model. Since 1972, the California Coastal Commission—the state agency in charge of regulating new construction and guaranteeing coastal access to the public—has kept a watchful eye on this cherished natural amenity. Despite recurrent budget cuts, constant litigation from wealthy homeowners and determined developers, and many lost battles, the commission, with the help of staunch beach activists, has protected and opened to the public miles of coastline that would otherwise have been lost to development or privatized.

Far from being a marginal location, the coastline is one of the major demographic, cultural, and economic nerve centers of the Los Angeles metropolitan region. It is even tempting to claim, as did British architectural historian Reyner Banham, that Los Angeles is "the greatest City-on-the-Shore in the world."[5]

Yet it was not always the case. As of the late 1920s, such a declaration would have seemed implausible to many observers. At that time, the beaches of Los Angeles were dirty, crowded, and eroded. Pollution from untreated sewage, industrial effluents, and oil extraction was a critical issue. Most of the coastline was private and inaccessible to the public. Erosion was so severe that some of the metropolitan region's famous beaches were on the verge of disappearing altogether. To make matters worse, the turn-of-the-century beach amusement parks that had once enthralled the public no longer appealed to the middle class that deemed them "cheap," "artificial," and "vulgar." This was hardly a phenomenon unique to LA. East Coast and midwestern lake beaches that had once attracted teeming crowds were also marked by deteriorating amusements and ravaged shores. In other words, in the early 1920s, urban beaches across America were experiencing some sort of a crisis.

Beginning in the 1920s, and reaching a peak in the postwar years, reinventing the beach for the metropolitan age became the obsession of a group of engineers, urban planners, businesspeople, politicians, and city leaders. The search for the ideal "modern beach" was a nationwide trend. The American Shore and Beach Preservation Association, one of the main vehicles for this mission, was founded in 1926 under the aegis of New Jersey officials. But, this book shows, these efforts were particularly dynamic in Los Angeles. There, the sad states of the shores unleashed a "sand rush" of sorts, that of self-appointed "beach experts" who saw the city's fate as tied to its coastline and set out to remake the region's beaches using modern planning and engineering methods. By the 1930s, what I call the "LA beach lobby" had coalesced around civic organizations such as the

California Beaches Association and the Shoreline Planning Association and involved prominent figures such as Berkeley engineer Morrough P. O'Brien and Los Angeles's superintendent of recreation George Hjelte. While LA beach enthusiasts first looked east for inspiration, they came up with their own innovative solutions to coastal issues in the late 1930s and 1940s. In the years following the Second World War, just as California was entering an unprecedented decade of rapid demographic and economic growth, the LA metropolitan region established itself as a national leader in beach planning, development, and preservation. Coastal engineers, together with business and city leaders, accomplished the remarkable feat of enlarging the beaches—up to four times their original size—by adding large quantities of sand. Within the span of a few years, a new coastal landscape sprang up: beautiful and vast sandy beaches, complete with large parking lots, sparkling-clean toilet facilities, and nearby freeways.

The modernization campaign's most cherished, if little known, legacy is the fact that it opened up vast public spaces for Angelenos to express themselves and show off their bodies. Thanks to a one-hundred-million-dollar state budget surplus, the list of public beaches grew exponentially in the immediate postwar period. Once widened and cleaned up, the shores became the training ground and exhibition stage for original beach cultures, from the surfing boom to the bodybuilding phenomenon. The "modernized" shores of Los Angeles soon became home to "modern bodies": slim, muscular, and tanned. This ideal spread far beyond the sandy shores through newspapers, radio, films, magazines, and word of mouth. In this sense, the beaches of Los Angeles—as places where these bodies were displayed and admired—played a fundamental role in creating and spreading contemporary standards of Western beauty.

By pushing for more public beaches, the LA beach lobby opened up large stretches of sand to Angelenos, but its members had a rather narrow understanding of the "public." Using the model of suburban shopping malls and theme parks, the lobby remade the beaches following the needs and desires of the white, middle-class nuclear family. By adapting the beach experience to the suburban age, they effectively prevented a much-feared white flight from the coast. These transformations adversely affected certain groups of beachgoers, including African Americans, gay men and women, and bodybuilders, whose presence on the sand did not fit what the beach lobby had in mind for the shores. The destruction or displacement of these often-overlooked beach communities speaks to the exclusionary tendencies of modernization impulses.

Sand Rush recounts the origins, consequences, and legacies of the formidable campaign that transformed Los Angeles into one of the world's greatest coastal metropolises, revealing how the city's man-made shores served as a central locus for the reinvention of seaside leisure and the triumph of modern bodies. It tells the story of a place—the coastline—and how local elites and ordinary city-dwellers fought over its meaning, uses, and role in their lives and in the urban fabric writ large. Inspired by Roy Rosenzweig and Elizabeth Blackmar's study of New York City's Central Park, it describes the beaches as a "social institution and space," conceptualizes them as an essential "aspect of the city," and centers the experiences of the people who used them on a daily basis.[6] It foregrounds the ways in which today's beaches are the product of dynamic interactions between humans and coastal ecologies. Most Angelenos are unaware of how their shores went from narrow slivers of sand, often closed to visitors and soiled by pollution, to the vast public beaches they can now enjoy without worrying about getting tar on their feet. Collective amnesia about the major transformations of the city's waterfront has obscured the ways in which beaches were both distinct ecologies characterized by constant movement and urban infrastructures that have relied on regular maintenance. In bringing this history to light, *Sand Rush* seeks to rescue our contemporary shorelines from oblivion. At a time when the climate crisis and rising sea levels threaten to obliterate these landscapes, understanding local ecological conditions and their histories can better help us plan for their future.

The following pages retrace the origins of the modern Los Angeles coastal landscape. By remaking coastal ecologies to suit their aspirations and needs, Angelenos also reshaped their city, and themselves, with farreaching consequences. What impulses were behind the transformation of the LA coastline in the twentieth century? What were the ecological, social, and cultural repercussions of these repeated interventions on the environment? How did Angelenos share and compete over this coveted space? Finally, how did the reinvention of the beach experience in postwar Southern California influence the nation and beyond? These questions lie at the heart of the book.

The phrase "Los Angeles's beaches" is used throughout as a shorthand to designate the seventy-five-mile Los Angeles County shoreline, from Point Mugu in Malibu in the north to the Palos Verdes peninsula in the south. This generic label simplifies a complex patchwork of political systems and shoreline ownership, with some beaches being part of independent cities (including Santa Monica, Redondo Beach, Manhattan Beach, and Palos Verdes), others part of unincorporated Los Angeles County (such as the Malibu shoreline before the city's incorporation in 1991), and a few located in the city of Los Angeles (Will Rogers, Venice, Playa Del Rey, Dockweiler, and Cabrillo).[7] The LA shoreline may be divided among countless stakeholders (including private owners who, in California, can claim ownership of the beach up until the mean high tide line), it nonetheless represents a single "littoral cell" from an ecological point of view. Conceptualized by scientists in the 1970s, a littoral cell designates a stretch of coast, often separated by two rocky headlands, that has the same supply of sand, littoral drift (how sand is transported), and sink of sediment (where the sand eventually flows).[8] The Santa Monica littoral cell, which stretches along the Santa Monica Bay from Malibu to Palos Verdes, happens to roughly correspond to the administrative boundaries of the county coastline and to the lived reality of metropolitan Angelenos. As a self-contained ecological system—with sand coming from the Los Angeles River, a southeastern littoral drift, and most of the sand lost offshore through the Redondo Submarine Canyon—the Santa Monica littoral cell provides an ideal vantage point from which to observe the transformations of a coastal landscape over a long period of time. Any change occurring at one point in the cell systematically affects the rest of the system.[9] By focusing on this space, with occasional forays outside of it to place the story in a broader regional or national context, this book reinforces the fact that environmental phenomena ignore human-made borders. At the same time, the Santa Monica littoral cell conveniently corresponds to what local residents identify intuitively as the coastline of Los Angeles and encompasses many of the famous beaches that have contributed to the region's reputation.

Chapters chronologically narrate the story of Los Angeles's beaches from the 1900s, when their development became a source of preoccupation for local elites, into the twenty-first century. As with any case study, this story is far from typical. *Sand Rush* highlights the idiosyncratic circumstances—including the city's belated coastal development, the influence of Hollywood, the dynamic postwar economy—that allowed the LA "beachscape" to stand out by mid-century. At the same time, Los Angeles, set against other seaside cities, allows for larger conclusions to be drawn about humans' changing relationship with leisure and nature in an urban context. As such, this book makes a contribution to the history of seaside leisure and mass recreation, urban history, California history, and environmental history.

What the beach lobby intended to accomplish on the eroded and sullied shores of LA was nothing less than reinventing the beach for the twentieth century. Seaside resorts date back to late eighteenth-century England, when aristocrats, often on doctor's orders, took to bathing in the cold ocean water. According to historian Alain Corbin, the "lure of the sea" soon proved indomitable.[10] Bathing machines (four-wheeled carriages used as dressing rooms that also brought bathers directly into the water) and bathing houses along northern European shores signaled that the sea and its adjoining territory were no longer regarded as frightening, chaotic places, where biblical monsters, foreign invasions, and winter storms lurked beneath the surface. Instead, they became spaces where contact with nature invigorated the body and spirits. By the middle of the nineteenth century, sea bathing had grown so popular that new beach resorts popped up all over Europe and on the East Coast of the United States. New waves of sea enthusiasts abandoned the old-fashioned bathing machines and embraced new built features and sensory pleasures that centered on the sandy part of the shoreline.[11] In the early twentieth century, Mediterranean beach resorts, with their promenades, piers, and grand hotels, perfected seaside urbanism and helped create a landscape of coastal chic across the industrialized world.[12] Meanwhile, the first beach amusement parks at Coney Island, Atlantic City, and Blackpool lured "playful crowds" to the shores.[13]

Inspired by the splendors of the Mediterranean Riviera and the popularity of Luna Park and Dreamland—the famous Coney Island amusement parks—LA businessmen developed Santa Monica, Venice, Ocean Park, Redondo Beach, and many other resorts. Yet, by the late 1920s, the appeal of these earlier models had somewhat faded, and new problems—erosion chief among them—challenged coastal communities. What happened afterward, and how such challenges were addressed, remains underexplored.[14]

The lack of attention to modern shorelines reflects the terrestrial bias long dominant in environmental history. Environmental histories in the 1990s and early 2000s largely focused their attention on farmlands, forests, parks, and "other places 'out there.'" In the 2000s, the rise of maritime and oceanic history brought attention to liquid spaces.[15] Yet coastal environments—existing in a liminal space between maritime and terrestrial—have too often fallen between the cracks. In the late twentieth century, the explosion of beach tourism and the advent of global container shipping radically transformed not only coastlines but also how they were perceived. In an essay on the promises of "coastal history," a term he coined to identify the unique challenges and opportunities found at the intersection of land and sea, Isaac Land notes that nostalgia too often dominates writings on modern coastlines. John Gillis's lamentation in his *Human Shore* for the shores "coloniz[ed]" by tourism and recreational activities in the twentieth century is representative of this trend. "The coast," he wrote, "has become a place with no memory of itself."[16] The tendency to perceive the recent coastal past as "ruined" and "inauthentic" also has a gendered component. The shorelines of the deeper past, associated with work and production, were peopled with fishermen and sailors. By contrast, the beaches of today—devoted to consumption, indolence, and sensual pleasures—are spaces more likely to be populated by bathing beauties than burly maritime workers. Soiled by these associations with feminine elements and values, our coastal present has long been neglected.

Complementing recent work on race and beaches and conflicts between tourism, fisheries, and industry that played out on the California shores, this book makes the case that Los Angeles was central to the reinvention of the modern beach experience and, more broadly, to mass leisure.[17] The beach lobby's efforts to "save" the beaches from decline combined with ordinary Angelenos' enthusiasm for the beach lifestyle, the influence of Hawaii, and the proximity of the movie industry and its legions of Hollywood hopefuls produced a distinct seaside model. By the 1960s, it had become a global reference for urbanism, engineering, design, visual culture, and body aesthetics. The Southern California "beachscape"—understood as the combination of unique geographical features and a powerful cultural imaginary—had set a new standard for beachgoing. The Southern California beach—with its wide and sandy strands; its somewhat exotic, yet domesticated, charm; and its population of lithe, suntanned beach bums—created a potent ideal, synthesizing previous models into a unique combination. Other seaside models have persisted or emerged since—the Mediterranean resorts, the Carioca beach culture, and the Australian beach lifestyle being the most prominent—but the Southern California shores have remained the embodiment of the ideal modern beach in the twentieth century, influencing leisure spaces in other settings and setting the bar for what a beautiful body should look like, both on and off the sand.[18]

Southern California looms large in understanding American leisure. The 1955 opening of Disneyland in Anaheim is frequently seen as the turning point that ended the era of public amusements, where heterogeneous urban crowds mixed (albeit with African Americans usually banned from the premises), and opened the way for a new model of segregated, privatized leisure.[19] Yet this narrative obscures the persistent popularity of a concurrent model of mass leisure, predicated on public access and crowd mixing. Just as Walt Disney was opening up the gates of his theme park, the public beaches of Los Angeles benefited from massive investments and were attracting more visitors than ever. They brought together amateur surfers, families, sunbathers, athletes, swimmers, and onlookers from far and wide. They symbolized a modern way of life centered on outdoor exercise, youth, and Hollywood glamour.[20] This book clarifies the relationship between these two leisure spaces by showing how Disneyland served as an important, if unacknowledged, model for the remaking of the Southern California beaches in the postwar period. It also highlights how simple replication was impossible and how the beaches, despite persistent patterns of racial and class segregation and exclusion, offered opportunities for truly democratic forms of leisure.

The persistent popularity of the LA beaches challenges the dominant narrative of urban recreation in the twentieth century. According to this narrative, turn-of-the-century amusement parks, beaches, ballparks, movie palaces, and swimming pools were extremely popular with working-class and middle-class city-dwellers.[21] By the 1920s, they had lost some of their novelty but still attracted large crowds. In the years following the Second World War, the first signs of decline began to emerge. Bankruptcies and fires soon followed. By the 1960s, urban public amusements "had vanished forever."[22] According to this "rise and fall" narrative, a combination of factors, including racial riots, white flight, and the inability to compete with suburban recreational offerings, was responsible for this decline. More recently, the fall has been blamed on racist violence perpetrated by whites who denied African Americans their right to occupy urban space. Moreover, historians insist, the early years of urban amusements were fundamentally based on the exclusion of racial others.[23] Yet the narrative's main conclusion—the "fall" of urban recreational spaces and their replacement by suburban recreation—has remained unquestioned.

While *Sand Rush* does not contend that a decline never took place, it argues that this was neither all-encompassing nor definite. The history of the Los Angeles beaches shows that throughout the twentieth century, despite racial tensions and occasional racial violence, the city's beaches remained attractive both to whites and nonwhites, the working class, and the middle and upper classes. More significantly, they remained associated with modernity, both as an essential element of a sought-after Southern California lifestyle and as an iconic urban landscape emulated around the globe. The long-standing popularity of the LA beaches was predicated on the success of the beach modernization movement, a system of racial relations that kept confrontations far from the sands, and their role as key public spaces where the new social, sexual, and bodily norms of the postwar era were produced and displayed.

The beach modernization movement was not an isolated effort to spruce up the city's coastline but an essential yet forgotten aspect of the massive efforts to modernize American cities in the aftermath of the Second World War. Postwar urban planners and business interests across the nation were extremely interested in and concerned about the future of urban beaches. Nowhere was the threat of a disorderly urban life more alarming than on the sand, where strangers from all walks of life, from different classes and races, undressed themselves and played in close proximity to each other. Complementing work on urban renewal and the remaking of postwar urban America, with its largely East Coast bias, *Sand Rush* shifts the focus away from the central city to shed light on the transformation of the coastal environment and the erasure of alternative communities in Los Angeles.[24] While inspired by the towering park builder Robert Moses's creations on the East Coast, the Los Angeles beach lobby eventually took the national leadership in setting the standards for the modern beach experience. Looking at urban renewal from the perspective of the coastline highlights the mobilization of the entire urban "metabolism" to revive declining cities and rearrange their spatial organization according to racial and ethnic hierarchies.

Centering on the city's largest public space necessarily offers a fresh perspective on Los Angeles, a city usually associated with privatism and racial and social segregation. This grim view of the City of Angels is part of the "noir" history on the city, to borrow historian Lawrence Culver's typology, best seen in the books by Mike Davis. In contrast to the "sunshine" view of the city, represented by Kevin Starr's *Americans and the California Dream* series, the noir reading of the city denounces its vicious social, racial, and environmental inequalities and condemns the ruling elite that has let them fester for over a century.[25] Even the beaches are not exempt from the noir treatment: "In the erstwhile world capital of teenagers, writes Mikes Davis in *City of Quartz*, . . . the beaches are now closed at dark, patrolled by helicopter gunships and police dune buggies."[26] When not excessively policed, the beaches in Davis's works are covered in sewage, going up in flames, or portrayed as Eden's lost garden. Yet this vision completely ignores the large public investments in the shoreline in the postwar period and the resulting increased proportion of beaches in the public domain. While, as Davis laments, the creation of a "social democracy of beaches and playgrounds" was never achieved in LA, the state has nonetheless benefited from one of the most progressive and stringent set of beach development regulations since 1972, when the Coastal Commission was established following a referendum.[27] However flawed and underfunded, the agency was the culmination of decades of campaigning for the preservation of the state's public shores led by Southern California groups.[28] The public for whom the beaches were acquired and protected may have been the white middle class in the minds of many beach lobbyists at mid-century, but Angelenos of all social and racial backgrounds eventually staked their claim to the public shore. While there were setbacks—some of which this book details—it would be attributing too much power to the city's elites to deny how empowering the opening of large stretches of sand proved to be over the long term for local residents.

Whether noir or sunshine, the literature on Los Angeles and its urban development tends to focus on its infamous landscape of sprawling inland suburbs and, occasionally, its long-declining and more recently revived Downtown area. By shifting the focus to the city's geographic edge—the Pacific coastline—the book argues for rethinking the city's urban growth and relationship to the environment. In addition to revealing the hitherto little-known story of LA's Westside, it shows that the region has not been a poster child for environmental destruction and unsustainability. In the 1930s, local beach associations took a leadership role in the national campaign to preserve shorelines. By comparison, Northern California—despite what geographer Richard Walker has termed its "green groove"—lagged behind, with little activity in relation to its coastline up until the postwar period.[29] Thinking of Southern California as a precursor in the nature protection movement may seem counterintuitive, yet the birth of the LA beach lobby emerged from early twentieth-century regional boosterism predicated on the promise that the city would provide its residents with gentle and abundant nature at their back door, in contrast with congested and polluted East Coast cities. As historian Clark Davis has shown, "deserted beaches and a deep blue sea" were essential elements of the boosters' discourse, which celebrated the region as a Mediterranean paradise.[30] When over one million newcomers settled in the region beginning in the 1920s, the county's extraordinary demographic growth threatened Los Angeles's unique urban promise. The perceived crisis over this shoreline prompted a forceful response from local businessmen and officials. As one LA official put it, the city "could not afford to neglect the goose that lay our golden eggs." The transformations that took place over the next few years were nothing short of spectacular.

Los Angeles's famed coastal landscape was constructed through a process of artificial sand nourishment. As such, the urban beach was another example of man-made nature within the city. Unlike generously funded and carefully planned-out sites such as New York City's Central Park, the vastly enlarged LA beaches are as much the product of neglect, lack of scientific understanding of coastal ecology, and, most crucially, chance, as they are the result of technological innovations. While the beach lobby produced countless reports and plans boasting grandiose visions for the shores, the reality is that the LA beachscape was created in fits and starts. The failures of 1930s' engineers to understand erosion processes fueled local elites' dissatisfaction with coastal management. Even more decisive for LA's coastal future was the presence of nearby dunes, owned by the municipality, which provided the raw material to rebuild the beaches. Foregrounding the errors and opportunities inherent in this story serves as a reminder that only a thorough knowledge of unique local conditions can provide sustainable responses to impacts of climate change.

Despite their artificial origins, LA's beaches have proved remarkably resilient, especially compared to their battered East Coast counterparts. *Sand Rush*, then, contrasts with the traditionally declensionist field of environmental history. On the Los Angeles waterfront, drastic human interventions on nature brought social and economic benefits to the region without long-term detrimental consequences on the environment. Yet the ongoing climate crisis and rapid sea-level rise will eventually force the city to reckon with past attempts at building ever-larger beaches. As scholars of the Mediterranean coast have recently put it, when it comes to histories of shorelines, "stabilization . . . [i]s never achieved once and for all."[31] Coastal dynamism continuously challenges those who believe the planet can be fully dominated and controlled by humans. Even in the so-called Anthropocene—the term proposed by some for a new geological epoch defined by humans' multifaceted impacts on the Earth system—shorelines can escape our control. While the Los Angeles beach lobby was able to "grow" the region's shores without concerns for major weather events and other disruptions throughout the twentieth century, this period of stability is coming to an end. In a 2017 article, a group of engineers and marine scientists who modeled shoreline response to climate change soberly concluded that "31% to 67% of Southern California beaches may become completely eroded by 2100" due to sea-level rise.[32] Like sandcastles, Angelenos' beloved beaches will only last as long as the tide keeps away. Losing the beaches to climate change would mean a lot more than just losing a place of outdoor recreation; it would annihilate the many stories this landscape tells about our relationship to nature and technology, and our ability to share space with others. By telling these stories, this book makes a case for seeing beaches as places of vital historical relevance whose value increases as erosion engulfs more and more coastal sites across the world.

Chapter 1, "Westside LA," narrates the history of mass leisure from a less frequently considered West Coast perspective. It shows how the urbanization of the coastline in the 1920s and 1930s and local developers' savvy promotional strategies produced the Westside, an attractive neighborhood where a hybrid lifestyle, both suburban and resortlike, took shape. The coast's proximity to Hollywood, LA's special relationship with Hawaii, and the regional cult of the body contributed to the emergence of a unique beach culture centered on beauty, fashion, and body performance. By the end of the 1930s, Southern California had pioneered a new model of seaside leisure, inspiring beach cultures well beyond the region.

Chapter 2 interrogates the beach as an urban public space where rules and regulations (whether formal or informal) were the subject of constant negotiations and, occasionally, violent confrontations. As the small resorts of the early twentieth century turned into residential communities in the 1920s and 1930s, a local elite sought to bring order to the seaside and reintroduce to the beach some semblance of class segregation. Setting up exclusive beach clubs did draw some lines in the sand, but new ordinances restricting certain behaviors often went ignored or unenforced. Racial segregation became more entrenched starting in the 1920s, and multiple attempts by middle-class African Americans to establish beach clubs and private establishments near the shoreline were squashed. By the early 1940s, the beach was not as strictly policed and regulated as other public spaces in the city due to lack of officers and the sheer expanse of land to patrol. But race continued to determine which spaces beachgoers could hope to enjoy without fear of harassment.

The influx of new Angelenos in the boom decades of the 1920s and 1930s also prompted the region's elite to declare the beaches in crisis. Chapter 3 chronicles the emergence of the beach protection movement and the rise of coastal engineering in reaction to this perceived crisis. During the 1930s, these self-proclaimed beach experts produced reports and studies lamenting the sad state of the shores and planning the ideal urban beach. In contrast to their East Coast equivalents, who timidly approached the issue of coastal access, the LA beach lobby championed the eventual acquisition of the entire California shoreline for the public. Moreover, this lobby advocated for a development program devised at the state level in order to take into account the inner workings of the coastal ecosystem.

The lobby's plans reflected a modern vision of the coastline, where wide-open spaces and parking lots would replace the dark corners of the old-fashioned amusement zones. Chapter 4 explores the postwar beach modernization projects and the movement for the acquisition of public beaches. During that period, Southern California positioned itself as the national leader for shoreline planning and public access to the coast. In the postwar period, thanks to lobbying efforts at the state level, large sections of the shoreline were bought for the public, artificially widened, and cleaned up. These vast, empty beaches allowed the planners to proceed with the next step of their plan: adapting the coastline to the postwar suburbanite values of cleanliness, privacy, and respectability. Taking their cues from newly opened Disneyland, they built modern accommodations and family-friendly recreational spaces on the sands, hoping to prevent the white middle class from "fleeing" the beach just as they had fled the city.

Yet beaches provided visitors with a very different experience than the popular theme park. Chapter 5 shows how, in the postwar era, the LA coastline became a public stage where subcultures reshaped notions of beauty, masculinity, and femininity. The concomitant rise of a youth beach culture—centered around late-night beach parties and annual Spring Break celebrations, the surfing phenomenon and its avatars in the music and clothing industries, and the birth of bodybuilding at Santa Monica's Muscle Beach—made the beaches of Los Angeles into places that produced and promoted modern standards of beauty and appearance.

This phenomenon was both facilitated and impeded by beach modernization objectives that disrupted long-standing local traditions and sought to make these spaces more homogeneous. The newly widened beaches and their brand-new sports centers, volleyball courts, and gym apparatus afforded more space for athletic activities. Yet not all beachgoers were welcomed on the modernized shores. Chapter 6 explores the ways in which beach modernization and new policing techniques contributed to the construction of the beach, both literally and culturally, as an exclusive space for the white middle-class nuclear family. More specifically, it shows how an alliance of real estate interests and city officials combined planning and policing strategies in order to turn Ocean Park, a section of Santa Monica that was previously a haven for gay, Black, and working-class beachgoers, into a semiprivatized playground for the white middle class.

Beach modernization, like other urban renewal efforts, had a short life span. Chapter 7 analyzes how the consensus behind beach modernization efforts imploded in the late 1960s under the triple pressure of the modern environmentalist movement, the rise of the New Right, and controversy over oceanside high-rises. By the 1970s, most Angelenos perceived the beaches as natural spaces with a unique history that needed to be protected from the assault of developers and the wrecking ball. Meanwhile, in Orange County, resistance against "big government" championed by the New Right resonated with local beach homeowners who felt that "their" beaches should be closed off to outsiders. By the late 1960s, public beach acquisitions had come to a halt.

From early twentieth-century businessmen's dreams of turning the Santa Monica Bay into the "Coney Island of the West" to 1960s' coastal residents' fears of seeing their neighborhoods morph into the "Miami of the West," the book chronicles the making and remaking of the LA coastline according to varying models, countermodels, and ideals. The epilogue explores recent controversies that have called into question the democratic character of the beaches. Today, the beaches of Los Angeles are more popular than ever. The COVID-19 pandemic, which led to temporary beach closures in Southern California in the spring of 2020, threw into sharp relief the essential role they play as spaces where anyone can cool off for free in a metropolis where rental and property prices have skyrocketed. Yet the "right to the beach" remains contested. Malibu beach owners continue to devise new strategies and file lawsuits to keep visitors off their precious beachfront property. Aggressive policing and new laws intent on protecting coastal residents' tranquility have been criticized for establishing new forms of spatial segregation that essentially turn some beaches into the exclusive preserves of the rich. From an environmental point of view, ocean pollution and rising sea levels threaten this beloved ecosystem. In spite, or maybe because, of the many threats to the shoreline, the beaches' reputation and allure in popular culture has only grown in the past few decades. In the 1990s, the *Baywatch* TV series revived for a modern audience the familiar "SoCal" seaside fantasies peddled by Hollywood from early in the century. Shapely bathing beauties, bleached-haired surfers, and colorful sunsets proved, once again, a winning recipe. Twenty-first-century influencers might prefer to display their tanned and toned bodies by the crystal-clear water of a private swimming pool, but the familiar LA coastal landscape continues to be a prized background for social media posts. Meanwhile, who gets to enjoy this picture-perfect, albeit artificial, playground remains an open question.

CHAPTER 1

⌇

Westside LA

Although its international reputation is inextricably linked to the shoreline, Los Angeles is not a traditional coastal city. Founded in 1781, the pueblo known as El Pueblo de Nuestra Señora La Reina de Los Angeles was in fact established along the Los Angeles River, about fifteen miles from the Pacific Ocean.[1] In the second half of the nineteenth century, the city center, Downtown, turned its back on the sandy beaches of nearby Santa Monica Bay, while most industrial and commercial port functions were restricted to distant San Pedro Bay, south of the city. As for the first tourists, they preferred the dry inland climate to the humidity of the coast and frequented the sanatoriums of the San Gabriel Valley. In the early twentieth century, few people lived on the Los Angeles littoral, and the beaches of Santa Monica Bay were isolated, little-frequented spaces far from the city's commercial, municipal, and cultural centers.

Yet thirty years later the coast had established itself as one of the metropolis's major demographic and economic hubs. This collection of neighborhoods and independent cities, better known today as the Westside—or "Surfurbia," as architectural historian and LA enthusiast Reyner Banham dubbed it—sprang to life due to a complex mix of economic, political, cultural, and environmental factors that shifted the city's center of gravity from east to west.[2] The westward move is most apparent in maps of the city. At the turn of the century, maps of Los Angeles focused on its Downtown area, leaving out the coast altogether. By 1920, cartographers struggled to contain the spectacular growth of the city, which radiated in all directions, but they never failed to picture the coast and its now famed resort towns. Ten years later, the metropolis was often presented as if seen from the Pacific, with the beaches in the foreground. From a continental outpost, Los Angeles had become a beach city.[3]

The rush to the ocean did not happen by chance. At the turn of the century, a group of local businessmen set about establishing beach resorts along the coast to attract visitors from the east and Angelenos looking to get away from the city. They drew inspiration from a vast reservoir of seaside models; from Coney Island to Atlantic City, from Nice to Brighton, the world's shorelines had already undergone considerable development. Indeed, "the invention of the beach," in the words of historian Alain Corbin, had already taken place. Drawing on cultural references, Venice was promoted as the "Coney Island of the West," while other resorts took on the more aristocratic airs of "Hollywood Riviera." But the coastline grew to become much more than just a simple tourist and leisure area. In the 1920s, the local political elites chose to abandon the traditional concentric urban form, where the city is organized around its central business district, and instead promoted decentralization and a low-density urban landscape. Developers seized this opportunity to turn the coast into a new node of the polycentric metropolis. To do so, they developed innovative promotional strategies that relied on two essential promises: that the coastline was a necessarily limited natural amenity, enticing Angelenos to buy property on "the last beach" of the region, and that resort living was possible year-round. Their hard work paid off. By the late 1930s, the beach resorts of yesteryear had morphed into multifunctional residential communities. The Westside was taking shape.[4]

As the city experienced rapid demographic growth and expanded its public transport networks, Angelenos in all their social and racial diversity headed to the ocean. They experienced traditional seaside pleasures while inventing new ways of enjoying the beach. Under the influence of the film industry, the local sports and fitness subculture, and the city's privileged relationship with Hawaii, a unique Southern California beach culture took shape. By the late 1930s, the Westside was much more than one of the city's economic and demographic centers: it was a state of mind and a lifestyle centered on beauty, fun, sports, and outdoor recreation.

Contrary to the widespread misconception that the city's horizontal configuration and infamous sprawl was the result of chaotic growth and lack of upstream planning, Los Angeles was, in fact, fundamentally shaped by the choices of early twentieth-century urban planners and elites. The new urban model was characterized by low density and the segregation of the city's industrial, commercial, and residential functions.[5] Like much of the rest of Los Angeles, the Westside was neither entirely planned nor left to grow without checks. Yet its trajectory is unique. Once on the geographical and metaphorical fringes of the city, it became an integral component of a polycentral metropolis while giving birth to a distinct lifestyle, partway between city and resort life.

COASTAL PERIPHERIES

Framed by two jutting headlands—Point Dume in Malibu in the north and the Palos Verdes Peninsula in the south—the sandy beaches of the Santa Monica Bay run for a length of about forty miles. Overlooked by the Santa Monica Mountains, which, at certain points, reach directly to the shore, Malibu beaches range from the tiniest of pocket beaches backed by steep cliffs to narrow barrier beaches running alongside lagoons and (now largely reclaimed) wetlands. Further south, from Santa Monica to Redondo Beach, the beaches have always been wider; they are part of the vast coastal plain known as the Los Angeles Basin, a depression that filled with sediment and rose above sea level due to tectonic activity about five million years ago. The flat surface of the basin provided optimal conditions for the establishment of human settlements and, in the twentieth century, a city. But the beaches themselves and their immediate surroundings long remained on the fringes of the basin's main population and economic centers.

In the first volume of his history of the Golden State, Kevin Starr claims that Southern California "was a land that rushed to the sea as if to an eager lover." While today's Southern Californians do love their beaches, the rush was not as self-evident as Starr made it sound. Up until the early twentieth century, the Los Angeles littoral was sparsely populated. It did, however, provide abundant resources for the five thousand to ten thousand Native Californians who inhabited the region prior to Spanish colonization. The Chumash, whose coastal territory stretched from Monterrey down to Topanga in Malibu, and the Gabrielino-Tongva, who resided in the Los Angeles Basin, used the beaches to hunt, harvest shellfish and other marine life, and gather plants. Sandy shorelines also provided the ideal launching pads for their plank boats, with which they fished and traveled to the Channel Islands. Even so, apart from a few exceptions, such as today's Ballona wetlands, Native villages were usually located inland. Spanish colonizers, who settled in the region starting in 1769, also favored the interior, establishing the San Gabriel and San Fernando missions in their eponymous valleys, where a water supply was more easily secured. In the following decades, as nearly all Natives either died of imported diseases; integrated (often by force) the Spanish missions, pueblos, and ranchos;

or left for the less populated interior, traditional lifeways declined. In the 1830s, under Mexican rule, the dismantlement of the missions meant that the land fell in the hands of the descendants of Spanish colonizers. Used as grazing land for cattle and sheep, coastal areas remained peripheral to the region's main population and economic center, the pueblo of Los Angeles. American occupation in 1848 did not fundamentally alter the situation. While some white pleasure-seekers did enjoy picnics on the beach starting in the 1860s, they remained few and far between.[6]

In the 1880s, the coastal ranchos were subdivided and sold. By then, the Los Angeles area was experiencing something of a boom fueled by aggressive land speculation. With the arrival of the first transcontinental railway in 1879 (the Southern Pacific Railroad) followed by a second line in 1885 (the Santa Fe Railway) and the steep decline in transportation costs from the eastern United States, the city attracted a motley assortment of visitors, among them tuberculosis patients, adventurers in search of opportunities, and a growing contingent of tourists. In fact, Los Angeles was making a name for itself as a tourist destination for well-heeled vacationers. So-called boosters, the notables and intellectuals who settled in the region and promoted it in newspapers, magazines, and novels, developed a distinctive visual imaginary around the southern half of the California. They sung the praises of the region's diverse landscapes, natural abundance, mild climate, and "tropical" charms.[7]

Even so, the coast was not yet an indispensable part of the Southern California tourism industry. Easterners who made the trip out west, many of them on doctors' orders, came to enjoy the region's balmy climate and improve their constitution or, more prosaically, escape the harsh New England winters. The dry climate, which was considered ideal to treat tuberculosis, could best be enjoyed inland, and thus Pasadena, not Santa Monica, became the center of a thriving hotel culture in the foothills of the San Gabriel Mountains. Tourists who braved the daylong carriage ride to Santa Monica in the 1870s found only canvas tents for accommodations. By the 1880s, journeying by train was possible, and hotels, mansions, bathhouses, pavilions, and shops started appearing along the coastline. City founder Senator John P. Jones of Nevada moved his family to Santa Monica in 1889 to a palatial mansion, Miramar, built on the bluffs overlooking the sea. A year later, the lavish Redondo Hotel opened in the South Bay with its eighteen-hole golf course and tennis courts on the beach. Yet inland Pasadena remained far more famous than any of the coastal communities.[8]

If Santa Monica Bay was not yet a major tourist destination, neither was it a major production center. Apart from a small Japanese fishing village founded in 1899 to the north of Santa Monica, there was not a substantial

population making its living from seafood products. Prior to its development in the 1900s, the shoreline was mostly used for grazing and recreational hunting and fishing. Some sources also indicate the use of coastal
lands in the South Bay for dry farming of barley and other crops. The bay
had also no major commercial or industrial activity. While there was a small
amount of salt production on the site of the future city of Redondo Beach,
it had disappeared by the early 1880s. Redondo served as a regional port
of call, but it had lost all its shipping business to the much bigger harbor in
San Pedro by 1912. The one exception was in El Segundo, where Standard
Oil Company built a refinery in 1911, laying the foundation for what would
become an "industrial suburb" of greater Los Angeles.[9]

Efforts to turn Santa Monica into Los Angeles's main harbor failed spectacularly not once but twice before the turn of the century. A first attempt
in the 1870s, under the helm of Senator Jones, came to nothing as railroad
magnate Collis P. Huntington, who owned the only railroad serving the
port of San Pedro, brought such furious competition that he forced Jones
to sell him his railroad and Santa Monica wharf. Twenty years later, when
the federal government decided to build a deepwater port in the region
to handle growing traffic and compete with San Francisco, Huntington,
who feared that his monopoly over San Pedro would be challenged, revived
the idea of turning Santa Monica into a major seaport. In 1893, the determined magnate built an impressive wharf extending 4,720 feet into the sea
from today's Will Rogers State Beach to sway government officials' final
decision. But Santa Monica, exposed as it was to ocean currents, was hardly
an ideal location. And San Pedro's partisans could easily point to the necessity of loosening the grip Huntington and his Southern Pacific railroad held
over the region. In 1897, the government selected the site of San Pedro as
Los Angeles's main port. While Santa Monica Bay suffered a setback in the
short term, the decision proved to be decisive over the long term. Its shores
were spared the industrial pollution a major port would inevitably have
brought; the bay would instead be entirely dedicated to leisure.[10]

This is a distinctive feature that the Los Angeles shoreline shares with
other developed New World coastlines, particularly in Australia and Florida.
Prior to their development for tourism, the Santa Monica Bay beaches had
served no major productive function. Unlike what happened in many areas
on European shorelines, where the surge in beach tourism came as an "intrusion" as the existing populations were driven out by newcomers, Los
Angeles's beaches offered a fresh and unencumbered landscape. This had
a lasting influence on how people used and perceived the beach. In Los
Angeles, no negotiations took place between local coastal populations and
beachgoers. Recreation dominated from the outset and was not connected

to a therapeutic tradition—which was concentrated in Pasadena and the interior valleys—or to a maritime past.[11]

FIRST RESORTS

The turning point for the Los Angeles coast came in the first decade of the twentieth century. A trip to the ocean had once involved a daylong excursion on dusty and badly kept roads that only a few adventurous visitors could afford. Rapid social and cultural changes combined with improved transportation made a beach trip accessible to Angelenos via an easy tram ride. Within a short decade, Los Angeles's major beach resorts—from north to south: Santa Monica, Ocean Park, Venice, Manhattan Beach, Hermosa Beach, and Redondo Beach—established their reputation as alluring playgrounds for wealthy East Coast visitors and day-trippers alike.

But before Los Angeles could turn into a beach city, it had to shed its reputation as the "Mecca of the afflicted," as one brochure put it. Until 1900, about a quarter of Southern California's new residents were "health-seekers"—consumptives or other diseased individuals. A decade later, however, the region's identity had undergone a critical shift as promotional materials presented Southern California as the ideal place for middle-class tourists who sought rest and relaxation. Boosters sought to present Los Angeles as a "frontier of leisure": a place where a lifestyle devoted to leisure and outdoor sports could be enjoyed, not only during holidays, but throughout the year. Some coastal vacation spots, such as the Coronado Tent City, even started excluding consumptive patients "to insure [sic] the fullest enjoyment and greatest benefit to its patrons." The sight of "tuberculars" swaddled with blankets on sun-loungers might not have been the best advertisement for a newly opened resort. This shift also aligned with new scientific discoveries and trends, as the heliotherapy movement gained wider acceptance in the United States and Europe in the late nineteenth century. Healthy adults and children, not just invalids, were encouraged to disrobe and spend time in the sunlight. In general, outdoor recreation was becoming an increasingly popular pursuit, especially among the middle and upper classes who answered President Theodore Roosevelt's call for the "strenuous life."[12]

The newfound popularity of ocean swimming and, eventually, sunbathing grew out of this particular moment. While coastal tourism had taken off in Europe and on the East Coast since at least the late eighteenth century, most visitors still contented themselves with a stroll or a picnic by the ocean, and many remained fully clothed.[13] Several factors may have emboldened Southern Californians to indulge in ocean bathing in the early twentieth century: the exploits of famous swimmers such as Australian phenomenon Annette Kellerman; the rise of a new mass culture in urban centers that encouraged more freedom of movement, whether in the dancehall or on the sand; and a new appreciation for heat and the summer season.[14] Southern California, where the swimming season could be extended over half of the year, offered a unique setting. While winter continued to be a popular season for seaside tourism in California and elsewhere, the beach bathing craze brought an increasing number of visitors to the Los Angeles coast in the warmer months, at least a full decade before this trend took hold in Europe.[15]

More than any other factor, ease of transportation transformed the Los Angeles shoreline from a periphery into a new center of the expanding metropolis. Unlike most European and East Coast beach resorts, which predated the arrival of the trains, many resorts in Florida and California were created by the railroad barons themselves to ensure the profitability of their new lines. The first Ocean Park pier in Santa Monica, for example, was built by the Santa Fe Railroad in 1892 to coincide with the opening of a line linking Downtown with the ocean in just 35 minutes. A year later, the company built cement promenades along the beach, an amusement pavilion, and a bathhouse.[16] Starting in 1896, electric streetcars were run out from Downtown to the coast. In the following years, as Los Angeles's interurban electric trolley system expanded and consolidated, traveling to the beach became increasingly easy and cheap. In the 1910s, the city's most popular trolley line was the "Balloon Route." For just one dollar, tourists were taken on a balloon-shaped tour from Downtown to the coast and back, visiting along the way no fewer than "8 cities—10 beaches," as the slogan promised. In the summer of 1909, an average of ten thousand excursionists per month enjoyed the route.

By then, ocean bathing was far from the only attraction. At the turn of the century, a "new mass culture" centered around commercial recreational pursuits such as movie theaters, amusement parks, and bathing facilities was emerging in urban industrial areas across the country. Eager for fun, the young generation of the early twentieth century rejected the Victorian values of restriction, temperance, and discipline and embraced a new ethos of leisure and consumption. Inspired by the success of Coney Island and Atlantic City, entrepreneurs rushed to create versions of them on the Santa Monica Bay. Between 1905 and 1909, three amusement areas opened on pleasure piers extending into the sea: Venice Pier (1905), Ocean Park Pier (1905), and Santa Monica Pier (1909). Of the three, "Venice of America," as it was originally called by its eccentric developer, Abbot Kinney, was the most original development. Enchanted by the beauty of the Italian city, Kinney used the money from his family's cigarette business to reproduce its likeness in California, including its canals and gondolas. Although his intention was to create a city of art and culture where visitors would attend lectures and plays, the public's indifference to his plans quickly led him to turn his Venetian project into an amusement park for the cheap leisure crowd. As historian Kevin Starr put it, "Most Southern Californians found the Ferris wheel more fun than Sarah Bernhardt and would always prefer the aquacade to opera, the shoot-the-chutes to *Camille*."[17]

In the 1910s, competition between the different resorts and amusement areas intensified as local entrepreneurs built new carousels, theaters, roller coasters, and restaurants to attract the pleasure-seeking crowds. Going to the beach did not necessarily require spending money on commercial amusements. The "beach party," one of Southern California's time-honored traditions, was celebrated by Angelenos in the summer but also in the spring. Santa Monica's local newspaper often reported on such occasions, offering readers a glimpse of the exciting social life on the sands. On April 22, 1900, for example, journalists reported on the "Jolly beach party" organized by Mr. and Mrs. Thomas "in honor of a number of Illinois relatives and friends . . . spending the winter in Southern California." On July 13, 1901, Santa Monica residents could read all about how local businessmen had invited about thirty of their Long Beach counterparts to a beach party and had even chartered a streetcar for the occasion.[18] Bonfires, sausages, marshmallows, baked potatoes, sunset walks on the beach—these became the indispensable ingredients of a successful beach party. In the 1900s, most beach parties were organized by wealthy families. But from the 1910s onwards, religious and charitable organizations as well as local schools took advantage of the beaches' proximity to organize picnics, a sign of the gradual democratization of the beach.

EVERYDAY SPACES

While the invention of the beach party and the increase in rail links between Downtown and the ocean brought Angelenos and their beaches closer, it was not until the 1920s that the coast became one of Los Angeles's essential public spaces at the metropolitan level. Between 1910 and 1920, the population of Los Angeles County nearly doubled from approximately 505,000 to more than 936,000. The pace of growth accelerated, so by 1930 more than 2.2 million people lived in Los Angeles County. By then, Los Angeles was the fifth-largest city in the country and the largest in the West.[19] This influx of new residents was linked to the development of intensive agriculture and the region's tourism, oil, and film industries. With vast swaths of cheap land available, the area also benefited from the booming real estate industry. Finally, the demographic boom combined with the absence of a strong union tradition in the city encouraged industrialists to set up factories there. In 1930, Los Angeles ranked first among West Coast cities in terms of industrial output.[20] This thrum of activity played an essential role in attracting migrants to the city.

At the same time, the city's elites adopted an original urban development plan that was radically different than the traditional concentric layout. In doing so, they set the path for a distinctive urban form characterized by low density and horizontality. While it is tempting to attribute the city's sprawl to the demographic explosion in this period, the deliberate decisions about decentralization were made only after numerous negotiations between groups with divergent interests.[21] According to historian Jeremiah Axelrod, Los Angeles in the early 1920s had a relatively traditional layout with a compact city center, Downtown, serving as the city's major economic, municipal, and cultural nerve center. A few years later, growing traffic congestion led the business elite and civic leaders to rethink the city's spatial organization. They decided instead to create a metropolis organized around several independent satellite communities, which would be well connected via private and public transportation. Doing so would ease congestion and preserve the region's hybrid landscape, halfway between the countryside and the city. Indeed, this sort of landscape had been singled out early on as an ideal for which the city should strive. In a prescriptive work titled *The Better City* (1907), Dana Bartlett, a booster and Methodist pastor, imagined Los Angeles as a morally superior city where easy access to nature would improve civility between residents. While the plans drawn up in the 1920s were not necessarily executed, they encouraged the sprawl and integrated coastal cities, once physically separated from Los Angeles, into its urban fabric.[22]

The transformation of Wilshire Boulevard, the key access route to the city's beaches in the nineteenth century, is emblematic in this respect. Built in the 1920s as a parkway between Downtown and the ocean, the boulevard was slated to become a residential zone in accordance with zoning ordinances.[23] Over the course of the decade, real estate developers managed to modify these ordinances and took advantage of Downtown traffic congestion to lure consumers to businesses they opened along the boulevard. The ease with which customers could access these businesses, aided by the construction of parking lots behind the stores and the erection of billboards large enough to be seen from an automobile, made Wilshire

Boulevard into one of Los Angeles's central east-west arteries. Initially designed to improve traffic flow in the city and separate its districts, the boulevard ended up contributing to Los Angeles's sprawl between the city and the ocean.[24]

As Los Angeles swiftly grew into a vast metropolis stretching over hundreds of miles, the city extended its administrative boundaries, using its access to water to gently coerce neighboring cities into annexation. Above all, local elites sought to expand toward the Pacific. "All [that is] now needed to make Los Angeles the most wonderful hostess city in America for the world's tourists is a municipal beach," asserted the *Los Angeles Times* in 1917.[25] In 1925, the city finally got its wish when it annexed Venice. While popular with the crowds, the resort was mired in financial difficulties linked to the upkeep of Kinney's canals, and annexation to Los Angeles promised much-needed access to a water supply. However, Los Angeles failed in its efforts to annex the City of Santa Monica, which feared losing its civic identity to an already vast metropolis. Other coastal cities (Redondo, Manhattan Beach, El Segundo) also maintained their independence. Thus, the bay remained divided among several municipalities, a situation that would become increasingly problematic as the coastline developed.

If Los Angeles failed to annex the entire bay, it nonetheless tightened its grip over the region. Between 1906 and 1930, the city's surface area increased from 43 to 442 square miles. The whole population had access to the beaches, thanks to the Pacific Electric vast interurban rail system. The Red Cars, the streetcars that crisscrossed the entire region—including the entirety of the Santa Monica Bay from north to south—linked together fifty communities in four different counties. Given the high rate of automobile ownership in Los Angeles—in 1920, one automobile for every 3.6 inhabitants—it was also possible to use a major thoroughfare that connected the city center to the ocean, like Wilshire Boulevard, to get to the beach.[26]

Whether they arrived by public or private transportation, the number of beachgoers increased dramatically. In 1925–1926, 2.7 million people visited the municipal beaches. By 1929–1930, this figure mushroomed to more than 10.3 million.[27] By the end of the 1920s, beaches had become essential public spaces visited daily by Angelenos. Hollywood narratives reflected the beaches' new status. Many of Mack Sennett's popular 1920s comedies filmed in Los Angeles included a scene at the beach inserted in the middle of stories otherwise set in the city. In *Photograph Story*, for instance, the first scenes take place in a city office where the main characters—a wealthy businessman and his young clerk—are introduced. Soon after, the clerk flirts with the businessman's daughter at the beach, a setting no doubt chosen to highlight the mixture of social classes on the sand. A comedic short, *Just as It Should Be*, ended with the main couple "in a loving embrace," riding a Red Car home from the beach after a series of misadventures.[28]

Accessible transportation routes and a booming population also turned the early-twentieth-century beach resorts into full-fledged residential communities. Starting in the 1920s, many observers noted the growing number of commuters who worked in Downtown but chose to live by the sea. The most famous were the Hollywood movie stars who built lavish houses along the coast, but the phenomenon was more widespread. Affluent families were joined by workers at the El Segundo Refinery who turned Manhattan Beach and Hermosa Beach into "black gold suburbs." Other signs pointed at the residential character of the coast. In 1925, author Marshall Breeden reported that his brother, "who is in the piano-business," told him that "Santa Monica uses more pianos than any other city of its size in the County." Santa Monica "has indeed become a home city," he concluded, and "is no longer simply a summer or winter pleasure resort." From tourist areas catering to seasonal visitors, coastal communities had become places to live and work. Real estate developers in search of profits quickly followed.[29]

PROMOTING THE COAST

While real estate speculation around Los Angeles's coastal properties began in the late nineteenth century, it accelerated sharply in the 1920s, in part due to the dismantling of the last big Spanish and Mexican ranchos. Automobile ownership also allowed speculators to develop land that was not necessarily near a trolley station. In 1927, the *Los Angeles Examiner* claimed that "seventeen large real estate firms and syndicate organizations [we]re in the midst of a beach development program which, conservatively, involves not less than $100,000,000." In five years, the newspaper warned, "reasonably priced beach lots are going to be scarce as hen's teeth." This prediction proved prescient. Rental prices in the Santa Monica Bay were skyrocketing, especially during the summer months when tourists joined with Angelenos looking for a place to live. In July 1936, the secretary of the Venice Realty Board reported, "We have people coming here and telling us that they have been up and down the beach from Manhattan to Malibu in search of a beach home and are unable to find anything."[30] After all, many midwestern transplants had never set eyes on the Pacific Ocean and, once in town, relished its sight. Freshly arrived from Wyoming, the Booths, for instance, decided that "[they] would only live near the ocean." "If we're in California," the father reasoned, "we might as well have the benefits of Southern California and the beaches."[31]

Even if many newly arrived Angelenos felt the "lure of the sea," transforming the beach into a residential area required a bit of imagination. Some coastal cities, like Venice and Ocean Park, seemed to cater more toward pleasure seekers than to respectable families. Others were little more than names. Early 1920s Palisades Del Rey (today's Playa Del Rey area), for example—a vast terrain of untouched sand dunes with no connection to water, electricity, and sewage lines—seemed especially unsuitable for residential development. If Angelenos dreamed of living on the beach, it was partly because real estate agencies, through their advertising and building campaigns, were in the business of selling that dream. Early twentieth-century developers touted a "population trend *toward the ocean*." The construction or expansion of east-west arteries such as Century Boulevard and Belleview (today's Imperial Highway) and the growing number of building permits issued in West Los Angeles were sure signs of this phenomenon. "Home sites near the ocean are already being snapped up by ready buyers," they warned interested parties. The impetus to live by the beach was so obvious that it deserved its own adjective: one could read in the spring of 1926 about the "City-to-Sea development" that was shaking up Greater Los Angeles.[32]

Real estate agents were also quick to tell potential customers that the coastline was a limited natural amenity. They repeatedly underscored the scarcity of coastal property along the county's seventy-one-mile shoreline. Prices, brochures explained, depended on the "law of supply and demand," and since "you cannot stretch the coastline," properties would only grow in value. According to some, "The time was not far distant when a piece of beach frontage w[ould] be as valuable as a piece of property of similar size on 7th and Broadway," in the heart of Downtown Los Angeles.[33] While typical of real estate boosterism, such claims were not completely baseless. The Santa Monica Bay was effectively hemmed in on all sides, so residential development could not easily spread. Blocked to the south by the industrial and commercial port of San Pedro and the independent city of Long Beach, development was also impeded to the north by the Santa Monica Mountains. The Cities of Santa Monica, Venice, Redondo Beach, Manhattan Beach, and Hermosa Beach were already well developed. By the 1920s, undeveloped land was relatively rare, found only in three places: in Malibu, where land remained effectively closed to development until the late 1930s; in Playa Del Rey, south of Venice; and in and around Palos Verdes, south of the bay.[34]

Perhaps the most striking example of the coastline being packaged and sold as a scarce commodity was the campaign led by Fritz Burns, Dickenson & Gillespie's vice president, in Palisades Del Rey. Starting in 1924, Burns, a prominent real estate developer and cunning salesman, invested all his energy in promoting the area. Billed as "The Last Three Miles"—that is, the last three miles of undeveloped coastal land in Los Angeles—Palisades Del Rey was sold as the last opportunity to buy an affordable home with an oceanfront view. Given that boosters had repeated the availability of cheap land in Southern California like a mantra, this slogan required some explanation. Burns thus made his case meticulously: "There is only one re-alty commodity which can never be manufactured, and that is Ocean Front; there can be—for all time to come—just ONE shoreline and ONE only." Further, prospective buyers could read that "Los Angeles ha[d] already consumed 93% of its available ocean front . . . to meet the demands of its first million population." The second million was "already on the way." "BUY NOW," urged the brochure.[35] According to the *Los Angeles Examiner*, Burns had "travers[ed] every foot of beach front from the Malibu Ranch on the north to San Clemente on the South" before declaring that "every worthwhile available foot of beach property is now being subdivided and marketed."[36]

This was not the first time that such a marketing ploy had been used on the bay. In 1921, developer Clifford Reid's project, the "Hollywood Riviera" (located in today's City of Torrance), had been marketed as "the last of the beaches on Santa Monica Bay." Hired by the Reid company to pen the pub-licity brochure for the new development, poet John McGroarty remarked on the rapid pace of development around the bay and the dwindling number of public shores: "our beaches have been allowed carelessly to slip into private hands. There is not much beach left open anymore that the public can call its own." In line with California law, which condones privati-zation above mean high tide line, large stretches of the Los Angeles shore-line were owned by private individuals and thus closed to the public. Yet the fact that the project McGroarty was extolling would privatize some of the last remaining beachfront for the exclusive benefit of the privileged few did not seem to bother the poet. Instead, his lines glorified the "exceptional beauty" of the private beach and rejoiced in the fact that future residents would have "their own beautiful club and their own wonderful community life in every way, safe from encroachments and the onslaughts of the out-side world."[37]

Being safe from the outside world was a very real concern for African Americans who wished to enjoy the beach. The scarcity of coastal land compounded informal racial segregation practices that prevented Black

Angelenos from frequenting the city's most popular beaches and confined them to Bay Street Beach, a small stretch of sand on Santa Monica Beach.[38] African Americans with means also had the option of patronizing private beaches, such as Bruce's Beach located in Manhattan Beach, and clubs. In 1925, a group of African American businessmen planned the construction of the Pacific Beach Club, a private beach club located on a piece of undeveloped ocean frontage in Orange County's Huntington Beach. In search of stockholders to make the project a reality, they published several advertisements and articles in the *California Eagle*, Los Angeles's premiere Black newspaper. Readers were warned about the rapidly vanishing beach frontage in the region: "Do you know that soon all the land facing the Ocean will be owned by private individuals and that beach frontage is the most valuable property today in Southern California?" While similar on the surface to the "scarcity" argument used by the Reid Company, the motivation behind it was different: for African Americans, privatization was the only way to enjoy the sands free from harassment and violence. The erection of a "beautiful six-foot ornamental fence" around the private beach and its attendant bathhouse, dance pavilion, and tents, the *Eagle* noted, guaranteed "security for the club's members and their families."[39]

Beyond scarcity, developers and real estate agents were also quick to point at the many health benefits of living by the shore. Their glossy brochures promised resort living just a stone's throw from the city. Located "within thirty minutes of Hollywood and Los Angeles," Rancho Malibu (a seventeen-thousand-acre seaside estate in Malibu) was touted as a happy middle ground for "those of exacting taste" who refused "surrendering the luxuries of a city dwelling or the delights of a peaceful environment." Similarly, a flyer for Long Beach explained that "after a long, arduous day in the office, nothing is more refreshing than a dip in the surf before dinner time." Far from distracting residents from work, proximity to the ocean allowed them to enjoy the rejuvenating effects of a beach vacation year-round and to return to the office rested. By the same token, proximity to Downtown was a key selling point, and real estate developers eagerly highlighted connections. In Palisades Del Rey, Fritz Burns produced original maps that showed just how easy it was to get from Del Rey to the city, whether by highlighting in red the "six major boulevards" commuters could take or by drawing concentric circles from Downtown to the ocean, drawing attention to the fact that Del Rey, located "WITHIN THE 13 MILE CIRCLE," was, undoubtedly, "LOS ANGELES' CLOSEST BEACH."[40]

Away from the hustle and bustle of the city, and yet near enough to work there, coastal residents would be able to engage in outdoor recreation on a daily basis. The Hollywood Riviera promised its residents a life filled with swimming races, yachting escapades, golf and tennis parties, and horse-back riding tours. At Rancho Malibu, space had already been set aside for golf clubs, yacht harbors, recreational parks, bridle paths and trails, and even "an old English hunting club." Real estate promoters worked up a sweat promoting the attractions of this new athletic lifestyle, sometimes quite literally. Every morning, Fritz Burns made his employees, in shirts and ties, practice their calisthenics on the beach at Del Rey. More than a simple teambuilding exercise, these morning workouts associated Burns's business with the active lifestyle of potential middle-class buyers for whom slenderness and health had become something of an obsession in the 1920s. The svelte and vigorous bodies of his agents symbolized that Palisades Del Rey was a new kind of neighborhood, built around recreation and athleticism.[41]

The *Palisades del Rey Press*, a newspaper launched by Fritz Burns to advertise his development, often regaled its readers with stories of its healthful residents. Climatic arguments, at a time when air conditioning was not yet widespread, were key. The cooler temperatures enjoyed on the Westside guaranteed a respite from the sweltering conditions of the city

Figure 1.1. Employees of the Dickinson & Gillespie real estate companies practice calisthenics on the beach at Playa Del Rey, mid-1920s. Fritz Burns Papers, box 5, folder 12, Department of Archives and Special Collections, William H. Hannon Library, Loyola Marymount University.

on the hottest days of the year. On February 1, 1926, the paper introduced readers to the "first baby born in Palisades Del Rey." Her beaming parents attributed their daughter's first prize at the most beautiful baby of the bay contest to the "delightful climatic conditions." Similarly, on November 10, 1928, the paper told the tale of the astonished husband who, witnessing "the pure air and the fresh ocean breeze bringing back a rosy color to the cheeks of my wife" as they were touring the area, decided to make a down payment on the spot.[42]

Such stories also painted a portrait of the sort of people the company wanted to attract to its development: healthy, athletic, and above all, white, middle- and upper-class families with young children. To draw them in, its advertising brochures clearly stated that several "restrictions," such as zoning ordinances forbidding the construction of industrial districts and "perpetual racial restrictions," guaranteed Palisades Del Rey's success.[43] In other words, the emerging Southern California beach lifestyle was not open to African American, Latino, and Asian Angelenos. Although technically illegal, racial covenants continued to be in force throughout much of the city in the 1920s. As a result, African Americans were almost entirely confined to the Central Avenue neighborhood west of Downtown.[44] The scarcity of beachfront property enabled real estate developers to drive up prices and to offer these spaces only to white families. The coastal real estate boom of the 1920s and 1930s turned the shoreline into luxury property reserved for a certain segment of the population defined by its skin color, income level, and special relationship with outdoor recreation and the ocean. By the late 1920s, the Westside was not just one of the city's newest neighborhoods but a state of mind and a lifestyle, inspired by resort living but fit for city-loving professionals.

A VAST REPERTOIRE OF SEASIDE MODELS

Devoid of a maritime past and without any significant shipping or industrial tradition, early twentieth-century Santa Monica Bay was built on a landscape with a relatively small human footprint. By contrast, the cultural background against which this process took place was rich and vibrant. The rise of seaside resorts in Europe and on the US East Coast in the eighteenth and nineteenth centuries, coupled with the spectacular success of Coney Island and its many copycats across the nation, provided local developers and elites with a vast repertoire of models from which they borrowed liberally to attract tourists and residents to the beach. As a result of this variety, communities were able to shape their own identities.

Coney Island was the most evocative of these models. In the early twentieth century, The Pike, Long Beach's main amusement park, and the Venice and Ocean Park amusement areas all claimed for themselves the title of "Coney Island of the West" or "Coney Island of the Pacific."[45] At the time, the New York resort, famed for its amusement parks (Steeplechase, Luna Park, and Dreamland), reigned as the "undisputed capital of amusement" in the United States. Whether through postcards, newspaper articles, photographs, or films, all Americans had heard about the carnival atmosphere that reigned on this two-mile spit of sand on the southern tip of Brooklyn. Coney Island was emblematic of the era's new mass culture that was challenging genteel cultural standards and values. With its varied entertainments and heterogeneous (although strictly white) crowds, Coney Island functioned as "an invitation to collective gaiety and release," a place where visitors could shed their inhibitions. California beach resorts sought to capture this same magic. Visitors to Venice could enjoy a circus, a pier with a Ferris wheel, an ice skating rink, a dance hall, a bathhouse, and a variety of fairground attractions, including a zoo with over two hundred monkeys. At Long Beach, they could profit from the "joyous cosmopolitan atmosphere" of the promenade. As at Coney Island, the different amusement areas also featured spectacles showcasing "exotic" peoples, such as the Ubangis from Africa, and "freaks" like the Monkey-Man and Fire-Eater. The resorts also mirrored Coney Island's tantalizing architecture, with its outlandish facades and Oriental buildings. Santa Monica's La Monica Ballroom, whose turrets recalled the silhouette of a Middle Eastern palace, might not have been as unusual as the elephant-shaped hotel built in Coney Island in 1884, but it clearly signaled to visitors that they had entered an extraordinary space.[46]

Comparisons with Atlantic City also evoked an atmosphere of gaiety and freedom from everyday norms. At the turn of the century, the New Jersey beach resort was renowned throughout the country for its famous boardwalk where visitors took rides in wicker rolling chairs and enjoyed the pleasure of seeing and being seen by the masses.[47] For example, in 1914 the *Los Angeles Times* claimed that the Venice boardwalk presented "an animated panorama of new spring suits and hats . . . as equally and as well patronized as Atlantic City."[48] But Atlantic City also offered the latest thrill with its mechanical amusement rides. As such, Long Beach claimed to be "known throughout the world as the 'Atlantic City of the West'" and was "living up to her reputation by keeping abreast of the times with needed amusement features."[49] The California beaches, like Atlantic City and Coney Island, sought to attract pleasure-seeking crowds and convey a sense of modernity and exuberance.

Although Coney Island was a commercial success, it could also turn off some visitors. The completion in 1920 of a subway line linking it to New York City, as well as repeated fires that damaged the amusement parks, changed the composition of the crowds. By the 1930s, Coney Island had become associated with working-class leisure, and its attractions were deemed "cheap" and "vulgar" by many contemporary observers. As it came to be known as the "Sodom by the Sea," several Los Angeles resorts sought to distance themselves from the Brooklyn amusement area.[50] Manhattan Beach, for instance, described itself in terms that stigmatized honky-tonk amusements: "Nowhere else in America is there a better place for the home lover. There are no typical beach concessions or cheap amusement devices or shows. The property owners and residents will always be free from having their beach spoiled by the cheap amusement crowd." Similarly, Hermosa Beach sold itself as "a quiet town . . . uncluttered by amusement concessions."[51]

The rejection of commercial leisure led some municipalities and developers to adopt radically different seaside models. Hoping to establish their reputation as peaceful and respectable residential communities, Santa Monica, Redondo Beach, and other bay cities sought more distinguished comparisons with the Mediterranean Riviera or the coast of Normandy in France. The former functioned particularly well as it perpetuated the "Mediterranean comparison," a well-established tradition among late nineteenth-century boosters who had touted the Mediterranean qualities of the region's climate. By the time Abbot Kinney had founded his "Venice of America," in 1900, the Mediterranean was already an inescapable reference in Southern California. While the two regions certainly shared some resemblances, the Mediterranean reference served a more immediate objective for a remote region in the process of establishing itself. According to Kevin Starr, it "invoked values of responsible order and conveyed a sense of impending civilization." Most importantly, the metaphor conveniently erased California's Mexican past in favor of a romanticized Spanish heritage, in which the region's "racial purity" could be safeguarded.[52]

The Riviera also embodied a coastal imaginary very different from Coney Island's. It brought to mind sun-drenched cypress trees and white sandy beaches, rather than bustling boardwalks. It conjured up the therapeutic qualities of the sea and ocean air and the genteel lifestyle of the European aristocracy, with its hotel receptions, balls, regattas, and leisurely strolls on attractive promenades. In the American context, then, the European leisure areas were the very antithesis of Coney Island and working-class leisure. Resorts and new developments drew on these associations to lure wealthy buyers, emphasizing the beauty of the surrounding landscape and the refined lifestyle of their residents. In the booklet promoting Rancho Malibu, photographs of Nice and Monte Carlo not only expressed an aesthetic ideal but also gestured at the promoters' intention of attracting an exclusive clientele. Similarly, the Reid Company's "Hollywood Riviera" was an ingenious combination of two worlds that stood for refinement and elegance.

Beyond its symbolism, the Riviera provided a concrete model for developers, urban planners, and architects. Opened in 1927, the Deauville Beach Club was not only French by name: its architecture mimicked that of a "venerable French castle," complete with whimsical side turrets, crenelated walls, and fortified entrance. According to a 1941 guide, Palisades Del Rey was "now almost entirely residential, with fine widely spaced Mediterranean style houses, along broad avenues."[53] The emphasis on the neighborhood's residential character distinguished it from more commercially oriented beaches, while the mention of wide streets and Mediterranean-style houses evoked the spacious avenues of Cannes or Nice. The Riviera model proved particularly useful to Santa Monica elites who sought to distinguish themselves from Venice and Ocean Park, their raucous neighbors to the south. Aiming to make their city "something more than another Coney Island," they adopted a development strategy inspired by the Mediterranean yachting culture.[54] In the 1910s, hoping to create a "luxurious meeting place for the nation's millionaire yachtsmen," local elites started raising funds to build a harbor just north of the city's famous amusement pier. When the harbor was finally opened in 1934 after many technical difficulties, the *Los Angeles Times* proclaimed that it was "the last touch needed to what we may now fairly call the American Riviera."[55]

Beyond creating powerful imaginaries—and striking buildings—such comparisons functioned as a subtle form of exclusion. Every claim by an advertising brochure that a community was not overrun by "the cheap amusement crowd" or that it was "on par with the Mediterranean Riviera" signaled the promoters' intention to create a space for the select few. Just as the Palisades Del Rey newspaper drew a profile of the community's ideal future residents, so too did the comparison with European resorts mark working-class and nonwhite Angelenos as undesirable visitors.

THE MAKING OF A SOUTHERN CALIFORNIA BEACH CULTURE

Although Coney Island and the Riviera remained essential references for describing the Los Angeles coastline throughout the first half of the twentieth century, Southern California quickly established itself as a new seaside ideal across the industrialized world. Unlike its predecessors, the Southern California beach culture was resolutely hedonistic. Gone was the preoccupation with medical and hygienist concerns: what mattered most on the beaches of Los Angeles was how good someone looked in a bathing suit and how much fun could be had. Hollywood, the cult of sport, and the emergent surfing community particularly influenced the local beach culture. But it was hardly more inclusive than those of the East Coast or Europe. Although African American, Latino, and Asian American beachgoers took active part in surfing, swimsuit contests, gymnastics, and bodybuilding, they were notably absent from the films and magazines that spread this culture throughout the rest of the country. From the early twentieth-century onward, the Southern California beach culture was firmly associated with whiteness.

Considering Hollywood's obsession with filming bodily perfection, the local movie industry unsurprisingly had a major influence on beach manners. From the moment the film industry relocated to the region in the late 1900s, the beach occupied an important place in film production. Moviemakers were enthralled by the freedom of movement and dress sanctioned by the seaside location. Vast and often empty during the winter, Southern California beaches soon became early Hollywood's favorite shooting locations. The first American feature-length film, *Enoch Arden* (1911, D. W. Griffith), was filmed on the beaches of Santa Monica Bay. Beaches were also ideal places to film car chases, essential scenes in "California slapstick," a brand of comedy that relied on comic physicality. For an industry that depended on its ability to transport audiences to far-away places, the beaches could usefully be transformed into a variety of landscapes, from the Riviera to the dunes of the Sahara. Local newspapers, such as the *Palisades Del Rey Press*, provide a glimpse into the filming activity between 1926 and 1928, when at least four film shoots took place on the sand.[56] In 1927, the newspaper described the neighborhood excitement when Al Nathan Productions came to film an orientalist romantic drama titled *The Queen of Queens*, and it included a photo of the entire crew posing on the beach. The shoot was so successful that the studio even bought a section of coastal land.[57]

Buying property on the beach was becoming increasingly common among Hollywood professionals in this period. Once a private ranch fiercely defended from trespassers, Malibu started attracting the likes of actresses Anna Q. Nilsson, Marie Prevost, and Clara Bow in the late 1920s. The area chosen by such illustrious residents eventually came to be known as "the Malibu movie colony."[58] A few miles to the south, Santa Monica's "Gold

Coast" was home to famous directors and actors such as Louis B. Mayer, Jesse Lasky, Douglas Fairbanks, Mary Pickford, and Marion Davies. By choosing to live at the beach—an unusual choice at the time—stars hoped to elevate their public profiles and benefit from the booming popularity of seaside recreation. Moreover, such a move attached an aura of mystique to any film star in need of a publicity boost. In the context of Hollywood's rising star system, which pitted actors against one other, living by the beach soon became an essential marker of a true movie star.[59]

By the 1930s, the beaches were so central to the movie world that bus companies, such as Allison California Auto Trips, organized tours titled "Hollywood and the Beaches," combining a visit to the inland studios with an excursion to the seaside.[60] Starlets posed on the beach, hoping to catch the eye of a producer while tourists headed to the shore with their autograph books, hoping to meet their favorite actors. In fact, so many movie stars lived in Malibu that the city had to station "uniformed guards . . . at every entrance" to protect their glamorous residents from "sight-seers and autograph hunters."[61]

One of the most enduring legacies of the close relationship between Hollywood and the coastline was the emergence of the bathing beauty as an icon of popular culture. Bathing beauties first appeared on tourist brochures promoting Southern California beach resorts in the early twentieth century. Although not unique to the region, Southern Californian bathing beauties wore more daring swimsuits and posed in a more flirtatious fashion than their counterparts on the East Coast, where conservatives had more influence over beach etiquette.[62] Moreover, the phenomenon soon took on another dimension in Los Angeles when filmmaker Mack Sennett, inspired by local beach cultures, started using the coast as a scenic background for his "Bathing Beauties," young, pretty, bathing-suit-clad actresses, frolicking on the sand.[63] These young women had little to do with any storyline; their presence essentially was an opportunity to display female beauty and seminudity. The ploy proved successful. Sennett's Bathing Beauties became so popular with the public that other studios quickly launched their own brigade of shapely actresses clad in fashionable swimwear. By the 1920s, the bathing girl had become an established screen type with its own subheading in the columns of *The Standard*, a casting directory.[64]

While the rise of the bathing girl reflected national trends, including the rising popularity of beauty pageants, it had a disproportionate impact on standards of beauty at the local level. In contrast to moviegoers in New York or Chicago, who admired the Bathing Beauties on the silver screen as abstract icons with no connection to their daily lives, Angelenos could encounter them both in the movies and in reality. Even if they didn't catch

Figure 1.2. The Mack Sennett Bathing Beauties posing on an automobile, circa 1919. National Photo Company Collection / Library of Congress.

a glimpse of the young ladies while Sennett filmed his movies, they could read about them in their local newspapers or see them make appearances at movie openings, automobile shows, and other local events.[65] In May 1919, Ocean Park theater patrons who came to see *Yankee Doodle in Berlin* were also treated to the "tuneful frolics" of the "famous Mack Sennett Bathing Beauties in person."[66] More significantly, Sennett often enrolled his Bathing Beauties in local beach beauty pageants. In 1917, members of his troupe took first, second, and third place in the Great Bathing Parade held in Venice. Sennett himself was often a judge at these events.[67]

Sennett was not the only filmmaker to use local pageants as an opportunity for publicity. All the studios entered "their prettiest girls" in the annual Venice Bathing Parade. If not already under contract, female contestants were often lured by the prospect of winning "a screen test in Hollywood." Indeed, according to the local press, many were entering "with the hope that it would prove a stepping stone into the movies." Hollywood even influenced the categories used in local pageants, with the 1928 Venice Bathing parade offering a prize for "most handsome male film extra."[68] In other words, Hollywood beauty criteria soon became the ultimate standards against which the beach bodies of local women (and men) were judged.

While the bathing girls on the silver screen were always white, local beach queens were more diverse. Black Angelenos took part in the nascent

Southern California beach culture despite persistent forms of segregation. Verna Williams, a young African American woman whose family relocated from Texas to Los Angeles in the 1920s, visited the Bay Street Beach in Santa Monica every Sunday. In photographs from her family album, Verna is clad in the most fashionable swimwear and poses languorously on the sands in a manner inspired by Hollywood movies. In one of them, she is even wearing a one-piece bathing suit with the word "HOLLYWOOD" sewn down the side of her chest.[69] In 1925, the short-lived Pacific Beach Club organized a pre-opening marketing event that included a well-attended "Bathing Beauty Parade," "the first ever given for our group on the Pacific Coast," according to the *California Eagle*, in which many "local girls" could demonstrate their "cinema aspirations." The following week, reels of the parade were shown at a movie theater in the mostly Black South Central neighborhood, turning the contestants, at least for the day, into stars of the silver screen. The dissemination, however limited, of such events certainly instilled a sense of pride in Black audiences. It also reinscribed Black bodies within regional narratives of the body beautiful.[70]

In early twentieth-century Los Angeles, then, going to the beach was a glamorous affair: it meant potentially meeting a star, or even becoming one. But it also decreed that Angelenos' bodies should always be ready for the camera. As a result, residents were acutely aware of the need to prepare and shape their bodies for public display, and many turned to physical exercise to achieve the beauty standards of the time. This phenomenon was national in scope. Since the end of the nineteenth century and the rise of the "muscular Christianity" movement, Americans had become increasingly interested in physical activity as a means of improving the body. At the same time, changing social and cultural mores meant that excess body fat was no longer seen as a sign of wealth, but instead as something to be mocked.[71]

While all Americans experienced these transformations, Angelenos were under particular pressure to conform. Not only were athletic prowess and slenderness more revered in Hollywood than anywhere else, especially as the "reducing craze" reached a peak during the 1920s, but Los Angeles's civic image was intimately linked to athleticism.[72] In 1904, it was the first city in the country to have a municipal service entirely dedicated to recreation and playgrounds. As early as the 1930s, it was widely accepted that Californians were more athletic than people from the East. Many contemporaries saw Californian bodies—powered by the nutrients from the region's agricultural products and tanned by the sun year round—as "naturally" stronger and more beautiful. Yet Los Angeles had fewer parks

Figure 1.3. Verna Williams at Bay Street Beach in Santa Monica (also known as "the Inkwell"), 1931. Shades of L.A. Photo Collection / Los Angeles Public Library.

than other large American cities. As a result, major athletes, as well as those just looking for fun, headed for the sands.[73]

The cult of sport that flourished in the region's athletic clubs also had a significant influence on Los Angeles beach cultures. The beach parties so typical of Southern California usually featured swimming, games, and races. The annual Catholic reunion at Ocean Park Beach in 1904, for instance, featured dancing, a pie-eating competition, and a baby pageant alongside the more strenuous running, boating, and swimming races.[74] The private African American beach known as Bruce's Beach was likewise a site for sporting events.[75] By mixing sports and recreation, Angelenos eliminated distinctions between fitness and fun, the practical and the playful. Throughout the 1920s and 1930s, municipalities began to provide more formal settings for children and adults to exercise, installing playgrounds and gym equipment on the sands. Wealthier residents had even more opportunities, as Downtown sports clubs started opening branches on the coast and adapted sports to the beach environment. In the 1920s, for example, the Santa Monica Swimming Club installed nets on the beach so its members could practice their golf swings on the sand.[76]

Although similar practices took place at European beaches, they held a different meaning. In early twentieth-century France, for example, the tradition of the "gymkhanas" presented opportunities for bourgeois adults and children to exercise. After the First World War, basketball and volleyball were introduced at some beach clubs. Yet such activities were organized with hygienic and military objectives in mind, ultimately with the goal of preparing the next generation of soldiers.[77]

Pacific coast recreation was intended instead to turn children into beautiful adults. This "Mecca of childhood," as the *Los Angeles Times* described the area, ensured the development of "perfect physical manhood and womanhood." Extolling the virtues of "aquatic sports," the paper presented "the winner of a recent thousand-dollar beauty prize" and native of Santa Monica, Miss Newkirk, as an example of this physical perfection.[78] Children as young as a year and a half were encouraged to "work out" as a means to secure a good place in local beauty pageants. A photograph of Venice toddler Larry Sims, with his angelic blond curls, freshly changed diaper, and pint-sized barbell, perfectly captures the combination of fun, showmanship, and body cult that characterized the LA beach cultures.

Adults were also encouraged to take part. Every Thursday in 1928, reported the *Santa Monica Evening Outlook*, women of the Elks Club could be seen "bending and twisting on the beaches" as they underwent "a course of body and beauty building."[79] The close relationship between beach exercise and beauty was reinforced by Hollywood stars like Marion Davies, who emphasized her athleticism by staging a ballgame photo shoot in front of her beach house.[80]

Exercising on the beach, then, was a way of strengthening one's body, "beautifying" it, and having fun while doing so. The phenomenon of Muscle Beach is particularly representative of this mindset. Located on Santa Monica Beach near the famous recreation pier, Muscle Beach was initially opened as a municipal playground where children could exercise on gymnastic equipment, such as rings and parallel bars. Starting in 1931, however, the site started attracting local gymnasts, athletes, and circus artists who wanted to practice their routines. With a lively vaudeville scene

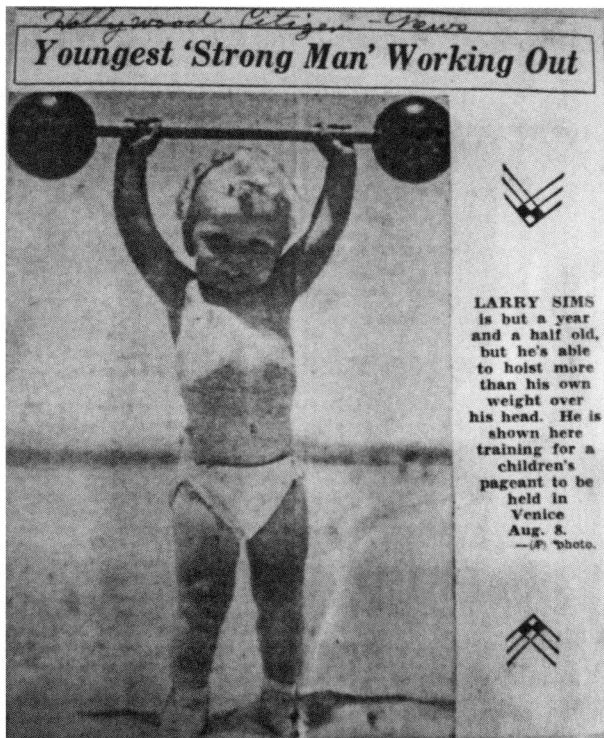

Figure 1.4. A young Californian hoists a barbell on Venice Beach, circa 1930. Clipping in scrapbook. Santa Monica History Museum Collection.

Figure 1.5. Marion Davies in front of her beach house in Santa Monica, late 1920s. Werner von Boltenstern Postcard Collection. Department of Archives and Special Collections, William H. Hannon Library, Loyola Marymount University.

in Downtown Los Angeles, several nearby wrestling and boxing arenas, a strong collegiate gymnastics presence at local universities, and scores of young men and women lured to Tinseltown by the appeal of a career in the movie industry, the playground drew from a large pool of potential recruits. By the mid-1930s, the local newspaper reported on regular "tumbling, flying rings, and horizontal bar exhibitions" taking place at the beach.[81] While many athletes practiced traditional gymnastics exercises, the most popular acts were the human pyramids and the "adagio," which consisted of gently tossing a swimsuit-clad woman in the air and having her land gracefully in the hands of a well-built male. In the words of one of its alumni, Muscle Beach was "a circus beneath a blue sky instead of a tent."[82] Unlike circus performers, who wore fanciful outfits and elaborate makeup, Muscle Beach habitués displayed their lithe and muscular bodies in ordinary bathing suits and wore the most natural form of makeup: their California tans. The popular Muscle Beach spectacles also differentiated themselves from more traditional gymnastic and acrobatic shows through their erotic appeal. Beautiful men and women performing feats of strength and balance in skimpy bathing suits could not help but elicit lustful appreciation from the audience. Looking was actively encouraged. Every year, Santa Monica organized an annual photograph contest, inviting visitors to take "camera shots of any activity from sunbathing to acrobatics."[83] Finally, there was no need for music and choreography, as sounds of the ocean background and the athletes' cheerful laughter made for a joyful spectacle. At Muscle Beach, physical exercise and outdoor living became a performance.

Physical exercise as performance was not a new phenomenon on the Southern California coast. As early as the 1900s, businessmen were routinely organizing swimming races and surfing and diving demonstrations to attract tourists to their beach resorts. Surfing was particularly popular with the crowds. As an ancient Hawaiian practice, surfing's exotic nature appealed to a primarily white audience. The first and most famous surfing expert of the time was undoubtedly Hawaiian swimmer and lifesaving instructor George Freeth. Upon arriving in California in 1907, Freeth was hired by businessmen Henry Huntington and Abbot Kinney to demonstrate his surfing tricks at their respective resorts along the coast, Redondo Beach and Venice.[84] His career inspired others to bring their surfing talents to the mainland. In 1912, Olympic swimmer Duke Kahanamoku also gave surfing demonstrations in the region.[85]

Although surfing exhibitions took place in Atlantic City, Europe, and Australia, surfing established its deepest roots in Southern California, where it resonated with the hedonism and showmanship of local beach cultures.[86] Moreover, Hawaii and Southern California had enjoyed close commercial relationships since the nineteenth century.[87] Following US annexation of the islands in 1898, a growing number of Californians took to vacationing on the beaches of Waikiki. By 1925, economic and cultural ties between the islands and the continent were so strong that Hawaii booster Lorrin A. Thurston declared Hawaii "the natural companion piece to, the supplement of, Los Angeles."[88] As young Hawaiians such as George Freeth and Duke Kahanamoku visited and eventually settled in the region, they parlayed their passion for water sports into a means of earning a living. With water safety turning into an essential part of Los Angeles's tourist and leisure economies, these young men were hired into the newly created posts of lifeguards and spread the practice of surfing among their colleagues.[89]

By the late 1920s, surfing was practiced by about a hundred, mostly male, lifeguards, swimming instructors, and professional swimmers in the region. Despite their small numbers, early practitioners of the sport were regular fixtures in the pages of the *Los Angeles Times*, which regaled its readers with tales of "mermen" riding the waves, and established the visual characteristics of the lifeguard/surfer as a modern icon.[90] Thomas Blake, a Wisconsin native who settled in Los Angeles in 1921, played an important role in this process by documenting the emergent Hawaiian and Southern Californian surfing communities in photographs and extolling the virtues of the sport for health and fitness. Like Kahanamoku and Freeth, Blake worked as a lifeguard for local beach clubs during the 1920s. Traveling regularly between the continent and Hawaii, he became fascinated with traditional paddle boards and surfboards. Over the following years, he publicized his own board designs in a book, *Hawaiian Surfriders* (1935), and published several articles in popular magazines and newspapers. His 1935 article on Hawaiian surfing in *National Geographic* featured a particularly striking photograph of Blake standing beside his collection of traditional Hawaiian surfboards.[91] As surfing scholar Kristin Lawler has described, his "beach-blond, tousled hair, tan healthy skin [and his] light-colored, baggy, simple clothing" came to epitomize the "relaxed, carefree look that is associated with the beach to this day."[92] In the 1930s, Olympic swimmer and actor Johnny Weissmuller further established the iconic image of the Southern California lifeguard as muscular, suntanned, and tall. Weissmuller, who rose to fame playing a broad-chested Tarzan in a dozen movies between 1932 and 1948, was a regular at Santa Monica Beach, where he trained with the lifeguards and even became an honorary Los Angeles County lifeguard in 1932.[93] By the early 1940s, the stereotype of the blond, muscular, and tanned lifeguard was so entrenched in the imaginaries of locals and tourists that thousands of cards were printed every summer warning beachgoers against "trying to get a tan like a lifeguard on your first visit to the beach."[94] Although two nonwhite men, Kahanamoku and Freeth— whose mother was half Hawaiian—had introduced surfing to Southern California and their Hawaiian-ness had been instrumental in the sport's early appeal there, by the 1930s, the representation of surfers in the media had completely erased the indigeneity of the sport.[95]

By the end of the 1930s, Southern California had emerged as a new model of seaside leisure, characterized by its emphasis on the display of beautiful, tanned, and fit bodies. Thanks to films, photographs, and advertisements, Americans across the country imagined the LA beaches as populated by glamorous film stars and intrepid surfers. This local beach culture would continue to evolve and spread, especially in the 1950s and 1960s, but its broad outlines were already cemented around a recreational culture of seaside fun and displays of healthy, attractive bodies. To a certain extent, the myth was based on reality, but photographs and films systematically erased the contributions of non-white Angelenos to the variety of bodily cultures. This contradiction between representation and reality would only grow starker in the postwar period.

By the late 1930s, the Westside, as it would eventually be called, was coming into its own. This new area of the city contained a motley collection of neighborhoods and towns, from the most exclusive beach communities to industrial suburbs and raucous amusement zones. But it possessed an unquestionably distinctive charm as the only place in Los Angeles where one could enjoy cooling oceanic breezes, beautiful homes, easy access to the city, and proximity to the Hollywood crowd. Being near the beach had undeniable benefits. The rise of the Westside coincided with the beach craze that took America by storm in the 1920s. In Los Angeles, where closeness to Hollywood upped the stakes, a beach afternoon was not just fun: it was a workout, a party, and a show all at once. Moving to the Westside meant being able to enjoy the pleasures of a beach afternoon on a daily basis. If Los Angeles, as historian Lawrence Culver argues, invented "leisure as a permanent way of life," then the Westside is where this lifestyle was brought to perfection.[96]

Of course, not everybody was welcome to the Westside. Racial covenants ensured that most of the area remained white. Beach clubs excluded nonwhite people from becoming members—and if legal means proved inefficient, strict racial boundaries were enforced through violence and harassment. Yet Black Angelenos also enjoyed the nascent Southern

California beach culture, whether within the bounds of segregated beaches or at private beach clubs. Although most Mexican Americans and Asian Americans lived far from the coast, they too took part in the beach craze. In fact, nonwhite Angelenos were central to the development of the Westside, as the influence of Hawaiian surfers Duke Kahanamoku and George Freeth shows. As much as residents tried to avoid encounters with racial others, the Westside's appeal was partially based on its connections with remote locales and nonwhite cultures.

CHAPTER 2

⌖

A Troubled Seaside Order

"Have a good time at the beach this year! Go as often as you please! Stay as long as you please. Swim as much as you like. Eat what you want; and soak up the sunshine." On July 5, 1936, the *Los Angeles Times* encouraged its readers to take refuge from the heat on the beaches of the metropolis and abandon all restraint. Yet even as it celebrated the freedom of the seaside, the article warned, "But remember just this, there is law on the beach and you are expected to observe it to the letter!" The rest of the article provided a list of the laws that applied to this specific area.[1]

This article highlighted the tensions surrounding the policing of beaches in a large metropolis: how could beach hedonism coexist with law and order? In Los Angeles, the seaside initially attracted little attention from law enforcement as the city first developed inland, about fifteen miles from the ocean. When the city experienced an economic and demographic boom that propelled it toward the Pacific in the mid-1920s, the first laws specifically regulating beachgoing behavior appeared in that context. As the small resorts of the early twentieth century turned into full-fledged, year-round residential cities, local elites—mainly composed of businessmen involved in tourism and city affairs, and religious leaders—established themselves as the guardians of respectability and good morals.

Meanwhile, beaches became spaces where bathers from all walks of life mingled. Among the newcomers who settled in Los Angeles in the first half of the twentieth century and headed to the beach were significant numbers of African Americans, Mexicans, Filipinos, and Japanese. In 1930, nonwhite inhabitants of Los Angeles (including Mexicans) represented 14 percent of the total population, a "proportion exceeded only by Baltimore among the nation's largest cities."[2] As the beach public grew more racially diverse, tensions heightened. By the 1920s, most urban beaches in the United States were segregated by race, leading to frequent battles over access, from small skirmishes to full-on riots. Most notoriously, the Chicago race riot of 1919 started on a segregated Lake Michigan beach when a white man hit a fourteen-year-old Black boy on the head with a rock.[3] Leisure spaces crystallized racial tensions because they encouraged playful flirting and could become the site of interracial sexual encounters.[4] Beaches and swimming pools were particularly fraught because they involved social interactions in a state of undress, especially after the 1920s when bathing suits increasingly revealed women's curves. In Los Angeles, the existence of invisible "color lines" on the sand sometimes led to violent confrontations between Black, Mexican, Asian, and white beachgoers.

Starting in the late 1920s, then, the increasing racial and ethnic diversity of the growing population and the concurrent mobilization of coastal property owners in favor of stricter beach rules forced local authorities to include the coastline in their policing strategy. At the same time, nonwhite Angelenos asserted their rights to enjoy the Southern California beach lifestyle, challenging prevailing ethnic and racial hierarchies in the city. As a liminal space far from the gaze of the authorities, where men and women mixed in a state of seminudity, the beach called into question not only traditional methods of policing but also the underpinnings of the social and racial order of the urban metropolis. Who had the "right to the beach" in an increasingly racially diverse Los Angeles? Who determined the parameters of beach policing as the metropolis integrated the Westside into its fold? This chapter argues that the beach order, rather than being a space of freedom from societal norms, was shaped by constant negotiations and confrontations between groups of beachgoers, local authorities, and coastal residents. As beaches became integral to Angelenos' sense of identity and daily life, encounters on the sand altered law enforcement practices, as well as social and racial hierarchies throughout the metropolis.

FREEDOM FROM RULES? INFORMAL REGULATIONS ON LOS ANGELES BEACHES, 1900S–1910S

Historians of the seaside have traditionally portrayed the beach of the nineteenth and early twentieth centuries as a lawless space where "the certainties of authority [were] diluted, and the usual constraints on behavior [were] suspended."[5] In this vision, a carnivalesque atmosphere prevailed on the sand, allowing visitors to transgress boundaries and abandon social proprieties.[6] To be sure, the seaside in industrialized countries represented at least until the Second World War a space outside the ordinary, where clothing and conduct followed looser rules and where encounters with social and racial others were possible. However, urban beaches did function according to unspoken racial rules and could become the site of violent confrontations with police intervention. For example, in Chicago in 1919, a riot erupted after a group of Black youngsters playing on a makeshift raft inadvertently crossed the unofficial boundary dividing the white part of the beach from the one where Black beachgoers were customarily confined. While Coney Island and other resorts did embrace the mixing of social classes and ethnicities, racial segregation, if not outright exclusion, was widespread on US coastlines. In that sense, rules, written or not, fundamentally shaped the modern beach experience.

In 1900s and 1910s Los Angeles, beach policing was not a major issue for local authorities. An informal segregation system kept violent confrontations at bay. Local boosters also prevented excessive policing, fearing it would scare off tourists and weekend crowds of pleasure-seekers.

The beach exerted a strong pull on nonwhite Angelenos. African Americans who settled in the region were just as eager as white newcomers to enjoy escapades in nature. In newspapers and magazines, Black boosters extolled the region's climate and beauty, as well as its vibrant industries, though they never failed to mention the many forms of discrimination African Americans still faced.[7] Moreover, Afro-Angelenos tended to be in a somewhat better economic position than many of their counterparts in other big cities, since only those with some means could make the long and costly journey from the South to the West. In general, they belonged to the "Black middle class" in terms of their values and lifestyle, if not their paychecks.[8] The coastline also proved relatively accessible even for those of modest means, thanks to the extensive tramway system.

The Black population in Los Angeles was relatively small at two thousand in 1900 and seventy-six hundred in 1910, but it was growing as quickly as the rest of the region.[9] No doubt taking note of the trend, white residents and developers sought to limit if not altogether bar the presence of African Americans in Los Angeles's coastal neighborhoods and towns. Through a mixture of legal means, such as restrictive covenants, and real estate agents' discriminatory practices, the city became increasingly divided between its eastern neighborhoods, where the vast majority of nonwhite residents lived, and western ones, which tended to be more affluent and white (with the notable exceptions of small African American communities located in Santa Monica, Venice, and Manhattan Beach). In a 1912 letter to the Black daily newspaper the *Crisis*, Louise McDonald testified to the pervasive racism in the region: "We suffer almost anything (except lynching) right here in the beautiful land of sunshine. . . . Civil privileges are here unknown." Places of recreation, in her account, were far from exempt: "You can't bathe at the beaches, eat in any first-class place, nor will the street car and sight-seeing companies sell us tickets if they can possibly help it."[10]

That same year, African American entrepreneur Willa A. Bruce, who had moved to Los Angeles from New Mexico with her husband, Charles Bruce, a few years earlier, bought a piece of land by the ocean in Manhattan Beach, taking advantage of the fact that restrictive covenants had not yet been introduced in the sparsely populated town. In 1913, the couple opened a small resort on their beach property, which they improved over the next few years by building a dance hall, café, and bathhouse. The lodge where they lived could also accommodate a few summer and weekend visitors. Despite constant harassment from white landowners in the vicinity, including city founder George H. Peck, Bruce's Beach, as it came to be known, was a success. In 1920, the Bruces expanded their business with the purchase of a second beach lot adjacent to their first acquisition.[11]

Other Afro-Angelenos, such as the stylish beachgoer Verna Williams, frequented Bay Street Beach in Santa Monica, known derogatively as the "Inkwell." On this small stretch of sand located between Bay and Bicknell Streets, the risk of harassment and intimidation by white beachgoers was lower than in other areas. Using the family car, Williams would meet her friends at the popular spot after school and on Sundays after church.[12] African Americans had used this stretch of beach since the 1900s, probably because a small Black community emerged at that time around Phillips Chapel, a Methodist Episcopal church located in Santa Monica's Ocean Park district. Located about half a mile south of the Santa Monica Pier, the beach was away from the main attractions at a time when the area was not well developed. Although African Americans also spread their towels at North Beach and Playa Del Rey, Santa Monica's Bay Street Beach had the advantage of being close to small Black businesses.[13] Black beachgoers could rent a bathing suit and get changed in La Bonita, a Black-owned bathhouse and lodge located nearby. A few blocks from the beach, George Caldwell's dance club, a popular African American establishment, provided nightly entertainment for beachgoers.[14] In the 1900s and 1910s, then, Afro-Angelenos managed to carve out their own spots for fun in the sun. The situation was far from ideal considering the informal restrictions Black beachgoers were subjected to, but there were few racist incidents on the sand compared to the daily, often bloody interracial encounters on Chicago's beaches and other recreational spaces.[15]

The police considered beaches a low priority because of the relatively small number of year-round residents living in coastal communities. At the beginning of the twentieth century, beach resorts such as Santa Monica and Venice relied almost exclusively on the tourism and leisure economy.[16] Given the stiff competition for visitors, municipalities did not want to scare off beachgoers by enforcing strict laws. On the contrary, tourist brochures touted "the exhilarating freedom which only the ocean [could] provide."[17] Given the small size of their police forces, coastal communities chose to concentrate their officers where they were most needed—on the streets. According to the Venice Chief of Police in 1917, "There are not enough police in the city to watch all the bathers."[18] The same situation existed in neighboring Santa Monica. In 1911, the resort town's mayor recommended that a police officer be stationed near the municipal bath-house, only to be told by the city council that such a measure could not be financed.[19] The communities that were part of the City of Los Angeles were underserved as well. Compared to other metropolises, Los Angeles had the lowest number of officers per capita in the country. Authority figures were sparse on the coastline. Not until the 1920s and 1930s were the first professional lifeguard teams organized.[20] While unspoken segregation rules did exist, visitors could engage in a range of activities—including dog walking, drinking alcohol, and starting a fire—for which no regulation existed.

The lax rules and minimal oversight explain why beaches were often the site of festive gatherings organized by schools, charitable organizations, and local residents. Overnight, the beaches could morph into large encampments with big bonfires and cars parked on the sand. Such events would never have been possible in urban parks, where behavior was much more tightly regulated. In New York's Central Park, for instance, guards around the same period were on the lookout for visitors who drank alcohol or dared set foot on the parks' lawns. Early twentieth-century beaches, then, enjoyed greater freedom than other recreational spaces in the city.[21]

Regulations regarding bathing attire did exist. In the early twentieth century, most beachgoers across the country, whether male or female, still wore dark, cumbersome outfits that concealed their bodies. Men wore loose-fitting trunks that reached down to their knees and sleeveless tops that covered their chests. Women wore voluminous dresses made of dark wool with elbow-length sleeves; this design guaranteed hips and thighs would remain unseen, even if the fabric got soaked. On some beaches, a swimming cap and stockings were recommended to complete a respectable appearance. Many municipalities, such as Santa Monica, did not actually enact any laws regarding bathing suits on the premise that the innate modesty of beachgoers rendered ordinances unnecessary.[22] Such attitudes were widespread beyond Los Angeles. In 1923, the Board of Recreation superintendent in Bridgeport, Connecticut, considered that "the public [was] fairly sane on [the] matter of [bathing suits] and prescribing the inches above the knee, etc. [was] all tommy-rot." In other words, the existence of profoundly internalized social norms precluded the need for a written rule.[23] In metropolitan Los Angeles, enforcing bathing-suit laws was complicated by the fact that the beaches belonged to different municipalities and thus enforced different laws. In 1930, a Public Beach Coordinating Committee attempted to formulate uniform bathing-suit regulations for the entire coastline but ended up abandoning the idea "in view of new styles being turned out by manufacturers every year."[24]

Negotiations surrounding bathing attire grew particularly tense when the one-piece swimsuit first appeared on the city's beaches in the late 1910s. A tightly fitting outfit of dark fabric better known today as the Annette Kellerman suit, after the Australian Olympic swimmer who made it famous, the one-piece suit left the legs bare and enabled women to swim far more easily than a dress and stockings. While the fashionable swimsuit was not widely adopted on most American beaches until the 1920s, when a new generation of daring flappers challenged Victorian standards of public decency, a significant number of young women in Los Angeles had already donned the notorious garment a few years earlier. Hollywood's influence combined with the local obsession with the outdoors meant that Angelenos were ahead of the curve when it came to sporting and swimming fashion. The region's reputation for liberal views on bathing suit etiquette was no secret. In 1916, the Sears, Roebuck & Co. catalog advertised its skimpiest women's swimsuits as "California Style."[25]

In this rapidly changing context, residents in Los Angeles's beach communities were divided. The younger generation—men and women who enjoyed the seaside pleasures on a regular basis—supported a flexible bathing suit policy. City council members, who were usually male and older, wanted to uphold moral values, with the support of local religious authorities and upper-class women's clubs. Beachgoers' daily acts of transgressions occasionally forced council members to renounce their plans, however. In 1912, for instance, the Venice City Council abandoned its plan to adopt an ordinance regulating the length of bathing suits when a petition opposing it gained traction.[26]

The most effective weapon bathers possessed was the local press and its power to make or destroy a resort's reputation. In the 1910s, controversies arose over ordinances that prohibited beachgoers from walking through the City of Santa Monica uncovered. While the police arrested many beachgoers (of both sexes but mostly female) who wore their bathing suits without a cover in the streets, trams, and shops of the city throughout the 1910s, they eventually stopped when the local business elite realized that newspaper reports of the arrests were damaging the town in the eyes of tourists. After all, as the owner of a local bathhouse remarked, was it prudent to send young people to jail for wearing fashionable bathing suits in the street when the city circulated brochures portraying young women wearing similarly suggestive outfits? In 1919, following the arrest of Mrs. Alta Johnson, a "very pretty and young matron" who had gone to fetch a loaf of bread in a shop while wearing a swimsuit and a knee-length bathrobe that did not cover her entire body, the local paper expressed fears that the news would turn the beach city into "the laughing stock of liberal minded persons." Following legal advice, Alta Johnson threatened the city with a lawsuit. As the local newspaper explained, "Scores of pretty girls walk[ed] on the promenade and [went] back and forth to the apartment houses without any covering at all over their bathing suits." Since the rules were constantly broken, argued Johnson's lawyers, they had lost all meaning. Given such negative media coverage of the arrest, the police felt compelled to drop the case and stop enforcing the ordinance. Strict policing of the beach proved not only impractical but also risky for a place dependent on a tourism and leisure economy.[27]

A NEW BEACH ORDER? IMPOSING SOCIAL AND RACIAL SEGREGATION ON THE BEACH, 1920S–1930S

While the marginal position of early twentieth-century beaches allowed for looser rules and easier social mixing, the situation changed rapidly during Los Angeles's boom years of the 1920s and 1930s. As the Westside towns and neighborhoods acquired a year-round population and the number of beachgoers soared (from 2.7 million annually to over 20 million between 1925 and 1935), tensions surrounding beach use grew more frequent. By opening private clubs and erecting physical barriers on the sand, upper-class beachgoers sought to distance themselves, physically and metaphorically, from working-class pleasure-seekers. The opening of several beach clubs may also have been racially motivated. As the presence of nonwhites on the shores became more noticeable, a wave of anti-Black animosity severely diminished African Americans' opportunities for recreation and entrepreneurial success at the seaside.

Los Angeles beaches of the 1920s and 1930s, like swimming pools in that era, were "social melting pots."[28] Going for a dip in the Pacific was free, and the vast tramway system took working-class Angelenos there from across the inland metropolis. Even those who could not afford the full price of a beach-bound tramway ticket found ways to partake. In his 1926 study titled *The City Boy and His Problems*, sociologist Emory Bogardus noted the widespread practice among the city's male adolescents of "begging a ride to the beach." One of Bogardus's interviewees readily admitted the common method he and his friends used: "We go on the street car as far as nickel will take us and then we walk a few blocks and then we catch a ride."[29] Moreover, by the late 1930s, owning a car was affordable for a wide swath of the urban population. In 1939, for instance, Celes King III, a fifteen-year-old African American high school student, was able to buy a used Ford Model A car for less than a hundred dollars, thanks to a loan he repaid with the help of his dad and the wages he earned working at a gas station on Saturdays. Many years later, King remembered in an interview how much this had changed his ability to enjoy the region's pleasures: "I was able to go to the beach if I chose to, and I could go down to Santa Monica, jump in the ocean, get back in the car, drive back and say, 'Oh boy, this California's great.'" Once at the beach, spending money was optional. Of course, many people splurged on rides and ate at restaurants in the amusement areas. But swimming was free, and food could be procured on the cheap. Joy Elliott remembered in an interview how, in the 1920s, vendors sold tamales hot from their carts for a dime at The Pike in Long Beach.[30]

While resorts prided themselves on their "democratic" atmosphere, the multiplication of beach clubs in 1920s Los Angeles suggests that some beachgoers did not enjoy rubbing elbows with the common crowds of merrymakers. Santa Monica, for instance, touted the fact that "people in all walks of life" enjoyed "every known marine sport" along the bay. The "ocean," the city assured in its promotional material, was "very democratic—appealing to clubs and Chautauquas, colleges and crowds, society and real American homes." Yet by the late 1920s, the city was home to at least eleven beach clubs "with a total membership of 25,000 persons."[31] Club openings were so frequent in that period—over twenty were launched between 1922 and 1927—that the *Los Angeles Times* joked that "there was a new club every morning, including Sundays and holidays."[32] As public beaches attracted more people, clubs provided their members with privacy and safety, while guaranteeing them more space to spread out their towels and personal belongings. According to the "prominent Los Angeles men" who launched the Santa Monica Swimming Club in 1923, the project was sorely needed due to "the prevalent congested beaches adjacent to Los Angeles."[33]

Nevertheless, exclusivity remained the main reason why upper-class Angelenos flocked to beach clubs. Lists of members included "city, county, and public officials, political figures, moving picture celebrities and magnates, and hundreds of business and professional men and women" or, in short, "everybody who is anybody."[34] Joining such an exclusive roster of people required paying high membership fees (about one hundred dollars per year or more, which amounts to eighteen hundred modern dollars accounting for inflation), as well as meeting a series of criteria that ensured the elitist nature of these spaces. Nonwhite Angelenos and Jews were not allowed to join. New members' applications had to be supported by one or more club members. Other rules seemed designed to preserve the good morals of the establishment. At the Bel Air Bay Club, for example, an unmarried man who was a member of the club was not allowed to invite another man to join, perhaps a rule designed to protect against any suspected homosexual activities.[35]

Such precautions were useless, however, if club members had to mingle with other beachgoers once they hit the sand. Key to a club's success was its ability to privatize a stretch of beach for its members. The Los Angeles Surf Club, for example, boasted "the largest area of private beach" in the region, "with frontage of more than a quarter mile." Most clubs had a wall or a railing surrounding their patch of sand. In its August 1925 newsletter, the Casa Del Mar Club proudly featured a photograph of its "Beach Wall with its handsome Art Stone Filigree and Iron lamps." The Westport Beach Club, in Playa Del Rey, went even further by building a wall enclosing its beachfront swimming pool and a monumental entrance, which faced the ocean and was closed at night.

Preserving a club's exclusivity was no simple matter. Beach fences and walls existed in a kind of legal limbo. While it was legal to privatize the dry part of the beach, no legislation spelled out whether private owners could enclose their lots. In the case of the Casa Del Mar, the wall was unofficially authorized by the municipality of Santa Monica because the club had agreed to build and maintain a lifeguard station nearby in return. Other clubs were less well-off. According to Frank A. Garbutt, the president of the Los Angeles Athletic Club, which took over the Venice Surf and Sand Club in the 1930s, the absence of a fence surrounding the club's stretch of beach had doomed the enterprise from the start. The club, he later explained, had been "overrun by undesirables who came from elsewhere with bathing suits under their clothes, misconducted themselves and littered the beach." After operating the club at annual loss of twenty-five thousand dollars for seven years, Garbutt eventually closed it.[36]

In the absence of a clear physical border between the private and public parts of the beach, clubs could resort to hiring private guards and posting signs on the sand. Yet evidence shows that these strategies often failed

Figure 2.1. Gate and wall at the Westport Beach Club in 1937, Herman Schultheis. Herman J. Schultheis Collection / Los Angeles Public Library.

to keep nonmembers out. For instance, preventing theft of members' personal effects was a major concern among club owners. Reports of youths entering beach clubs and stealing "cigars, cigarettes, and chewing gum" were not uncommon.[37] Another sign that the clubs had difficulty maintaining tight borders is the emergence of the beach club interloper as a trope in popular films and novels of the time. Mack Sennett's short comedy *The Beach Club* (1928), for instance, poked fun at the alleged exclusiveness of this kind of establishments. In the first scene, Billy Doolittle, a penniless man who nonetheless enjoys the finer things in life, is immediately asked for his card as he enters the "Bluepoint Beach Club," his garish clothes an obvious giveaway. Doolittle proudly hands his member's card to the club's employee, where the audience can read that he still owes $990 out of the $1,000 membership fees. The employee has no choice but to let him enter. In the satirical novel *City of Angels* (1941), a lowly but handsome lifeguard meets the wife of a wealthy real estate magnate when she jumps above the "ornate fence that cut off a smart swimming-club and its private sands from th[e] public beach."[38] In popular culture, intruders could come from both sides of the fence.

While walls and fences could not deter the most determined con artists, they did provide a clear boundary and acted as a powerful deterrent. In the case of the Casa Del Mar, the "concrete and iron fence" built at the foot of Pico Boulevard was even more critical as it was located one block north of the Bay Street Beach. Despite mounting hostility against what some argued was a blatant appropriation of public space, the fence remained in place throughout the 1920s and 1930s. In fact, the mayor of Santa Monica justified its existence in 1936 by arguing that lifeguards needed the area around their tower (itself maintained by the club) to be free from crowds.[39] The fence was more likely a useful structure to distance the club members, both physically and metaphorically, from seeing African American beachgoers enjoying a picnic and sporting the latest bathing suit styles.[40] Even so, club members could comfort themselves with the thought that they, at least, were on the right side of the fence. Indeed, membership in a Los Angeles beach club remained a white prerogative for most of the twentieth century.[41]

While far from a golden age, the first two decades did provide opportunities for Afro-Angelenos to take part in the nascent beach culture, but as the racial climate changed in the 1920s, these opportunities shrank.[42] In the summer of 1919, twenty-six racial riots erupted across the United States. Around the same time, a resurrected Ku Klux Klan recruited several million white native-born Protestants. At the local level, the arrival of waves of Black and white migrants from the South heightened racial tensions in the city. As the African American population grew more visible and "race enterprises" more successful, white demands for Jim Crow legislation multiplied. With coastal real estate booming and available space by the ocean diminishing, Los Angeles beaches became a crucial battleground for racial equality in the Roaring Twenties.

Signs of a new wave of bigotry appeared across the region, as they did nationally. On Memorial Day, May 20, 1920, Arthur Valentine, an African American chauffeur, was savagely beaten up and shot by three sheriff's deputies on a beach north of Santa Monica. Not only did Valentine survive, but he sued and was able to testify that he was not trespassing on private land, as the deputies had claimed, but had refused to leave a beach customarily frequented by whites where he was picnicking with relatives. Although the deputies were indicted, the charges against them were eventually dismissed in 1923. The Valentine story proved typical of the racial climate in 1920s LA: victories were often followed by immediate disappointment, or the other way around. As historian Douglas Flamming put it, "Racial conditions for Black Angelenos usually got better and worse *at the same time*."[43] Around this period, Black newspapers printed stories about the revived Ku Klux Klan's plans to establish itself in Southern California. Evidence that it had arrived on the Pacific coast soon appeared. In June 1922, the *Los Angeles Times* reported that "Caucasians" had founded the Santa Monica Bay Protective League with the goal of "eliminating all objectionable features or anything that now is or will prove a menace to the bay district."[44] In Manhattan Beach, just as white residents were petitioning to condemn Bruce's Beach and turn it into a public park, Ku Klux Klan members were reported handing out threatening pamphlets along the shoreline.[45]

Between 1922 and 1927, four Black-owned beach enterprises and projects suffered crushing defeats. Plans for a Black-owned resort in Ocean Park were nipped in the bud in 1922. Three years later, an El Segundo beach amusement park project was also squashed.[46] Even more traumatic was the 1926 fire that razed the brand-new Pacific Beach Club, a Black enterprise that was set to open in Huntington Beach and was already attracting praises from across the nation for its excellent location and lavish accommodations.[47] The final blow was the decision by the Manhattan Beach City Council to seize the Bruces' beachfront property, as well as that of other Black families in the immediate surroundings, on the pretext of establishing a park. For years, the Bruces had withstood harassment from white residents—from cross burning to threatening telephone calls. But the condemnation proceedings, which officially began in 1924, left no recourse for the couple and their Black neighbors.[48]

By the spring of 1927, just after the Bruces held their "closing out party" featuring wiener bakes and an orchestra, the situation on the ground remained tense.[49] Rather than building the park it had promised, the city leased the Bruces' beach frontage to a man named Oscar C. Bassonette, who installed a "No Trespassing" sign on the sand and called the police whenever African Americans came down for a swim. According to the *California Eagle*, the deal had been concluded because white residents were consumed by jealousy. A few months earlier, the newspaper claimed, a Black couple had "erected a modern, up-to-date 10-room house, much better than the homes owned by the lazy, poor-white, race haters." Since then, a "seething war [was being] waged against Negroes at Manhattan Beach."[50] On Memorial Day 1927, the police sought to intimidate the twenty-five Black bathers present by taking their names and addresses. "Sooner or later," mused the *California Eagle*, "the bathing question must be settled. Why not now?"

A few weeks later, on July 4, a nineteen-year-old African American student named Elizabeth Catley went for a swim on the former Bruce's Beach and was arrested and pushed into a police car while still in her swimsuit. Another Black man, who was said to go swimming at the same beach every Sunday, was also arrested. According to the *Eagle*, these were the first arrests ever made in the City of Los Angeles for bathing in the Pacific Ocean. The reaction of the local branch of the National Association for the Advancement of Colored People (NAACP) was swift. A few days later, with the branch president (dentist Henry C. Hudson) at its helm, a swim-in was organized at Bruce's Beach to expose the city's unlawful segregation practices. Bassonette, as expected, called the police. Hudson and others were arrested and charged with "resisting an officer." Yet the affair eventually turned into a victory for the NAACP. At the court hearings, police officers testified that Bassonette had specifically asked them to keep "colored people" off the beach. On August 19, 1927, the *California Eagle* announced that the Los Angeles County Court had overturned the judgment of the local court that had initially found Hudson and his group guilty. Around the same time, the city fathers revoked the Bassonette lease and proclaimed their intention to make the city's beachfront available to all members of the public, regardless of race.[51] The NAACP's swim-in was critical in forcing the city to end its Jim Crow–style practices. In the mainstream press, however, the affair was presented as a triumph of the city's democratic spirit over private interests, with no mention of the role the Black organization had played in the city's turnaround. In fact, the *Times* praised "the financial foresight" of the city's trustees for opening two miles of beach frontage to the public and keeping it "free from private exploitation or the erection of barriers." All beach cities, readers were told, ought to follow "Manhattan's fine example." At a time when beach clubs were multiplying and beachfront property prices were skyrocketing, the city could easily pass off its backpedaling as a wise decision preserving a finite resource for the benefit of the public.[52]

African Americans were not the only racial minorities who wished to enjoy the beach. Evidence is scant, but it is likely that anti-Mexican and anti-Asian discrimination was not as systematic as attempts to implement Jim Crow–style segregation. In fact, when African American student Elizabeth Catley was arrested on Manhattan Beach, she told journalists that she had been "bathing in the ocean along with Japs, Mexicans and whites," who were allowed to remain in the water. Four days after the arrest, the *California Eagle* published a cartoon denouncing the police's actions, but also striking a blow at the preferential treatment allegedly given to Japanese Americans. They were portrayed enjoying the water with a sign describing them as "non tax paying aliens," while "a tax paying citizen" (Catley) was dragged off the beach by a police officer three times her size.[53] The cartoon reflected the sense of injustice many African Americans felt at their second-class-citizen status, but it also hinted at their animosity toward Japanese Americans, many of whom did not have access to US citizenship.[54]

Other examples testify to the presence of Asian American beachgoers on the Los Angeles coastline. Historian Valerie Matsumoto, in her study of LA's Nisei girl clubs in the first half of the twentieth century, found that that "picnics and beach outings were a staple for Southern California clubs." Young Korean Americans also enjoyed the beach. A striking photograph in the "Shades of LA" collection, dated July 4, 1931, shows a group of nine Korean teenagers and children posing in their wet swimsuits on Venice Beach, surrounded by white beachgoers. Other photographs from this period show similar groups of smiling Korean beachgoers.[55] In a 2001 memoir, a Chinese American author who grew up in a large, upper-middle-class family in Los Angeles in the first half of the twentieth century, recalled fond memories of beach weekends with her father and her siblings in 1920s Ocean Park and Long Beach. As a teenager, she would later take the Red Cars to Venice Beach with her maid and would happily spend the two dollars her mother gave her on rides, hot dogs, and cotton candy. However, she also recalled an incident during a beach date when she was refused entrance to an Ocean Park dancehall by the man at the ticket booth who proclaimed the place to be "whites only."[56] Restaurants, movie theaters, and other commercial venues routinely refused entrance to Asians or demanded that they stay in a specific area.[57] Humiliating experiences like these may explain why, in the 1930s, Brighton Beach on Terminal Island became a gathering place for the local Asian American population. Before its residents were evacuated and sent to internment camps in 1942, the island had been home to a small community of Japanese American fishermen and their families, providing an ideal setting for a resortlike area with a boardwalk and pavilions for dances. In an oral interview conducted many years later, Chuck Furutani, a young Terminal Island resident, remembered that "[Asians] could come there and be right at home."[58]

This example aside, feeling "right at home" on the beach was never a given for nonwhite Angelenos, though they persisted in making beach culture a part of their lives. Picking the "right" beach could make or break an outing. African Americans suffered by far the most systematic forms of exclusion and harassment. At least four African American beach clubs and resorts were forced to close or prevented from opening due to discrimination. Starting in the late 1930s, racial violence was common on the oceanfront. From small scuffles to full-on riots, such incidents brought the police more frequently to the beach, an area they had long considered marginal to their operations. By then, coastal residents demanded a greater police presence and petitioned for beach rules—from camping bans to nighttime curfews—to be enforced. Yet enforcement remained intermittent and contested.

RACIAL TENSIONS AND NEW BEACH LAWS, 1930S–1940S

By the early 1930s, the small beach resorts of the Westside had established themselves as full-fledged residential communities. With the development of the movie industry, oil industry, agriculture, and aircraft manufacturing, the region's economy had grown increasingly diverse. Attracting more visitors ceased to be the beach cities' primary concern. Instead, local elites cared more about bringing order to the communities. Coastal homeowners began to see how their own interests, particularly the value of coastal real estate, were linked to the policing of the beach. City leaders wanted to project an aura of respectability in order to attract wealthy residents and tourists.

Within a few years, a legal arsenal was created that regulated behaviors on the beach and indirectly excluded the working class and any beachgoer who did not conform to the ideal image of a tourist. The first beach laws emerged in the late 1920s in reaction to the presence of squatters, who previously had never appeared in council minutes. By banning fires and closed tents, beach cities hoped to chase squatters from the sands without inconveniencing tourists (who used tents to protect themselves from the sun). In 1926, the superintendent of the Los Angeles Board of Playground and Recreation proposed such an ordinance, arguing that closed tents "resulted in committing nuisances, which have called forth numerous complaints."[59] While the declaration was not specific, it targeted both those who used the beach as a camping ground and those who might have been using tents to have sexual relations. Similarly, in 1927, the Los Angeles City Council voted in a new law banning beach fires. While many bathers did complain about charcoal left buried in the sands, the law was intended to discourage squatters and working-class beachgoers who enjoyed "wienie bakes" on the beach.[60] It did not affect upper-class beachgoers with access to private beach clubs, where fires remained legal. In Redondo Beach, beach fires were banned in the 1930s after coastal residents complained of the odors wafting up to their houses from the shores.[61] For local homeowners, beaches were not merely public space but their backyards, which they believed they had the right to supervise.

Beach laws multiplied in the 1930s and 1940s, often in response to the demands of local residents.[62] Some regulations pertained to bathers' safety, as was the case with the beach fire ban and other laws banning dogs, alcohol, and hard balls from the sands. Others were more concerned with respectability: peddling, organizing meetings, begging, and boisterous behavior were all forbidden.[63] Beyond their immediate aims, all these laws framed the beach as a space exclusively reserved for the enjoyment of middle- and upper-class beachgoers. Until then, the beach had served multiple functions: a site of sociability for the working class, a temporary camping ground for homeless people, and a recreational space for wealthier people. Such a mix became increasingly problematic in the eyes of local elites. This change did not impact all beachgoers equally. Only working-class visitors, who lacked access to private beaches and could not afford to live by the sea, had to comply systematically with these new rules.

With new rules also came new enforcement measures. In Santa Monica, for instance, lifeguards were given the power to arrest bathers in 1932, and an officer was assigned on the pleasure pier beginning in 1940.[64] In some other coastal cities, beach supervision was not as well funded, and seasonal lifeguards did not double as police officers. Only on special holidays, such as New Year's Eve and Independence Day, were police officers specifically assigned to the beach.[65] On more than one occasion, police representatives on the Westside had to explain to lawmakers that their new beach ordinances would not be enforced. On August 18, 1927, for instance, a representative of the Los Angeles Police Department warned the city council that the beach fire ban would not be enforced due to a shortage of manpower. A year later, the captain of the Sawtelle Division used the same argument when facing the Recreation Commission.[66] The shortage of police in a rapidly expanding city was an acute problem at the time; in 1937, the Los Angeles police chief claimed that, despite the city's rapid demographic growth, the number of officers had barely changed since 1926.[67]

Multiple sets of rules up and down the coastline also made enforcement difficult. It was precisely to avoid confusion that in 1936 the *Los Angeles Times* published its special report on beachfront regulations, which compiled a guide of sorts for the wandering bather. Based on this article, it seems fair to assume that many beachgoers broke the law—consciously or not—on a regular basis.[68] In fact, some rules were never truly enforced. In Venice and Ocean Park, for instance, beachgoers played all kinds of ballgames despite the existing ban on such activities. "Why do guards sit idly and watch these games in progress with no effort to interfere?" asked an angry mother in a letter to the Parks and Recreation Commission. Similarly, a 1940 article published in a local newspaper demanded tougher measures against visitors who rode their bicycles on the pier and jumped from it.[69] Even when the city's safety was at stake, laws were disregarded. During the Second World War, many beachgoers failed to respect the regionwide ban on beach fires, which could have allowed the enemy to identify buildings and people on the coast.[70]

The interviews given by Westside police chiefs to local newspapers, while essentially serving to legitimize police work, provide insight into why the police focused on certain tasks rather than others. According to the Redondo police chief, who spoke in 1936 to the *Los Angeles Times*, only those ordinances that guaranteed beachgoers' safety needed to be systematically enforced. In Manhattan Beach, the local police chief similarly claimed to ignore minor violations but that he "[would] make arrests of anyone whom [he found] breaking bottles at the beach" since broken glass posed an obvious risk to barefoot visitors. According to the reporter, this flexible approach to beach policing was linked to the necessity of maintaining the resorts' popularity: "The hot dog merchant, the games proprietor and the fishing barge owner depend upon the good will of the public toward their community. They must do a whole year's business in four months."[71] While the region's economy had grown more diverse over the years, coastal communities still relied to some extent on tourist dollars.

Even without taking tourist spending into account, all police chiefs interviewed for this 1936 article agreed that, on the beach, police officers had to be more patient and understanding: "Most people get into trouble because they play too hard. Beach judges and beach police proceed on that theory." What mattered in the end, explained the Santa Monica chief of police, was the beachgoer's "attitude": if he was "sarcastic or surly when the officers made the arrest it may go hard with him."[72] Such comments, printed in a very public forum, had two consequences. First, they explicitly condoned the discretionary power of police officers in the field and authorized them to treat beachgoers differently based not only on their actions but also on their class, race, sex, and age. Second, they retroactively justified the flexible approach adopted on the beach and, at the same time, responded to citizens' demands for tougher enforcement. Police leaders thus managed to defuse citizens' accusations of inaction while acknowledging their own inability to enforce beach laws in their discussion with city lawmakers. They may have wanted to believe (and make others believe) that their tolerant approach was chosen after careful consideration, but police leaders revealed in their communications with the city that they were, for the most part, forced to adopt this pragmatic policy because of a lack of staff available to patrol such a vast public space. The adoption of new laws thus did not put an end to the unique status of the coastline within the metropolis. But it did lead to justifications for their work, most notably equating police flexibility on the seaside with pragmatism.

Meanwhile, episodes of racial tensions and racial violence continued to bring the police to the shores. Even after Manhattan Beach proclaimed solemnly its intention to keep the coastline open to all bathers, white residents harassed the few African American families who had managed to stay in the seaside town. In October 1927, just a few months after Black newspapers declared victory in the Manhattan Beach affair, the *California Eagle* reported that the Ku Klux Klan was terrorizing Black homeowning families by setting buildings and crosses on fire.[73] There is evidence that white residents in the adjoining city of Hermosa Beach used similar tactics. In 1939, a local scandal revealed residents' attempts to keep African Americans off their beach. That year, plans to turn the "swanky Hermosa Biltmore Hotel" into a dormitory for the National Youth Administration, a New Deal government agency providing training and employment opportunities to American youths, sparked an outrage in the small resort community. When two hundred "underprivileged boys and girls" moved into the hotel, residents protested vociferously, arguing that such a move "would lower property values." While the affair most obviously demonstrated residents' wish to keep the poor away from their community, it soon exposed their racial prejudice as well. At a public hearing, Frank A. Garbutt, the president of the Los Angeles Athletic Club in charge of the hotel's lease, denounced local residents' bigotry, explaining that, a few years ago, "law-abiding citizens" had bragged about chasing African Americans from their town "by force and by threats." Later on, he explained that he had initially considered leasing the hotel to a "group of respectable colored citizens" who wished to establish a beach club, but he had accepted the NYA's offer as an act of patriotism.[74]

The Hermosa affair shows not only that the Westside remained hostile to any attempts by African Americans to establish themselves and their businesses in the area, but also that a beach club continued to be a sought-after aspiration for the Black middle class. As Afro-Angelenos attempted to create and sustain leisure spaces outside of the city, Black businessmen and women were constrained by racial discrimination and limited access to credit.[75] Socializing with their peers in a beautiful setting and enjoying the lifestyle available to white people of means were obvious perks of belonging to a club, but membership meant more than this for well-off Afro-Angelenos. Racial discrimination may have been outlawed on the sands after the 1927 swim-in, but a club protected its members from the more subtle indignities Black beachgoers could suffer and the very real possibility of being caught in the middle of a beach brawl with implicit, or more often explicit, racial undertones. While sparse, evidence shows that beachgoing continued to be fraught for African Americans throughout the 1930s and 1940s, especially for young working-class men, whose presence on the shore could be perceived as an intrusion by young white locals.

The 1940 Ocean Park Pier brawl illustrates the hostility that Afro-Angelenos could face as soon as they stepped out of the narrow borders of Bay Street Beach. On Saturday night August 25, 1940, Black members of the junior choir of Pleasant Hill Baptist Church headed to Ocean Park for a "wiener bake" on the beach. At midnight, twenty of them decided to go to the amusement area on the Ocean Park Pier, where the roller coaster and other typical fairground attractions attracted youths year-round. What exactly happened at that point is unclear. According to the *Los Angeles Sentinel*, a Black newspaper, a crowd had already formed around two white youths who had been attacking a young Black boy. As the police were handcuffing the boy, a white woman spat on one of the choir members, which quickly launched a general brawl in which white people vastly outnumbered African Americans. The local Santa Monica newspaper presented a different account of the incident. Following exchanges of insults between two groups, it reported, a fight had broken out involving a "crowd of some 200 persons of both races." The *Los Angeles Times* put the onus squarely on the African American group, alleging that two of them had slashed four white youths with razors. The "riot," as white newspapers labeled the event, resulted in the arrest of two African Americans, while four (or five, depending on the account) white boys were taken to the hospital. Although their accounts diverged, both white and Black newspapers agreed that this was far from an isolated occurrence. "Long-brewing ill-feeling" existed in the area, the *Times* admitted. For the *Sentinel*, this was part of "a systematic attempt extending over the past few years to deprive Negroes of their right to use the beaches in Los Angeles County." African Americans, the newspaper concluded, ought to "make a determined stand now" or else be forced off the beach.[76]

That the Ocean Park Beach fight was part of a pattern of interracial confrontations on the coastline became apparent in the subsequent years, eventually culminating in a series of altercations during the 1943 Los Angeles zoot suit riots. After the United States entered World War II, national campaigns supported by Black institutions brought to light the chasm between the wartime rhetoric of freedom and equality and the reality of Jim Crow at home. Victory abroad was not enough; African Americans demanded "double victory," against the Axis and against racial prejudice. This new mood of militancy reinforced a widespread sense of injustice among Black and Latino urban youths whose daily lives were punctuated by racist incidents. Meanwhile, the Second Great Migration brought new waves of Black migrants to major industrial cities, exacerbating the competition for housing and causing rapid shifts in the racial geographies of working-class neighborhoods.

The zoot suit riots, which erupted in several cities during the summer of 1943, emerged from these tense conditions. Zoot-suiters were Latino and Black working-class youths who took to the streets sporting a distinctive style: ballooning pants tapered to the ankles and hanging high at the waist, and wide-shouldered coats that hit mid-thigh or fell down to the knees. In Los Angeles, the style was associated with Mexican American youths, called Pachucos, and was also worn by women (Pachucas), with some adaptations. In the context of wartime fabric rationing, wearing a zoot suit carried a political message of defiance toward seemingly hollow calls for patriotism, whether they came from white society or the Black bourgeoisie.[77]

The zoot suit riots unfolded roughly along the same patterns in different places: groups of young white servicemen and civilians patrolled the city and attacked and, in some cases, "de-panted" Black and Latino zoot-suiters while the police observed passively or even aided the violence. But local context mattered. In Los Angeles, "anti-Mexican hysteria" stirred by the local press in 1942 and the opening of a training school for an all-white navy in the middle of historically Mexican neighborhoods heightened racial tensions.[78] In fact, much of the violence took place on the Eastside and in the Downtown district. Yet episodes of racial hostility and violence also took place along the coastline before and after the main riot days of June 3–8. On May 10, 1943, hundreds of white sailors, servicemen, and high school students gathered on Lick Pier, at the border between Santa Monica and Venice, following a rumor that a Pachuco had stabbed a sailor to death. Police failed to contain the crowd and a fight broke out. Twenty-one zoot-suiters, ages eighteen to twenty-seven—the majority of Mexican descent—were arrested. The following Saturday, acting on the information that zoot-suiters were heading to Venice for revenge, the police stopped and took the names and addresses of over a hundred youths before sending them home. Eight white boys, most of them from Venice, were also arrested for carrying concealed weapons. On June 25, another beach fight took place near the Santa Monica Pier, pitting local whites against Mexican American youths (including women). Fifteen Mexican boys and girls were arrested, most of whom gave West LA and Culver City addresses.[79]

Unlike the incidents that unfolded on the Eastside, where sailors who did not normally reside in the city took the lead and local zoot-suiters stood up to them, the beach hostilities involved residents from the Westside who were very familiar with the beach area and its amusements. In other words, the zoot suit riots revived older racial rivalries between Westside youths (and youth gangs) of different races. As Black and Latino youths were emboldened by the militant atmosphere that permeated wartime Los Angeles, they took a more offensive posture toward white youth aggression, hitting back when attacked and seeking revenge when driven off their turf. The spring 1943 beach fights were part of the decade-long rivalry between white and nonwhite youths over who could lay claim to the popular oceanfront amusement parks and their immediate surroundings.

The 1943 events also highlight the fact that African Americans were not the sole racial group whose presence on the shores was contested. Following his arrest in the aftermath of the Lick Pier brawl in May 1943, Alfred Barela, a young Mexican American, wrote a letter to the judge in charge of his case denouncing the longtime routine harassment on the shoreline to which he and his friends had been subjected: "Ever since I can remember I've been pushed around and called names because I'm a Mexican. I was born in this country. Like you said I have the same rights and privileges of other Americans. . . . We're tired of being pushed around. We're tired of being told we can't go to this show or that dance hall because we're Mexican or that we better not be seen on the beach front."[80] Indeed, Mexican Americans were common targets of discrimination and prejudice in 1940s California, especially in leisure settings that involved interracial mixing. In many cities, Mexican Americans were barred from accessing municipal pools except for the day before the water was drained, the same day that African Americans were allowed in the water, for fear that they would contaminate the white public.[81] Denied access to these public facilities and recreational spaces, Mexican youths would "adopt any body of water they could find as their place to swim and relax." The reservoir at the Williams Ranch in East Los Angeles—where José Díaz was found unconscious in August 1942, leading to the infamous Sleepy Lagoon trial—was one of them.[82] As reflected by Barela's letter, exclusion from recreational spaces was felt particularly strongly by US-born youths, who resented their status as second-class citizens.

Not all Mexicans were treated the same way at the beach and in other leisure settings. Age, class, gender, and demeanor all affected the enforcement of racial boundaries. According to some accounts, women and families seem to have enjoyed the coastline mostly undisturbed. For instance, Della Ortega and Ramona Frias, Mexican American sisters who grew up in the

San Fernando Valley in the 1930s, spoke fondly of their family trips to the beach, although these were usually taken in Oxnard rather than in Los Angeles because camping was allowed on the Ventura County beach. Joined by five or six other families, they would stay overnight and sit around a fire singing Mexican songs. Even though they couldn't afford bathing suits and swam in the ocean with "whatever [they] had on," one of the sisters remembered the outings as "the best time of [her] life." Similarly, historian Eric Avila writes that in the 1940s his grandmother, Mary Gonzales, enjoyed her regular trips to the Pike (the beachfront amusement park in Long Beach) with her friends, all women of Mexican descent.[83] By contrast, working-class young men who sported the provoking outfits and manners of Pachucos, and who were thus perceived as delinquents by white Angelenos, suffered the harshest forms of discrimination and police harassment, at the beach and elsewhere.

———

In the first half of the century, the Los Angeles coastline became the scene of constant negotiations and conflicts over what uses of the beach were appropriate and who could legitimately use it. At the beginning of the century, no one complained about groups of merrymakers barreling down to the beach in cars, setting up tents, and lighting bonfires for traditional marshmallow and wiener bakes. Nor was social mixing much of an issue. The existence of Bruce's Beach and other successful "race enterprises" by the ocean attested to the fact that Los Angeles offered pockets of respite from racial prejudice and violence.

As urban expansion toward the Pacific transformed small beach resorts into coastal municipalities in the 1920s and 1930s, the local elite pushed for order and propriety. As the *Los Angeles Times* sternly reminded its readers in 1936, "The police department and the court must protect the beach community and its citizens from law-breaking and mischief."[84] Yet local authorities lacked sufficient staff to enforce new ordinances and knew better than to fine visitors whose dollars were essential to the tourist industry. Beach clubs provided a more luxurious and protected setting. By privatizing entire stretches of the frontage, they kept "undesirables" out of sight, if not out of mind. In the end, local elites never completely achieved their goal of turning beaches into regular urban spaces, policed as strictly as street corners and neighborhood parks. But they did prove more successful in extending the urban regime of informal racial segregation to the coastline. Through legal means as well as police harassment and everyday violence, African Americans were repeatedly reminded of the fact that the

California dream was not intended for them. By the late 1930s, young Black and Brown beachgoers grew more determined to enjoy all that Los Angeles had to offer, but they found themselves subjected to threats and assaults by their white counterparts when they attempted to use coveted parts of the shoreline. As far as these young citizens were concerned, an update of the beach order was overdue.

CHAPTER 3

✧

The Emergence of the Los Angeles Beach Lobby

In 1930, after a decade of feverish growth, the distinctive natural elements of the Los Angeles region—its wooded hills, quiet arroyos, tranquil coastal plains, aqua-blue lagoons, and sandy shorelines, to name but a few—were rapidly changing as a continuous stream of new residents arrived from all corners of the nation and as building to accommodate all these new Angelenos continued. That year, the Los Angeles Chamber of Commerce unveiled a gloomy report warning that haphazard growth would cause the region to be "less and less attractive."[1] From the mid-nineteenth century on, Anglo-Americans had actively managed the region's ecology, inspired by visions of Southern California as an earthly paradise. While some of these transformations were perceived as augmenting the region's natural riches (such as citrus orchards covering the hills and valleys), others were understood as a necessary evil (oil derricks blanketing entire neighborhoods), while others still were framed as defending the metropolis against the destructiveness of nature (channeling the Los Angeles River). All contemporary observers agreed, however, that what was happening along the city's shoreline was a disgrace.[2] Erosion, rampant beach privatization, oil drilling, and sewage pollution were the principal causes for concern. Beyond its environmental consequences, LA's rampant growth considerably transformed the beach experience. Crowded, dirty, and lacking adequate parking, the beaches strained to accommodate the soaring number of Angelenos. By the early 1930s, these various developments prompted local elites to declare the beaches in crisis.

The dire situation, to their mind, required new solutions and new experts. Soon, a beach lobby coalesced around Los Angeles city (and, more broadly, Southern California) officials, engineers, urban planners, and businessmen who wanted to tackle these challenges head-on. Attempts to save the coastline from the ravages of urban modernity were not unique to Southern California. From the beaches of the Eastern Seaboard to the shores of the Great Lakes, local groups across the nation worried about erosion, congestion, and pollution. While Southern California initially lagged behind the East Coast, several local beach preservation associations were formed in the 1930s. At the same time, California engineers took the lead in establishing coastal engineering, a new subfield focused on the unique challenges of developing coastlines. By the 1940s, the most radical and innovative ideas concerning shoreline acquisition and development were coming from Southern California. Los Angeles had become the epicenter of a movement to reinvent the beach for a modern era.

LOCAL ELITES SOUND THE ALARM

In the late 1920s, Los Angeles elites grew increasingly concerned that growth, without careful planning, endangered one of the key elements that distinguished Southern California cities: easy access to and enjoyment of the outdoors. Of all the region's natural assets, the coastline was perhaps the one that visitors and residents alike most valued. At the end of the 1920s, the City of Los Angeles Department of Recreation and Parks confirmed that the city's beaches were "the most popular of all recreation places in Southern California," way ahead of its mountains, playgrounds, and parks.[3] Whether directly or indirectly, they represented a source of revenue for every business on the coast. A 1939 article in *Western City* magazine calculated that if each of the six million visitors to Hermosa Beach that summer spent just ten cents at the resort, local businesses would take in six hundred thousand dollars. As *Life* magazine put it succinctly in 1937, "Bathing Is Big Business."[4]

No doubt profits were on the minds of members of the Los Angeles Chamber of Commerce when, in 1927, they commissioned the landscape architecture and city planning firms Olmsted Brothers and Harland Bartholomew and Associates to write a report on the "Parks, Beaches, and Playgrounds of Los Angeles." But other motives also animated their initiative. The authors justified their approach by invoking nature's benefits to society. Echoing the hygienist and Olmstedian traditions, they saw public parks as "the lungs of the city" and positioned their recommendations as benefiting the "moral welfare" of Los Angeles residents, especially those living in "the most saturated neighborhoods."[5] By engaging the services of two of the most prestigious East Coast city planning firms, the Chamber of Commerce hoped to obtain a dispassionate assessment of the impact of urban growth on the region and thus to influence decisions made at the city and county levels. In doing so, the Chamber essentially acted as an interest group, protecting its members' assets in tourism, real estate, and other ventures connected to the region's appeal.

For three years, the firms had carried out an inventory of the region's beaches and parks with the help of a Citizens' Committee mostly made up of members of the Chamber of Commerce. In 1930, two hundred copies of the report were finally released under the title *Parks, Playgrounds and Beaches for the Los Angeles Region*. Its findings were disturbing. The authors lamented "the present crisis in the welfare of Los Angeles and the surrounding region." Los Angeles, they explained, was suffering from an acute park shortage, with only 1 percent of its area dedicated to parklands. The situation required bold measures: the report advocated the development of a metropolitan-wide system of public parks connected via parkways to nature reserves along the Pacific and further inland. Concerning beaches specifically, the report deplored the number of private beaches and overcrowded public shores. To solve this problem, it recommended that the state acquire more than thirty-two miles of coastline at a cost of fifteen million dollars.[6] The authors further recommended creating an independent commission to implement the plan on a citywide scale.

The report went too far. Some members of the Chamber were critical of the idea of an independent commission with such a colossal budget, to say nothing of the taxes required. They actively sought to limit the report's circulation and influence.[7] LA historian Mike Davis calls the report a "window into a lost future." If implemented, it could have ushered in a "vigorous social democracy of beaches and playgrounds." Instead, the report was effectively ignored, and the remaining copies in the city's archives stand as a sad reminder of the tragic environmental history of the region, or "How Eden lost its Garden."[8]

Although the report did not lead to immediate measures, it did lay the groundwork for future action. In 1936, the founding declaration of the California Beaches Association (CBA)—some of whose members had served on the Citizens' Committee—used language similar to what appeared in the 1930 report. In its first bulletin, it warned that "if the glory of the beaches is not to be lost, people of California must be impressed with the gravity of the crisis that faces them."[9] Unlike the Olmsted-Bartholomew report, however, the CBA discussed two glaring problems that the earlier document had ignored: erosion and pollution. Gaining in prominence in the 1930s, the two phenomena deepened the sense of crisis hanging over local elites.

"SWALLOWED BY THE WAVES"

Erosion undoubtedly brought about the most dramatic changes to the Los Angeles shoreline in the first half of the twentieth century. In the late nineteenth century, before coastal development got underway, the beaches of Santa Monica Bay were relatively narrow. In a memorandum to the US Senate, George Davidson from the US Coast and Geodetic Survey wrote that, when he had visited the bay from Santa Monica to Point Dume in 1872, "the high bluffs and cliffs came so sharply to the shore, and the arroyos there so deep that no road was practicable above high water, and I had to travel along the beach at low water." In fact, according to A. G. Johnson, beach design engineer for the City of Los Angeles, the bay beaches, "in their natural state, before changes occurred to activities of man," had a uniform width of about seventy-five to one hundred feet, a far cry from today's five-hundred-foot beaches.[10]

Between the 1870s and the 1910s, the erection of wharves, jetties, breakwaters, and piers as part of the commercial and touristic development of the region significantly altered the coastal ecosystem. The pace of construction was frenetic: between 1898 and 1929, at least eleven piers were built on the bay. Developers soon discovered that building on the shores was tricky business. Sandy beaches are essentially moving landscapes, constantly shaped and reshaped by the wind and waves. Sediments found one day on a beach might be at the bottom of the sea the next day and vice versa. Beaches also function according to seasonal cycles. Narrow in winter, they are replenished with sand in summer, thanks to littoral currents that transport sediment. Generally speaking, obstructing this natural motion causes changes to a beach's shape.[11] By interrupting the sand's natural flow (the littoral drift system), piers, jetties, and other similar constructions built out into the surf disrupt the shoreline's "natural equilibrium," creating the perfect conditions for down-drift erosion and its twin phenomenon, accumulation of sand (known as accretion) up drift or, in the case of a breakwater, behind the structure. In the case of Santa Monica Bay, a littoral cell dominated by southeast currents, the beaches north of hard structures benefit from accretion while those to the south erode rapidly.

One of the first examples of this implacable logic took place in 1905 when businessman Abbot Kinney had a breakwater built twelve hundred feet offshore to protect the amusements on the Venice Pier. Soon, the beaches north of the pier tripled in width seaward, eventually reaching the breakwater. Inevitably, the beaches south of the breakwater suffered from erosion. By 1909, however, a jetty had been built at Playa Del Rey just south of Venice. The eroded beaches soon regained some of their width as they retained the sand transported by the littoral currents. The problem then shifted to the beaches south of Playa Del Rey.[12] The same sort of chain reaction was set in motion at several locations along the bay: a landowner or municipality built a feature that interrupted the littoral currents, which forced the landowner to the south to do the same to prevent the erosion of his beaches, which in turn led to the erosion of still further beaches, and so on.

Although this initial development caused changes to the coastline, they were still not enough to cause a stir. It was only in the 1930s, when the construction of several breakwaters had disastrous consequences for famous beaches, that local elites sounded the alarm. Amid a national craze for boating in the late 1920s and early 1930s, three Southern California beach resorts—Santa Barbara, Santa Monica, and Redondo Beach— set out to build yacht harbors, seeking to attract wealthy tourists and residents. Yet the cities' dreams of re-creating the Riviera on the Pacific coast soon turned sour. In fact, the three faulty structures acquired such notoriety that they quickly became known to the coastal engineering community as the "Southern California breakwater fiascoes."[13] The first of these breakwaters, built in Santa Barbara between 1928 and 1930, not only caused the destruction of a "Million-Dollar Beach" in a matter of months, but it also led to sand accumulation within the harbor, rendering it useless only three years after it opened.[14] In a baffling move considering this precedent, the City of Santa Monica set out to build a harbor using the same process three years later. The same methods begot the same results: an impressive sand salient more than five hundred feet long gradually formed on the beach north of the breakwater, while those to the south fell victim to erosion.[15] On April 10, 1939, the Los Angeles City Board of Playground and Recreation carried out a comparison of two aerial photographs of the same stretch of coast, taken in 1933 and 1939. Placed side by side, they showed the dramatic changes to the coastline that had occurred in only six years. Shocked by their findings, the members of the council decided that the photographs should "be indexed and deposited in the fire vault . . . with the understanding that they are not to be taken out for use except upon written order of the Superintendent of this department, or at the request of the city engineer."[16] The stakes were high: the shores most affected by erosion were those of Venice, which was part of the City of Los Angeles. In other words, the photographs were irrefutable proof that Santa Monica,

Sand Rush

Figure 3.1. The Santa Monica Breakwater and its consequences for the shoreline, circa 1940. From US Army Corps of Engineers, "Santa Monica Breakwater Feasibility Report," 1995, plate 8. Santa Monica Public Library.

with its faulty harbor, had siphoned off sand from its neighbor. In 1940, the City of Los Angeles claimed that Venice beach had lost 138 feet to erosion.

Despite these two "blunders"—as John Anson Ford, a member of the Los Angeles County Board of Supervisors, referred to the two harbors in a letter—the City of Redondo Beach repeated the same mistake in 1939. In October 1940, less than a year after the harbor's inauguration, the damage was already considerable. Nearly 330,000 cubic yards of sand had disappeared from the beaches south of the breakwater.[17]

This series of failed projects reveal the rapidly changing perceptions of the coastline in the 1920s and 1930s. For the local business elite, the development of the bay was considered a necessity, even a given. "Our big attraction is the ocean. Are we never going to use it?" exclaimed Frank Bundy, a wealthy Santa Monica property owner who campaigned endlessly for the construction of a leisure harbor in the city.[18] The shores, it was believed, could only be improved by human action. Yet the structures' disastrous consequences quickly tempered the "technological enthusiasm" of the period.[19] These failures also demonstrate how little attention had been paid to beach erosion prior to the 1920s beach craze. The phenomenon, of course, was well known. As early as the seventeenth century, scientists had sought to decipher "the laws of nature" in an attempt to devise coastal

Figure 3.2. Aerial photograph of the Santa Monica Harbor in 1949. Madigan-Hyland, "Recreational Development of the Los Angeles Area Shoreline. An Engineering and Economic Report to the Mayor and the City Council," 1949, 85, box 1380, Los Angeles City Archives—Records Management Division—Office of the City Clerk.

structures in harmony with the littoral drift.[20] But the focus had been on avoiding the silting up of harbors to ensure the navigability of sea routes. Beach erosion—at a time when beaches were considered at worst repulsive and frightening places and at best subsistence areas—was of little importance.[21] It took the rise of a thriving beach economy in the early twentieth century for engineers to turn their attention to the issue of human-made erosion. The disappearance of the shoreline came at a cost. Every beach that slipped beneath the waves robbed a coastal community of a significant portion of its income and an essential element of its brand. As the mayor of Santa Barbara reminded conference-goers in 1936, the city's survival depended "on the people who come to visit us and spend their time here, and we are not getting these people anymore, because we haven't beaches."[22]

By the end of the 1930s, erosion had become a central preoccupation of local scientists, engineers, businessmen, and officials. Coverage of the phenomenon soon made its way into local newspapers. In 1938, the *Los Angeles Times* warned that the region's beaches, visited by millions of bathers every year, were at risk of being "swallowed by the waves."[23] Coastal matters were no longer a subject reserved only for specialists. The consequences of erosion could be seen firsthand by visitors when their favorite beach disappeared in front of their own eyes.

"A 'NO MAN'S LAND' OF STENCH AND CORRUPTION"

Beachgoers could also unfortunately observe for themselves the effects of oil and sewage pollution on the shores. By the mid-1920s, bathing in filth—which many Angelenos kept on doing as much by habit as by ignorance about its detrimental health effects—grew increasingly unacceptable to Los Angeles elites. At the same time, oil companies worked hard to convince the public and city officials to allow drilling near and on the beach. While nuisances linked to the oil industry initially set off the most contentious debates, it was ultimately sewage pollution that led the State of California to declare the Bay's beaches in crisis.

The discovery of rich pools of oil along the coast of Southern California in the 1920s raised difficult questions for residents, landowners, and officials in beach communities. "Would beaches trump oil?" as historian Paul Sabin put it, was no doubt a central one. In the end, the answer depended largely on the timing of oil discoveries and location. Venice and Santa Monica took dramatically different paths. In the 1920s, clashes between beach conservationists and oil companies had resulted in some important victories for the former, including a 1921 state ban on drilling in tidelands located in front of a city and a 1928 ban on drilling from piers. Yet as coastal onshore fields' productivity declined, pressure grew to open up offshore drilling. Another issue, beyond protecting beaches, was the depressive effect of drilling on property values.[24] By the summer of 1930, six months after the first oil lease had been granted in what would become the Venice Beach–Del Rey oil field, such wisdom was keenly felt by local residents. Although oil companies had pledged that there would be "no pollution of beach or ocean," they struggled to contain spills and blowouts.[25] In theory, Los Angeles's zoning regulations banned oil drilling in residential areas. Yet oil companies circumvented such restrictions by promising high returns to property owners who leased their land and pressuring the city to deliver special permits. As historian Sarah Elkind explains, the "law of capture," according to which oil belonged to the person who mined it from the ground, even if that oil was actually located under another person's property, incentivized the erection of derricks in close proximity in the same area. By the summer of 1930, the "destruction of Venice," as it was billed, was well advanced.[26] Oil derricks were located so close to the beach that the city considered leasing it, using the royalties to acquire public shorelines elsewhere. The proposal prompted fierce debates. While some residents pushed for all drilling restrictions to be lifted, others denounced plans to "prostitute the scenic beauties of Venice for monetary gain."[27] Most famously, Hollywood star Lewis Stone, whose Venice home fronted the beach, successfully sued the city. Of course, opposing drilling was as much about preserving the shoreline from pollution as protecting real estate prices. But the issue did signal a line most Angelenos were not willing to cross: beaches should remain free of drilling equipment.

Venice's fate provided an object lesson for its neighbors, most immediately Santa Monica, where explorations were already underway. In 1931, the Santa Monica newspaper commented that "the experience of Venice property owners . . . had served to change the opinion of many Ocean Park residents who were originally in favor of the oil-drilling program." Over the next few years, opposition to the "oil invasion" grew louder, eventually culminating in Santa Monicans approving "the strongest possible ban on oil drilling" on February 18, 1939. Santa Monica was choosing its future as a "residential seaside community," prioritizing long-term prosperity over short-term gains.[28] Beyond Santa Monica, the business community in several residential areas of Los Angeles in the 1930s (including Redondo Beach) successfully supported drilling bans to protect property values. Nevertheless, the oil industry won a major victory when slant drilling (a technique that allowed for the exploitation of underwater oil from the land) was legalized in 1936. Arguing for the method's safety, proponents of the law included a well-received clause stipulating that half of the revenues from tidelands leases would be used to purchase parks and beaches for the public. Even the beach protection movement supported the new law.[29] Even so, it did not trigger the beach oil boom many feared, in part because, a year later, Congress initiated a lawsuit to claim ownership of tidelands over the States of California, Texas, and Louisiana. But oil drilling soon got another boost when the United States entered World War II, making oil production a national priority. Faced with the demands of industry and the military, municipal authorities were not in a strong position to enforce zoning ordinances. During the war, the Los Angeles City Council would authorize new oil wells throughout the city, including in Venice.[30]

Beach communities in Los Angeles were hardly more successful at fighting sewage pollution. Since 1894, most sewage produced by Los Angeles residents was poured into Santa Monica Bay at Hyperion, south of Playa Del Rey, through an outfall. Yet leaks appeared almost as soon as it was opened. In 1925, the city built a screening plant and extended the outfall to five thousand feet, but spills remained a problem. Disposal of raw sewage in large bodies of water was common practice at the time. Before the 1930s, most engineers believed that diluting sewage in seawater, if done far enough from shore and in accordance with the tidal cycle, posed little risk of contamination. In fact, it was considered cheap and efficient. According to C. G. Gillespie, chief of the California Bureau of Sanitary Engineering, a city saved up to ten dollars per resident by using the "diluting and oxidizing powers of the ocean."[31] Engineers were far more interested in pollution affecting drinking water (which posed an immediate health risk). Floating solids, because they could affect the public's view of a particular beach, ought to be filtered—but from a public health perspective, their presence was perceived as benign.[32]

By the early 1940s, the city's frenetic growth had strained the wastewater management system to the breaking point. Between 1925 and the end of the war, no improvements had been made to the wastewater system even though the population it served grew from 500,000 to more than 1,787,000.[33] In 1940, it was estimated that close to 20 percent of all sewage leaked from the outfall. Because of the southeastward littoral currents, South Bay beaches were most affected. As early as 1924, a quarantine zone had been established on Venice beaches due to the accumulation of waste on the sands. By 1943, the situation was so dire that a study found that most of the bay's beaches were contaminated. Those around the outfall itself were quite simply "unusable."[34]

Throughout the 1930s and early 1940s, South Bay residents attempted to hold the City of Los Angeles accountable. When the city failed to respond, the municipalities finally turned to the state. The State Board of Health received reams of letters describing the nauseating odors wafting from the ocean and forcing residents to keep their windows closed. The same letters also lamented the unhealthy color of the contaminated water, and the waste (condoms, fruit peels, toilet paper) found on the sand. Bathing in such filthy conditions was hardly inviting, as one Venice resident explained: "I do not like the idea, when I go in bathing of getting my hair, eyes, ears, nose and mouth full of the diluted sewage of over a million and a half people, and of needing a very thorough bath afterward." In fact, South Bay residents spoke of the need to undergo a "gasoline bath" after a swim due to presence of sewage grease in the ocean. Even walking along the ocean was out of the question in the immediate vicinity of the outfall, where the beach turned into a "veritable 'no man's land' of stench and corruption."[35] The letters were not written in vain. In September 1940, after several warnings, the State Board of Health indefinitely suspended the city's authorization to discharge its waste into the Hyperion sewer.

While the Los Angeles City Council finally recognized the "urgency of the 'sewer problem,'" that same year the electorate voted down a tax to repair the Hyperion sewer.[36] For most residents—those who did not suffer the daily nuisances created by sewage and who could simply avoid the most contaminated beaches—beach pollution was not worth raising taxes for. Hoping to convince Angelenos of the need for such a levy, a mayoral committee hired independent engineers to conduct a study of the pollution in Santa Monica Bay. In the meantime, the State Board of Health advocated posting signs on polluted beaches and forming patrols to discourage people from visiting them.[37] The City of Los Angeles again turned a blind eye and took no action, even when the independent report, a year in the making, found that the North Outfall at Hyperion was "cracked to the point of bursting" and that typhoid organisms were present in the water.[38] A year later, under pressure from the South Bay coastal communities, the State Board of Health finally established a ten-mile quarantine zone from Brooks Avenue in Venice in the north to Fourteenth Street in Hermosa Beach in the south, citing the risk of a typhoid or dysentery outbreak. The desperate municipalities welcomed the measure. Closing their beaches was the only way to draw the public's attention, and consequently the attention of the City of Los Angeles, to the "sewer problem."

If the city dragged its feet, it was due partly to the administrative division of the coast—the Los Angeles City Council could afford to ignore angry letters from residents of South Bay cities—and partly to social and racial segregation. Not all Angelenos were equally impacted by beach pollution. The shores most affected were precisely those used by working-class Angelenos (those south of Venice in particular) and racial minorities. In 1942, for example, pieces of grease and excrement washed ashore on the beach formerly known as Bruce's Beach, which continued to be frequented by African Americans.[39] In contrast, the beaches of Santa Monica, home to private clubs and up the coast from the Hyperion sewer, were largely protected from sewage leaks and were excluded from the quarantine area. It is likely that the Los Angeles City Council would have reacted more quickly had local elites experienced the filthy conditions of the South Bay beaches. That is not to say, however, that the African American population was indifferent to pollution. In 1935, for example, the *Los Angeles Sentinel*, one of the city's Black newspapers, alerted its readers to the need to combat oil pollution along the coast.[40] Most likely, enduring patterns of environmental racism prevented their voices from being heard. Even so, the closure of ten miles of beach frontage represented a major blow to local businesses dependent on seaside activities, from swimsuit manufacturers to ice cream vendors. Combined with the oil industry invading Venice and Playa Del Rey neighborhoods, sewage pollution was one of the essential elements of the "beach crisis" that mobilized local elites in the 1930s.

A DETERIORATING BEACH EXPERIENCE

Beyond its environmental impact, the growing population also affected the beach experience. By the early 1930s, beaches were synonymous with big crowds and traffic congestion. In the "pre climate-controlled summer," the beach was a rare oasis where Angelenos could flee what scientists today call the "urban heat island effect." In some contemporary photographs of the region's popular beaches, beachgoers and their dark umbrellas are so tightly packed that there is no sand in sight. The problem was so acute that the Chamber of Commerce decided to obtain exact figures as part of the Olmsted-Bartholomew report. On July 4, 1928, Boy Scouts were sent to Santa Monica Beach to conduct a census.[41] The results were shocking: they counted 47,670 people on the beach at one time, with an average of fifteen square feet of sand per person. By comparison, aerial photographs of Atlantic City beaches showed an average of seventy-eight square feet per bather. And each bather at Coney Island—dubbed "the world's most heavily used beach" in the report—enjoyed fifty-six square feet on average.[42] By choosing to conduct their census on the national holiday, the report's authors knew they would obtain impressive figures. Another study carried out by the Regional Planning Commission on a "not particularly favorable beach day" in 1940 provided different figures; it found that visitors to Santa Monica had on average access to seventy square feet of sand.[43] Using Coney Island as a reference point also heightened the sense of a congestion crisis: all Americans, whether they had ever been to the famous New York resort, had seen widely circulated photographs and films of its crowded beaches. By comparing Los Angeles's beaches to their East Coast equivalent using a supposedly objective standard, the report's authors hoped to galvanize public opinion and convince other officials of the need to repair the unacceptable conditions. Los Angeles's reputation as a national tourist area was at stake.

The most obvious way to reduce congestion was to open new beaches. Against the background of the 1920s coastal real estate boom, the proliferation of private beach clubs, and the destruction of large swaths of coastline due to oil exploitation, meeting this objective became all the more urgent. The opening of the Venice oil field, lamented the Los Angeles Board of Playground and Recreation, had essentially obliterated "25% of the already limited beach owned by the city." Bathing near "noisy machinery and unpleasant odor" was hardly ideal.[44] Nor was it pleasant to get told off by "bewhiskered gentlemen with long guns" for trespassing on private land—an all-too-common experience for beachgoers.[45] The public trust doctrine, a legal principle with roots in Roman law and validated by the US Supreme Court in 1892, guarantees the public ownership of all tidelands and submerged lands. The exact point where public land becomes private property has been interpreted differently in each state. In California, courts declared that the demarcation would be drawn at "mean high tide line." Yet the exact location of what some called this "strange, mysterious and elusive line" remained a matter of controversy.[46] As the number of beachgoers soared, fences and barbed wires became a common sight on the shoreline. The coastline, the Los Angeles Times reported in 1926, had been "literally 'chopped up' with the ownership barometer registering in favor of the private owner." Figures compiled in the 1930 report confirmed the newspaper's claims: out of the seventy-two miles of shoreline in Los Angeles County, only fourteen miles of beach were public. Even in Santa Monica, a city known for its large public beach, 63 percent of the coast was in private hands. Worse still, "two iron fences, each higher than a man's head," blocked off a strip of 350 feet between the Casa del Mar and the Edgewater Beach Club.[47] In 1922, following reports that concessionaires were routinely charging beachgoers fifty cents for the privilege of seating on the beach, Santa Monica elites launched a campaign with the objective to "own every foot of ocean sand within the city limits." A similar movement took off in Los Angeles in 1925, but these initiatives remained local and short-lived, and their achievements were limited.[48]

At the state level, the preservation movement was agitating for more public parks. But beaches figured low on the list of priorities. The mighty forests of redwoods seemed more worthy of attention than sandy shores teeming with pleasure-seekers. Yet the movement's first victory, in 1928, also benefited beaches. That year, California voters voted on a referendum to spend six million dollars (to be matched by an equal amount of public or private funds) acquiring parks and beaches.[49] Two years later, one million dollars from the state park bond was spent on a 3,333-foot beach lot located north of the mouth of Santa Monica Canyon. In accordance with the matching principle, Los Angeles County donated to the state a contiguous beach lot of equivalent value, resulting in the opening of what the *Los Angeles Times* declared to be "the largest continuous public bathing beach in Southern California." Using the same process, another half-mile lot was acquired and opened to the public at Manhattan Beach. By 1933, however, the state park funds had almost run out, and Los Angeles officials condemned the inequitable allocation of the funds, with Northern California receiving the lion's share. As far as Southland beaches were concerned, the campaign fell short of expectations.[50]

Spreading crowds out along the coastline was another strategy to relieve congestion. But this required building more roads and parking lots. In the 1930s, the rise in automobile ownership and the declining popularity of the Red Cars prompted officials and urban planners to reflect on the problem. All interested parties agreed that the main thoroughfare through Venice, an eighteen-foot alley ironically called the "Venice Speedway," was thoroughly inadequate. In Malibu, the state highway was more spacious, but it was separated from the public beach by a continuous strip of private land, preventing public access and blocking the view from the road. In the words of planning adviser Hugh Pomeroy, "The tourists' view of the Pacific Ocean [had] become a series of fences and back yards."[51] Santa Monica beaches were, by far, the most easily accessible in the region. But this came at a cost: "Come a hot day here and what happens?" remarked a local town planner. "We have 100,000 to 200,000 automobiles in two hours that will concentrate on Santa Monica and these other towns." Once more, the famous Brooklyn resort acted as a foil, with talk of local beaches becoming just "like Coney Island in the movies." Echoing the conclusions of the Olmsted-Bartholomew report, Pomeroy advocated in 1936 for the construction of a "magnificent parkway along our shores."[52] But acquiring right-of-way along the beach had only grown more complex in the six years since the report had been published.

Finally, crowded beaches also meant filthy beaches. This posed a particularly challenging problem to small independent cities like Santa Monica, which had to shoulder the upkeep of a vast public beach visited by hundreds of thousands of people every year. In 1924, the local newspaper published an editorial denouncing the "deplorable condition" of the beaches and proposing "to put a gang of men at work at midnight every crowded day at the beach."[53] In Venice, which had merged with Los Angeles in 1926 and relied on it for beach maintenance, beaches were littered with trash after hot summer days. In 1934, the LA Board of Playground and Recreation

Commission noted that Venice's beaches were "very badly in need of cleaning." The Great Depression no doubt had something to do with the squalor, the beach having been "neglected due to financial difficulties."[54] By 1942, when the pollution study was released, beach cleanliness was still a prominent problem, with multiple mentions of the "good deal of lunch litter" left on popular beaches.[55]

From picnic scraps left on the sands to entire beaches slipping beneath the waves, the consequences of rapid demographic growth and urbanization on the Santa Monica Bay amounted to a "crisis" in the eyes of local elites. By establishing minimum acceptable standards for the beach experience, whether for accessibility, cleanliness, or congestion level, officials and planners hoped to regulate growth and preserve the region's distinctive landscapes. This progressive impulse was not unique to Los Angeles. In 1928, for example, the authors of the regional plan for New York's recreational facilities were the first to calculate the average square footage of sand per bather on the region's beaches.[56] The beach preservation movement precisely emerged around that time to ensure that these new scientific norms would be taken seriously. By the 1930s, a beach lobby, centered on the Los Angeles region, was coming into its own.

THE BEACH PRESERVATION MOVEMENT

As the birthplace of American beach tourism, the East Coast first experienced the erosion issues that accompanied coastal development. Starting in the late eighteenth century in the states of Rhode Island and New Jersey, and accelerating in the nineteenth century, Americans headed to the beach for health and recreation.[57] By the early twentieth century, the New Jersey coastline was substantially developed. When three hurricanes and four tropical storms battered the state's coastline between 1915 and 1921, local authorities were forced to contend with the new problem of beach erosion. In 1922, the state Board of Commerce and Navigation created the Engineering Advisory Board of New Jersey and tasked it with conducting a comprehensive erosion study. Around the same time, the Division of Geology and Geography at the National Research Council (NRC) formed a Committee on Shoreline Studies to research the matter. The committee helped New Jersey governor A. Harry Moore convene eighty-five representatives of sixteen Atlantic and Gulf states in Asbury Park in October 1926 to discuss coastal problems. The meeting resulted in the creation of the American Shore and Beach Preservation Association (ASBPA). The first organization dedicated to promoting "sound, far-sighted and economical development and preservation" of ocean, lake, and river shorelines, the ASBPA was a direct product of the beach boom and the changing perception of the coastline. R. S. Patton, chair of the Committee on Shoreline Studies, put it best during its foundational meeting: "Only a few years ago our beaches were desolate, barren wastes of sand-dunes and underbrush. Now, they contribute annually to the welfare and happiness of millions of our people."[58] Beaches, once part of a distant and frightening "coastal frontier," had morphed into premier engines of the economy.[59]

As a direct threat to the tourism economy, erosion was the catalyst for the creation of the ASBPA. In the 1920s, few people understood the role humans played in beach erosion, and even scientists like Patton believed "the ocean" and its "tireless attack" to be the root cause. "Man," he urged, "must come to the rescue of the beaches."[60] The goal of the ASBPA was precisely to act as a clearinghouse for scientific and technical information related to coastal matters, which it made available to different municipalities primarily through its journal, *Shore & Beach*, published quarterly beginning in 1933. In addition, the organization functioned as a lobbying group for obtaining federal funding to conduct erosion studies and repair damaged shorelines. Following intense pressure from the association and New Jersey officials in Washington, DC, Congress eventually voted on July 3, 1930, to establish the United States Beach Erosion Board (BEB), a commission tasked with studying and preventing coastal erosion. The association was able to exert more influence amid the New Deal and the federal government's growing involvement in society. With the passage of the Emergency Relief Appropriation Act in 1935, the ASBPA succeeded in its efforts to ensure that shore protection would be included among eligible relief projects. A year later, the passage of the United States Beach Improvement and Protection Act formalized the process through which coastal communities could appeal to the BEB to conduct studies and claim federal funding for coastal protection works.[61]

California was initially left out of these initiatives. In 1926, the ASBPA focused only on American shorelines from "Maine to Texas."[62] Several beach associations were established in California in the 1920s, but they were usually centered on a specific, local issue and had limited life spans. The turning point came in the mid-1930s with the failures of the Santa Monica and Santa Barbara harbors. In 1935, ASBPA members elected Los Angeles superintendent of recreation George Hjelte to the position of vice president. Thanks to his influence, Los Angeles hosted 160 members of the association for its 1936 annual convention. Playing host provided the impetus for the creation, that same year, of the California Beaches Association (CBA), the first statewide association in California, which published its own newsletter and soon organized two conferences.[63] This flurry of activity was no coincidence: George Hjelte was one of the founding members of the CBA, and his involvement in the ASBPA was a major factor in the creation of an association worthy of the name in California.

Unlike previous regional associations, the CBA championed an ambitious twelve-point agenda. Some of its initial objectives echoed those put forward in the Olmsted-Bartholomew report: improving public access to beaches, creating more beach state parks, and preserving the "natural beauty of the ocean shores." Unsurprisingly, several members of the citizens' committee behind the 1930 report were also CBA members. Hugh Pomeroy, for example, a regular contributor to *Shore & Beach* and the *California Beaches Association Bulletin*, served as the committee's executive secretary. Yet the CBA differed in its emphasis on combating erosion. The organization was intent on lobbying at the federal and state level for the conduct of erosion surveys and passage of legislation "for beach improvement and protection." In addition, the association took a stand against all forms of pollution, including oil and sewage contamination.[64]

Like Pomeroy, many CBA members demonstrated a sustained interest in beach issues. A. G. Johnson, beach design engineer for the City of Los Angeles and the author of two articles for the association's bulletin in 1936, had conducted beach erosion surveys since at least 1930. Many CBA members, including Johnson and Hjelte, worked for the local government and dealt with coastal issues on a daily basis. Another important contingent was the region's political and business elite, including directors of charitable organizations, prominent journalists, real estate promoters, hotel owners, and other businessmen with connections to the coast. The association also welcomed into its ranks scientists and engineers interested in the shoreline, such as Dr. Floyd I. Beckwith, its first president; U. S. Grant, professor of geology at the University of California, Los Angeles; George F. McEwen, professor of physical oceanography at the Scripps Institution of Oceanography in San Diego; and Morrough P. O'Brien, professor of mechanical engineering at the University of California–Berkeley and a member of the BEB. Several naval officers also joined. With this influential group, the CBA effectively functioned as a beach lobby that championed the coast both at the local level and in Sacramento.

Although its activities and membership were concentrated in Southern California, the association's initial ambition was to represent the entire state. After conferences held in La Jolla and Santa Barbara in 1936, the association planned a third one in San Francisco.[65] Its first bulletin also announced that the CBA would be opening an office in San Francisco, in addition to the one in Los Angeles, a clear signal of its statewide ambitions.

As its president remarked, "There is no alternative. The job is so big and so complicated that we must go at it in a big way." By the end of 1936, the association had over three hundred members. But its reach was much broader: its bulletin was distributed free of charge to over seven thousand people, and its activities were regularly covered by newspapers throughout the state.[66]

A PROTEAN RHETORIC

Borrowing from a variety of traditions within the nature movement, the California Beaches Association defied easy classification. While the association professed "to preserve the greatest natural asset that California possesses . . . from destruction, contamination, pollution, and despoliation," its members did not intend to halt human exploitation of the coast. Its utilitarian aim was to "develop the beaches as tourist attractions."[67] As such, the association shared traits with the early twentieth-century conservation movement whose "essence" was "rational planning to promote efficient development and use of all natural resources."[68] In the conservationist vein, it argued for a "scientific approach" to coastal planning. At the association's first conference, President Beckwith delighted in the fact that "the very atmosphere of this place [was] permeated with scientific research." "Suppose we think of ourselves today as in college again for one brief day," he proposed. The conference attendees were the "student body" and the speakers the "very distinguished faculty, a group of men that have devoted their lives to scientific research." This approach not only guaranteed the preservation of the shoreline but also benefited the state's finances. "As state-wide economic benefit, the value of California's beaches is incalculable," insisted editor W. R. Stewart in the association's first monthly bulletin.[69] In fact, the CBA had close ties with industrial interests. George D. Smith, owner of the Fairmont Hotels in San Francisco, for example, praised the group's efforts in its March 1936 bulletin. As owners of coastal real estate or tourism businesses, many members' economic fortunes rose and fell with the health of the coastline.[70]

But the economic argument was never advanced on its own. Beaches, Beckwith explained, paid "huge dividends now in money, health insurance and opportunity for open-air exercise."[71] In this sense, CBA leaders were inspired by the recreation movement and the late nineteenth-century preservation or wilderness movement. In the minds of preservationists, American wilderness was to be found in the supposedly uninhabited forests and mountainous areas that were protected by national parks.[72] Crowded beaches hardly fit this ideal. Yet if CBA members wanted to attract federal funding, they needed to be able to speak the language government officials wanted to hear. As ASBPA member Colonel Marcel Garsaud lamented in 1933, the National Park Service "could not see where the interest of the federal government was in the question of beaches, and all they were interested in . . . was the national parks and forests." CBA members thus regularly made explicit references to forests. In May 1936, oceanographer McEwen regretted that "President Roosevelt's far-seeing policy of conservation" had preserved "great areas of virgin forest" while completely ignoring beach areas despite their "comparable recreational value."[73] A few months earlier, Hjelte had pointed to the many similarities between beaches and forests: "Both are great national and natural resources. Both are essential to the economic and recreational welfare of the adjoining populated areas; the forests of more economic importance, perhaps, and the beaches of more recreational importance." Four years later, he went so far as to compare beaches to "national monuments like Yellowstone Park."[74] Comparisons sometimes turned competitive. During the 1936 ASBPA convention, John C. Porter, former mayor of Los Angeles and a member of the State Park commission, declared that the beaches, not the Redwoods, the celebrated sequoia forests of northern California, were the "greatest and most important part of the state parks."[75] Besides, more people visited beaches than state and national parks. In the words of Garsaud, "A man will visit a national park perhaps once in his lifetime, perhaps twice. . . . But he will go to a beach, one beach or another beach, three years out of five during his vacation time."[76] CBA members also drew on the goals of the recreation movement, which advocated for the opening of parks and play areas to provide youths with recreational alternatives to vice-ridden streets. In fact, the beach lobby indiscriminately used arguments from the conservation, preservation, and recreation traditions, as the questions posed by Colonel Charles T. Leeds in the March 1936 CBA bulletin illustrate:

> Are the beaches worth preserving? What does it mean to you as citizens to have an attractive ocean frontage to look at, to have a beautiful, smooth beach on which to bathe, swim, or lie in the sunshine, rather than a bare rocky shore? What is the difference in taxable value between ocean front property with an attractive beach in front and the same property without a usable beach? How much is a beautiful coastline worth as an attraction to tourists?[77]

While Leeds's questions were rhetorical, of course, he left it up to readers to decide if preservation was an economic issue to encourage active recreation or was simply because humans needed a beautiful landscape to admire.

Switching between different discourses allowed for the beach lobby to appeal to different sensibilities and stakeholders. But it also reflected the complexities of what they were attempting to defend. Beaches were all at once natural landscapes in need of protection, natural resources requiring efficient exploitation, and recreation areas ready for development. Beaches were in-between spaces, and the beach lobby borrowed from all strands of the nature protection movement in supporting its pragmatic position.[78]

Despite its initial successes, the CBA began to encounter difficulties in its second year. Beginning in February 1937, its bulletin ceased publication. After this date, the association virtually disappeared from public view, suggesting that it may have dissolved. Its rapid decline can be attributed to several factors. The CBA does not seem to have gained traction in the northern part of the state; the San Francisco conference never took place, and the San Francisco office was shuttered by the end of 1936. The fact that the association was relatively unsuccessful in implementing its agenda at the ASBPA's annual convention held in Los Angeles only added to its troubles. By welcoming members from around the nation as well as representatives of the BEB, the CBA had hoped to get the federal government to make a concrete commitment to funding erosion works in the region. Yet the association's bulletin glumly noted, "No action was taken by the conference."[79] Furthermore, the BEB was clearly neglecting the Pacific Coast: all of the eleven studies it had undertaken had focused on the Atlantic Coast or the Gulf of Mexico. Even worse, West Coast beaches were almost completely left out of the program of public works projects carried out by the Works Progress Administration (WPA) put in place during the Great Depression. Finally, the CBA was perhaps too ambitious for an association set up by an anonymous benefactor and funded through subscriptions to its monthly bulletin. Long-term projects—such as the plan to establish committees of experts specializing in erosion or pollution—were simply not viable without the stable financial resources of a much larger organization.[80]

The dissolution of the CBA, however, did not mean that the LA beach lobby was unraveling. Another group, the Shoreline Planning Association (SPA), quickly filled the void. Founded a year earlier than the CBA, in 1935, the Santa Monica–based group languished until 1940, when a conference on erosion organized by Los Angeles County gave it a new lease on life.[81] Previously focused on local issues, the association expanded its activities to include all Southern California counties. Although wartime demands limited its ambitions, the SPA would play a particularly important role in the postwar period.

In sum, by the mid-1930s, the state's elites finally took seriously problems that had plagued coastal municipalities for years. From then on, these influential figures constituted a veritable beach lobby, active at the local, state, and even national levels through the CBA and later the SPA. Los Angeles members were particularly active, holding leading positions in both associations. Scientists and engineers interested in the shoreline found that their expertise was highly valued, and the associations sought funding for their studies. In this way, the beach lobby proved critical for establishing coastal engineering as its own subfield of civil engineering.

BETWEEN LAND AND SEA: THE EMERGENCE OF COASTAL ENGINEERING

"Not so many years ago one did not think of the science of engineering as having much to do with a day's outing at the beach," mused A. G. Johnson in 1936. By the time he made that comment, however, engineers had become central players in shoreline development and in the beach protection movement at large. Engineers had been involved in coastal works before the twentieth century, dredging harbors; building lighthouses, ports, and other navigational structures; and protecting shorelines. But beaches had always been marginal to their practice. Sand was either seen as a nuisance, when it hindered navigation, or as a useful defense, when it broke the power of waves. In short, sand was incidental to navigation.[82]

By the turn of the century, sand had taken on a new meaning. When accumulated, it became the beach, a most precious asset that lured crowds of visitors in the summer months. At the same time, hotels, houses, boardwalks, bathhouses, and other structures near the shoreline quickly proliferated. The two phenomena were, of course, linked. But they were fundamentally at odds. Protecting coastal buildings from storms required "armoring" the shoreline, that is building seawalls and other hard structures. This is what residents of Galveston famously did after a deadly hurricane struck the Texas city on September 8, 1900, killing over six thousand people. Yet as author Cornelia Dean explains, "Beaches and seawalls cannot coexist for long. The reason is as simple as it is inexorable: an eroding shoreline is dynamic, but a wall is fixed." By 1920, Galveston had lost one hundred yards of sand. All that was left from its wide beach was "a narrow strip of sand at low tide and a gloomy vista of waves on rocks when the tide was high."[83] All of a sudden, engineering was closely related to a day's outing at the beach. Defending the coastline could not come at the cost of losing a beach, and engineers were tasked with finding a way to protect both.

Several major projects were carried out in the 1920s and early 1930s, including the first beach replenishment operation in the United States at Coney Island in 1922 and the construction of the esplanade and seawall at Ocean Beach in San Francisco.[84] In creating the BEB in 1930, the federal government gave a critical stimulus to the emerging field by bringing together the best engineers in the country focusing on erosion issues to conduct "the first worldwide systematic investigation of coastal phenomena."[85] Morrough P. O'Brien was one of the three civilian members first appointed (the board was composed of four officers from the Army Corps of Engineers and three civilian engineers). After obtaining his engineering degree at the Massachusetts Institute of Technology and pursuing two years of graduate studies at Purdue University, O'Brien had spent over a year studying in Germany and Sweden, where he learned about river hydraulics. Upon his return to the United States, O'Brien pioneered the study of fluid dynamics and applied it to coastal engineering.[86] He was one of the first engineers to promote the use of models in coastal development, highlighting their utility in predicting a built structure's effects on a given coastline. Alongside his work with the BEB, O'Brien became a leading figure in the California beach lobby, helping to organize the first CBA conference on erosion, writing articles for the CBA and ASBPA bulletins, and maintaining close ties to the SPA.[87] Perhaps even more significantly, he trained a whole generation of engineers at Berkeley in the 1930s and 1940s on beach erosion issues. Omar Lillevang, who entered Berkeley in 1937, was one such student. On O'Brien's advice, he and fellow student Roger W. Brant, a Santa Barbara native, studied changes to sediment transport brought about by the construction of Santa Barbara's harbor. The pair built a miniature hydraulic model of the affected coastline to imitate the littoral currents driving erosion.[88]

But O'Brien was not alone in laying the groundwork for this new subfield. At the local level, many of the engineers working for coastal municipalities in California were increasingly aware that specific knowledge was required to work on coastal sites. This was especially true of A. G. Johnson, who carried out a series of shoreline studies in Los Angeles from 1930. He inventoried all of the shoreline constructions while simultaneously gathering all existing documents related to the Santa Monica Bay coastline, including photographs, maps, and reports.[89] These local initiatives were reinforced by the work of associations like the CBA, which coordinated and mobilized people who cared about the beaches. Starting in 1936, anyone interested in coastal issues could read in the pages of the *California Beaches Association Bulletin* about the problems that California coastal cities faced. Moreover, the ASBPA journal, *Shore & Beach*, devoted numerous articles to the California coastline. These publications played an essential role in

CALIFORNIA BEACHES ASSOCIATION MONTHLY BULLETIN

Beach Experts at La Jolla Conference

Principal speakers at La Jolla gathering: Left to right, sitting—Dr. Robert T. Knapp, Dr. Floyd I. Beckwith, Dr. T. Wayland Vaughan. Standing: Dr. M. P. O'Brien, Dr. George F. McEwen, A. G Johnson, Col. W. W. Crosby. (San Diego Sun Photo.)

Figure 3.3. Coastal engineers at the La Jolla Conference on erosion, March 1936. Morrough P. O'Brien, who played a crucial role in the emergence of coastal engineering, is on the top left. A. G. Johnson, who devoted his career to coastal erosion in Los Angeles, stands second from the right. *California Beaches Association* 1, no. 4 (April 1936): 3. Morrough O'Brien Collection, box 14, file 100, Water Resources Collections & Archives, Special Collections & University Archives, University of California–Riverside.

creating and facilitating an informal network of coastal engineers at the state and national levels.

ENGINEERING BY INTUITION

Despite this flurry of activity, coastal engineering was not recognized as a separate field of engineering until the postwar period. In fact, the term did not appear in print until October 1950 when a conference titled "The Institute on Coastal Engineering" was held in Long Beach. Even O'Brien, writing in the conference proceedings, refused to consider it a "separate branch of engineering." According to him, coastal engineering was "primarily a branch of Civil Engineering which leans heavily on the sciences of oceanography, meteorology, fluid mechanics, electronics, structural mechanics, and others."[90]

O'Brien may have resisted the idea, but engineers involved in coastal works had already started to conceive of themselves as a separate breed in the 1930s. For one, engineers who straddled the boundaries between land and sea all faced the same difficulties when it came to finding scientific and technical information. Between 1876 and 1936, only five articles on beaches and erosion were published in the *Transactions of the American Society of Civil Engineers*, the profession's flagship journal. Even scientists still knew little about coastal morphology. In 1927, engineer Henry S. Sharp stated that "the engineer who wishes to attack his [shoreline] problem scientifically finds that science has done very little to help him. He is almost entirely without trustworthy facts and must work up his data from hasty studies of his own."[91] Until the 1970s, there was no generally accepted theory of how erosion worked—or rather, there were too many. O'Brien's account of his appointment to the BEB illustrates the problem:

> In 1929 the Beach Erosion Board found that all the civil engineers and every member of the board has his own version of beach erosion, and they decided that if they got anybody who knew anything about it, he would have too many opinions. So, they looked around and selected a mechanical engineer. I think I can still qualify in knowing nothing about it, but, unfortunately, I have some opinions.[92]

In fact, few engineers of the time, regardless of subfield, paid attention to scientific theories. Many used the trusted trial-and-error method, relying on what had worked elsewhere.[93] However, when it came to coastal development, accumulated experience was of little use. As Sharp warned, "A structure successful at one place may be a dismal failure at another." Due to the variations from one coastal area to another—including the direction of littoral currents, their strength, and the waves' angle of attack—the "rule-of-thumb methods [were] sure to give a large percentage of failures." Given such a bewildering number of factors, most coastal engineers of that period readily admitted that they "went about [their] work . . . intuitively."[94] Even new techniques such as miniature modeling did not resolve the issue. During the March 1936 CBA conference on erosion, O'Brien admitted that models still involved "an element of judgment." The remark sparked a lengthy technical discussion among the participants, with President Beckwith apologizing: "I just wanted to let you see how complicated these things are." A shout from the back of the room—"Maybe it's right to guess about them!"—caused great hilarity. The anecdote reflects the position of most of the engineers involved: when it came to building on the ocean, a good guess was almost as effective as complex calculations.[95]

The intuitive approach necessarily led to numerous errors, but these errors in turn provided an opportunity to learn more about how erosion worked. A. G. Johnson, for example, was able to estimate the average daily volume of sediment transported by the littoral currents in the Santa

Monica Bay thanks to the breakwater erected by the city, which retained sediments normally transported downdrift.[96] By the end of the 1930s, coastal engineering and science had made massive strides.

LEARNING FROM FAILURES

One of the first lessons coastal engineers learned from the many failed experiments of the 1930s was that the foreshore differed markedly from terra firma. Principles that worked for constructions built on static land did not apply to the shoreline. A beach, explained O'Brien in *Shore & Beach*, "is merely part of a stream of material in process of being transported from the land surface to the ocean depths." Another way to put it was to speak of beaches as "river[s] of sand," as the BEB did in a 1933 report. The term quickly caught on. Awareness of the fluidity of this zone was an essential prerequisite for understanding the true causes of erosion.[97]

In the early twentieth century, the notion that human activities caused erosion was not understood. In fact, coastal morphology in general was a highly debated topic. In his *Shore Processes and Shoreline Development* (1919), geomorphologist Douglas Johnson noted "the widely conflicting opinions and observations relating to those most puzzling forces."[98] In the 1930s, engineers continued to be baffled about "the mysterious things that cause[d] erosion (winds, currents, tides)," with some blaming "ocean currents working in their mysterious ways" for Santa Barbara's disappearing beaches.[99] By the early 1940s, however, it was widely accepted that human constructions had caused the most egregious cases of erosion on the coastline. Aerial photographs, especially those A. G. Johnson carefully preserved in the city's vault, provided incontrovertible proof that human choices had a direct impact on sediment transport. Waves, it was now understood, played a fundamental role in how littoral currents operated: if they were eliminated—by a breakwater, for example—sediments would be "trapped," and beaches downdrift would start eroding.[100] This realization led to numerous studies on waves and how their speed and angle affected beaches. Coastal engineers complemented observations of their studies on the coasts of California by monitoring other shorelines. In 1929, for example, Taggart Aston, a consulting harbor engineer hired by Santa Monica, traveled to Europe to visit harbors in England, France, and Spain.[101]

However, California with its beautiful sandy beaches and countless erosion problems, represented the most formidable "beach erosion laboratory" that coastal engineers could hope for. In 1936, O'Brien used the state's coastline in developing a rudimentary version of the concept of the "littoral cell," a core principle of coastal morphology.[102] In the 1970s, Douglas Inman, a prominent professor of oceanography, defined a littoral cell as "a coastal compartment that contains a complete cycle of sedimentation including sources, transport paths, and sinks." If the "budget of sediment" is balanced within the cell (that is, if as much sand moves into the area as moves out of it), then the beach is in a state of equilibrium. However, if more sand moves out of an area than moves into it (for instance, if it is interrupted by a breakwater upcoast), then erosion occurs.[103] Although the exact terminology was not fixed until scientists such as Inman published comprehensive studies on the topic, O'Brien established the concept's general framework. According to him, the coastline of California was "divided naturally into sections which appear to be integral units as regards beach erosion and related phenomena." Each of these units, he explained, "differ in exposure to wave and wind attack, in plan form, in character and supply of beach material, etc." A hand-drawn map highlighting each of these "sections" along the California coast accompanied his article, with the Monterrey, Santa Barbara, Santa Monica, San Pedro, and San Diego cells all neatly identified.[104]

Around the same period, a series of lawsuits related to the consequences of the Santa Monica harbor's construction on nearby beaches clarified the legal implications of sand erosion and accretion. Watching ever more of their beaches wash away each year, several private property owners sued the city. More surprisingly, other property owners—whose land was located north of the breakwater—blamed the harbor for enlarging their beaches. The Los Angeles Athletic Club, which owned two beach clubs, claimed their clients "no longer [found] sea bathing convenient," having to walk for "miles" to reach the ocean.[105] By 1940, when the lawsuits were heard, the city's liability was well established. Both sides acknowledged that the changes to the beaches' shapes had been caused by "the breakwater interfering with the littoral drift." Yet none of these lawsuits led to a conviction, and the court ruled in favor of the city on every issue. This was partly because the judges, relying on witness reports given by coastal engineers, including Morrough O'Brien, were forced to acknowledge that it was impossible to determine where the mean high tide line would lie "in a natural state of equilibrium."[106] The municipality did have in its archives a topographic survey dating from 1876, before the boom in coastal development. But this lacked a date indicating which month it was drawn up, so it was impossible to establish whether it corresponded to winter beaches, temporarily eroded by storms, or to the wider summer beaches. Moreover, the engineers and scientists called to testify agreed that the area that had been eroded as a result of the harbor was probably not "natural" and did not exist when the owners had bought their beaches. Much of the shoreline in question, they claimed, were accretions related to the multiple man-made structures built on the coast since the late nineteenth century. Since, according to California law, artificial accretions (unlike natural ones) belonged to the public, the judge ruled that the lost sand had been city property all along.[107]

The lawsuits contributed to a larger conversation about how best to define and locate the mean high tide line. Legal experts conceded that "the law of this state [was] not settled as to what constitutes the ordinary high-water mark . . . or how such a line may be located upon the ground." Another complication stemmed from the fact that, unlike on the Atlantic coast, the two daily high tides and low tides on the Pacific coast did not reach the same levels. As a result, "Decisions in jurisdictions bordering on the Atlantic Coast [were] of little benefit to [people] on the Pacific Coast."[108] In the end, both sides acknowledged that the exact location of that line was "uncertain." Even so, coastal engineers' testimonies served to clarify and reaffirm the public trust doctrine: no one could privatize the foreshore.

As the Santa Monica breakwater lawsuits testify, coastal engineers were key members of the LA beach lobby. Together with local officials and businesspeople, they produced countless conferences, bulletins, plans, reports, and studies. Taken as a whole, these documents provided a detailed portrait of what the ideal modern beach should look like, as well as the road map required to get there.

JONES BEACH, THE FIRST MODERN BEACH

An ideal modern beach to study was already available to the California experts. When Jones Beach, a stretch of the Long Island shoreline about thirty-four miles from New York City, was inaugurated on August 4, 1929, it quickly became a new benchmark for coastal development. Developed at a cost of over fifteen million dollars by Robert Moses, New York's City park commissioner, Jones Beach was an instant success. A few days after its inauguration, the journalist Ernest Biehl gushed in the New York Times, "I have visited nearly all of the important beach resorts in this country and I must say that nowhere on this continent is there a public or private beach that is even comparable to the one that the State under Moses has built."[109] Jones Beach was, indeed, a marvel of engineering. According to biographer Robert Caro, Moses had taken a "barren, deserted, windswept sand spit" and transformed it into "what may be the world's greatest oceanfront park and bathing beach."[110] One of the first artificial beaches in the nation, it was enlarged using a new technique involving dredging up sand from the ocean floor. In the 1920s, many experts claimed that deposited sand would immediately be swallowed up by the waves. Jones Beach silenced the naysayers: not only did the beach survive the hurricane that struck the East Coast on September 21, 1938, but the accumulated sand actually protected nearby structures.

At Jones Beach, Robert Moses also applied the principles that had guided his work in the New York City Department of Parks and Recreation. A fierce advocate of public recreation, he envisioned Jones Beach as the anti–Coney Island: a family-friendly leisure area where the urban middle class could relax on a clean, strictly regulated beach. Journalists invited to the inauguration were astonished to find "no concessions, no booths, no bawling hot-dog vendors." The beach was expansive, with each visitor having on average a minimum of sixty-four square feet of immaculately clean sand all to themselves.[111] Dressed in sailor uniforms, the beach's staff made sure that the rules were enforced and that the sanitary facilities and two large bathing establishments were kept spick-and-span. Local students during the summer months picked up the trash that visitors left. The surest sign that Moses aspired to make Jones Beach the ideal middle-class beach was undoubtedly the two giant parking lots. The architect allegedly had bridges along the Southern State Parkway built too low for buses to drive underneath, thus ensuring the beach's social and racial exclusivity.[112] While this claim has since been challenged, the massive parking lots did signal that the needs and wishes of middle-class motorists were at the core of the design. Aerial photographs of the parking lots, twice as large as the beach itself, spread throughout the country. In the opinion of the *Los Angeles Daily News*, Jones Beach was unquestionably "the nation's best municipal beach."[113]

The Los Angeles beach lobby was quick to take note of Moses's innovations. As early as 1940, it was widely acknowledged that Jones Beach was "a superior development." In the view of A. G. Johnson, the Southern California beaches lagged "twenty years behind."[114] In 1946, George P. Larsen, secretary of the SPA Inc., claimed that the group's goal was "to equal the magnificent achievements of commissioner Robert Moses."[115] Will Rogers State Beach, a stretch of beach located north of Santa Monica Bay, was dubbed the " 'Jones Beach' of the California shore." As construction was underway on the new beach, plans called for building amenities remarkably similar to those at the Long Island beach, including "152 lockers, showers and toilets." A museum was even envisioned where smelly hotdog stands had once stood.[116] Following Moses's lead, the beach lobby could not envision opening a beach park without a minimal number of amenities. Jones Beach

Figure 3.4. Aerial photograph of Jones Beach on July 4, 1939. Hagley ID, J. Victor Dallin Aerial Survey collection (Accession 1970.200), Audiovisual Collections and Digital Initiatives Department. Courtesy of the Hagley Museum & Library.

changed the perception of what a modern beach should look like. Sun, sea, and sand were no longer enough.

The Jones Beach model also prompted West Coast engineers to experiment further with artificial beach construction. Some of them, such as A. G. Johnson, traveled to the East Coast to survey the latest innovation in sand pumping technology.[117] Upon his return in 1936, Johnson conducted the first large-scale beach nourishment operation. Funded by the Works Progress Administration, the project consisted of pumping sand from the dunes at Hyperion Beach to the eroded beaches at Venice. Seven hundred WPA employees were employed, working two six-hour shifts, five days a week. "Moving a mountain of sand into the seashore" seemed like magic to those gathered to watch the process at work. After six weeks, longtime visitors could already see that "the beach within a half-mile of the project [had] been made 30 feet wider."[118] Results were particularly spectacular at Del Rey, where the beaches tripled in width. That same year, Cabrillo Beach, in the San Pedro Bay, was celebrated as "a nearly perfect example of an entirely man-made strand" after a successful nourishment operation transformed what was "formerly a rocky shore" into a "fine bathing beach." Success made local engineers more confident in their ability to create beaches from scratch. From the early 1940s on, the most daring proposals in coastal design came from Southern California.[119]

A HOTBED OF INNOVATION: SOUTHERN CALIFORNIA IN THE 1940S

In the early 1940s, Southern California emerged as a hotbed of ideas and proposals for how best to manage and develop the coastline. One of the most daring proposals to arise at the time was put forward by A. G. Johnson. The LA city engineer's plan involved excavating more sand from the Hyperion dune field and depositing it on the beaches of Santa Monica and Venice, where a new coastal highway would be built. As he conceived it, the plan would solve "three major problems" simultaneously: the highway would relieve weekend traffic; the excavated sand would help to reverse erosion caused by Santa Monica Harbor; and the leveled dunes at Hyperion Beach would, it was hoped, enable a new sewage treatment plant to be built.[120]

Outlined in a 1940 report, Johnson's proposal was innovative in several ways. It required displacing over 12 million cubic yards of sand, far more than the 1.8 million cubic yards of sand transported four years earlier during the WPA-funded project. Further, it called for widening the beaches from 75 to 275 feet, a substantial undertaking that would require close coordination among seven different administrative municipalities.[121] Additionally, no study had been conducted to assess the highway's feasibility, and no precedent existed for a road of that magnitude to be built entirely on artificial strands. Several public figures, including John Anson Ford, a member of the Los Angeles County Board of Supervisors, spoke out against the plan, which he considered too risky. "The idea is beautiful. . . . But is it economical and sound from an engineering standpoint?" worried Ford.[122] The Santa Monica harbor fiasco was still too fresh in people's minds for them to blindly put their trust in engineers. In addition to these arguments, many coastal residents balked at the idea of a highway marring their view of the ocean.[123] While the project was ultimately abandoned, it nevertheless testified to the willingness of local coastal engineers to experiment. In the face of erosion, all solutions, even the most audacious, were on the table. Moreover, the innovators knew the beach lobby could be counted on to promote their ideas to local officials, from the county level all the way to the halls of the state capitol.

From the 1930s onward, the LA beach lobby exercised a powerful influence on county and state beach policies. By the late 1930s, their persistent

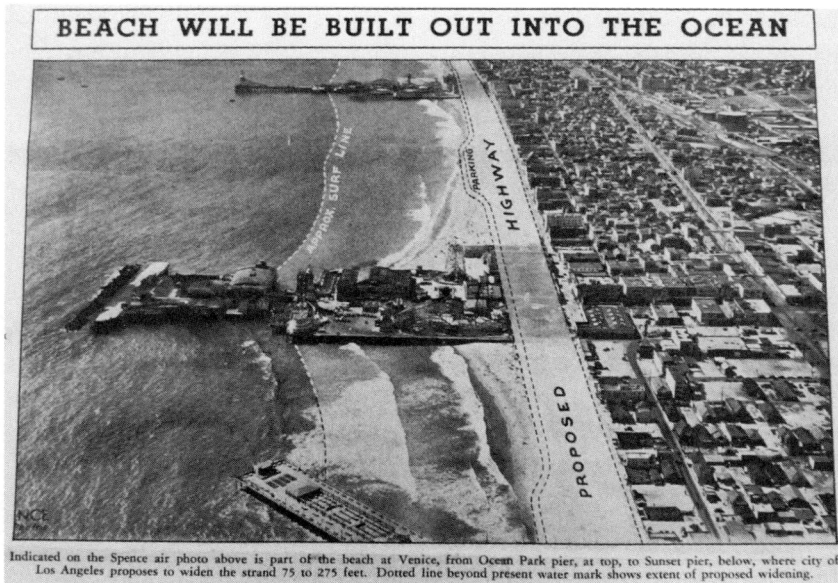

Figure 3.5. Diagram of the highway project on an artificial beach in Santa Monica. *California Beaches Association* 1, no. 11 (November 1936): 1. Morrough O'Brien Collection, box 14, file 100, Water Resources Collections & Archives, Special Collections & University Archives, University of California–Riverside.

pressure had brought about notable successes. In 1938, responding to pleas from the beach associations to abandon fragmented planning, the Los Angeles County Board of Supervisors ordered the Regional Planning Commission to come up with a shoreline development program that would include all the region's beaches, whether belonging to a city, county, state, individual, or company. By taking this initiative, the county was satisfying one of the beach lobby's long-standing demands. The Olmsted-Bartholomew report had already recommended action at the regional level, but it was above all the CBA that most vigorously denounced the "system of piecemeal, haphazard growth and improvement."[124] A revived SPA also advocated a holistic approach and was directly involved in bringing the plan to fruition. Two years in the making, the "Master Plan of Shoreline Development for the Los Angeles County" was released in 1940 to great acclaim. Far from simply mimicking an East Coast model, the document offered a new vision. By bringing on board all major players in coastal development—the cities, the county, the State of California, and private property owners—the plan allowed local leaders to plot the shoreline's long-term development while simultaneously considering ecological phenomena, such as littoral drift, that cut across jurisdictional lines. Upholding the idea that ecological forces, such as waves and currents, superseded man-made borders, the report represented an early example of environmentally informed policymaking.

The plan rapidly established itself as the gold standard in shoreline development. *Shore & Beach*, the official publication of the ASBPA, published it in its entirety in 1941, calling it "one of the most progressive shorefront utilization programs ever conceived." The national association even encouraged its readers to "copy [the LA Master Plan] with suitable local modifications."[125] A year later Orange County followed suit.[126] Not only was the plan pioneering in its regional focus, but it also called for acquiring virtually the entire shoreline for the public. From an engineering point of view, the plan backed Johnson's call to deposit sand excavated from Hyperion on eroded beaches, but omitted the controversial highway built on artificially enlarged shores.

At the state level, the "shoreliners," as SPA members called themselves, managed to get several historic measures enacted. The state recognized that it was necessary to "acquire all possible ocean frontage for use by the public for recreation purpose"—quite a radical ambition for the era. It authorized the expenditure of five hundred thousand dollars for beach acquisition on the condition that all coastal counties release a master plan of shoreline development—a condition that Los Angeles County had already met. The state's Division of Parks was renamed the "Division of Beaches and Parks," a largely symbolic move that acknowledged the status of beaches as natural landscapes worthy of preservation and validated the shoreliners' long campaign. Finally, the state committed to increasing the share of revenue from coastal oil development that went toward purchasing public beaches from 30 to 70 percent. By endorsing the principle that all beaches should be accessible to the public, the state, following in the footsteps of Los Angeles County, set the policy agenda with respect to the coastline for the next fifty years.[127]

Looking back on the field and his career in the 1980s, coastal engineer William Herron claimed that Southern California had been "more receptive to research and original thinking in coastal engineering than many parts of the US." According to Herron, this openness was linked to the proximity of leading universities and research centers such as the Scripps Institution of Oceanography in San Diego, the University of California–Berkeley, and the California Institute of Technology in Pasadena.[128] Although private and public investment in research certainly fostered innovative thinking in coastal engineering, it does not wholly explain the region's leadership in the domain of shoreline development. The advocacy of the LA beach lobby played a key role in supporting coastal engineers' most ambitious visions.

Throughout the 1930s and 1940s, the lobby put sustained pressure on local and state politicians to preserve, acquire, and develop beaches. Yet its work has largely been forgotten today, leaving few tangible traces on either public memory or scholarship.[129] In part this was because the local business and civic leaders who made up the beach lobby perceived of themselves as "the voice of the people" and saw public beaches as part of a greater good.[130] Yet the power of business groups like the CBA and SPA over state and federal policies reveals the undemocratic nature of American politics in the twentieth century. While most ordinary Californians did love beaches, their voices remained unheard. The beach lobby's vision of the ideal modern beach reflected its members' social and racial backgrounds. As such, it did not take into account the desires of working-class beachgoers and racial minorities. As the lobby realized its goals in the postwar period, the region's coastline would be cleared of any activities and groups that did not fit their narrow vision for the modern seaside.

By the early 1940s, the birth pangs of a new seaside model were being felt on the beaches of Los Angeles. Of course, it was not entirely new. The modern beach remained indebted to the Riviera model, with its wide boardwalks, palatial hotels, and picturesque marinas. Jones Beach, with its artificial strands and huge parking lots, provided some key elements of reference as well. The Southern California model represented a synthesis and a culmination: it stood for public and clean beaches equipped with modern facilities and stabilized, if not enlarged, thanks to extraordinary feats of engineering.[131] Even so, Los Angeles's beaches were far from the ideal modern shoreline described in the beach lobby's plans. Erosion had reached a crisis point; beaches remained overcrowded and coastal roads were famously congested; pollution was so dire that the South Bay beaches were cordoned off in 1942. Military exigencies meant that coastal development and beach acquisition were near the bottom of politicians' priorities. The situation on the eve of the US entry into World War II was therefore highly paradoxical. On the one hand, the beach lobby had managed to get several measures into law, and ambitious plans were being drawn up. On the other hand, the beaches themselves were in a sorry state. Not until the 1950s and 1960s would their vision for the California coastline begin to flourish.

CHAPTER 4

⌘

A Beach for the Suburban Age

In March 1950, *California Coast*, the monthly bulletin edited by the Shoreline Planning Association, offered a sad commentary on the State's public shores: "the phrase 'public beach' calls up in the minds of many people an unpleasant picture. . . . Whatever the locale, many visualize the details as identical: over-crowded, littered up, inadequate parking, very noisy, small and unsanitary facilities, the whole nourished by smelly ramshackle hot dog stands skilled in the preparation of dubious hamburgers, underdone wieners, stale coffee, and dispensing the most synthetic of soft drinks and tasteless 'ice cream' consisting largely of air bubbles."[1] Just a year earlier, the city planning firm Madigan and Hyland had reached a similar conclusion in a report commissioned by Los Angeles County: "The local beaches offer the prospective visitor traffic jams, parking problems, crowded conditions, inadequate and low-grade food stands, honkey-tonk amusements and sand in the shoes."[2] In his address to the 1948 annual convention of the Shoreline Planning Association, August E. Henning, chief of the California Division of Parks and Beaches, called the beaches a "sorry mess," a pithy phrase local newspapers eagerly adopted for their headlines.[3]

This was hardly the kind of publicity California resorts desired. In fact, these descriptions stood in sharp contrast with the publicity brochures circulated by the All-Year Club of Southern California, a nonprofit organization promoting the region as a tourist destination. Preferring to ignore the effects of postwar growth on natural landscapes, the All-Year Club relied on its tried-and-true prewar advertising message selling California as an idyllic setting, with brochures showing "small groups or couples soaking up the sun on a deserted beach."[4] While this strategy made sense in the short term, the SPA refused to conceal the reality. The appalling state of the beaches risked jeopardizing the region's reputation as a paradise for outdoor recreation. What would tourists think once they set foot on a California beach and realized that they were far from "deserted," in addition to being polluted, dirty, and eroded? Concerns about these conditions were hardly unknown, but all the measures planned to address the shoreline problems had been postponed during the war.

In the immediate postwar years, the beach lobby, with the support of the state and county, strove to bring image and reality into alignment. Thanks to the SPA's lobbying efforts at the state level and California's booming postwar economy, which generously fed state coffers, the Los Angeles beach lobby was finally able to put its plans into practice. The results were spectacular. Within a decade, large swaths of the shoreline came into public ownership, sewage pollution radically abated, and beach enlargement progressed rapidly. To the delight of the millions of new Angelenos who settled in the city after the war, entire strands of beach literally emerged from the water. At the same time, coastal development proceeded in line with the new principles in suburban planning. Like the new shopping centers and theme parks popping up across the country, the city's beaches were redeveloped to attract white middle-class families.

The beach modernization campaign echoed contemporary urban renewal efforts to remake the cityscape of major industrial cities. Hoping to retain and attract investors, middle-class shoppers, and wealthy residents, proponents of urban renewal bulldozed countless inner-city neighborhoods labeled as "slums" to make room for urban freeways, baseball stadiums, and high-rise apartment buildings. On the coastline, modernizing impulses targeted the nineteenth-century beachscape characterized by old piers, "ramshackle hot-dog stands," and the much decried honky-tonk amusements. By getting rid of these remnants of the seaside past, artificially enlarging the beaches, and building modern accommodation on the sands, the Los Angeles beach lobby attempted to create a beach experience that met suburbanites' expectations, in the hopes of preventing them from "fleeing" the coast as they had "fled" the city.[5] Unlike most urban renewal projects in central cities, "beach renewal" was largely effective. Los Angeles's beaches continued to attract the white middle and upper classes at a time when many other urban recreational spaces were perceived as declining. In the end, beach renewal did more than alter the landscapes of the Santa Monica Bay. It fundamentally reshaped expectations of what a beach

outing should be, further distancing visitors from forging an ecological relationship with the coastline.

BAYWATCH: THE SHORE AT WAR

The Second World War represented a fundamental turning point in the history of the Los Angeles metropolitan region.[6] Long isolated from the more
established urban and industrial centers of the East and Midwest, the city
became second in the nation in industrial output and the largest metropolis in the American West during these years. While the entire state experienced a "Second Gold Rush" during the war, Southern California benefited
the most from defense spending, thanks to its proximity to the Pacific theater and the heavy presence of the aircraft and shipbuilding industries in
the region. Within four years, Los Angeles welcomed more than 780,000
new residents, many of them African Americans, attracted by the prospect
of higher wages in the war industries.[7]

News of the Japanese attack on Pearl Harbor on December 7, 1941, put
all Americans on a war footing, but California's proximity to the Pacific
warfront and its strategic importance as a major industrial and military
center made it particularly vulnerable. As early as December 18, Japanese
submarines carried out a series of operations against US ships in West
Coast waters. The nearby presence of the enemy heightened the sense of
danger experienced by those who lived near the coast. Fears soon turned to
the skies and the possibility of a Japanese raid on Southern California's defense plants and military bases. On February 25, 1942, the army informed
the civil defense authorities that enemy planes were headed toward the
city. All soldiers and volunteers of the Office of Civilian Defense were put
on high alert. Although no attack took place, the incident—known today
somewhat humorously as the "Battle of Los Angeles"—gave Angelenos the
impression that the war could arrive on their doorstep at any moment.[8]

Concerns about espionage and sabotage from the inside, heightened by
a long-standing anti-Japanese sentiment, had dramatic consequences for
Japanese Americans who lived on the Pacific Coast. On the day of the Pearl
Harbor bombing, thirty-one-year-old photographer George Fukasawa, a
second-generation Japanese American and UCLA graduate living in Santa
Monica, was enjoying a Sunday beach outing with his new wife when
he heard the news on the car radio. As a member of the Santa Monica
Auxiliary Police, he reported immediately to the police station and later
worked with intelligence agencies on cases involving Japanese individuals
suspected of subversive activities. Around fifteen hundred leaders in the

community (mostly men) were rounded up and arrested in the immediate aftermath of the bombing. In early 1942, rumors about Japanese American fishermen gathering data on the shape of the coastline and the seafloor led to the passage of new fishing rules to prevent noncitizens from going out in boats. All Japanese Americans, regardless of their age, profession, or citizenship status, were considered suspect. Although there was no evidence that the Japanese would attack the Pacific coast or that US-based saboteurs were ready to help them, the combination of war fever and anti-Japanese prejudice in the region led some individuals in the army and in civil society to advocate for harsher measures.[9] On February 19, 1942, President Roosevelt signed Executive Order 9066 authorizing the removal of all people of Japanese ancestry from two newly created "military areas" in the Western United States. Despite George Fukasawa's active involvement in Santa Monica's civic life, he was also "evacuated." He and his wife spent their honeymoon in Manzanar, one of ten incarceration camps that the US authorities established to detain over 110,000 Japanese Americans.[10]

Concerns about wartime sabotage shone a spotlight on the importance of the coastline and its beaches. The shoreline was regularly patrolled by the army, and some beaches, such as Playa Del Rey, were closed to the public for military exercises.[11] Moreover, a number of hotels and apartment buildings located on the bay were requisitioned. The La Monica Ballroom, for example, became a bivouac for the troops in charge of coastal surveillance, while the Miramar and Edgewater Hotels hosted soldiers on leave from the front. Civilians also had a part to play. As the summer season came into full swing in July 1942, the local press urged readers to "keep a close watch for enemy agents who may attempt to land on the Southern California coast." Alertness was especially important "whenever [you] are on the beach or near the shore." All "suspicious incidents" that occurred on the shore, "such as abandoned boats, rubber boats, abandoned clothing and other evidence pointing to unauthorized landings" were to be reported to the Office of Civilian Defense.[12]

While most beaches and amusement parks remained open throughout the war, their atmospheres were obviously less festive than during peacetime. Beginning in late May 1942, local authorities started imposing nightly dimouts in San Pedro, West Los Angeles, and Venice in order to deprive enemy aircraft of easy targets and prevent submarine activities along the coast. Although amusement piers were allowed to operate at night, their bright lights were dimmed starting in July 1942. Streetlights were painted black, residents were encouraged to cover their windows with dark curtains, and motorists were told not to drive near the shore. The Santa Monica Chamber of Commerce went even further, vowing to blackout (rather than simply dim) all signs and show windows in the city.[13] In late March 1942, the City of Los Angeles beefed up the surveillance of beach activities and prohibited all beach bonfires (as well as the use of flashlights along the shores) for fear that "spies could operate among picknickers." Even without the presence of spies, bonfires could inadvertently aid the enemy by "silhouetting moving vessels, making them easy targets for submarine attacks." Beach wienie bakes, as the Santa Monica newspaper humorously put it, ended up as "a war casualty."[14]

For some visitors, the dimouts were not without their advantages. Members of the Bel Air Bay Club were pleased to rediscover the beauty of "the phosphorescent display of the waves at night." Of course, "this [had] been going on for years," but people had failed to notice it due to the "bright reflections of well-lighted cities around the bay, which more or less hid this display of nature." Meanwhile, young lovers had more privacy for their amorous dalliances on the public beaches. As one amusement operator busy covering up lights on the Venice and Ocean Park Pier noted, "We'll have dimout rides now and I believe the young folks will like that!"[15]

Young people's revelries on the coastline attracted the attention of local authorities. Concerns focused on the rising tide of juvenile delinquency, which many attributed to "the great increase in the number of employed mothers."[16] Such discourses reflected broader anxieties over the wartime disruptions of the traditional family order. In response, local authorities took strict measures, including a new ban forbidding all youth under eighteen from patronizing dance halls after midnight, and a general curfew closing all dancing establishments at 2 a.m. This dramatically reduced the "swing shift," so-called because factory workers whose shifts ended at midnight would often go straight to dance until the 6 a.m. closure.[17] Nightlife was more tightly controlled, but not necessarily less lively. Unemployment was minimal during the war, and defense workers enjoyed high salaries. Many workers spent their money in the dance halls and amusement parks where the summer seasons continued to offer new attractions.

Even with the restrictions, people continued to flock to the beach. Gasoline rationing, for instance, had the paradoxical effect of increasing the number of visitors to the shore. While Angelenos could no longer go on long road trips, many of them had enough in their gas tanks to get to the beach. As one Venice resident remarked in 1943, "The curtailment of gas has resulted in our beach becoming the vacation spot for everyone."[18] On July 4, 1942, a crowd estimated at more than 250,000 gathered on the city's beach to celebrate the national holiday, the highest figure in the past three years. In June 1943, a massive traffic jam even blocked the entrance to the Santa Monica Municipal Pier, causing the police chief to exclaim, "You never would have guessed that we have gasoline rationing to look at the traffic we had!"[19] Despite having to turn away nonmembers due to food rationing, the summer of 1944 at the Bel Air Bay Club "[was] one of the biggest seasons we have ever had."[20] Even fabric rationing could be circumvented: "don't you worry and get wrinkles, my beamish bathing beauty, over wool and rubber shortages," admonished the Santa Monica newspaper, wartime rationing "only speeded up a trend toward rayon fabrics in swim suits, now blossoming out in the shops." To the relief of fashion victims, "beach glamour" need not be sacrificed in wartime Los Angeles.[21]

THE BEACH AS PATRIOTIC SYMBOL

The sight of these crowded beaches while so many globally lived amid a brutal conflict must have been quite shocking to Los Angeles's many European refugees. In her autobiography, Austrian Jewish actress Salka Viertel bitterly described the "hairless bodies glistening and brown" of the "unconcerned sunbathers on the beach."[22] Nonchalant beachgoers notwithstanding, the shore was not simply a place where people went to forget the troubles of war, but a space endowed with patriotic symbolism.

Urban parks and streets were key sites where Americans expressed their patriotism during the war. On June 14, 1942, for instance, four hundred thousand Chicagoans proudly paraded in the city's streets to commemorate Flag Day and "demonstrate the city's irreproachable spirit of national unity," emblematic of the competition between industrial cities to attract federal dollars.[23] While no such demonstration took place on the nation's shores, beaches located near urban areas played an important part in the conflict, particularly in Los Angeles, home to war production plants and troops in transit to the Pacific front. In fact, the war contributed to making the beach a symbol of the American way of life, laying the groundwork for massive postwar investments in the coast.

The beaches were favorite leisure spots for soldiers based in the region who had the opportunity to stay at the Santa Monica army recreation camp. In 1944, the army was authorized to reserve a portion of the beach frontage between Ocean Park Boulevard and Fraser Street for the soldiers and to build a "winterized hutment" to accommodate them. The camp was so successful that an estimated sixty-eight thousand men had stayed there by 1943, a number that exceeded the entire population of Santa Monica. The camp was free, and as Major Robert J. Kennedy explained in the local newspaper, "soldiers looking for a place to sleep [could] be sent there at any hour of the day and night." Kennedy presciently commented that "many of them [were] eager to come back" once the war was over. In fact, many soldiers who had trained or relaxed in Santa Monica chose to return after the war and settle permanently in the city.[24] In addition to the camp, the United Service Organizations (USO), whose role was to boost the morale of the troops, organized regular beach parties at the bay's various private beach clubs, featuring softball and volleyball games, swimming, dinner parties, and dancing. "USO girls" also collected the towels and bathing suits necessary for the soldiers' stay at the beach and were always "on hand to entertain the boys."[25]

Soldiers enjoying seaside fun proved an ideal topic to explore for the American media, which was under pressure to focus on positive news and lift the population's spirits.[26] The beach outings of soldiers on leave were the subject of two photo essays in *Life* magazine in 1942. The first of these, published in April, focused on six "fortunate young soldiers whom the rest of the U.S. Army [could] regard only with the grossest envy." Arriving from Camp Callan, just north of San Diego, the men were met at LA's Union Station by "five starlets from Universal Studios," who took them to Santa Monica for some beach fun, followed by dinner at a Hollywood nightclub. A few months later, as the beach season was in full swing, *Life* published "A Girl's Guide for Entertaining Soldiers," featuring twenty-one-year-old actress Marjorie Woodworth, who was sent to visit a Southern California army camp. Far from "going Hollywood on the boys," the young woman was depicted serving food to the soldiers, trying on unflattering overalls, and enjoying a beach romp.[27] In both cases, entertaining soldiers was presented as the patriotic duty of women, especially Hollywood actresses. Described as the ultimate "good sport," Marjorie was the model whom all "other girls involved in this type of war effort" should follow. As it happened, *Life*'s spring beach outing coincided with the release of hostess Janet Blair's first movie, a patriotic comedy set against the backdrop of the war. Marjorie Woodworth was also about to see her first feature film hit the screens. Entertaining soldiers was thus good business for the studios. It provided free publicity and reinforced the industry's explicit backing of the war effort.[28] Doing so on the beach only made sense since it offered the perfect excuse to show off the latest starlets wearing revealing swimsuits.

Fun from the shores of California also offered a reassuring counterpoint to battlefield stories. The photographs accompanying both articles depicted the soldiers engaging in beach activities such as "blanket-tossing," the bouncing of a young woman on a blanket held by four or five men (to which both Janet and Marjorie were subjected), and the "human cannonball," which involved two men holding a woman's ankles and wrists and projecting her forward. The soldiers' interest in these beach games was self-evident. Above all, the activities reinforced traditional gender roles, as a passive young woman "[squealed] joyfully" at the mercy of "husky soldiers." For all their sexual allusions, the hijinks staged for *Life* also recalled the world of childhood, with the beach depicted as a place where acting like a kid was encouraged. Games of leapfrog and exhilarating sprints in the surf with soldiers and actresses running hand in hand gave the whole affair an aura of innocence, while also emphasizing the nation's unity in fighting the enemy. The "human cannonball" gave a subtle nod to the very real fighting to which soldiers would soon be returning. Finally, the two articles reminded readers of what the brave G.I.'s were fighting for: the American way of life. For *Life*, an afternoon at the beach was, as the saying goes, as American as apple pie. To be sure, wartime propaganda promised defense workers and soldiers a future of material abundance, picturing reunited couples finally achieving their dream of owning a house and a car. But as these two photo spreads exemplified, an afternoon at the beach could also be effectively used for patriotic mobilization.[29]

Defense workers, who were considered almost as essential to the war effort as soldiers, were also encouraged to come and relax on the sands. In its 1944 annual report, the Los Angeles Department of Playground and Recreation pointed out that "the warworker or waiting serviceman's wife can keep herself in shape and sustain her morale at one of the Southland beaches."[30] The report's image of a bathing beauty striking a graceful pose on the sand echoed the traditional tourist brochures, but it also served to convey a patriotic message: some beach fun and rest were necessary for the men and women powering the Allied war effort.

For its part, the City of Santa Monica introduced a program of festive events for defense workers during the summer of 1943. That same year, the members of the Venice Chamber of Commerce implored the State Board of Health to lift the quarantine on the coast: "Many defense workers and children of Los Angeles County have been deprived of the use of the beach."[31] Local residents agreed. On April 12, 1943, Rosalyn Rankin, a Venice resident, sent a letter calling for the city council of Los Angeles to end the quarantine: "As you know doubtlessly, residents of this area are mostly war workers, many of whom work on the night shifts, and the beaches have been their only recreation."[32] For this woman, it was only fair that the sacrifices required for the war effort—such as working nights due to round-the-clock production schedules—should be offset by relaxing moments at the beach. Another Venice resident called for the city to finally address the erosion problem since "most of the people living at the beach are people working in the defense plants and need their rest."[33]

All-Year Club photo

THE WARWORKER or waiting serviceman's wife can keep herself in shape and sustain her morale at one of Southland beaches.

Figure 4.1. The war worker (or soldier's wife) enjoys the beach, 1944. From "Life Worth
Living" foldout, Department of Playground and Recreation, box C2012, Los Angeles City
Archives—Records Management Division—Office of the City Clerk.

This kind of discourse was not lost on the advocates of beach modernization. The beach lobby seized on this rhetoric to convince California's
governor Earl Warren to fund their projects. As early as 1942, SPA executive secretary George P. Larsen was delighted at the "[r]ecognition . . . now
being accorded to beaches as healthful recreation facilities by the Army."
He enthusiastically recalled the many military camps on the coast and was
pleased that the authorities were finally coming around to the views "which
many beach advocates have had for a long time."[34] SPA members also
appealed to defense workers. In a July 7, 1943, letter to the Los Angeles

City Council, they expressed their outrage that funds to hire summer lifeguards had been cut: "With thousands of defense workers who can get to the beaches for healthful recreation . . . there should by all means have been increases rather than any reduction."[35] With momentum building, the SPA took advantage of Warren's presence in Santa Monica in the summer of 1943 to take him for a private lunch where the "whole beach program was fully explained to him."[36]

By late 1944, with victory all but certain and the prospect of demobilization drawing nearer, the SPA began to modify its discourse for a postwar world by integrating the figure of the harried veteran seeking peace and quiet on the seashore. In August 1944, the association's letterhead included the following slogan: "SAVE THE BEACHES. Beaches are saving us in war. SAVE OUR BEACHES FOR PEACE!"[37] The idea that beaches played a role in "saving" Americans during the war was yet another reference to the beneficial effects a day at the beach had on soldiers on leave or defense workers. It might also have been a nod to the role of Normandy beaches as landing grounds on D-Day. In any case, the last part of the slogan showed that the SPA was already looking ahead to the postwar period and the imminent arrival of millions of veterans. In 1944, for example, George P. Larsen followed a list of the damage caused by erosion with an emotional appeal to his audience: "What a picture! And Why? Who made it so? What are the men, women and children, and the returning soldiers going to do with such desolation?"[38] Two years later, Larsen touted California's coastal development program, which, he believed, "[would] prove highly beneficial to the returned men and women of our armed forces." This time he went even further. In order to finance the program, Larsen proposed turning public beaches into "Living War Memorials" on the model of those commemorating World War I. In the immediate aftermath of the Great War, many cities had built community centers and libraries and opened public forests and highways that doubled, thanks to a plaque, flagpole, or some added sculptural element, as memorials commemorating the fallen soldiers.[39] Similarly, donations to the state could be used to purchase new beach areas, which would then take the name of the generous donor. Larsen even suggested that weapon manufacturers "who have profited greatly during the war" should consider "granting funds to the State for beach acquisitions and developments as living memorials."[40] By integrating into its discourse the figures of the fallen soldier and the tired veteran, the association hoped to raise the funds necessary to implement its program. After all, shoreline development, including beach acquisition and dealing with erosion and pollution, did not come cheap.

WARTIME WOES AND POSTWAR PLANS

By 1946, *Life* ran yet another photo essay on a beach. Focused on Long Island's Jones Beach, the article reflected on "the first postwar August." This time, all Americans deserved the rewards of a beach outing. After "six straight summers of crises," commented the journalist, "everybody needed a rest."[41] While the war consecrated the beaches' new status as patriotic places of rest, its effects on the shores were catastrophic. By halting all projects not directly related to the war effort, the conflict aggravated the pollution and erosion problems in Los Angeles. In September 1942, the War Production Board refused to authorize a project to move sand from the Hyperion Dunes and the Santa Monica Harbor to rebuild the eroded beaches of Venice. Four years later, "the damage amount[ed] almost to a catastrophe," and many residents feared that their homes would be washed away. A January 1942 letter from Venice resident Beatrice A. Irivino pointed out that "there is not much difference if your home is destroyed by a bomb or if it is washed out by the ocean, it is still destroyed."[42] Whether spurred by such letters or by the prospect that popular beaches enjoyed by defense workers and soldiers alike would slip beneath the waves, the cities of Los Angeles and Santa Monica finally acted in 1943, transporting thousands of tons of sand from the dunes at Hyperion Beach by truck.[43]

While this emergency measure stabilized Venice beaches, the issue of sewage pollution remained unaddressed. On April 3, 1943, the State Board of Health established a ten-mile quarantine zone from Venice to Hermosa Beach. Paradoxically, the outbreak of war initially led to a reduction in coastal pollution. The rationing of grease and oil meant that less of these fluids ended up in the sewers.[44] Yet the rapid increase in population during the war, coupled with the decision to abandon plans to build a new sewage treatment plant and to repair the outfall at Hyperion, pushed the system to its breaking point. In 1945, the quarantine zone was extended 1.3 miles to the south and 2.9 miles to the north as high bacterial counts were recorded in new areas.[45]

The health risks were not insignificant, although they were difficult to prove scientifically. According to a 1942 report, a study of the origins of the cases of typhoid, dysentery, and poliomyelitis—intestinal diseases linked to the presence of bacteria such as E. coli in the water—in the Los Angeles area was all but impossible to undertake since it would require several years of research as well as the cooperation of all people—including tourists—who frequented the beaches. Nevertheless, the survey did uncover several suspicious cases among local lifeguards, three of whom had been forced to temporarily abandon their posts due to severe

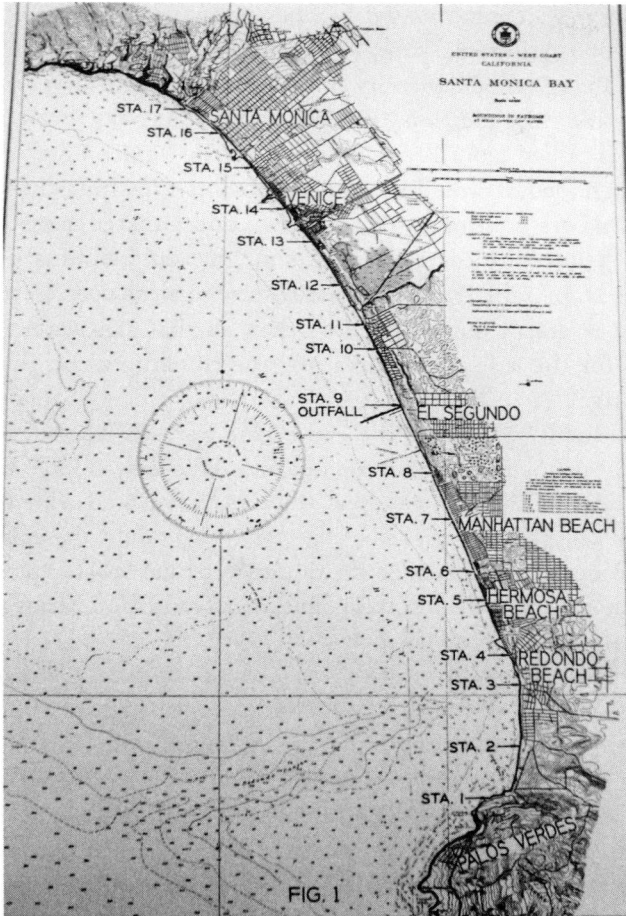

Figure 4.2. Map showing the monitoring stations set up as part of the 1942 study to determine the level of pollution on the beaches. The quarantine was eventually established between stations 5 (Hermosa Beach) and 14 (Venice). Elmer Belt, "A Sanitary Survey of Sewage Pollution of the Surf and Beaches of Santa Monica Bay," 1942, 9.

dysentery. In all three cases, the lifeguards showed symptoms after they had performed a rescue operation in a heavily polluted area. A study that made the rounds in the press beginning in 1943 even claimed that intestinal diseases were three times more common in Los Angeles than in San Francisco.[46]

Despite the media coverage, many visitors continued to swim in the polluted water. In April 1943, the city placed warning signs throughout the quarantine area, but to no avail.[47] One report stated that on August 7, 1943, 3,650 bathers and more than 19,500 visitors in street clothes went to the bay's contaminated beaches, a figure lower than the usual attendance, but still remarkably high for an area that had been declared off limits. That October, the city hired guards to inform visitors about the quarantine.[48] In addition, the quarantine zone's northern boundary marker was moved from Brooks Avenue to the Venice Pier, where, the city council hoped, it would be more noticeable.[49] Despite these efforts, some beachgoers continued to visit the contaminated beaches. Many Angelenos believed (incorrectly) that sunlight could eliminate bacteria, and recent immigrants from the Midwest, who were used to swimming in polluted rivers, "c[ouldn't] believe that 'all that salt water won't kill bugs.'" As for the rest of the violators, the thinking went, they simply "d[id]n't care."[50]

The situation improved at the end of the war. On April 3, 1945, Los Angeles voters finally authorized a tax to build a new sewage treatment plant. In addition, the following year the city started a chlorine treatment program to reduce the presence of bacteria.[51] No doubt the extension of the quarantine to the edges of Santa Monica's popular beaches played a role in its implementation. In any case, pollution in Santa Monica Bay remained a pressing concern after the war.

In the eyes of members of the beach lobby, the situation was desperate to say the least. As one of the many reports published during the war put it, one could only find "disfigurement and blight" where "miles of wide beaches of clean white sand" had once been.[52] This sad spectacle only strengthened the resolve of the supporters of shoreline development, however. According to a report financed by the Haynes Foundation on the proposed plans for the future of the shoreline, it was high time to "clean up the mess!"[53] Lobby members understood that a clear plan for action had to be put in place if they were to have any chance of securing postwar funding. In this, they were following the advice of Robert Moses, who, in an October 1943 article in *Shore & Beach*, explained that if the necessary preparatory work was done, "beaches in the postwar construction program will take their place alongside highways, buildings, and other public works."[54] The editorial preceding the article reinforced Moses's message: "War does not completely end with the cessation of hostilities. Postwar problems . . . are part of war itself. This need for planning cannot be emphasized too strongly."[55]

The war years were a very prolific period of shoreline planning in the state. Between 1944 and 1946, six different plans for the future of the California coastline were produced, including five entirely dedicated to Los Angeles. The county's shoreline development plan, first published in 1941, was reworked on a more local scale, leading to a revised version in 1946.[56] A preliminary Master Plan for shoreline development for California as a whole was also published that year.[57] This frenzy of activity was linked to the beach lobby's legislative victories in Sacramento. In fact, the association's entire legislative agenda was adopted between 1940 and 1945, spurred on by a rosy financial picture. In 1944, the state announced that it had a one-hundred-million-dollar budget surplus to spend after the war. A commission was appointed to allocate the money, and prominent SPA member Morrough P. O'Brien headed the subcommittee on beaches.[58] O'Brien was evidently convincing: California governor Earl Warren designated ten million dollars of the state budget for beach acquisition. Los Angeles County, where the beach lobby was particularly active, alone received four and a half million dollars.[59]

Considering the "dollar-for-dollar" matching provision, according to which any sum spent by the state on beach acquisition would be matched by local entities, the county stood to acquire 9 million dollars' worth of beachfront. Flush with cash, county officials viewed almost the entirety of Santa Monica Bay as potential areas to be purchased. In addition to the projects included in the 1941 plan—such as large-scale beach replenishment operations and a new sewage treatment plant—the revised development plan called for the construction of a gigantic 350-hectare harbor, to accommodate more than five thousand boats, in the marshy area north of Playa Del Rey.[60] The plan also identified "blighted areas" that spoiled the coastline. "Idle and rotting" amusement areas were destined for demolition.[61] Instead of these outdated facilities, the plan envisioned Jones Beach–style infrastructure—sanitary facilities, lifeguard towers, and parking lots.

As supporters of coastal development mobilized for the postwar era, the beaches' newfound popularity as patriotic places of rest and relaxation for war worker and soldier alike reinforced their recommendations. With the return of peace, local officials, city planners, business leaders, and engineers all pushed for beach improvements. A strong consensus animated the beach lobby's goals of acquiring the entire coastline for public use, undertaking a massive program of beach replenishment, building a new sewage treatment plant and yacht harbor, demolishing the dilapidated amusement areas, and most importantly, developing modern beaches to attract upper- and middle-class whites. The changes during this period were swift and dramatic. In the 1950s and 1960s, Southern California established itself as a national leader in the planning and development of public shorelines.

"BEACHES BELONG TO THE PUBLIC": BEACH
ACQUISITION IN THE POSTWAR ERA

Although returning veterans led to a temporary rise in unemployment in California, the state's economic growth quickly recovered—indeed, boomed—in the postwar decades thanks to new federal orders for military equipment linked to the Cold War and the Vietnam War. Unlike the major eastern and midwestern cities that experienced a downturn in their industrial activity from the 1960s on, the military-industrial complex consolidated in Southern California. The resultant economic growth supported investment in outdoor recreation and tourism throughout the period. In addition to the state's surplus spending, the beaches benefited from coastal oil revenues. From 1943 on, the state devoted 70 percent of its offshore drilling revenues purchasing parks and beaches.

The region's staggering population growth in the postwar period, coupled with the return of veterans and the threat of a sharp increase in real estate prices, added a sense of urgency to public beach acquisition. The beach lobby soon made it its first priority. In fact, the SPA's new slogan left no room for doubt: "The Beaches Must Belong to the People."[62] The association's long-time work in the Los Angeles region paid off. As early as 1946, Los Angeles County ceded its title to 14,647 feet of public beaches to the State Division of Beaches and Park.[63] Taken together, the land was valued at more than $2 million, which the state had to match by purchasing an equivalent amount. At the same time, the City of Manhattan Beach agreed to transfer all its beaches to the state, a significant conveyance. According to a local newspaper, the cession "clear[ed] the way for the acquisition by the state of virtually all remaining privately owned beach between Topanga Canyon and Palos Verdes."[64] Shortly thereafter, the state committed to purchasing eleven sections of private beach at various points along the coast.[65] Once completed, the number of miles of public beach in the county increased from 20.71 miles in 1944 to 27 miles two years later. With 40 percent of its coastline now in public ownership, Los Angeles County became a leader in the movement for a free and accessible shoreline.[66] The percentage of public beaches in Los Angeles was particularly substantial when compared to East Coast states. For example, in 1945, only 3 percent of the Massachusetts coastline was publicly owned, and in New York, only 15 percent of beaches were public.[67] General Glenn E. Edgerton, president of the Beach Erosion Board, crowed on a visit to Santa Monica in 1949 that "California [stood] in the forefront of states which recognized the value of public ownership of beaches." As for the East Coast, it was "just beginning to wake up to it."[68]

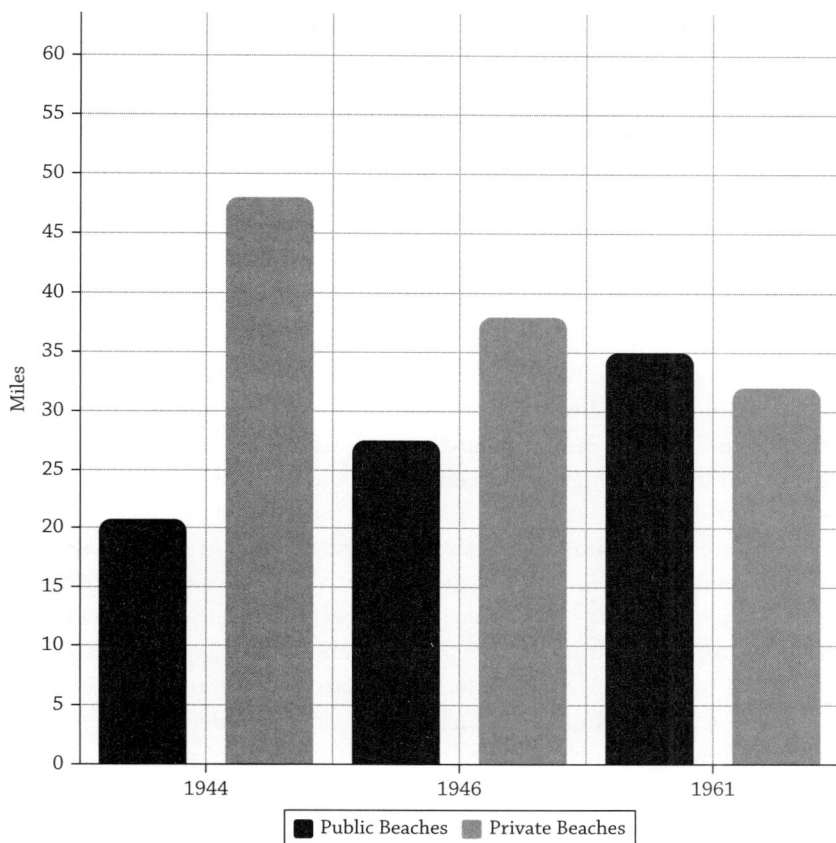

Figure 4.3. Public and private beaches in Los Angeles County, 1944–1961.

In the years that followed, the SPA played a critical role in the beach acquisition campaign by encouraging and reporting on state action. Progress was swift: between 1946 and 1948, the state acquired an additional 3 miles in Los Angeles County; in 1949, it bought two strategic lots of the "Gold Coast," the famous strand of coastline where Hollywood stars owned palatial beach homes, thus opening up access to the public beach in front of them. In 1952, the Abbot Kinney Company sold a three-acre beach strip in Venice to the state.[69] By 1955, the ten million dollars was exhausted. The state assembly set aside an additional sum of forty million dollars for the purchase of parks, beaches, and forests.[70] By 1961, Los Angeles County could finally boast that more than half of its shoreline—51 percent to be precise (38.2 miles)—was open to the public.[71]

The record was more mixed at the state level. In 1960, only 28 percent of the coast was in public hands.[72] Although new initiatives were undertaken to continue procurement, there were indications that the campaign was running out of steam. In 1964, the state put a bond issue on the ballot to buy and develop more parks and beaches. Beach acquisition was no longer to come out of the general fund but to be paid for by a new tax. In other words, the state put the matter in voters' hands. In order to convince Californians of the measure's importance, the state printed brochures that depicted the future of the coast in a bleak light. Public access was increasingly precarious, the beaches "Too Few for So Many."[73] The state pledged to focus its attention on Southern Californian metropolitan areas where prices were particularly high. Voters approved the measure, and twenty million dollars in bonds were issued. Yet by 1969 only 37 percent of the California coastline was publicly owned.

The acquisition campaign also remained somewhat conservative in other respects. The SPA did not question the existence of private beach clubs. In 1946, George P. Larsen, its executive secretary, had clarified the association's position: while "all available beach land" ought to be purchased for public use, "beaches which are already encumbered with costly clubs . . . and beaches which are already occupied with extensive private homes obviously do not follow in that category."[74] Considering that many SPA members were themselves members of the region's beach clubs, it should come as no surprise that the group stopped short of undermining them. Larsen's justification was based on what he considered self-evident financial considerations: state dollars were better put to use elsewhere. Acquiring these lots would also have gone a step too far, challenging a commonly held assumption that the rich and famous should be able to buy seclusion and quiet for themselves. Malibu beaches, supposedly due to their narrowness, also remained outside of the campaign's purview. "While this area contains some stretches of beautiful beach," a 1944 report noted, "almost none of it is suitable for the accommodation of large crowds without unjustifiable expense in development costs." Geomorphic and financial considerations aside, Malibu beach homeowners, many of whom were influential in the movie and business worlds, categorically refused to see the area opened to the public.[75] Despite the internal contradictions of the beach acquisition movement, its impact on the California coast was undeniable. By the early 1960s, almost all the beaches of Santa Monica Bay were open to the public. This new legal situation paved the way for the state to carry out major beach replenishment projects.

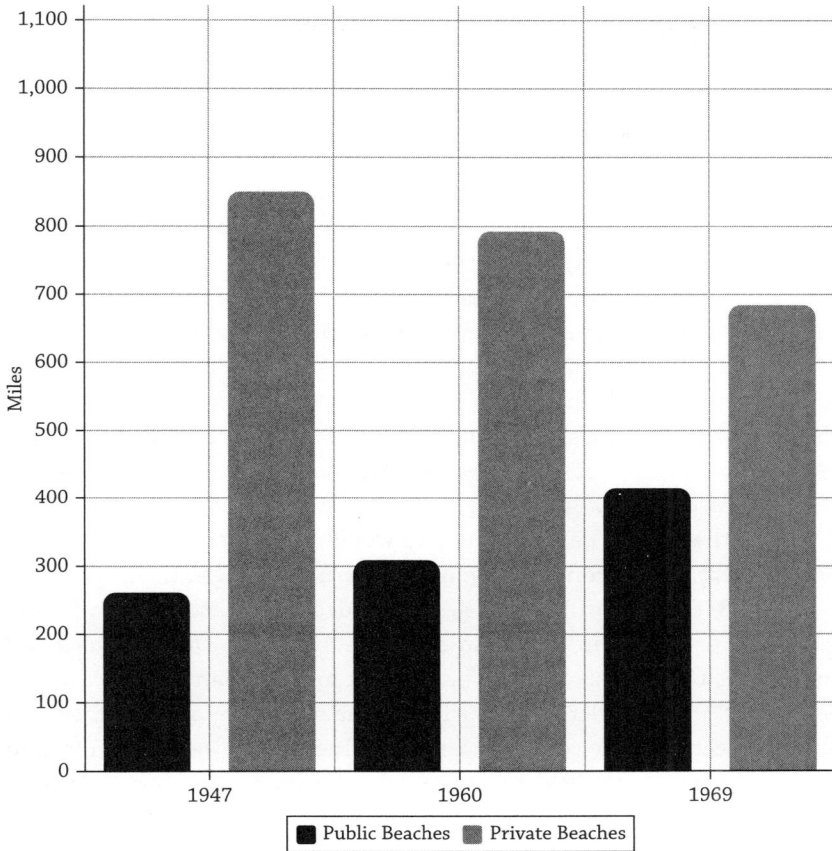

Figure 4.4. Public and private bin California, 1947–1969.

"MOVING SAND AROUND IN A BIG WAY": ENLARGING THE BEACHES

In the postwar period, the Los Angeles beaches were massively enlarged in a process that was both typical of major operations undertaken on the American coasts at that time and unusual. Typical was the use of artificial beach replenishment (or nourishment)—the most common technique engineers used to modify the coastline. As early as 1953, a report issued by the Beach Erosion Board claimed that it was the most effective method to protect beaches from erosion.[76] Even so, the scale of the Los Angeles project was unprecedented. In the space of two decades, the beaches of Los Angeles were widened by hundreds of feet, with the new sand holding firm. This technical achievement was not solely the result of the engineers' ingenuity; it was also the product of a combination of ecological conditions specific to Santa Monica Bay, one-time opportunities, and, to a certain extent, chance.

During the war, the state of the eroded South Bay beaches was so serious that local authorities organized an emergency beach replenishment operation. Trucks rushed back and forth between the Hyperion Dunes and the beaches at Venice, dumping a million cubic yards of sand on the shore. While carried out hastily, the operation was a resounding success: the sand stayed put, protecting the houses built along the shoreline. The successful experiment guided future decisions. The Hyperion Dunes, long perceived of as useless areas, became the go-to source as a natural provider of sand for projects. Not only did they seem to be inexhaustible, they belonged to the City of Los Angeles, and thus the sand was free. This operation also presented advocates of a new wastewater facility, such as City Engineer Lloyd Aldrich, with a golden opportunity. By pumping sands from the dunes to the eroded beaches, the city would both expand the shore and pave the way for the construction of a modern sewage treatment plant.[77]

In 1948, the City of Los Angeles proceeded to extract and pump fourteen million cubic yards of sand from the Hyperion Dunes, which was then deposited over six miles of beachfront between Santa Monica and El Segundo.[78] The fill widened the surface of the beaches by approximately six hundred feet over the course of a month. The results were so miraculous that, according to the SPA, it was not enough to see it for oneself; for best effect, you had to take people to the shore to see "their eyes pop open in amazement." "This is what happens when you begin moving sand around in a big way," exclaimed *California Coast*. The beaches were "not twice as wide, not three times as wide, but four times as wide as before." Before-and-after photos accompanying the article allowed readers to take in the magnitude of the changes. Taken at the same spot one month apart, the first showed ocean water, the second a broad, sandy beach.[79]

In 1950, a third component of the development program—the dredging of the Santa Monica Harbor, where sand had accumulated since its construction in 1934—was carried out. In total, 960,000 cubic yards of sand were removed and deposited on the beach immediately to the south, widening it by an average of three hundred feet. One three-hundred-yard stretch was even widened by seven hundred feet. Yet even the removal of the sediment could not keep the harbor from remaining a failure. Insufficiently protected from storms, pleasure boats no longer anchored there. Only commercial and fishing vessels continued to use it.[80]

Beach replenishment operations continued into the 1950s and 1960s. In 1956, the construction of a power plant on the El Segundo coastline entailed

Figure 4.5. Beach replenishment according to the Shoreline Planning Association: "Before" and "After." *California Coast* 2, no. 5 (July 1948): 3. University of Southern California.

removing 2.4 million cubic yards of sand, which were then deposited by bulldozers on the eroded beaches south of Ballona Creek. Between 1960 and 1963, the construction of the gigantic Marina Del Rey harbor required the removal of 10.1 million cubic yards of sand, which were distributed on Dockweiler Beach.[81] Major construction on the coastline became less frequent thereafter, and other sources of sediment had to be found. In 1969–1970, for instance, a stretch of the Redondo Beach coastline was widened with 1.1 million cubic yards of sand dredged from an offshore source.[82]

In total, between 1945 and the late 1960s, nearly 30 million cubic yards of sand were deposited on the beaches of Santa Monica Bay. Studies carried out in the 1960s showed that the sand had remained on the beaches, unlike on other coastlines. For instance, in Mississippi, similar replenishment projects were wiped away overnight by hurricanes or, over longer periods of time, by erosion. After the 1960s, the newly enlarged Los Angeles beaches required only occasional maintenance operations. As of the 2020s, the 1948 beach replenishment operation remains the largest ever carried out in the bay. Of course, such drastic transformations of the natural environment entailed some inconveniences. The new beach came with a steepened slope, which made it difficult for lifeguards to keep an eye on cusps and rip currents as well as bathers going beyond their depth. The material deposited on the beach also contained high levels of magnetite, which can resemble oil deposits and greatly displeased beachgoers. Finally, some people complained "that they burned their feet walking across what seemed like miles of desert," while others complained "of the wind-blown sand and dust." But such complaints were easily dismissed considering the enlargement's many benefits. The ASBPA recognized the program's success by devoting the December 1959 issue of Shore & Beach to Santa Monica and holding its annual conference there the following year.[83]

More than any other factor, the rapid advances made in coastal engineering made this success possible. In the 1950s and 1960s, the field underwent a period of rapid expansion and institutionalization. Omar Lillevang, one of the pioneers of the field in California, recalled that, before the end of World War II, he had devoted only 30 percent of his time to coastal projects; by 1960, the demand became so great that he and his partner "were devoting all our time to sea coast and harbor matters." In 1950, the first conference on coastal engineering was held in Long Beach, showcasing the explosion of scientific work in the field.[84] A decade later, the first courses devoted to the discipline were taught at engineering schools. In 1963, the Beach Erosion Board was dismantled and replaced by two bodies, the Coastal Engineering Research Center and the Coastal Engineering Research Board, a sign that the discipline had come into its own.[85]

The success of the sand replenishment operations in Los Angeles was also linked to specific ecological and human factors that were difficult to replicate elsewhere. Several recent studies indicate that, due to complex geological factors, artificial beaches have greater longevity on the Pacific Coast than on the Atlantic or Gulf Coasts.[86] Santa Monica Bay also possesses its own unique characteristics: it is surrounded by two rocky headlands that act as barriers, and the sediment currents that do enter the bay deposit relatively modest amounts of sand. On the land, the channelization of the region's rivers and streams over the course of the twentieth century has decreased the amount of sediment that replenishes the beaches naturally. Out in the sea, tides have slowly chipped away at the breakwaters and jetties built over the years, which means that their impact diminished over time. By the late 1950s, a new equilibrium had established itself: very little sediment entered the bay naturally; sand introduced artificially flowed freely and held firm when deposited on the beaches, rarely, if ever, disturbed by winter storms. Borne out of the entanglement of human and natural processes, this equilibrium has provided stability in what used to be a highly mobile coastal ecology. In the bay, littoral currents have been reduced to a minimum. If beaches are "rivers of sand," then the Los Angeles coastline amounts to a lethargic stream. Of course, this equilibrium remains fragile and is subject to the forces of the climate crisis, melting glaciers, and rising sea levels. Without human intervention, scientists estimate that between 31 percent and 67 percent of Southern California beaches could be lost to erosion by 2100.[87] Nevertheless, as unsustainable as this equilibrium may be in the coming years, the metropolitan coastline expanded dramatically and relatively sustainably between the late 1950s and the early twenty-first century.

OF CIGARETTE BUTTS AND BEER CANS: CLEANING UP THE BEACHES

These vast beaches would not lure visitors if they remained soiled by sewage and waste. In 1950, the inauguration of a new state-of-the-art sewage disposal plant appeared to solve the problems. Built at a cost of forty-two million dollars and taking up more than thirty hectares on Hyperion Beach, the plant was the pride of the city.[88] Some of its most famous residents even wrote lyrical paeans to this monument of human ingenuity. According to novelist Aldous Huxley, it was "one of the marvels of modern technology, its effluent purity of 99.7 percent exceeds that of Ivory Soap." Huxley knew what he was talking about. He could vividly remember how, in 1938, as he and fellow writer Thomas Mann were walking on a South Bay beach, they had found themselves surrounded by "ten million used condoms" discharged from the leaky outfall.[89] As components of the sewage plant were activated in the run-up to its official opening, the quarantine on the beach was gradually lifted. On June 16, 1950, Los Angeles mayor Fletcher Bowron officially announced that the beaches of Venice were no longer under quarantine, and on July 24, 1951, all beaches were finally opened to the public. From then on, 250 million gallons of sewage a day would pass through the plant before being discharged into the ocean more than a mile offshore.

At this point, officials were confident that the new plant would be able to handle the region's wastewater for years, if not decades, to come. "Venice beach will never be under quarantine again," the head of the state health department promised.[90] Such confidence was soon put to test. By the mid-1950s, population growth was so rapid that the plant was no longer up to the task. In 1954, the cities of Manhattan Beach, Hermosa Beach, and Torrance Beach issued several complaints to the Los Angeles City Council regarding the presence of kitchen grease and detergent-type foam in their waters. The council dismissed the charges, first explaining that the incidents reported were related to a "red tide" event, a natural phenomenon whereby the growth of microscopic marine plants results in the discoloration of water, and later, when complaints persisted, attributing the grease to other sources. By early 1956, however, South Bay citizens were "outraged" when the tide deposited "offensive sewage solids on their beaches." Leaks were not the culprit this time around. The releases had been deliberately created when the system was overtaxed following heavy rains. This explanation angered Manhattan residents, who suggested that the city discharge the overflow "into its own streets and rivers rather than upon its neighbor's beaches." Later that year, South Bay cities filed a joint lawsuit against Los Angeles, demanding that the council explain exactly "what's going on in the cesspool called Santa Monica Bay," as the mayor of Manhattan Beach put it. This show of force had the desired effect. By the end of the year, work had been carried out to double the plant's treatment capacity. This upgrade was intended to serve the city until the year 2000 and to discharge the treated sewage five miles offshore.[91] Still, these problems testified, in the words of an editorial published by the *Los Angeles Examiner*, to a "habit of indifference and negligence" on the part of the city vis-à-vis the surrounding environment.[92]

In addition to the sewage treatment, standards of beach cleanliness were generally brought up to date in the postwar decade. As middle-class Americans moved en masse to new suburban homes with modern appliances and bright walls and surfaces, they became obsessed with hygiene and cleanliness as a marker of respectability and social standing. American housewives devoted considerable energy to "chasing dirt" from the smallest corners of their immaculate homes. Outside of their homes, however, middle-class Americans rarely picked up after themselves. In the early 1950s, litter—aggravated by the exponential rise of plastic packaging—was not yet perceived as a personal responsibility.[93] Expectations of public cleanliness were nonetheless high, and if the beach lobby wanted to keep the white middle class on the sands, it had to align itself with these new suburban sensibilities. The topic attracted broad interest. In 1949, for instance, *Life* magazine featured the latest invention used to clean California beaches: the "sand sweeper," a "tractor-towed beach sanitizer" invented by a former navy officer and Hollywood stuntman, processed sixteen hundred tons of sand a day.[94] In the "6-foot swath of clean sand" left in the sweeper's wake, three bathing beauties posed in languorous positions, embodying the contemporary reverence for machines that freed humans from such laborious tasks.

Even so, financing beach maintenance proved difficult. Acquiring beaches was a popular measure, but neither the county nor the cities wanted to deal with cleaning the coastline from picnic leftovers—a Sisyphean and costly task. A public beach, SPA president Geoffrey Morgan would often say, "is like an automobile or a safety razor, or a wife—it isn't so much the first cost; it's the everlasting upkeep."[95] The sexist quip, uttered to what must have been exclusively male audiences, worked like a charm. In the end, responsibility for the upkeep often fell to the cities themselves. Small, image-conscious municipalities, such as Newport Beach, Redondo Beach, and Santa Monica, prided themselves on their spotless streets and beaches. In 1954, the local Santa Monica newspaper claimed it was not uncommon to hear a tourist exclaim, "What clean beaches you have! They're much nicer than those in the East."[96] Newport Beach residents were adamant about the importance of cleanliness and "pleasant living conditions"; according to resident Ray R. Reeves, who wrote to the city council in 1946 to share his opinion on how the annual budget should be spent, "clean beaches were much more important than a new city hall."[97] By contrast, the maintenance of many large East Coast beaches was handled by much larger entities. Revere Beach, whose clean-up was under the purview of Boston Metropolitan Parks, was described by a group of nearby residents in 1962 as "a real disgrace . . .—it is littered with beer cans, whisky bottles and unmentionables."[98] Going swimming in such a poorly maintained area was out of the question for the white middle class. Cigarette butts and beer cans were simply not compatible with the modern beach experience.

DEATH TO THE HOT-DOG STAND: DEVELOPING MODERN BEACHES

With the opening of the new Hyperion treatment plant, C. P. L. Nicholls, Los Angeles's supervisor of beach operation, could finally rejoice that the city's beaches were "clean and ready for development." While Nicholls's declaration may have been premature, his ambition for the coastline was widely shared by beach lobby members. With beach acquisition on the right track, development seemed like the natural next step. In his 1948 message to his fellow "shoreliners," SPA president Geoffrey P. Morgan hammered home the association's new priority: developing beaches that measured up to "modern standards." By his account, California beaches were falling short: "All up and down the coast one may find long stretches of ocean frontage which have nothing but sand and seaweed to offer by way of recreational facilities." As far as Morgan and his acolytes were concerned, "sand and seaweed" did not make a beach. In fact, bare shorelines amounted to a "waste space" and certainly did not deserve the title of "state park." Morgan concluded his presidential message with a warning. If the Los Angeles coastline was to become a "worthy rival to the famous Jones Beach," it desperately required equipment, including roads, parking areas, rest rooms, and other facilities.[99]

Installing modern equipment along the entire Californian coastline required significant funding. In the early 1950s, when tidelands oil royalties were impounded due to litigation, the state struggled to provide regular funds for beach maintenance, let alone for coastal development. In 1953, when the lawsuit was resolved in favor of the state, it seemed to signal a new era for beach development in California. The division of Beaches and Parks was set to receive 70 percent of oil royalties, and the SPA fought off multiple attempts to redirect the funds elsewhere. In 1955, a beach development bill, which would have appropriated over fifteen million dollars of oil royalties for new park projects, was vetoed by the governor. Indeed, some Sacramento legislators and taxpayers' groups considered park and beach expenditures of that magnitude "wasteful consumption" and advocated instead for parks to be operated on a self-supporting basis. In 1956, their side won another victory when the legislature voted to cap the oil royalties directed to beaches and parks at seven million dollars annually.[100]

Failing to develop "modern beaches" did not just bring discomfort and "sand in the shoes," the beach lobby contended. It also risked attracting the wrong kind of people and activities to the shores. In August 1949, *California Coast* published a photograph of "Roadside Rest," a section of Santa Monica Beach deemed "especially popular with teenagers." "All the facilities that should be present to care for a crowd of this size—access roads, parking areas, sanitary facilities, bathhouses, sport and playgame areas—are sadly deficient," read the caption. While Roadside Rest was evidently too crowded for comfort, the problems lay more with the crowd's composition and deportment than with its size. Figuring prominently in the center of the image was a group of eight girls, in various state of undress, eyeing a group of teenage boys. By picturing seminaked teenagers in close proximity at a moment when juvenile delinquency was a primary concern among parents and politicians, the SPA suggested that beaches lacking modern facilities attracted young people of dubious character—typically the kind of "rebels without a cause" who defied authority and engaged in premarital sex. Game areas and other amenities, so the logic went, would improve the character of the crowd as well as provide respectable forms of recreation for young Angelenos. In fact, that same year, the Madigan-Hyland report highlighted this segment of the population: "Beaches are a natural haven for youth," the authors argued. "However," they warned, "they must be continually active. To channel their energies in healthful directions, facilities must be at hand which will hold their interest, given them an opportunity to show off and display their prowess." To be sure, beach improvement was not "the only answer to juvenile delinquency." But, the authors insisted, "it would help toward a solution."[101]

Beach development was not just about adding new accommodations to the shoreline. It was also about clearing the shoreline of what currently existed and greatly displeased the beach lobby and other middle-class observers. In the late 1940s, the beachfront promenade running almost uninterrupted between Santa Monica and Venice was made up of low-grade

August, 1949   *CALIFORNIA   COAST*   *Page Three*

NOT CONEY ISLAND – BUT SANTA MONICA ON A HOT SUNDAY

This section of Santa Monica beach is known as "Roadside Rest" and is especially popular with teenagers. All the facilities that should be present to care for a crowd of this size—access roads, parking areas, sanitary facilities, bathhouses, sport and playgame areas—are sadly deficient. Better than all the words in Webster, this photograph proves that beach development in Los Angeles County, as elsewhere, is an immediate, pressing problem.   —Pacific Press Photo.

Figure 4.6. In the eyes of the beach lobby, areas frequented by teenagers such as Roadside Rest, with its lack of recreational facilities and packed crowds, represented everything that was wrong with beach development. *California Coast* 3, no. 3 (August 1949): 3. Morrough O'Brien Collection, box 14, file 101, Water Resources Collections & Archives, Special Collections & University Archives, University of California–Riverside.

bars and food stands, novelty stores, dilapidated bathhouses, small apartment buildings, motels, and movie theaters, interspersed with parking lots and the occasional beach club and Hollywood star's beach house. Packed close together in some areas, this hodge-podge of buildings and commercial establishments represented everything that was wrong with public beaches in the eyes of the beach lobby. Authors of the Madigan-Hyland report noted that the Ocean Park beaches had "long since passed their prime" and that these "run-down neighborhoods" represented a "fertile field for revitalization."[102] UCLA geography student Charles Stapleton, who investigated the area when writing his 1952 master's thesis, shared their distaste for the Santa Monica amusement area. "The pier and the ballroom," he wrote, "have a general run-down and unkempt appearance."[103]

No beachfront establishment inspired more contempt than the humble hot-dog stand. The stands and their "characteristic odor of very stale grease" were regularly denounced in *California Coast* as a scourge that plagued public beaches statewide. Beloved by working-class beachgoers, reviled by the beach lobby, the hot dog stand was an iconic symbol of the early twentieth-century beach experience in all its festive vulgarity. In the classic LA noir novel, *Farewell My Lovely* (1940), the barking voice of the "hot dog man" and the smell of "hot fat" were key details that Raymond Chandler used to bring to life the distinctive atmosphere in nighttime "Bay City," a pseudonym for Santa Monica. Standing on a pier "tickling wienies with a long fork," the hot dog merchant was the kind of informant who could direct private detective Philip Marlowe to the nearest brothel or gambling joint.[104] In their vision of the future shoreline, beach lobby members imagined white middle-class families enjoying nutritious picnics of sandwiches, potato salad, coleslaw, and hard-boiled eggs lovingly prepared by housewives. Hot-dog stands, associated as they were with grimy street food and petty crime, hardly fit that picture.

Public opinion diverged with regard to the bathhouse. The two large and modern bathhouses erected at Jones Beach—the first ever to include diaper-changing rooms—were generally regarded as magnificent public infrastructure. But many beachgoers in Los Angeles considered bathhouses "a thing of the past," a holdover from a time when people did not own their own bathing suits and had to rent them. Most Angelenos instead changed in the privacy of their parked cars. Nonetheless, authors of the Madigan-Hyland report noted that older beachgoers would "prefer to drive home in dry clothes." As for the existing bathhouses, many of them in shabby condition and suspected of harboring homosexual activities, it was understood that they would have to go.[105]

Popular representations of the beach amusement areas and their immediate surroundings were hardly more positive. In novels of the period, descriptions oscillated between nostalgia and disgust at the state of affairs along the coastline. In Maritta Wolff's *The Big Nickelodeon* (1956), the Venice boardwalk was described as this "cement promenade lined with nondescript, weathered little buildings, souvenir stores with abalone shell jewelry displayed behind the dirty window glass, seafood restaurants, palm readers, salt-water taffy, bathing suit shops with great rubber flippers and goggles hung from the doorways, and the innumerable, tiny, open-air stalls with popcorn machines and faded, hand-lettered signs that advertised coffee and sun oil and beer."[106] But in Hollywood films, amusement areas were truly lost to the dark side. Film noir of that period, as historian Eric Avila has noted, "emphasized the seedy side of urban life," thus reinforcing the cultural and racial divide between suburbs and inner cities.[107] In that context, Ocean Park and other piers proved ideal movie settings. One of the first scenes of the movie *Mildred Pierce* (1945), for instance, was filmed on an unspecified amusement pier where shady bars and sideshows lit up the dark night. This is where Mildred, played by Joan Crawford, comes to contemplate death. It is also where, later in the film, her daughter degrades herself by performing in a dive bar in front of an inebriated male audience.

Despite their continued success with the crowds, the beach amusement areas could not withstand such contempt for too long. Like countless urban districts deemed "blighted," they were perceived as remnants of the past, obstacles to be removed on the way toward progress and modern living. In the immediate postwar years, federal policies, new wrecking technology, and general public support for redevelopment gave birth to a "culture of clearance" that radically transformed the nation. Bulldozers tore down cities, suburbs, and rural landscapes.[108]

Beaches were not spared. One after the other, most amusement piers and fairgrounds in the region were torn down. Broadly speaking, the entire beachscape from earlier in the century was slated for the wrecking ball: disused railway lines, saltwater plunges, bathhouses, old beach bungalows, the decaying Santa Monica breakwater, and the infamous hot dog stands. The process actually started before World War II. In 1941, the tracks of the Pacific Electric Railway, which had once hugged the shoreline and taken merrymakers from one resort to the next, were dismantled. In 1946, the Venice Pier was condemned as part of a neighborhood beautification program. That November, a fire sealed its fate. Six years later, the City of Los Angeles demolished the Abbot Kinney Pier in Venice.[109] In addition, dozens of restaurants, wooden barracks, and bathing establishments were deemed dilapidated and demolished. Such was the fate of the Crystal Beach bathhouse, shuttered in 1951 by the city of Los Angeles as part of a modernization program; it was also targeted for being a known homosexual hangout.[110]

These newly widened, bulldozed beaches allowed the lobby to enact the next step of their plan: adapting the coastline to the postwar suburbanite values of cleanliness, privacy, and respectability. As a growing share of American families benefited from the booming economy and gained access to a middle-class suburban lifestyle that used to be reserved to a privileged few, mainstream culture put a renewed emphasis on family entertainment, traditional gender roles, and homeownership. By building modern accommodations and family-friendly recreational spaces on the sand, the beach lobby hoped to prevent white flight from the beach. In Venice, the lifting of quarantine in 1950 was the perfect occasion to unveil the Venice Athletic Beach Center, a new seaside recreation facility. Inspired by Santa Monica's Muscle Beach, but with an emphasis on family-friendly game areas, it included handball, volleyball, table tennis, and basketball courts, as well as a weight room for amateur weightlifters. On the expanded beach, a huge parking lot with room for over one thousand cars typified the trend toward the "automobile-beach."[111] That same year, the City of Los Angeles unveiled its plans to turn Will Rogers State Beach into "the 'Jones Beach' of the California shore." Designed by Paul R. Williams, a pathbreaking African American architect, the North Beach Center, with its modernist aesthetic, would stand as a symbol of "the trend in modern beach design." In contrast to the "grimy hot dog stands" and "flimsy wooden bath houses" that attracted a largely working-class clientele, the "strictly modern, multipurpose building" would appeal to a middle-class public. By providing all the accommodations necessary for a family trip to the beach (including comfort stations, changing rooms, cafetarias, and telephone booths), the building also reflected middle-class aspirations of cleanliness and propriety. "Many more such 'centers,'" boasted *California Coast*, "[we]re planned along the shoreline."[112]

While the North Beach Center typified the continued reverence for Jones Beach in the world of beach design, a new model in the realm of mass leisure had emerged by the mid-1950s. Opened to widespread acclaim in July 1955, Disneyland had far-reaching influence over all recreational spaces, including beaches. Walt Disney deliberately designed his theme park as "the very antithesis of Coney Island." Echoing the discourses found in the SPA's *California Coast*, Disney detested traditional amusement parks, these "dirty, phoney places run by tough looking people." Coney Island, with its titillating atmosphere, mixed crowds, dilapidated buildings, and sideshow barkers, embodied the cosmopolitan culture bred in big cities, for

The above is not a trick photo. Yes, what you see is really parking space for 1000 cars at the beach. The location? The newly opened Venice Beach in the City of Los Angeles. Quarantined for more than 5 years due to sewage pollution, the beach was widened several hundred feet for a distance of about 7 miles by the simple expedient of placing on it excess sand from the site of the new sewage treatment plant. A great variety of games and recreation equipment has been installed and the beach is proving extremely popular.

Figure 4.7. A large parking lot built in 1950 on the newly expanded Venice Beach. From *California Coast* 4, no. 4 (August 1950): 4. Morrough O'Brien Collection, box 14, file 101, Water Resources Collections & Archives, Special Collections & University Archives, University of California–Riverside.

This architect's drawing of the building to be erected by the City of Los Angeles on Will Rogers Beach about two miles north of Santa Monica, gives a graphic idea of the trend in modern beach design. Gone are the flimsy wooden bathhouses, the grimy hot-dog stands which saturated the air with the characteristic odor of very stale grease, and the inadequate sanitary facilities. To cost about $60,000, the building will be ready for the 1951 season.

Figure 4.8. Drawing of a modernist-style building to be built on Will Rogers State Beach. From *California Coast* 4, no. 2 (May 1950): 2. Morrough O'Brien Collection, box 14, file 101, Water Resources Collections & Archives, Special Collections & University Archives, University of California–Riverside.

which Disney had nothing but contempt. By contrast, Disneyland reflected its creator's nostalgia for small-town America and enshrined its most sacred values: patriotism, tradition, and family togetherness. In searching for the ideal site for his new endeavor, Walt Disney had specifically rejected beach locations, fearing that people would show up in their bathing suits and degrade the general atmosphere of innocence and wonder he sought to create. Eventually, Disney settled on Anaheim, a distant agricultural community in Orange County. By building his kingdom far from the city and public transportation but, crucially, along the planned route of the Santa Ana Freeway, he ensured that his park would be easily accessible to suburban families with automobiles and unreachable for those without cars. Disneyland, with its separate areas dedicated to different "themes," presented "a controlled landscape that orchestrated the movement and vision of park visitors."[113] In contrast to the amusement piers, where disparate shows had differing prices and styles, Disneyland charged a single price for entry to the park where everything, from the color scheme to the well-kempt employees, was standardized. By building an amusement park that was clean, orderly, homogeneous, and devoid of dubious recreational activities, Walt Disney redefined mainstream leisure for the suburban era.

That Disneyland represented a source of inspiration for beach design became abundantly clear in July 1958, when Pacific Ocean Park (also known as "P.O.P."), a brand-new amusement park, opened on the Ocean Park Pier. In 1949, the authors of the Madigan-Hyland report had recommended the construction of a "major high-class amusement center." Almost a decade later, the project finally took off when the city of Santa Monica offered a twenty-five-year lease of the pier to the Los Angeles Turf Club and Columbia Broadcasting System (CBS) to replace the "dwindling carnival-like attractions" with a "large family type amusement area." While P.O.P.'s managers claimed their project would be "totally unlike that in Anaheim" due to its oceanic theme, it was heavily influenced by ideas developed at Disneyland. For one, P.O.P. also sought to distance itself from traditional seaside amusement areas. It would be "very different from the old 'try your luck' sort of things of the early days," promised the executive vice president of the Turf Club. Much of the old Ocean Park Pier was demolished in early 1958, and, as publicity releases emphasized, "aside from the old roller coaster which will be completely overhauled . . . everything will be entirely new." Contemporary observers could not help but notice that P.O.P.'s rides were "similar to those at Disneyland." For instance, the ocean highway ride—an over-water ride that involved "hydromatic, gas-powered, miniature American or foreign automobiles"—recalled Disneyland's Autopia, a ride modeled on real-life freeways.[114] In addition, like Disneyland's

"Frontierland," which featured colorfully dressed "savages," P.O.P.'s most popular rides, such as the "Banana Train," drew on stereotypes of non-white cultures to appeal to a white audience fascinated by the exotic other. Finally, P.O.P. was clean (its restrooms were dubbed "the most beautiful public facilities in the world"), orderly, and closely supervised by park attendants in uniform.[115]

By the time P.O.P. opened its doors, most of the plans proposed in the 1945 Master Plan of shoreline development had been successfully completed. With its wide and clean beaches, high-class theme park, and attractive public facilities, the Santa Monica Bay finally realized the beach lobby's ambitions. One crucial element, however, was still missing: a pleasure craft harbor big enough to sustain the postwar yachting craze. In the 1950s, rising incomes and increasing leisure time paired with technological advances in boat design that enabled the fabrication of cheap, home-assembly vessels, turned the once-elitist sport into a democratic sailing boom. The need for a modern marina to replace the failing Santa Monica and Redondo harbors was pressing; according to the Madigan-Hyland report, the number of boats owned by Los Angeles County residents berthed at Newport Harbor had increased by 145 percent between 1938 and 1948.[116] Plans to build a major yachting center in the marshy areas south of Playa del Rey found ready supporters at the SPA, which set up its own Small Boat Harbors Division in December 1950. In the context of the Cold War, Morgan argued that harbors were not only about recreation; the navy, he insisted, considered them "as an integral part of the national defense." But, as Morgan was forced to concede, sailing was also "big business in California."[117]

By the mid-1950s, the SPA's advocacy started to pay off. In 1954, Los Angeles County created a new Department of Harbors and Marinas to oversee the development and financing of the twenty-five-million-dollar Marina Del Rey harbor. Yet financing pleasure harbors remained a daunting task, and some legislators criticized such recreational development as wasteful spending. The financial arrangement behind Marina Del Rey typified the compromises made to win over even the most hesitant. For one, the federal government, under pressure from the beach lobby and keen to beef up auxiliary harbors for defense purposes, agreed to pay half of the cost of building the navigation facilities. The State of California also contributed two million dollars from tideland oil royalties for the land. Finally, the marina was conceived as a self-supporting facility. By leasing the land around the harbor to private companies, the county would repay a thirteen-million-dollar revenue bond. This arrangement ensured that Marina Del Rey would become much more than "the largest small craft harbor in the world." It was touted as a "multi-purpose urban activity center." To attract wealthy yacht owners and young professionals, the project included upscale shops, hotels, and high-class apartment buildings equipped with swimming pools, saunas, and cinemas. Projecting an atmosphere of opulence and leisure, yachting provided the perfect backdrop to develop what essentially became a gated community for the rich. After six years of construction, Marina Del Rey welcomed its first residents and sailing enthusiasts in 1963. As far as members of the beach lobby were concerned, Marina Del Rey was the coastline's crown jewel.[118]

Marina Del Rey was part of a larger pattern of commercial and residential development that cities undertook to combat white flight and attract capital and wealthy residents to their central neighborhoods. City officials focused their efforts on amenities and residential developments conjuring a "suave lifestyle of urban consumerism and indulgent leisure." Working in collaboration with corporate interests, city governments bet on marinas, luxury hotels, and "ultramodern" baseball stadiums to revitalize the urban core and bring in new jobs and tax revenues. In Los Angeles, where the local business elite sought to establish the region as a world-class urban center and to contain the suburban boom attracting families to new subdivisions in the San Fernando Valley and Orange County, these efforts resulted in the construction of Dodger Stadium and the Westin Bonaventure Hotel, among other projects. In both cases, federal urban renewal subsidies were used to clear the sites, thereby condemning two working-class immigrant communities, Chavez Ravine and Bunker Hill, respectively. These were not unusual examples. Such operations so frequently involved the eviction of people of color that urban renewal came to be known as "Negro renewal."[119]

In the case of Marina Del Rey, no human residents were evicted from the marshy area when dredging equipment dug the harbor's channels and basins. However, as a spokesman for the Audubon Society noted over a decade later, "an enormous population of mammals, waterfowl and shorebirds" lost their habitat. Few people, if any, sounded an alarm during construction. While a 1944 report conceded that the harbor would destroy "a refuge for over 80 species of water fowl," it concluded that a choice would have to be made "between two sets of values." A choice was evidently made in favor of the marina. To the untrained eye, the marshland was only home to "clouds of insects" that needed to be eradicated. The ecological needs of other species were bypassed in favor of creating tax revenues and fueling the sailing boom. As the buzz of Playa Del Rey mosquitoes faded into the background, a new relationship was being forged between Angelenos and their coastline. While many more people would be able to sunbathe on the newly enlarged beaches and sail along the bay, other forms of connection with the coastal landscape and its nonhuman inhabitants were lost forever.[120]

In 1964, as the owners of Steeplechase, the last amusement park in Coney Island, announced it would soon close its doors to the public, Southern California beaches were celebrated with the release of two popular "beach party" movies, *Bikini Beach* and *Muscle Beach Party*. On one coast, public beaches were synonymous with "'unsafe subways,' 'teenage hoodlums,' 'bad weather,' 'inadequate parking.'" On the other, the beach was presented as an alluring playground where sun-kissed, white, middle-class youths boasted enviable physiques and played with the latest consumer products—seemingly oblivious to the antiwar protests and civil rights battles convulsing the nation. By adapting the Los Angeles coastline to suburban sensibilities, the beach lobby had firmly associated it with safety and modernity.[121]

Of course, unlike Disneyland, which provided the sense of suburban safety only tall walls and turnstiles could provide, the beaches of Los Angeles were, for the most part, public and accessible to all. Yet the beach lobby and its allies in local government ensured that the shoreline, or at least its most desirable parts, would remain free of "undesirable" elements.

CHAPTER 5

✦

Beach Bodies

On a late Sunday afternoon in August 1962, President John F. Kennedy took a swim in the Pacific Ocean. The president's "impromptu dip" surprised all parties involved, including the FBI and Secret Service, as well as the beachgoers who happened to be out that day. Kennedy was on the last day of a short trip through the West, and he was visiting his sister and brother-in-law at their beach house in Santa Monica. After a relaxing afternoon spent lounging beside the couple's private pool, the young president "made the snap decision to try the ocean waters." Leaving the safety of the house's fenced yard behind, he jogged toward the Pacific. Passersby caught sight of him quickly taking off his polo shirt, wearing "blue boxer swim trunks," and plunging headfirst into the surf. "It's him! Look how handsome!" sunbathers reportedly exclaimed. By the time the president was splashing around in the ocean, a crowd had formed, and scores followed him into the water. This was *Los Angeles Times* photographer Bill Beebe's lucky day. Despite being dressed in a business suit, he dashed into the water "up to his waist" and snapped candid photographs of the president and the delighted beach crowd. The next day, the photographs made national headlines. A few days later, *Life* magazine featured the most striking of the series as its "picture of the week." Flashing a Hollywood-worthy smile revealing his sparkling white teeth, the president was pictured jogging back from his swim in his dripping trunks, surrounded by beachgoers and exchanging a friendly glance with a beautiful woman in a polka-dot, two-piece bathing suit.

The president's spontaneous decision to disrobe and go for a swim turned into a fantastic media opportunity for the White House. Upon his return to Washington, DC, the *Los Angeles Times* noted, the president had "left in his wake many an awestruck bather." The photograph humanized a president caught in an unguarded moment of boyish playfulness. It also allowed the nation to see itself as an open, democratic place where the most important man in the country could mix among ordinary citizens in his swimming trunks. Emphasizing the nation's reputation as a beacon of freedom, *Life* proudly commented that such "a moist mob scene . . . could take place, surely, only in the U.S."[1]

The photograph also garnered attention because it caught a youthful president in the flattering light of the setting sun, emphasizing his healthy

Figure 5.1. This photograph of President John F. Kennedy on Santa Monica Beach was picked up by *Life* magazine as its photo of the week in 1962. Bill Beebe, *Los Angeles Times* Photographic Collection, Library Special Collections, Charles E. Young Research Library, University of California–Los Angeles.

tan and trim physique. In the early 1960s, the Southern California beach culture was on display everywhere, from music album covers to movies and magazine advertisements. The summer after Kennedy hit Santa Monica Beach, surf music duo Jan and Dean topped the charts with "Surf City," and American teenagers swarmed theaters to see the first installment of what would become a series of youth-targeted beach movies, which extolled the lifestyle of local surfers and beach bums. By revealing his deep tan and fit body—*Life* commented approvingly that "he still [had] only a modest displacement"—the president showed that he was perfectly at ease in this environment. No doubt the photograph's reception would have been quite different if Kennedy had sported unflattering tan marks and a paunch. With his broad smile and relaxed demeanor despite the commotion around him, Kennedy conveyed his mastery of postwar youth hipness: maintaining a good-natured nonchalance in all situations. Despite his many physical ailments (which he carefully kept from the public), Kennedy possessed what many Americans had started to covet: a California tan, a youthful look and attitude, and an enviable beach body.

For a short period between the early 1950s and the mid-1960s, America was obsessed with Southern California beach bodies. More precisely, Americans were fascinated by the bodies—young, tanned, white, and fit—on display on the state's southern shores. This obsession was part of the enormous cultural influence California exerted nationally during the postwar period. With its burgeoning suburbs, automobile-centered lifestyle, bountiful jobs, and youthful population, the Golden State came to embody the boundless opportunities that peace and economic growth had to offer. Furthered by the surfing craze and the popularity of beach "teenpics," Southern California beach cultures emerged as the perfect metaphor for the good life. With its sweeping beaches and cinematic palm trees, Southern California appeared to be a great place in which to escape from Cold War threats of nuclear annihilation and racial tensions linked to the nascent civil rights movement. Yet mere escapism does not fully explain this postwar fascination. What made California beaches so appealing to local and national audiences, this chapter argues, was their role in producing and displaying the new social and bodily norms of the postwar era. Kennedy's beach romp may have been an exceptional event, but it confirmed what many Americans already sensed: the best, hippest, most attractive bodies were to be found on the sands of Los Angeles.[2]

Although Southern Californians' enthusiasm for physical health, fitness, and beauty was not a new phenomenon, the local beach culture had yet to form into a coherent body aesthetic. This transformation took place in the aftermath of World War II as an increasing number of Angelenos searched for meaning, pleasure, health, and community at the beach.

The beach lobby's actions supported that trend: the clean, widened beaches and their brand-new sports centers, volleyball courts, boardwalks, and gym apparatus afforded more space for athletic activities. For parents, officials, and experts worried both about juvenile crime and the decreasing fitness levels of the next generation, keeping youth active was a priority. And active they were. Multiple bodily cultures emerged in the 1950s, while older ones gained popularity. In addition to surfing, droves of Angelenos took up beach volleyball, bodybuilding, water-skiing, diving, boating, and beach acrobatics. On Newport Beach's Balboa Island, over eighty thousand high school and college students celebrated Bal Week, the local version of Spring Break, on the beaches of the otherwise quiet resort.[3] Spring-breakers, surfers, and other beach bums not only relaxed and forged friendships on the shores. There they sought to shape and display their bodies by combining traditional seaside hedonism with an ethos of bodily discipline. In Southern California, men and women prepared their beach bodies while on the beach, transforming what was perceived elsewhere as a place of rest into a site of exertion. Going to the beach offered the opportunity to observe—and participate in—the transformation of beauty standards that gripped postwar America. In addition to being clean, wide, and conveniently equipped with parking lots, the modernized beaches of Los Angeles offered another unique advantage: it was there that modern bodies were sculpted.

For the vast majority of Americans who lived far from the West Coast, the postwar beach and surfing craze was experienced primarily in the media. Thanks to the film, music, fashion, and advertising industries, US residents could observe and enjoy the bodies of Californians from afar, and the most dedicated could emulate their beauty regimens and diets. The emergence of a teenage consumer market in the postwar period was instrumental in spreading the ubiquitous image of the California "clean teen." By the 1960s, in the words of one historian of fitness, "the California lifestyle was transformed into a physical aesthetic: thin, tan, taut bodies with sun-bleached blond hair and pearly white teeth."[4] In the process of becoming a commercially packaged lifestyle and look, the California beach culture also became synonymous with whiteness, even though many nonwhite Angelenos were just as dedicated to the beach life. This chapter grounds this media phenomenon in the actual places where Southern California bodies, in their ethnic and racial diversity, were shaped, displayed, and observed. In the end, the combined real and fictional world of beach bums intensified Americans' engagement with the new corporeal ideals associated with California.

FROM BOBBY-SOXERS TO BEACH BUMS: THE TEENAGE BEACH CULTURE IN SOUTHERN CALIFORNIA

California was not the only state that attracted national attention for its beautiful beaches and year-round sunshine in the postwar period. Florida experienced a parallel demographic explosion, promising prospective residents a suburban lifestyle, spotless shores, and balmy winters in an exotic yet air-conditioned setting. Despite its beautiful sandy beaches, however, Florida never developed a beach culture to rival the one that flourished on the Southern California coast. As historian Gay Mormino notes, California was unique in that it was home to Hollywood, which ensured its role as a "cultural incubator," but the main reason for its popularity lies elsewhere: "From St. Petersburg to Miami Beach to Boca Raton, Florida's beaches were more likely teeming with retirees than teenagers."[5]

The flowering of a Southern California beach culture at mid-century was, first and foremost, the product of demographic trends. California's population was undeniably young: in 1948, it led the nation in youth population increase and boasted the third-largest number of children under the age of eighteen. Schools, the *Los Angeles Times* reported in 1958, stood as "one of the largest single items in the Southland's building picture." Despite spending one hundred thousand dollars a week on new construction, the Los Angeles Board of Education could not keep up with the new crops of youngsters.[6] Unlike Florida, which became the nation's retirement capital sometime in the late 1950s, the Golden State attracted large numbers of baby-boom families. Exemplifying long-standing beliefs about the importance of fresh air and sunshine for good health, the "indoor-outdoor" living associated with the southern half of the state was considered ideal for raising the next generation. In fact, according to *Life* magazine in 1951, the entire Pacific seaboard was "a wondrous place for kids to grow up and live." No doubt this was the prime reason why the West Coast, with its "abnormal rates of birth and migration," was "growing by leaps and bounds and millions."[7]

Nowhere was this demographic trend more obvious than on the shores. In his book *The New Society* (1963) dedicated to the new societal trends emerging out of California, Remi Nadeau noted with no small amount of disapproval that "the age level [had] been gradually dropping [at the beach]." "Up to World War I, the sand was occupied by adults, with a preponderance of the middle-aged." But the boom of the 1920s had "brought people of all ages of California," and "the beach scene changed accordingly." Thereafter, "California's beaches became so fearfully crowded that they were, not a place of relaxation, but a scene of human indignity. . . . Most other adults sought out distant and less accessible spots. Only the teenagers were left. They loved crowds and had developed neither a sense of dignity nor a yearning for privacy."[8] Like many of his contemporaries concerned by the rebellious baby-boom generation, Nadeau held youths in contempt. Still, his observation that local beaches were packed with young people contained a kernel of truth. Even author Tom Wolfe, a keen observer of the Sixties youth, agreed with him: the beach where his "pump house gang" congregated was "segregated by age . . . verboten for people practically 50 years old."[9]

Of course, the region's youth had always enjoyed spending time by the ocean. The Spring Break phenomenon originated on the West Coast in the late 1920s when large delegations of students from all colleges and universities and most of the high schools of Orange, Los Angeles, Santa Barbara, and Riverside counties started spending their Easter vacation week on Newport Beach's Balboa Island, a sandbar in Newport Bay connected to the mainland by a bridge. During "Collegiate Week," as it was known back then, students used the local beaches "for their wild and noisy parties," to the great indignation of residents and the police. The phenomenon prompted adult observers to identify the age-specific leisure habits, music, dance, fashions, and lingo with the "collegiate crowd." Such youthful revelries, however, were reserved for the social elite in the interwar period; most youngsters could only dream of renting a pricey beach home for a holiday with their peers.[10]

By the 1940s, Collegiate Week still remained out of reach for many, but a growing cohort of "bobby-soxers" (the nickname bestowed upon swing-crazed high schoolers) and "teen-agers" enjoyed greater personal freedom, a small allowance, and access to the family car. The majority of youth also attended high school, allowing for more leisure time with their peers. As a distinct group with its "own age-related tastes, styles, and social concerns," this first generation identified as teenagers yearned for nothing more than a social space of its own. In Southern California, that place was the beach. Free, accessible to all, and far from the gaze of parental authorities, the beach was the ideal place for youths to demonstrate their independence from the world of adults.[11]

Some sections of Los Angeles's beaches were claimed by white high school and university students as their own private play areas. The practice was already well established by 1940. That year, *Life* dedicated two richly illustrated pages to "U.C.L.A.'s beach," a "200-yd strip of public sand reserved by students by the process of snubbing interlopers." Propped against what was described as their " 'private' wall on Santa Monica Beach," the students were photographed sunbathing with their open textbooks resting on their knees. While the beach atmosphere was hardly an ideal study environment, the magazine did not chastise the students, but instead gently teased them and noted that books often went "back to the campus with sand in their bindings, their pages not always so well read." The magazine relished in identifying the markers of this burgeoning beach-focused youth culture, including items of clothing ("play suits or pajamas"), leisure activities (volleyball for the boys; acrobatics and gossip for the girls), and favorite consumer items ("note pad, textbook, sandals, radio"). What *Life* had missed, however, was the stiff competition over territory that lay beneath the seemingly lazy beach afternoon. In the next issue's letters to the editor, former Santa Monica Junior College student Jack Gabrielson denied UCLA students' domination of the coveted strand. "I ought to know," he wrote, "because I spent during the spring semesters more time . . . at this beach than I did in classes."[12] Generally speaking, white high school and college students congregated on the same stretch of beach located north of the Santa Monica Pier, but those from different schools clustered around different physical landmarks. Hollywood High School students, for instance, hung out near Lifeguard Tower #13, while nearby Roadside Beach, so called because of its proximity to a café named the Roadside Diner, was the preferred haunt of the students from Santa Monica and Venice High Schools.[13]

Beaches popular with teenagers were hardly the most attractive strands. Roadside Beach was considered by families and older beachgoers too crowded for comfort and lacked even the most basic sanitary facilities, but this mattered little to the growing wave of postwar beach bums. Teenagers could find there a variety of free leisure activities: from swimming, sunbathing, and chatting to surfing and beach volleyball. Even dancing became an option as beachgoers brought their transistor radios and portable record players. In Venice, where a group of young (and not so young) beatniks settled in the 1950s in search of cheap rent and artistic inspiration in the "dilapidated grandeur" of the once famous resort, dancing to the tune of the bongo drums was another favorite beach activity.[14] Venice also offered more conventional and adult-approved forms of exercise at its new Athletic Center, with its "three paddle tennis courts, four volleyball courts, rope climb, flying rings, horizontal bars, tumbling mats and weights." A few miles north, at Santa Monica's Muscle Beach, young people could take classes in "body building, weightlifting, apparatus technique (high beam, rings, parallel bars), hand balancing, head balancing, adagio, pyramids and chess."[15] In fact, "teen-aged muscle men" were such an important part of the bodybuilding communities that a Junior Mr. Muscle Beach contest (and its equivalent in Venice, the Junior Mr. Surfestival contest) was introduced in 1951.[16] Meanwhile, at Playa Del Rey, the newly built fire rings were particularly popular with groups of youngsters who enjoyed roasting wieners under the moonlight. Above all, the beach was a relatively unregulated space far from the parental gaze where it was possible to develop strong friendships and to build one's sense of personal identity through identification with a collective. Whether someone was a surfer, a beatnik, a Muscle Beach body worshipper, or simply a beach bum, the beach was the place to find one's crowd.

The opportunity to meet members of the opposite sex in a flirtatious setting was another advantage the beach offered local youth. It was the ideal setting for first love: young people went to the shore in groups, which gave teenagers more opportunities to meet someone of the opposite sex, while beach games allowed bodies to touch. Like many other Angelenos, Sandra Odor, a young high school student from Burbank, remembered how when she went to the beach with her sister and friends, their goal was always the same: "to pick up boys."[17] Lois Warner, a Venice High School alumna, met her future spouse on the beach, as did countless other Southern Californians.[18] The annual ritual of Spring Break, in particular, offered chances for meeting new people and dating. The owners of rental homes on Balboa Island, where students headed to celebrate Bal Week, were well aware of the phenomenon: most preferred to rent to boys, under the impression that since boys were the ones who called on the girls to spend an evening with them—under the more or less watchful eyes of chaperones—there would be less wear and tear on their properties.[19]

The beach had another major advantage for teenagers in search of a discreet place to go necking. Unlike movie dates, which could come at a hefty price for young men, the sands were completely free. Given the high level of automobile ownership in Southern California, the beach was accessible to teenagers across social classes. In a 1945 *Life* article dedicated to the "California way of life" and profiling three families of different socioeconomic levels, all the youngsters described a similar pattern of shopping, going to school, and heading to the beaches in their leisure time. Not all teenagers had access to a "fan-shaped pool adjoining their home," like the kids in the wealthy Stothart family, but "Californians [did] not have to make $50,000 a year to enjoy swimming" since "nearly all of them [lived] within driving distance of Pacific beaches."[20] The myth of the beach as a classless site of youth camaraderie suffused popular culture. In the teen movie *The Careless Years* (1957), filmed on location at Santa Monica High School, a teen beach party was the background against which upper-middle-class

Emily and working-class Jerry shared their first kiss. In contrast to the private party where they initially met and where evidence of Emily's parents' wealth was on display, the beach provided a neutral ground where their young love could flourish, sheltered from class differences.

Racial differences were a different matter. Teen movies of this period portrayed the beach as an entirely white space, but the reality was of course more complex. In its May 1948 issue dedicated to the best vacation spots in California, *Ebony* magazine claimed that "all of the beaches in the immediate Los Angeles Area—Santa Monica, Ocean Park, Castle Rock—are city-owned and there are no restrictions." The cover of the issue seemed to confirm these claims: an interracial pair of bathing beauties, "both Los Angeles residents," proudly posed in colorful swimsuits on the deck of a sleek mahogany speedboat.[21] Yet the fact that the magazine singled out Lake Elsinore and Val Verde, two inland African American resort communities as, respectively, the "best Negro vacations spot in the state" and the "most popular Negro weekend spot for Southern Californians," intimated that informal forms of segregation persisted in some areas. As a matter of fact, everybody at "Roadside Rest" was white. At least, this is what Ann Winfield, a 1960 Venice High School graduate, remembers, and photographs of the popular hangout corroborate her account. Some Malibu beaches, another popular hangout for teenagers, were also off-limit to nonwhites (and even, to some extent, to nonlocals) well into the 1950s.[22]

Even so, Black teenagers enjoyed beach parties similar to the ones held by their white peers, though they usually took place in other, less coveted strands, such as Cabrillo Beach in the San Pedro Bay or Playa Del Rey.[23] The beaches located immediately south of the Santa Monica Pier, where the historically Black beach stood, were also popular with Black beachgoers. The crowd of spectators at Muscle Beach was relatively interracial. Some Latino and Black bodybuilders took part in the famous Mr. Muscle Beach contests held on the platform, and a few even won first place.[24] For a young girl like Sandra Odor, who lived in lily-white Burbank, Muscle Beach was the only place where she remembered being around African Americans. Occasionally, interracial youth beach parties took place elsewhere. On July 13, 1947, for instance, Black youths affiliated with Lincoln Memorial Congregational Church hosted two white groups from the region for a beach party at Redondo Beach, where they swam and ate hot dogs.[25]

Black and interracial beach parties were not always the carefree occasions participants desired. Black teenagers, unlike their white peers, could be subjected to police brutality and racial profiling. On May 27, 1961, for instance, when a fight broke out at an interracial beach party held at Cabrillo Beach, the police arrested seven young Black men, five of whom were later charged with assault, disturbing the peace, and causing a riot. According to the police, the group of Compton youths had stolen a record player and records from a white group, which had led to an interracial brawl. Yet the father of one of the young arrestees denied the police account, explaining that there was "a fight, yes, but no interracial riot, no gang war" and that the group was composed of "friends of long standing who had gone to school together."[26] Black teenagers could take part in the local beach culture, but their behavior had to be beyond reproach at all times. Frank Edwards, a Black surfer from Hermosa Beach who was the subject of a portrait in *Ebony* in 1965, was a model in that respect. The eighteen-year-old was not only gifted on the surfboard but also secretary of the Bay Area Surf Club, class president, and a college hopeful. But, as *Ebony* noted, he was "one of a minute number of Negros who have taken up the sport of surfing." Even at the height of the surf boom, the legacy of beach segregation, combined with the LAPD's entrenched racism, prevented most Black teenagers from taking up the sport.[27]

Although most young Americans lived far from the Pacific Coast, the teenage beach culture could still be part of their cultural milieu. By the early 1960s, almost all had read a novel, watched a film, listened to a song, or bought a piece of clothing inspired by this youth culture. The phenomenon was largely triggered by the late 1950s surf boom. With the advent of lightweight, polyurethane foam boards, which were far less expensive and easier to maneuver than their balsa wood predecessors, surfing drew an increasing number of devotees to the shores. According to most accounts, the true origin of the surfing craze was the release of *Gidget* in 1959. Adapted from a hit teen novel published two years earlier, the movie follows the adventures of fifteen-year-old Francine, who befriends a group of Malibu surfers, earns a new nickname (Gidget, the girl-midget, due to her small stature), and discovers the "thrill of shooting the curl," while also experiencing the joys and heartbreaks of first love. As the first color film to convey the joyful energy of the postwar Southern California beach and surf culture, *Gidget* drew packed audiences of teenagers to the theaters. A year later, the box office success of MGM's *Where the Boys Are* (1960), Hollywood's first movie depicting the Spring Break phenomenon, confirmed the bankable value of filming teenagers frolicking on the beach (even if, in this particular case, the beach was in Florida).[28]

Eventually, a small-budget film company called American International Pictures (AIP) perfected the genre with the box office hit *Beach Party* (1963). Set on an unnamed Southern California beach, the film follows the adventures of a teenage couple, Frankie and Dee Dee (played, respectively, by pop singer Frankie Avalon and Annette Funicello, a former host of the television show *The Mickey Mouse Club*), as they fight and make up while on their summer vacation with their gang of surfer friends. A mash-up of surfing shots with musical numbers, cartoonish brawls, improbable subplots, and references to contemporary fads, from hot-rodders to beatniks, the film was unanimously dismissed as a mindless comedy of little redeeming quality beyond the fact that it was shot "on a magnificent strip of California shoreline." But the film was a "monster-sized hit" for the small studio.[29] AIP's producers rushed to exploit this success. *Beach Party* was soon followed by another six films based on the same formula. Its basic ingredients were simple: a group of tanned (and thus invariably white), swimsuit-clad teenagers, some surfing scenes, a soundtrack that included popular surfing bands, trendy cars, and, of course, a pristine Southern California beach. Other Hollywood studios tried to ride the wave and produce their own surf and beach movies, including 20th Century-Fox's *Surf Party* (1964) and Paramount's *The Girls on the Beach* (1965). Meanwhile, *Gidget* spawned two film sequels and a television show. At a time when Hollywood struggled to compete with television and new suburban leisure attractions, the beach movie cycle was a much-needed boon to ticket sales.

The music business also gravitated toward the beach. Starting in 1961 with Dick Dale's "Let's Go Trippin'," considered by many to be the first surf song, surf music established itself as a mainstay in the music charts.[30] Unlike Dick Dale, who was a bona fide surfer, many members of surfing bands had never set foot on a board, and some surf bands such as the Astronauts hailed from landlocked states. But it didn't matter. By then, surfing had strayed beyond the actual act of riding the waves. Sounding or, even better, looking like a surfer was a must. Soon, the fashion, swimsuit, and cosmetics industries stepped in, selling "surf beach or deck pants" and "California blues" eye makeup to beach bum wannabes across the nation.[31] From a teenage subculture rooted in daily practices, the beach and surf culture had become a full-on national craze, inspiring young Americans everywhere to take up a new sport, change their looks, or simply dream of a romance in a beach setting.[32]

While it reflected the liveliness of local beach cultures, the Gidget-inspired media frenzy erased the active participation of nonwhite teens in the beach scene. In the over sixty surfing-inspired teen movies Hollywood produced in the 1950s and 1960s, none featured a Black or brown beach bum. African Americans were only allowed to appear in Hollywood's fantasy beach world as musical acts, safely removed from the beach and completely covered up. For instance, a fourteen-year-old Stevie Wonder made brief appearances in *Bikini Beach* (1964) and *Muscle Beach Party* (1964), while James Brown played with his band in *Sky Party* (1965). Other nonwhite characters included Frankie's Tahitian girlfriend in *How to Stuff a Wild Bikini* (1965), though she is abandoned by the end of the movie when he returns to his trusted Dee Dee, and a Chinese servant who also doubles as a detective in *For Those Who Think Young* (1964). The lack of racial and ethnic diversity in beach films was only matched by the total absence of nonwhite people in surfing music. Hollywood ironically portrayed the beach as a "segregated oasis" just as the civil rights movement was reaching its peak.[33] In fact, the beach teenpic mania coincided with several wade-ins staged by African Americans to desegregate beaches in Mississippi and Florida, some of which ended in bloodshed.[34] From the point of view of adults who produced the movies and music that fed the beach culture phenomenon, seminaked teenagers dancing next to each other seemed a lot less threatening if nonwhites were not part of the picture. Adults may not have been able to regulate all that was happening on the shores, but the cinematic beach remained a controlled, and thus largely whitewashed, environment.

YOUNG, REBELLIOUS BODIES

As the teen culture grew more visible in the late 1950s and early 1960s, adults became obsessed with deciphering its meaning. In newspaper articles and magazine features, the adult society observed with a mixture of curiosity, pride, and alarm the rise of the Southern California beach bums—a ubiquitous term in this period that designated young loafers who chose to forgo school and work to spend time on the beach. For some, the sight of vigorous adolescents goofing around on the sands reflected the energy of a youthful nation poised for greatness. This was the "West Coast youth" as profiled by *Life* magazine in 1951, with its "buoyant optimism of spirit" and "supreme confidence in its ability to get on in the world." For others, including author Remi Nadeau, the beach bum phenomenon was a sign of the nation's moral decline. In shirking responsibilities and succumbing to the deadly sin of idleness, the beach bum embodied a dangerous morality of pleasure that undermined traditional values of work, self-discipline, and moderation.[35]

Either way, the fixation on the teenage beach culture was rooted in its physicality. In the context of the Cold War, many parents and public officials worried about the perceived decreasing fitness level of American youth compared to their European counterparts. The "soft American," as journalists dubbed the phenomenon, was endangering children's health and, more worryingly, the nation's security. Just as suburbanization and increased reliance on the automobile fundamentally altered how Americans moved their bodies on a daily basis, postwar abundance and technological advances made it easier and cheaper than ever to bring tasty food to the family table. As teenagers wolfed down hamburgers and sugary ice creams and drank generous servings of soda, they were becoming noticeably heavier than preceding generations. In contrast, California's teenage beach bums, with their trim and tanned bodies, seemed impossibly healthy. Even Nadeau had to acknowledge the beauty on display. California youths, he conceded, "dominate the beaches with an arrogance that springs from their obvious physical superiority." With their ascendency, the beaches had become "the great show window for American physical fitness."[36] Yet devotion to the beach life could veer into excess. Too much time loafing in the sun could alter one's mind, leading youths into a dangerous spiral of juvenile delinquency, sexual promiscuity, and underage drinking. In fact, the classless world of the beach, like the much-decried rock 'n' roll concerts, risked bringing respectable high school kids into contact with lower-class teens and their delinquent ways. Contemporary observers gazed intently at the youthful physiques on display on the sands, searching for signs of defiance and licentiousness.

Surfers undoubtedly represented the most feared categories of all beach bums. In the postwar period, the chasm between surfing's image as a healthy outdoor sport and its simultaneous condemnation as a gateway drug to the delinquent lifestyle widened. "Are surfers good, clean American youth having fun at South Bay beaches? Or are they gangs of rowdies defying parental and school authority?" as one journalist put it.[37] As far as local residents were concerned, the latter was closer to reality. By the late 1950s, Malibu residents were growing increasingly frustrated with the "rowdiness, drinking, and carousing [that] prevailed at the surf rider rendezvous."[38] In Topanga Beach, residents complained of "teenaged surfers using private property as shortcuts to the beach and refusing to cooperate with residents when asked to do so."[39] According to the *Los Angeles Times* it was no longer a matter of shouting, "Keep your children off the street," but "Keep your children off the beach."[40] In the early 1960s, new regulations establishing surfing areas and temporary surf bans improved relations between surfers and authorities, but the sport continued to be associated with juvenile delinquency.[41] As a journalist observed in 1963, "The surfer ha[d] replaced the ducktailed motorcyclist and the beatnik as public parasite number one." Under the influence of the counterculture, surfing became closely associated with sex and drugs. By the late 1960s, surfers were often dismissed in the mainstream media as "addicts" and "beachniks."

For all the negative coverage surfers received, journalists could not help but acknowledge the sport's positive impact on the body. In fact, the best publicity for surfing was to be found among its most ardent devotees, the "new set of young businessmen" who supplied teenage surfers with their surfboards and magazines. With his bronze suntan and boyish smile, John Severson, the successful founder of *Surfer Magazine*, was presented by *Life* magazine as the finest example of "the beneficent results of the good California beach life that he espouses." Meanwhile, surfboard makers Tom Flaherty and Dale Velzy were described as "good-looking, bronzed, sea-loving men."[42] These comments found echoes in AIP's *Beach Party* movies. In *Bikini Beach* (1964), for instance, the gang of teenage surfers finds an advocate in Miss Clemens, a teacher at the local high school. When the gang faces off with Harvey Huntington Honeywagon, a curmudgeonlike character inspired by railroad baron Henry Huntington who accuses surfers of being juvenile delinquents, Miss Clemens defends them by pointing to their healthy physiques: "Those surfers are building strong, healthy bodies. What's wrong with physical fitness? You should try it sometimes."

If riding the waves could turn teenagers into vigorous adults, then surfing could find its way to redemption. In fact, this was the logic behind the introduction of surfing in the physical education curriculum of local high schools and universities. Advocates of this curriculum looked positively on the strenuous exercise regimen of some practitioners. After all, learning how to surf was "no small job," and mastering its intricacies required daily practice: "After school, after work over a weekend, or just at any time at all [surfers] trek down to the beach."[43] "Keeping fit," explained a San Francisco native who swam a mile several times a week and ran a mile every other day, "was vital to survive in this sport."[44] Most importantly, surfing was ideal to achieve a thin body. This was no small benefit considering that, in the 1960s, thinness was becoming "a signifier of status, personal style, and beauty." "You never see a fat surfer," commented a young swimming instructor. In contrast, the "sand bug," a disparaging term in the surf lingo used to designate a beach bum who didn't own a surfboard and never went in the water, was "usually fat and [lay] underneath a beach umbrella."[45]

California girls especially touted the weight-loss benefits of surfing. In fact, if they were "the prettiest, biggest, lithest, tannest, most luscious girls this side of the international date line," as *Life* magazine claimed in 1962, this was due to exercise. There was no better example of the link between a beautiful figure and sports than Laurie Hoover, a sixteen-year-old surfer from Pasadena who was shown in the corresponding photo spread demonstrating an elaborate acrobatic stunt with a well-muscled male friend.[46] Surfing combined with a strict diet could do wonders to one's waistline. By "surfing more and eating just two small meals a day," Malibu surfer Mary Lou McGinnis claimed she had managed to drop from 140 pounds to 124. Gudrun Wilcke, a "shapely green-eyed Glendale blond," was another splendid female specimen of the Golden State. Interviewed in 1963, the seventeen-year-old surfboard champion considered surfing "an excellent form of exertion to keep the figure trim." Even so, Wilcke regretted, few girls actually took up the sport seriously as many "feared unattractive muscular development from the exercise."[47]

As Wilcke's comments suggest, American women in the early 1960s received conflicting messages about the importance and role of exercise in achieving a trim body. A growing number of fitness experts recommended that women take up a gentle routine of repeated movements to tone and shape their bodies. But strenuous activities such as surfing increased appetite, which defeated the ultimate purpose of losing weight, and risked causing dramatic changes in women's bodies. An excessive muscle mass, in particular, challenged conventional standards of feminine attractiveness, predicated on a dainty figure. In that respect, the fact that Gidget was played on the silver screen by petite actress Sandra Dee not only fit the character's nickname but also assuaged any fears about the sport's unpleasant consequences on the female body. In addition, surfing was an outdoor sport, which involved exposing the body to the elements. A *Los Angeles Times* article on female surfers not only warned of the risk of becoming "muscle-bound" (a common misconception at the time of the potentially paralyzing effects of exercise on the body) but it also emphasized the "long-range physical risk to these girls from sun, wind and salt water." Female surfers were susceptible to cracked skin, dry hair, and "the infamous 'knobs,' or calcium deposits, that appear on their shins from kneeling on the Fiberglass board." Knobs (or knots), a status symbol for male surfers, were considered ugly on the female body. Toni, a fifteen-year-old blond surfer from Los Angeles, proclaimed, "A girl has to keep her knees nice."[48] Thinness could not come at any price. The female surfers profiled in popular magazines inspired respect for their athleticism, but they had to be well kempt when they stepped off the board.

The scars left by surfing on the bodies of California youths might have been a source of pride for the most passionate surfers, but, for adult observers, the scars signaled an intensity that bordered on psychologically unhealthy. Surfing to stay fit was a laudable pursuit, but excessive devotion was not just a disease of the mind but of the body. In fact, local authorities and experienced athletes alike often identified the dangerous elements among surfers by their corporeal markers. According to "clean-cut surfer"

Lindy Bulger, this small minority was composed of "school dropouts who . . . dye their hair blond and use abusive language to symbols of respectability." A Huntington Beach chief lifeguard identified the problem surfers by their "long, shaggy hair."[49] As these remarks indicate, hair evidently held the key to identifying the wholesome surfer from his evil twin, the hanger-on, also known as the "gremmie" or "ho-daddy" in surfing lingo. At a time when high school rules mandating short hair for boys were challenged in court by students who wanted to mimic the hairstyles of their rock idols, such considerations were far from trivial.[50] In the eyes of local officials and journalists, sporting long hair that "looked like it belonged on a sheepdog" was a political statement and a sign of rejections of middle-class values of respectability. Hair length was not the only issue. Color also denoted controversial references and a nonconformist streak. According to a 1961 *Los Angeles Times* article, surfers also attracted scrutiny for "the so-called neo-Nazi activities popular among [the] surfing fraternity such as painting swastikas on their shoes and walls or bleaching their hair." As author and surfing enthusiast Daniel Duane has remarked, surfing has troubling, yet little-known historical connections with white supremacy. In the 1960s, bleaching one's hair through exposure to the sun (or peroxide, if it failed) was a sure sign of belonging to the surfing community—according to the Beach Boys' 1963 hit "Surfin' USA," a surfer's key attributes were his "huarache sandals" and "bushy bushy blond hairdo." But it also could be interpreted as a distant echo of racist fantasies of the blond, blue-eyed Aryan's genetic superiority. While local officials acknowledged that Nazi references may not have been fully understood by teenage surfers, they interpreted such behavior as part of a wider problem: "defiance of authority."[51]

Surfers were not the only beach bums who attracted comments about their bodies and styles of dress. The thrill-seeking adolescents who trekked down to Balboa Island and surrounding beach towns every Easter also captured the attention of reporters. Of course, much of the coverage was focused on the youth's mischief. Every year, the young revelers' antics resulted in a surge in calls to the police, who spent much of the infamous week "chasing speeders, hauling drunks, breaking up fights, and in general keeping teen-crowded Balboa and Newport from becoming anything more than a minor Dante's inferno." As the phenomenon grew in the postwar years—from eight thousand spring-breakers in 1948 to twenty thousand in 1955 to eighty thousand in 1960—the number of arrests reached unprecedented levels. Yet, for all the tales of students using mattresses as surfboards and burning holes through the floors of their beach cottages, the press also wrote admiringly of the young people's energy as reflected in their "magnificent young bodies."[52] According to some accounts, Balboa beaches during Easter week were akin to the grounds of a major sports competition. They "[seethed] with volley ball games, impromptu baseball contests and football throwing" while other Bal Week celebrants chose to "ride the roller coaster breakers on surfboards, skin-dive, fish, swim or just wade in the spring-chilled water."[53] Photographs of students engaging in "a brisk tug of war," building human pyramids on the sand, carrying pretty girls on their shoulders, dancing the conga, hopping on a sailboat, climbing on top of their rental houses' roofs, or participating in a game of blanket tossing were featured prominently in local newspapers and national magazines.[54] "Despite the inevitable charges of wild parties," commented a Newport journalist, the youngsters "presented a glowing picture of young America having a lot of fun."[55]

Adults also noted with concern the popularity of skimpy bikinis and blood-red nail polish. In the mid-1960s, some remarked that it had become difficult "to tell the boys from the girls by the length of their hair." Ultimately, however, the vagaries of fashion were seen as mere signs of the passage of time rather than symbols of rebellion: "There really isn't much difference between Easter vacation 1961, and Easter vacation 'way back when,'" reflected a journalist sent to report on the celebrations. "It's still the old, old story of boy-meets-girl. . . . The girls are wearing muu muus this year and blue eye shadow. But they eat ice cream cones and go barefoot. The boys wear skimpy swim trunks and sometimes wispy beards. But they still chomp hot dogs. And everybody eats frozen bananas coated with chocolate."[56] If trouble did happen, the blame was squarely placed on "a small minority," an "older element" composed of nonstudents who took advantage of the revelries. Anyway, the "toughies" became less of an issue when the city council, in the mid-1950s, enacted a series of strict ordinances regulating Easter rentals and traffic. Pressured by the growing population of year-round residents organized into the Balboa Island Improvement Association, the police also strictly enforced curfew laws starting in 1960, sending thousands of juveniles to jail. By then, Bal Week, with its high rental prices and heavy police presence, attracted mostly white, middle-class youths, as was evident by the "top-down convertibles and flashy, polished-to-the-hilt sports cars" cruising down the island's narrow streets. At a time when the high school population in California was becoming more socially and racially diverse than ever, Bal Week thus presented a limited vision of teenage America focused on the "sweat-shirted youths"—that is, white "clean teens" enrolled in local high schools and elite universities. The infamous week functioned as an annual ritual allowing society to reassure itself about its young people as tanned, fun-loving, and ultimately law-abiding teens. In that sense, coverage of Bal Week echoed the Hollywood "surfsploitation films" of the early 1960s.[57]

Contemporary observers saw California youths' bodies as signs to be identified, interpreted, and in some cases repressed. The main plot of *Beach Party* (1963), the first of AIP's beach movies, involved an anthropologist (complete with pith helmet) observing the teenagers' every move, with the aid of a telescope, on the pretense of writing a book about the surfing subculture. The long-haired male surfers and their unkempt female peers were perceived as walking embodiments of the new teenage rebellion. By displaying unsightly knobs and spreading thick layers of zinc oxide on their noses, male and female teenage surfers challenged conventional expectations of masculinity and femininity. In a world made up of "men in gray flannel suits" who conformed to society's standards and fulfilled their familial and professional responsibilities, male surfers represented an alternative ideal of masculinity centered around hedonistic enjoyment and athletic prowess. Broadly speaking, surfers modeled new standards of beauty borne out of their privileged relationship with nature. The allure of female surfers was not that of the polished movie star with her impeccable curls and smooth, milky-white skin. Makeup free, tanned, and sporting a wild mane of beach locks, the real-life Gidgets embodied an authentic beauty free from artifice and accessories, which appealed to a growing number of young people attracted to countercultural values, environmentalist ideas, and non-Western cultures and philosophies.

As unconventional as they may have appeared in the eyes of adults, teenage beach bums possessed something many Americans had come to admire and yearn for by the early 1960s: youthful bodies and attitudes. In a society where young people made up almost half of the population and where teenage tastes seemed to dominate the music, fashion, and film industries, looking young, or acting young, was a sought-after trait. By taking part in the beach youth subcultures, many older Americans sought to prevent the passage of time or, at the very least, to retain some qualities of their younger days.

"FOR THOSE WHO THINK YOUNG": THE BEACH AS FOUNTAIN OF YOUTH

In the postwar period, youthfulness was no longer exclusively linked to a specific age group, even if the baby boom and the rise of the lucrative teenage consumer market were crucial factors in this shift. It was also a way of speaking, dressing, and styling one's hair, as well as a nonchalant, if not openly defiant attitude toward the conventional strictures of middle-class society. The new slogan adopted in the 1960s by a leading soft drink manufacturer was emblematic of this development: Pepsi was the drink "for those who think young." "Thinking young," as the slogan clarified, was about adopting "a wholesome attitude, an enthusiastic outlook." As such, it was a fundamentally ageless quality: "It means getting the most out of life, and everyone can join in." Of course, the inclusiveness of Pepsi's campaign made sense for a company seeking to attract the largest possible consumer base. But it was also emblematic of the 1960s, when many corporations sought to associate themselves, even if only performatively, with the countercultural youth leading the charge against conformism. Drinking Pepsi made anyone young, cool, and "hip."[58]

Of course, not everyone was born cool, but it was a state of mind that could be cultivated. At mid-century, Los Angeles's beach cultures offered entrée into this universe. From Venice beatniks to Malibu surfers, the various tribes that populated the region's beaches all refused to bend to dominant social norms and cultivated a more immediate relationship to the body and nature. This phenomenon had actually started before the Second World War. In the eyes of the press, the first Californian surfers of the 1920s and 1930s already formed a separate group with its own relaxed, in-tune-with-nature lifestyle. But the establishment of a third Beat scene in 1950s Venice—following those of New York's Greenwich Village and San Francisco's North Beach—was even more consequential in spreading contrarian ideas among local beach bums. In the early 1950s, Venice's cheap rents and proximity to the beach attracted artists and misfits who wished to abandon the pretense of bourgeois respectability and live according to their own rules. Venice was, as Beat poet Lawrence Lipton famously called it, "a slum by the sea," and thus the perfect place to distance oneself from the materialism of the mainstream society. Within a few years, Venice became a magnet for young West Coast bohemians and influenced the local surf culture. By the time Lipton published *The Holy Barbarians*, his account of the Venice Beat lifestyle, in 1959, the phenomenon was attracting widespread interest nationally. Before too long, the beats became the "beatniks," a popular culture stereotype symbolized by sandal-wearing, bearded young men who played the bongo drums on the beach. Even *Life* sent a reporter to Venice in 1959 to investigate the "rebellion of the beatnik." This kind of richly illustrated photo essay cemented the association in the contemporary imagination between the region's beaches and the nonconformism and romance of a bohemian lifestyle.[59]

It was not necessary to become a full-time Beat or surfer to stay young, but by embracing the beach bums' distinctive marks one could achieve something akin to youthfulness. Tanned skin, sandals, and rumpled clothes for the Beat; cut-off jeans, wool Pendleton shirts, and a surfboard hanging out the back of a "Woodie" for the surfer—these were signs of a young and hip lifestyle. "This active, youthful styling," as the *New York Times* explained to its readers in 1964, could be adopted "by the trimly-built man of any age."[60] As for Remi Nadeau, who skeptically eyed the new beach tribes, there was no question that the adult surfer considered surfing "a holdover from his youth." By 1965, the phenomenon of older, respectable adults taking up surfing and the style of dress associated with surfers was becoming increasingly visible. As "one tanned and bearded young man" told a journalist on Hermosa Beach, "The white collar types are taking over. Surfing is becoming too damned respectful."[61]

By the mid-1960s, looking and acting young had become something of a prerequisite for beachgoers, young or old, male or female, ordinary citizens or presidents. As such, John F. Kennedy's 1962 visit to the Santa Monica Beach fully conveyed his energetic and independent personality and his youthful state of mind.[62] When President Richard Nixon, himself a California native, attempted a similar move in January 1971, he failed to generate the same reaction. While on vacation at his San Clemente home, Nixon was photographed strolling on Trestle Beach in Orange County. Arranged by his team to commemorate his fifty-eighth birthday, the photo op, with its beach background and his dogs in the shot, was intended to give the president a relaxed, yet dignified air. The setting seemed ideal, but the picture was a failure: Nixon was immortalized walking stiffly on the beach while wearing a tie, a dark windbreaker, black pants, and wingtip shoes, "which, at one point," the *Los Angeles Times* mockingly noted, "were soaked by the surf."[63] Nixon had made the mistake of not respecting the dress code and hip insouciance demanded by the environment. His photo, in contrast to Kennedy's, only emphasized his age and clumsiness. The failed photo op was in keeping with Nixon's general distaste for anything that smacked of youth rebellion. When presented with a Hobie surfboard by his daughters on Father's Day 1969, the president reportedly said the board "didn't impress him a bit, and that he might end up giving it to his press secretary."[64] Elected to restore law and order, Nixon did not need, or wish, to adopt the traits of the hip youth.

The obsession with being young and cool was a key theme of 1960s beach movies. It featured in the title of one of its first iterations, *For Those Who Think Young* (1964), directly inspired by the Pepsi slogan. Even more important, it was conveyed through the constant physical and stylistic transformations of adult characters into more youthful versions of themselves. In *Beach Party*, Professor Sutwell (played by Robert Cummings), the bookish anthropologist who observes the young surfers, is easily distinguished from his subjects of study by his long beard, glasses, bow tie, and gray suit. After what he calls his "first contact" with his study group, Sutwell seems to take stock of his outdated looks and asks his assistant whether he is "an old man." Despite his age, Dee Dee takes an interest in him, hoping that Frankie will get jealous (and he does, calling Sutwell an "overaged fuzzy-face"). Taking Sutwell under her wing, Dee Dee decides to turn him into an attractive, fashionable man. Armed with an electric razor, she suggests he gets rid of his beard because he has "such young eyes and such an old chin." Once clean shaven, the professor is not only "the coolest" in Dee Dee's eyes but, as he declares himself, a "whole new me." Having "gone native," the professor has regained his youth and rushes off to kiss his young assistant, who was secretly in love with him all along. In *How to Stuff a Wild Bikini* (1965), a similar rejuvenation takes place. Two advertising executives dressed exactly the same in black bowler hats, three-piece suits, and ties arrive at the beach in search of someone to be the face for a new motorcycle. They stand in sharp contrast with the group of surfers wearing colorful swimsuits. Infatuated with Dee Dee, the younger of the two executives returns to the beach the next day, this time wearing casual beach clothes and looking much younger. He claims he finally feels like "the real me." In both films, the transformations serve as a humorous reminder of the generation gap that contrasted parents raised in the Depression and their carefree children. The scenes also reveal the power of the beach and surf culture to cure academic stuffiness (for Professor Sutwell) and the stifling conformity of corporate culture (for the young executive).

The idea that the world of beach bums could offer entrée to a more exciting, youthful life was hardly unique to Hollywood. Portraying the encounter of an uptight character, a "square" in the parlance of the time, with the liberating world of the Beat community or the surfing culture was a recurring theme in novels of the period, starting with *Gidget*. By taking up surfing, flat-chested, "nice girl" Francine becomes "the Gidget," a much cooler (and tanned) version of herself. In Allison Lurie's *Nowhere City* (1966), East Coast history professor Paul Cattleman makes a much smoother transition to life in sunny, sprawling Los Angeles than his headache-prone wife (at least initially), thanks to his chance meeting with artist Ceci, who initiates him to the alluring world of the Venice Beats. Paul soon adopts the Beat look, sporting "dirty clothes, sandals, beard almost two days old," and hangs out in the community's hip coffeehouses. While he may not look younger than his wife, who refuses to go to the beach and spends hours locked in their dark bedroom recovering from sinus headaches, he is definitely "in the thick of it."[65]

In a society obsessed with youthfulness, the beach provided an inexpensive fountain of youth. There was no need to even go to the seashore: all that was necessary to live a "young" lifestyle was to sport a tan and toned muscles and to display the latest fashionable accessories, whether sunglasses, sandals, or surfboards. As Nixon's beach stroll exemplified, not all adults were infatuated with the beach youth subcultures. But for those who wished to bridge the generation gap, putting on a swimsuit and getting a tan was a quick and easy trick to shed a few years. As long as the destabilizing elements of the youth beach culture were kept at bay—promiscuous girls, surf Nazis, and unemployable Beats—an older generation could freely sample its rejuvenating powers.

ACTIVE, DISCIPLINED BODIES

Being young, or at least looking young, was only one of the many injunctions that weighed on postwar beach bodies. All LA beach bums worth their salt also needed to be tanned, thin, and muscular and know how to best accentuate their assets by striking the right pose. This was true not just at the shores but in all public and private spaces. Whether donning shorts for high school P.E. or lounging by the neighbors' swimming pool, Angelenos knew better than to expose pale skin and flaccid muscles. Yet the summertime migration to the shores remained the ultimate test, especially starting in the 1950s, when women's magazines turned getting a "summer body" into an annual ritual. By then, glancing at other people's bodies on the sand had become part and parcel of the seaside experience. The "visual pressure" of the beach, as one anthropologist phrased it, heightened the stakes. In Los Angeles, where Hollywood had turned the shores into a favorite location, the pressure to look good was more intense than anywhere else.[66]

Such a devotion to the body beautiful often raised eyebrows and occasionally elicited outright disgust. Take the reactions to a photograph of five Muscle Beach bodybuilders published in the January 1951 issue of *Life*. Shown wearing tight briefs and flexing their biceps, the five men were mocked in the accompanying text for "carrying the body cult from the sublime to the absurd." Clearly, the *Life* journalists were unimpressed by such a display. So was Ludie Irene Lindsey, a reader from Fort Worth, Texas, who sent a letter to the editor, printed in the next issue, criticizing this "vulgar display of brawn." But it was undoubtedly another reaction that says the most about the primacy of the body beautiful in Southern California's beach culture. Charles Flynn, a subscriber from Pawtucket, Rhode Island, felt compelled to send a photograph, reprinted in the journal, to "show . . . West Coasters how the east coast youth enjoy themselves at the beach."[67] In stark contrast to the tanned and brawny Muscle Beach athletes, Flynn's black-and-white snapshot showed eight men of medium build—one of them with a visible paunch protruding from his T-shirt—lounging lazily on the beach while drinking cans of beer. In this reader's mind, this was a far more relaxing way to spend an afternoon at the beach. The two photographs highlighted the transitional status of the muscular body in the 1950s, when it had yet to become a marker of respectability and sexual appeal for middle-class heterosexual men.[68] More importantly, this juxtaposition drew attention to the growing distance, both physical and metaphorical, between Southern California and East Coast beach bodies. On the East Coast, the beach experience was associated with idleness and relaxation. In contrast to the strict discipline that regulated bodies at the office and in the factory, going to the beach meant freeing one's body from social prescriptions and sartorial rules. In Los Angeles, going to the shore was a serious matter, requiring bodies to be appropriately groomed, shaped, and clothed for the viewing pleasure of others. Far from a place of carefree indolence, Southern California beaches called for active, disciplined bodies.

Of course, not all Angelenos went to the same lengths as Muscle Beach bodybuilders. But if there was one ritual that they indulged in without restriction it was tanning. The desire for sun-kissed skin began in earnest in Southern California in the 1930s, but it became a true essential in the postwar era. According to Nadeau, refusing to tan amounted to "a sacrilege against the sun-god." "Nor is it acceptable," he wrote—in a style that mimicked that of a tourist guide describing an exotic land—"to punch an umbrella in the sand, unless you are one of the old folks. Beach umbrellas . . . are considered an obvious insult to the sun." Overall, Nadeau insisted, "you must exhibit some evidence of the outdoor life" and avoid looking like you "just got off the train." "Even if you are not a beachgoer," he warned, "the possibility of being invited over to a neighbor's pool is a powerful incentive to get a tan." In sunny Los Angeles, where opportunities to disrobe were legion, sporting the external signs of a beachgoing life, whether one actually frequented the seaside or not, was associated with success and happiness.[69]

Tanning in postwar California, then, was a serious affair. Young women coated themselves with a mixture of baby oil and iodine—a recipe that guaranteed a uniform tan. For young Angelenos, the goal was clear: to become as "dark" as possible. At Santa Monica High School, as alumna Merry Ovnick remembers, it was crucial to have the most tanned legs in gym class. Sandra Odor, who lived in Burbank but spent many afternoons at Santa Monica Beach in the 1950s, also remembers that "everybody wanted to be tanned." Even going too far was considered "cool": having peeled skin on one's nose or wearing zinc oxide on it—a common practice among surfers—ensured popularity. Sun-bleached hair was another sought-after marker of an active beach lifestyle. Some high school girls smeared fresh grapefruit or lemon juice on their hair before going to the beach so that it would turn blonde in the sun.[70] Achieving the right look required a genuine devotion to beach life. William Asher, AIP director and producer, claimed he had recruited most of his *Beach Party* films' extras on Malibu beaches because, he insisted, the only way to get such a tan is "to live on the beach."[71]

To be sure, the tanned look was not to everyone's taste. In Alison Lurie's *The Nowhere City*, New England native Katherine, who struggles to adapt to Los Angeles and doesn't like "the sun shining all the time in November," contemptuously observes the "muscular people in bathing suits" walking on the sidewalk, "most of them burnt to the colour of furniture." When she meets her husband's colleagues, she notices a woman whose tan is "so deep that her features were almost invisible." But her husband, Paul, quickly becomes a convert. After a few weeks in Los Angeles, he finds his pale wife "not attractive." "Maybe," he notes, "his standards of comparison had changed—the good-looking girls here were all deeply sun-tanned, outdoor types, glowing with light and life." Yet by the end of the novel, Paul returns to Boston, disillusioned by the superficiality of LA, whereas Katherine, who has found love and purpose at UCLA, decides to stay. Her skin is now "brown," and her hair is blonde, although not dyed, she insists, "only bleached by the sun." In *The Nowhere City*, suntanned skin becomes a metaphor for one's ability to acclimate to the region and its strange denizens.[72]

Of course, the ability to transform one's skin color from fair to brown was a privilege only white bodies could claim. In that sense, Brown and Black Angelenos could never quite acclimate to Los Angeles and sport the deep tan in vogue at the time. At the beginning of the twentieth century, tanning had given wealthy white tourists in exotic locales an opportunity to put on the skin of the racial other. Historian Catherine Cocks writes that "pale-skinned people's suntanning constituted a kind of 'brownface,' a playful experiment in becoming nonwhite that stemmed from, encouraged, and literally embodied a renovated relationship between civilization and nature."[73] Domesticated by Angelenos, who worked hard to achieve the ideal golden glow, "brownface" constituted a form of social capital tinged with exoticism. Like the Hawaiian dresses and shirts of the 1960s, tanning evoked the enticing, erotic, and mysterious world of the South Pacific. Yet the more it became associated with "Californian" blondness, the less it was linked to the racial other. While Black Angelenos could not change their skin color to take part in this trend—lightening skin products remained popular with African Americans throughout the 1960s—some did organize

"Hawaiian luaus," strum on ukuleles, don floral shirts, and dance the Conga. In 1957, for instance, a chapter of the Black sorority Alpha Kappa Alpha turned Santa Monica's Deauville Club into a "little Hawaii" (complete with palm branches and a diving show) to host the Black fraternities of Kappa Alpha Psi and Alpha Phi Alpha.[74] Going skin deep may not have been possible, but many Black Angelenos engaged actively with the beach culture's exoticism.

Another characteristic of Southern Californian beach cultures was the premium placed on thin bodies and taut muscles. In the 1950s and 1960s, the beaches of Los Angeles were a mecca for those looking to sculpt their bodies. Surfing, beach volleyball, and swimming were not simply fun pastimes but ways for people to work on their physical appearance. For those who did not want to ride the waves, other sporting activities abounded. Beach parties offered the perfect opportunity to play volleyball, baseball, or badminton; cities also organized numerous sporting events, such as the annual Santa Monica Sports Festival, launched in 1962, which took place largely on the sand.[75]

While sports initiatives and equipment existed on other city's beaches, only Los Angeles had Muscle Beach, an internationally famous site for bodybuilding and acrobatics.[76] Located on Santa Monica Beach immediately south of the famous recreation pier, Muscle Beach earned its reputation during the New Deal era. A popular place to come and admire impromptu demonstrations of acrobatics and human pyramids, the place was unique in bringing together a diverse range of performers—professionals and amateurs, male and female, old and young, all dedicated to the pursuit of the perfect routine. In 1940, the city-sponsored shows featured the "leading acrobatic gymnasts of the country" and included varied numbers such as "hand balancing, strength demonstrations, the adagio, tumbling, flying ring exercises, ring muscle exercises, and bar exercises."[77]

Acrobatics remained an essential component of the Muscle Beach activities throughout the 1940s and 1950s, but the site achieved national fame with the arrival of a contingent of bodybuilders and weightlifters in the immediate postwar years. Previously, weights had often been used at the beach, including by women, but they had mostly been a means to an end: building up one's strength in order to perform more spectacular tricks.[78] In the postwar period, the display of muscular physiques prevailed over acrobatics, at least in the media coverage of the phenomenon. Some of the newcomers, such as Steve Reeves and George Eiferman, who won the Mr. America title in 1947 and 1948, respectively, were bona fide stars in the world of bodybuilding. Their beach workouts were publicized in physique magazines such as *Health & Strength* and *Muscle Power*, which led

Figure 5.2. The wooden platform at Muscle Beach, circa 1947. *Los Angeles Daily News Negatives* (Collection 1387), Library Special Collections, Charles E. Young Research Library, University of California–Los Angeles.

to the arrival of an even greater number of weight-training fans to Santa Monica. Seymour Koenig, a wrestler who came to Muscle Beach in 1952 at age eighteen, recalled that it was through these magazines that he heard of the beach and decided to leave his native Brooklyn to try his chance out west. Eventually, a weightlifting pit was added south of the platform to accommodate the newcomers, and a weightlifters' club was established in 1955. In 1957, it boasted nearly one thousand dues-paying members.[79]

By the early 1950s, Muscle Beach was, in the words of Ralph Story, a Los Angeles television personality, "an institution," "a civic landmark."[80] Held on the Fourth of July, the Mister and Miss Muscle Beach contests

Figure 5.3. Gymnastics apparatus at Muscle Beach, circa 1947. *Los Angeles Daily News* Negatives (Collection 1387), Library Special Collections, Charles E. Young Research Library, University of California–Los Angeles.

(begun in 1947) attracted up to five thousand spectators. The site grew so popular that it inspired imitations like the Venice Beach Athletic Center, which hosted its own "Mr. Venice" contest.[81] More than just a local attraction, Muscle Beach earned national acclaim. "Practically every American ha[d] seen or heard of Muscle Beach," claimed *Strength and Health* in 1957, "because, like Brooklyn, it is standard joke equipment for wise-cracking comedians of stage, screen, TV and gossip columns from Coast to Coast." According to an oft-recounted legend, this stretch of beach was so famous that you could "mail a letter from anywhere in the world to someone at Muscle Beach, USA," and it would arrive to its addressee.[82]

The pursuit of the body beautiful at Muscle Beach held a unique fascination. The athletes' hard work clashed with people's expectations of what a beach afternoon was supposed to look like. Most beach lovers, explained journalist Joel Sayre, went to the ocean to enjoy a variety of pleasures: "casual swimming and wave riding, acquiring a tan, snoozing off a hang-over, gossip, picnicking, letting the kids blow off steam, playing a little volleyball, sizing up the pretty girls, and so on." But the pleasures of Muscle Beach athletes "[were] not precisely those that most people go to beaches for." According to Sayre, the regulars were "too serious and too busy for such frivolous pastimes," and Muscle Beach itself "serve[d] far less as a beach *per se* than as a unique three-acre, open-air gymnasium." All commentators agreed that such dedication to the body was both admirable and excessive. Self-discipline was key to becoming a respected member of the tribe. Many regulars had started learning acrobatics from as young as three and exercised every single day. Some, like veteran coach Barney Frey, "concocted special vitamin pills" and stuck to a rigorous diet.[83] Others had careers in professional sports and strove to reach their maximum potential, while those dreaming of a Hollywood career sculpted their bodies accordingly.[84] Whatever the ultimate goal, the results were astonishing, as exemplified by extraordinary stories like that of Dave "Hymie" Schwartz. Once a "physical wreck weighing but 85 lbs. as a result of yellow jaundice and malaria contracted . . . during the war," the young man had worked assiduously for three years at the beach to turn himself into an accomplished weightlifter.[85] The beach was a place for fun, but it also functioned as a site where one could parlay one's body into a career or overcome bodily ailments.

Like surfing, beach acrobatics and bodybuilding spoke to contemporary anxieties about the decreased level of youth fitness and rising numbers of heart attacks among adult males.[86] Unlike the strongman phenomenon of the early twentieth century, which relegated spectators to be passive admirers, Muscle Beach was a place where participation was encouraged. The site offered a weekly schedule of classes, including "Adult Body Building Instruction" and "Children Apparatus Instruction."[87] Similarly, the Venice Athletic Center offered opportunities to take up weightlifting. According to the local newspaper, it was the ideal place where "the head of the house, if he's threatened with a pouch, can tighten flabby muscles and trim off pounds."[88] In fact, the beach park benefited from the growing obsession with "reducing." TV shows that encouraged weight loss, such as KTLA's *Waistline Miracle*, came down to the beach to document the athletes' techniques for shedding extra weight. According to legend, Muscle Beach regular Abbye Stockton (nicknamed "Pudgy" since childhood due to her weight) had slimmed down in only a few months thanks to her daily exercise at the beach. By the late 1940s, she was the figurehead of American women's bodybuilding and touted the merits of strength training for women in a monthly column in *Strength & Health*. The athletes' exceptional physiques were the most effective advertisements for sports and exercise. Certainly, many who strolled past Muscle Beach were inspired to pick up dumbbells. That was how the site recruited new regulars—a process detailed in Ira Wallach's 1959 novel, *Muscle Beach*. The protagonist, Carlo Cofield, newly arrived from New York City, describes his reaction to seeing the bodybuilders on the beach: "I felt suddenly puny. My quite respectable biceps blushed and hid behind my skin. My chest, with which I have lived in harmony for years, appeared grossly inadequate."[89] Later, Cofield takes up weightlifting and throws himself fully into the bodybuilding lifestyle.

While the hard bodies on display at Muscle Beach inspired many Angelenos to lift a barbell, others were confused or even repulsed by the sight of women with visible biceps and well-oiled men wearing skimpy briefs. Throughout the first half of the twentieth century, "physical culture," as it was initially known, was perceived as a strange, seedy subculture practiced mainly by inmates and gawky adolescents. Lifting weights

Figure 5.4. The winners of the Mr. Muscle Beach contest in 1951. Bodybuilders were often photographed next to beautiful women looking adoringly at their biceps. *Los Angeles Herald Examiner* Collection, University of Southern California Digital Library.

was done in private, if at all. In fact, in the 1940s and 1950s, physicians still disagreed on the necessity of exercise and how strenuous it should be.[90] In addition, caring excessively for one's appearance—as bodybuilders seemed to do—was perceived as an act of vanity or, worse, a telltale sign of homosexuality. In the 1950s, the multiplication of pocket-size magazines targeting a gay readership and using physical culture as a cover increased the suspicions surrounding musclemen.[91] Muscle Beach bodybuilders did not escape speculation. In a 1951 *Life* article on the phenomenon, the journalist noted that the bodybuilders "flexed their muscles for their mutual admirations," hinting at the athletes' potential homosexuality.[92] Moreover, at a time when traditional gender roles and norms, including the male breadwinner, were being reinforced, male athletes were often denounced for shirking social expectations. "What do the muscle men do for a living?" wondered a Santa Monica journalist in a column. "'As little as possible,'" he noted disapprovingly.[93]

The men of Muscle Beach walked a thin line between adhering to and challenging gender norms. Both the press and the athletes sought to downplay the disturbing connotations attached to muscularity. In a veiled reference to homosexuals who might try to infiltrate the beach, *Strength & Health* claimed that any member of the Muscle Beach weightlifting club "who prove[d] to be a liability" was excluded.[94] The press also chose photographs that paired musclemen with beautiful women looking adoringly at their biceps. Women, either as contest judges or groupies, guaranteed that muscles would be interpreted in a heteronormative context. Moreover, to prevent any attempt at appropriating the bodybuilders' bodies for the visual pleasure of gay men, journalists emphasized the heterosexual appeal of the musclemen. "Why should men have all the fun looking?" remarked a journalist, thus insisting on the fact that the shows were reserved for the visual pleasure of women only.[95] The musclemen themselves insisted on their success with the ladies. In interviews, they claimed that "girls parade[d] up and down" in the Muscle Beach vicinity and eagerly accepted dates, including those who initially made fun of the men's bulging biceps.[96]

Conversely, the female athletes at Muscle Beach quite literally upset the period's gendered hierarchies when they were pictured supporting two or three men on their shoulders. The media occasionally chastised the female athletes who used barbells in public, as strength remained a masculine quality. In a portrait of Beverly Jocher, a sixteen-year-old who had "grown up at the beach," a journalist explained that she could "skate, run, swim, dance and lift weights but, he wondered, can she sew?"[97] Jocher had to be reminded of what truly lay at the heart of women's role in the American society: marriage and family life.

Although they challenged society's conventions and most physicians' advice, Muscle Beach women who lifted weights fascinated the public. Photographs of pretty blondes and brunettes handling heavy barbells offered a study in contrasts. But for female muscularity to be palatable to the wider public, it had to be domesticated. Athletes toned down their muscularity by posing with their children or next to their equally strong boyfriends. The shapely young women who paraded on the Miss Muscle Beach stage dressed and wore their hair in conventionally feminine styles.

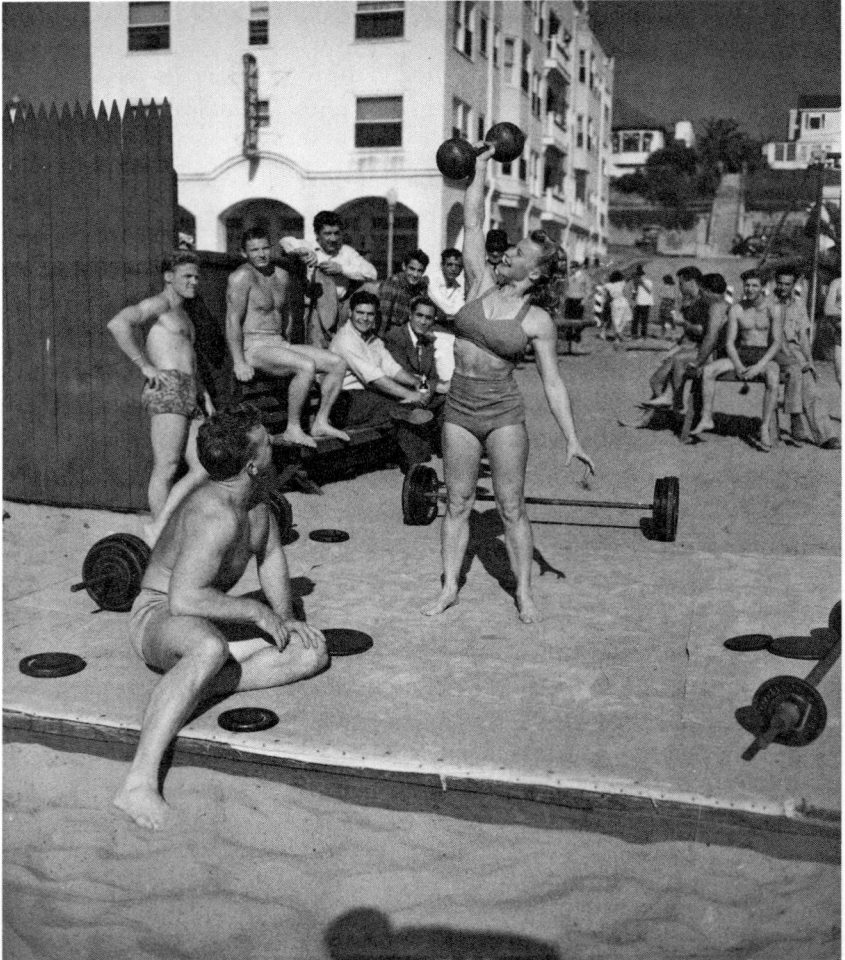

Figure 5.5. Abbye "Pudgy" Stockton with her admirers at Muscle Beach, circa 1947. *Los Angeles Daily News* Negatives (Collection 1387), Library Special Collections, Charles E. Young Research Library, University of California–Los Angeles.

Many were Hollywood models who collected beauty queen titles on the side, and all boasted ideal bust, waist, and hip measurements. As a TV reporter sent to cover Miss Muscle Beach 1954 explained, the winner had to "combine beauty with muscle," but there was a clear understanding that the "emphasis [was] on the beauty."[98] Once married, Muscle Beach women actually made for "gentle and devoted wives," explained one article. Marilyn Thomas was one of them. Despite her busy training schedule, she "k[ept] the house and cook[ed] all the meals." Ultimately, the women of Muscle Beach conformed to most of the dominant expectations of their gender. If anything, working out at the open-air gymnasium made them more feminine. Yet by showing off their strength in public and juggling babies with their fitness goals, the women of Muscle Beach projected an alternative model of femininity that reconciled muscles with sex appeal, marriage, and motherhood.

Void of its dangerous connotations, muscularity offered a ticket into the glamorous world of California beaches. From this point of view, the popularity of Muscle Beach, where bodies previously confined to prison gyms and working-class garages were displayed in public, marked an important step in the muscular body's entry into modern visual culture.[99] In a very real sense, the thousands of Angelenos who watched the annual Miss and Mister Muscle Beach contests were participating in the creation of new beauty standards, accelerating the process whereby the muscular body came to be not just acceptable, but desirable.

BODIES ON DISPLAY

Whether they found the bodies of Muscle Beach bodybuilders attractive, funny, or "vulgar," passersby were drawn to the beach stage. With its raised platform and bleachers, Muscle Beach directed observers' gaze toward the beauty on stage. The phenomenon was not entirely new; beauty pageants had been taking place on the sands since the 1920s. But from the 1940s on, it seemed as if all beachgoers, not just beauty contestants, were putting their bodies on display. As "Hollywood starlets who sun[ned] themselves at resorts frequented by movie directors and producers" knew all too well, "beach-lolling" was not "an idle pastime." Attracting the right attention to one's figure could potentially make one into a star.[100]

The attention of spectators was crucial for Muscle Beach regulars. Most of them did not train on the beach itself, but in gyms near the beach.[101] There they found spaces in which to perform the most physically arduous of exercises. According to bodybuilder Armand Tanny, the beach was reserved for lifts that required less concentration.[102] Muscle Beach was more important as a space where one could meet likeminded athletes and exchange information about local sporting events or the latest diet fad. Most importantly, it offered regulars the chance to be admired and photographed.

Many photo enthusiasts frequented the Muscle Beach stage. For photographers like Cecil Charles and Artie Zeller, the site served as a launching pad for careers in fitness and sports photography.[103] Others, including internationally recognized professionals such as Richard Avedon and Max Yavno, used Muscle Beach as an opportunity to document the California look, "an ideal of tanned, taut, and well-toned bodies." Both photographers are remembered for the iconic shots they snapped there: while Avedon focused his lens on a strong man holding up a toddler using solely the strength of his erect arm, Yavno captured the beach crowds milling around the stage, contrasting the passive, pudgy bodies of the spectators with the fine, toned bodies of the acrobats in the background.[104] Muscle Beach and Venice Beach also served as a playground for amateur photographers. Beginning in 1951, the City of Los Angeles organized annual "photography days" on Venice Beach. Contestants had three hours to take photographs based on one of the themes suggested: "bathing beauties, pretty senoritas, barnyard animals, weightlifting muscle men, statues, beach and shaded-dell scenes, and wild animals." The beach, then, regularly doubled as a photography studio, with the city literally putting a dozen pretty young women in bathing suits at the disposal of budding photographers.[105]

For the cities of Santa Monica and Los Angeles, the bodies displayed on the beach were a veritable boon. In 1954, a local journalist claimed that the Muscle Beach athletes "have gained for Santa Monica worldwide recognition. . . . As a publicity medium, it's invaluable and gains magazine, film, radio and TV time and space that it would be impossible for the city to purchase." In a short film shown to prospective travelers by United Airlines, "one full minute [was] devoted to the acrobatic activities at Muscle Beach."[106] Likewise, the fame of Santa Monica's lifeguards, who often staged lifesaving demonstrations on the beach, drew positive media attention to the city. It was even claimed that after four articles in *Life*, two short films, and five MGM movies on the lifeguards, the city could dispense altogether with its fifty-thousand-dollar advertising budget.[107]

Muscle Beach athletes, surfers, and lifeguards were not shy about posing for the camera, as a winning shot could attract the attention of Hollywood producers. By the 1950s, several Muscle Beach habitués, such as gladiator film actor Steve Reeves and television's fitness expert Jack LaLanne, had hit the big time. Their stories encouraged Hollywood hopefuls who entered the

Mr. and Miss Muscle Beach contests yearning to be "discovered." The local press contributed to spreading this reputation, reporting in 1951 that a representative from 20th Century-Fox Studios had requested the telephone numbers of the winners of the Miss Muscle Beach contest.[108]Although less famous than Reeves and LaLanne, many other regulars belonged to the movie world. Acrobats Russ and Pattie Saunders, for instance, were "in constant studio demand for their stunting virtuosities." Bodybuilders were also sought after. In 1954, Mae West raided Muscle Beach to recruit nine musclemen for a series of shows across the country.[109] Literally in Hollywood's backyard, Muscle Beach was a place where one could potentially approach celebrities or become a star oneself. Its regulars weren't the only ones with cinematic ambitions. Surfers too could hope to parlay their skills and physiques into movie roles. In 1966, for instance, the Los Angeles Times profiled Mary Lou McGinnis, a twenty-four-year-old "movie starlet surfer" who kept her figure svelte and her skills sharp with a specific goal in mind: to land the endorsement of one of the many companies looking to cash in on teenage enthusiasm for the surfing trend.[110] She hoped to follow in the footsteps of famous predecessors, from legendary Duke Kahanamoku to "bad boy" Miki Dora.

Hollywood could not get enough of the postwar beach bums. In turning their camera toward the Pacific, filmmakers perpetuated a long tradition of using the local beach scene as a source of inspiration. William Asher, who directed several of AIP's 1960s beach teenpics, readily admitted that his films were "updated versions of Mack Sennett's bathing beauty silents."[111] As one beach film after another reached the screens nationwide, the beauty standards of Hollywood increasingly projected those of LA's beach devotees. Prewar corporeal prescriptions and beauty standards were already tilting in favor of young, thin, and tan bodies, but these expectations intensified as the American visual landscape was crowded with surfers, bodybuilders, and their bikini-wearing admirers. Blond hair and a healthy glow were no longer enough; sun-bleached hair, a golden-brown tan, and a toned body were the sought-after markers of a modern, Californian lifestyle. In the early 1960s, Los Angeles's beach bums dictated the beauty criteria of the day.

———

In the postwar era, the Los Angeles coastline became a central theater of performance for subcultures that reshaped notions of beauty, masculinity, and femininity. A visit to the shores was a guarantee to get an eyeful. Other coastal regions also harbored self-styled beach bums and beauty queens.

But the Southern California beach culture was distinct in that it combined strict body discipline and sultry hedonism. In that sense, the postwar beaches morphed into outdoor factories, sculpting "beach bodies" for the immediate consumption of onlookers and, eventually, television and film audiences.

To be sure, not everyone in Los Angeles was happy with the casual display of seminaked bodies on the beach, as beautiful as they might have been. Throughout the 1950s, a number of residents disparaged the Muscle Beach athletes, particularly the bodybuilders. The "muscle heads" were criticized for their unnatural physiques, for blurring the "natural" distinctions between men and women, and for doing nothing all day apart from making a spectacle of themselves. Despite the growing centrality of a morality of pleasure and self-conscious display within postwar American culture, a conservative faction of the American middle class still prized the values of work and modesty. According to the anti–Muscle Beach crowd, the athletes' unhealthy "exhibitionism" was also attracting "undesirables" to the beach and cheapening the general atmosphere of the area. In 1958, Muscle Beach's critics scored a major victory when the open-air gym was shut down and the shows cancelled on the pretext that five Muscle Beach habitués had been accused of sexual misconduct. As it happened, not all beach bodies were welcomed on the modernized shores of Los Angeles.

CHAPTER 6

༄

Who Has the Right to the
Modern Beach?

Ocean Park was not like other beaches. In the early 1950s, this one-mile section of Santa Monica Beach was exceptional in its concentration of alternative uses of public space, marginalized communities, and various illegal and semilegal activities. To many visitors, Ocean Park was synonymous with its most famous attraction: Muscle Beach. To others, Ocean Park was home to Bay Street Beach (also known as the Inkwell), an informally segregated beach located a few hundred yards from Muscle Beach that had provided a safe haven for African American beachgoers since the early twentieth century. To others still, Ocean Park was known as the home of Los Angeles's unofficial gay beach, also known as Crystal Beach, where old-fashioned bathhouses and ramshackle bars served as vibrant spaces of sociability for gay men and women. Finally, marking the border between the city of Santa Monica and Venice was the Ocean Park Pier, a traditional amusement area where semilegal games of chance sat alongside the usual carnival attractions. The geographic convergence of these activities and groups was no coincidence. As a multiracial and working-class neighborhood of Santa Monica, Ocean Park served as a buffer zone between the lavish houses of movie stars and private beach clubs up north and the declining beach resort of Venice farther south. While few white and straight beachgoers were aware of all the facets that made Ocean Park unique, most agreed that its vibrant atmosphere set it apart.

By 1958, these worlds had ceased to exist. Within a few years, the City of Santa Monica had erased Ocean Park's alternative communities

OCEAN PARK - 1955

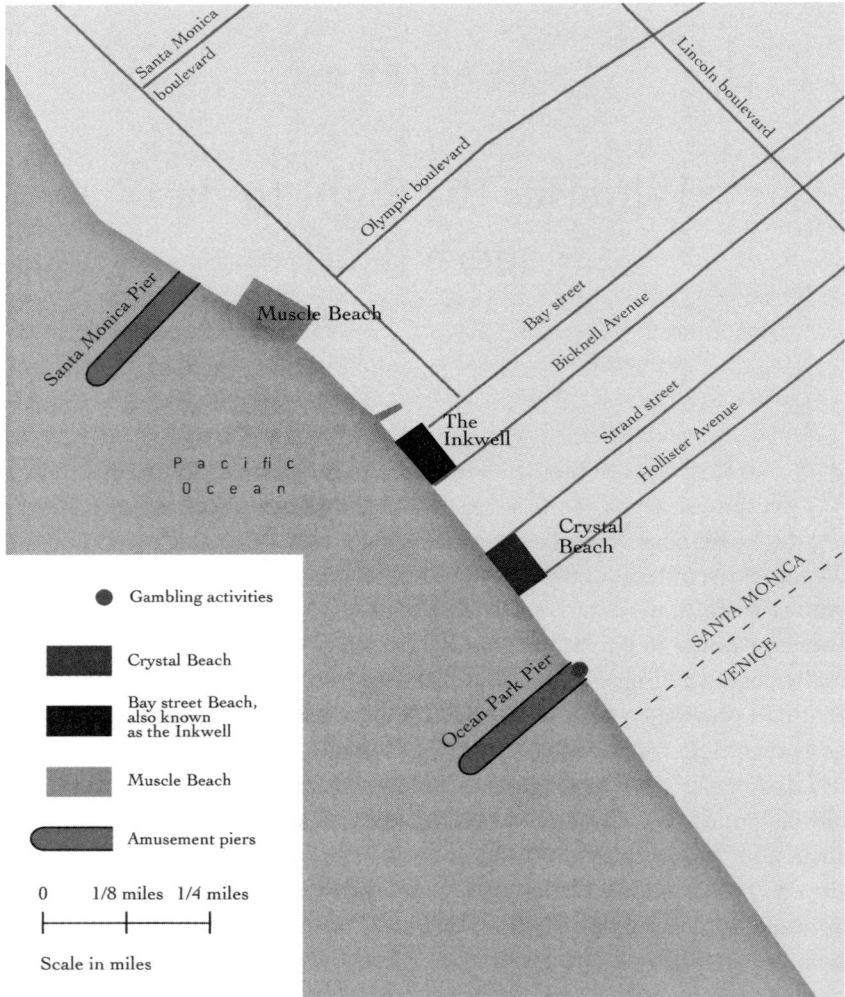

Figure 6.1. Map of Ocean Park in the mid-1950s. © Clémence Devienne

and illegal activities from the map. The Muscle Beach equipment was destroyed, Crystal Beach's gay bars and bathhouses had been raided, and the gambling parlors were closed. As for Bay Street Beach, its existence was challenged through a combination of different strategies, including seizure by eminent domain. As the Ocean Park "clean-up" was ongoing, city officials and local real estate interests planned for Ocean Park's "rebirth," envisioning gleaming high-rises with ocean views. Although they only partially succeeded in implementing their plans, their efforts left a lasting imprint on Ocean Park.

The object of massive investment, the coastline played an important role in the competition between cities and suburbs to attract middle-class residents and public and private capital in the 1950s and 1960s. Just as inner-city neighborhoods deemed blighted were subjected to "urban renewal" in an attempt to prevent white flight to the suburbs, so too were Los Angeles beaches "modernized" to keep the "respectable public" on the shore. The consequences of this process were keenly felt in Ocean Park, where certain groups of beachgoers—Muscle Beach athletes, Crystal Beach homosexuals, Afro-Angelenos, and the young and working-class crowds that frequented the amusement area—were forced to seek refuge on other shores.

This chapter uses Ocean Park to show how local urban elites—the public officials, businessmen, and engineers who made up the beach lobby—joined forces with self-proclaimed defenders of morality to "clean up" the coast from "undesirable" elements. Indeed, this alliance's dual agenda of urban renewal and reinforcing the gender and sexual norms undergirding the nuclear family met with startling success.[1] By removing Ocean Park's alternative beach cultures, Santa Monica officials delivered a victory to the city's conservatives and offered a clean slate for private interests. This process was not isolated to Santa Monica's beaches. Throughout the region, the modernization campaign was accompanied by increased surveillance and regulation of behavior on the sands. In the hour of the beach lobby's triumph, the scope of what was allowed on the shore was narrowing.

CLEANING UP OCEAN PARK

The Ocean Park clean-up was embedded in major demographic, ecological, economic, and cultural developments taking place at both the highly local level and the national level. The impulse to transform Ocean Park's amenities and the type of visitors attracted to this beach was part and parcel of a larger phenomenon that historian Andrew Kahrl dubbed "coastal capitalism." As coastal engineers grew more confident in their abilities to tame and shape the shoreline in the postwar decades, private and public investments in coastal communities soared. Across the nation, shores were promptly divided up into bathing beaches, oceanside residential developments, and urban marinas, boosting the real estate market and entire regional economies.[2] In Santa Monica, the coastline had always been at the center of the business elite's growth strategy for the city—whether as the ideal site for Los Angeles's commercial and industrial port in the late nineteenth century or as a resort when that initial plan failed. By the 1950s, Santa Monica's coastal capitalists held high hopes that the allure of a newly widened beach would hasten the city's transformation from a mere LA suburb into a multifunctional urban center. Standing in the way of this bright future were the dilapidated hot-dog stands, seedy bathhouses, suspicious "bridgo" parlors, and other subpar beach facilities scattered along the shoreline.

Ocean Park figured high on the list of beaches requiring an upgrade. In the late nineteenth century, tobacco manufacturer Abbot Kinney had developed Ocean Park as a popular tourist resort. Modeled after Coney Island's famous amusement parks, Ocean Park Pier offered thrill rides and sideshows to tourists and day trippers. Once an independent municipality, Ocean Park was eventually annexed by the neighboring City of Santa Monica.[3] Over time, as North Santa Monica attracted private beach clubs, Hollywood types, and wealthy residents, Ocean Park became a low-income residential neighborhood for commuters as well as a major entertainment zone for the entire region. By mid-century, Ocean Park was a hodgepodge of oceanfront motels, food and drink concessions, cheap apartment-style buildings, and old-fashioned beach bungalows. According to geography student Richard Stapleton's 1952 study, attendance at recreational facilities along the Ocean Park shoreline was high, but the area was "not attractive, for a dirty and crowded appearance prevail[ed]."[4] More concerning, Ocean Park's dilapidated urban landscape seemed to attract sleazy and criminal characters. According to a 1968 report, the neighborhood had long suffered from the "highest concentration of crime . . . in the city."[5] On the pier, gambling concessions masquerading as "games of skill" proliferated, despite regular police raids.[6] Hollywood also promoted Ocean Park's amusements as places of shady dealings and moral degeneration, in such films as *T-Men* (1948) and *Quicksand* (1950). Despite this beach area's bad reputation, its function as a buffer zone between the affluent section of Santa Monica and the declining neighborhood of Venice—which was part of the Los Angeles municipality—meant that the City of Santa Monica left it untouched throughout the 1930s and 1940s. For a while, gambling had persisted in other parts of Santa Monica, most famously on gambling boats such as the S.S. *Rex*, which was anchored just off the coast and was closed down following an epic police raid in 1939. But by the 1940s, gambling was done on land, and as long as it was contained within its limits, Ocean Park was simply ignored.[7]

In the 1950s, however, Santa Monica civic leaders started to investi-gate the possibility of using federal funds to clean up Ocean Park. Since the 1920s, when Santa Monica had resisted annexation by the municipality of Los Angeles, the city had prided itself on its independence, its exclu-sive atmosphere, and "its own 'personality' due . . . to the pleasant social background of open air sport and recreation."[8] Throughout the 1930s and 1940s, Santa Monica had teetered on the brink of seediness. Noir author Raymond Chandler best described Santa Monica's duality in *The Lady in the Lake* (1943). Bay City (the pseudonym for the town in his detective novels) was "a very nice place" with "a very nice jail," and "a very nice city hall," but it was also home to "waterfront dives . . ., sweaty little dance halls, . . . mari-juana joints, . . . and pimps and queens on the board walk." During the war, the city's rapid demographic growth prompted the adoption of the council-manager form of government in 1946. According to the *Evening Outlook*, the local newspaper, such a change allowed the city to be run "on a busi-nesslike, rather than political basis."[9] The change galvanized the local busi-ness elite. For the Santa Monica Chamber of Commerce, which had close connections to the council and *Evening Outlook* editor Robert E. McClure, it presented the opportunity to finally realize the full potential of the city.[10] In 1957, the city's new Master Plan reflected the local leaders' ambitious vision for the beach community. Recommended projects included making the city the western terminus of the projected freeway from Downtown Los Angeles, rebuilding city hall, and renovating the commercial zones and recreational areas.[11] Ultimately, civic leaders hoped to establish Santa Monica as a major economic, residential, and cultural center of the metro-politan region, thus avoiding the sad fate of floundering beach resorts such as Venice.

The question of Ocean Park's future first emerged during the Santa Monica municipal elections in the spring of 1955. Two candidates, Baptist pastor Fred Judson and twenty-seven-year-old lawyer Rex Minter, denounced the "laxity and apathy in law enforcement" on Ocean Park Beach. They accused Mayor Tom McDermott and Police Chief Hubert W. Hutchinson of turning a blind eye to the numerous "Bridgo" parlors—the popular gambling stands on the pier. The candidates also exposed the beaches' homosexual activity, previously hidden from public view.[12]

The string of establishments between Hollister and Strand had catered to a gay clientele since at least the 1940s. In the 1930s, several Ocean Park bathhouses suffered from neglect, and middle-class beachgoers started avoiding them. At the same time, erosion caused by the construc-tion of the Santa Monica yacht harbor diminished the beach's appeal. As the area became less reputable, it attracted a new clientele of men and women looking for same-sex sexual partners. A not-so-subtle sign of the beach's popularity as a cruising ground were advertisements on several of the aging bathhouses for "nude sun baths." By the early 1940s, some in-the-know beachgoers referred to the strand by suggestive names such as "Bitches Beach," "Queer Alley," or "Queens Beach." But most people called it "Crystal Beach" due to its proximity to Crystal Pier, which was eventually demolished in 1948 as part of the county's Master Plan of shore-line development.[13] According to the local newspaper, Crystal Beach was subjected to police scrutiny when several gay bars and taverns opened in the 1950s.[14] The threat to society posed by the gay beachgoing community was heightened amid a Cold War atmosphere in which any challenge to the heterosexual nuclear family model was perceived as a direct attack on American values. The anti-homosexuality hysteria led to purges in government employment in Washington, DC, and police raids on gay and lesbian establishments across the country. In LA, Chief of Police William Parker became famous for his unrelenting harassment of gays and lesbians. Police raids usually happened just before or after elections, and the Ocean Park situation proved no different.[15] Initially using vague terms for the "immoral situation at our beaches," the political candidates employed more pointed language during a March 1955 debate, when they accused the city council of "fostering and protecting homosexuals." More specifically, Reverend Judson criticized the police for refusing to enforce an ordinance, which, according to him, not only authorized the closure of establishments where "sex perverts" congregated, but also banned "dancing with a member of the same sex and impersonation of the opposite sex."[16] In reality, Parker and his police hounds were more than happy to repress cross-dressing and other behaviors associated with homosexuality, but California and LA courts were more liberal and often pushed back on arrests made on those grounds.

Despite the focus of the election appearing to be morality, the underlying issue was Ocean Park's economic future. Until that point, the Santa Monica City Council had favored a pragmatic policy, tolerating gambling venues and other dubious activities so long as they remained in the circumscribed limits of Ocean Park and brought visitors' dollars to the city coffers. This did not satisfy Minter and Hudson, who proposed a vastly different vision. In the words of Minter—the more ambitious of the two candidates—Ocean Park was "the logical place for development." Hinting at the availability of federal funding, Minter claimed that "we can have beautiful hotels and apartments here with the aid of the state." But in order for Ocean Park to become the "resort city" he proposed, undesirable elements had to go.[17]

In April 1955, Minter and Judson both won seats on the city council and proceeded to make good on their promises. Several anti-gay police raids were conducted on Ocean Park beach establishments over the next few months, resulting in over two hundred arrests. One of the most aggressive raids took place in December on the Rendezvous Ballroom, a popular dance-hall and bathhouse, where eleven men were arrested. The establishment was closed, and the owner's commercial lease revoked. Yet officials deemed these measures insufficient. A few years earlier, the dilapidated Crystal Beach bathhouse, which used to face the Rendezvous Ballroom, had been demolished as part of a shoreline modernization program.[18] Razing the Rendezvous Ballroom as well would simultaneously ensure the definitive elimination of an undesirable situation and advance the modernization objectives of city officials. Over the next few years, these objectives became so closely intertwined as to be virtually indistinguishable.

Raids resumed with renewed vigor in 1956, following the murder of a ten-year-old boy named Lawrence Rice by serial killer Stephen A. Nash. Nash had met his prey on the beach and offered him a burger and soda before luring him under the Santa Monica Pier, where he undressed the boy and stabbed him.[19] In the eyes of city officials, the crime was inextricably connected with Crystal Beach. Postwar "sex crime panics" conflated the activities of sexual criminals and gay men who engaged in consensual sex.[20] Rice's murder reinforced this association between homosexuality and deviancy when Nash admitted to having sexual relations with men. In fact, a local police officer went so far as to claim that, "while the average homosexual was as indignant over the murder of little Larry Price as anyone else, any one of them under a given set of circumstances [wa]s capable of murder."[21]

In the minds of city officials, the crime was also linked to the "blight" on the oceanfront. In a virulent editorial in the *Evening Outlook*, Robert McClure, who supported the council's aggressive stance toward homosexuals, demanded a "lasting cleanup" of the beachfront and "upgrading of the Ocean Park amusement zone as well as the carrying out of a long-range beach improvement program." Cleaning up meant both the literal demolition of inferior buildings and the metaphorical destruction of the Crystal Beach underground gay world. Over the following months, several bars and bathhouses accused of catering to "sexual deviants" were closed and bulldozed.[22] Other measures also served the twin purposes of infrastructure improvement and policing. For instance, Santa Monica's city manager justified the installation of lighting in nearby Palisades Park by explaining it would "make the park much brighter and easier to police at night, thereby depriving undesirables of one of their favorite hunting grounds . . . [and] improve the appearance of Ocean Avenue and make it safer for pedestrians."[23]

The conflation of modernization and policing continued during the next two years, when the council ordered the demolition of most of the eighty concession stands on Ocean Park Pier, including the Bridgo parlors that had garnered such criticism during the 1955 election, and the closure of the famous Muscle Beach playground.[24] Unlike Muscle Beach's controversial shutdown, however, the decision to renovate Ocean Park Pier was fairly consensual. In February 1957, nostalgic throngs took their final outings to enjoy the rides and games on the pier. By July of the following year, Pacific Ocean Park, a nautical-themed park dedicated to "wholesome family pleasure and relaxation," opened its doors to the public.[25]

CLOSING DOWN MUSCLE BEACH

The new theme park faced serious competition from the weekend shows at nearby Muscle Beach. Tolerance of Muscle Beach declined following the murder of Lawrence Rice. As panic spread among Santa Monica's parents, a cloud of suspicion fell on the entire Ocean Park Beach area. In a letter published by the local newspaper just a few days after Nash's arrest, a woman testified to witnessing "on nearby Muscle Beach . . . a bearded fat man attired in a scanty G-string pick up two 11-year-old girls and go off the beach with them." In light of the recent election debates and Rice's murder, the once-beloved athletes were perceived in a different light. The police issued a declaration that the playground had to close, and vice squad officers were sent to infiltrate the Muscle Beach crowd. Around the same time, the city council announced its decision to raze the Muscle Beach bathhouse (also known as Pounds Bathhouse), located next to the playground platform. The athletes were outraged that the decision had been made because of rumors that the establishment was "a hangout for deviates." The city's general manager immediately denied the rumors and emphasized that the destruction of the building "had been considered for over a year as part of the beach redevelopment plan." In this case, beach modernization served as moral and legal justification for eliminating establishments deemed suspicious by the local authorities.[26]

The beginning of the end for Muscle Beach came in 1957, when the city council announced its ambition—as part of the recently approved Master Plan for the city's beaches—to build four new beach parks, one of which would become the new and improved Muscle Beach.[27] Moving their stage to a new location, farther south from the Santa Monica Pier, was strongly opposed by athletes. The pier, they argued, protected them from wind and brought tourists and onlookers to the platform. The issue was raised during several city council meetings in 1958, but by the end of the year, no clear resolution was in sight.[28]

In the summer of 1958, the Mr. and Miss Muscle Beach beauty competitions took place as usual and weekend shows continued. On December 16, five bodybuilders were arrested for sexual misconduct against two African American girls, ages twelve and fourteen.[29] Four of the men were charged with sexual misconduct, while another was charged with a misdemeanor involving the possession of photographs of male nudity. According to the victims' testimonies, the girls had met the athletes on the beach before going to a nearby beachfront apartment and a motel where the crimes had taken place. Although the activities had not happened on-site and incriminated only a handful of the Muscle Beach regulars, the famous playground was immediately blamed. Within a few days of the arrests, the Santa Monica City Council decided to close down Muscle Beach. A pile of dirt was dumped on the site to deter athletes from coming back.[30]

Using the scandal as a pretext for getting rid of an attraction they had long despised, a coalition of conservative citizens led by Councilwoman Alys Drobnick, editor Robert McClure, and Police Chief Otto Faulkner campaigned for the definitive elimination of the playground, arguing that it "attracted bad elements to the area."[31] In the pages of the local newspaper, they accused the performers of attracting "perverts" or, worse, of harboring "sex deviates" who partook in "sex orgies."[32] While other city councilors held more nuanced opinions, noting that "you could not blame [it] for the whole morals problem on the beach," the anti–Muscle Beach coalition proved adept at dominating the public conversation about the affair. By publishing the angry letters of local residents, McClure kept the Muscle Beach issue in the spotlight throughout the following year.[33] The arrests thus provided the anti–Muscle Beach coalition with the opportunity to reshape the narrative on the beach and its habitués, despite all charges against the bodybuilders being reduced or dropped due to lack of evidence.[34] In reframing Muscle Beach as a hangout for "drifters" and sex offenders, they reactivated prejudices against muscularity that had been dormant during the playground's golden years.

One indication that muscular prejudices shaped the treatment of the affair was the narrow focus on weightlifters and bodybuilders, rather than on all the athletes who came to the beach. According to Police Chief Faulkner, the Muscle Beach problem could be solved through the "elimination of the weight-lifting element."[35] Similarly, Adela Bower, chairman of the city's Recreation Commission, insisted that "the weightlifting phase of Muscle

Beach should be minimized."[36] Two of the five men arrested were indeed weightlifting champions. But the divide between weightlifters and acrobats at the site was less clear than these detractors indicated. Many acrobats and gymnasts used weights to build up strength, and some musclemen occasionally took part in acrobatic acts.[37] Yet this nuanced understanding of Muscle Beach activities never made its way into the newspapers. The focus on "musclemen" became so intense after the incident that cracks started to appear within the usually tight-knit Muscle Beach community. According to the *Evening Outlook*, some gymnasts and acrobats were considering asking the city "to oust the weightlifters in order to retain other facilities [at the site]." Two days later, the city announced that the site's closure "only applied to the weightlifting platform and that other activities might continue."[38] Considering that a large pile of dirt had rendered the site inaccessible, it was unclear how acrobats were supposed to go back to their activities. The announcement ultimately served the purpose of further dividing the athletes and demonizing musclemen.

The strategy worked. A few days after the arrests, following a two-hour hearing attended by more than one hundred people, the city council voted to keep Muscle Beach closed pending an in-depth study of what Police Chief Faulkner termed the city's "terrific sex deviate problem."[39] A year later, the inauguration of the new and improved Muscle Beach—a few yards south of the original location—revealed the city's determination to keep bodybuilders and performers away from the beach. As a "family-style outdoor gym area under strict municipal supervision," Beach Park No. 4— the playground's official name—had little in common with its predecessor. Three supervisors were on duty at all times, and no performances of any kind were permitted. In contrast with the multigenerational and multiracial crowds that had gathered on the Muscle Beach platform, the *Los Angeles Times* pictured white children playing on the new beach under the watchful gaze of their mothers.[40] With its run-down equipment, disheveled crowds, and informal shows, Muscle Beach did not fit the vision of the modern beach that the beach lobby expounded.

FAREWELL TO THE INKWELL

In 1958, another incident occurred in Santa Monica's Ocean Park neighborhood, one barely noted by the press. In May 1957, Black entrepreneur Silas White acquired the old Elks Club building located on Ocean Avenue, just a few yards from Bay Street Beach—the Inkwell.[41] While the police had tried to impose segregation on the beach in the late 1920s, this practice had ceased following a 1927 wade-in organized by the local National Association for the Advancement of Colored People (NAACP).[42] African Americans still favored the area, which probably provided them with a feeling of safety from potential violence.[43] Silas White's idea was to offer an exclusive experience to those middle-class African Americans who could afford the fees at his proposed Ebony Beach Club. Two months after White acquired the site, the City of Santa Monica used its power of eminent domain to purchase the building, claiming it needed to provide parking spaces for the nearby civic center. White protested the decision by erecting a giant sign on the building accusing the city of racial discrimination, but in November 1959 the city won its case in court.[44] In the meantime, the city had gone ahead with the construction of a two-thousand-car beach parking lot just south of Bay Street.[45] As for the parking lot that was intended for the Ebony Beach Club site, it never materialized. More likely, the city feared that an African American beach club would have increased and further institutionalized the Black population's presence at Bay Street Beach. As a city boasting peaceful race relations—municipal brochures featured African American children learning to swim—Santa Monica may well have viewed Bay Street Beach as an uncomfortable reminder of the nation's segregationist past. Moreover, the goal of beach modernization was to impose order and homogeneity on the shoreline. Bay Street Beach, with its concentration of Black bodies on the sand, represented a blatant incongruity. By building a huge parking lot nearby, the city ensured that many white beachgoers would patronize the beach. Combined, the two decisions contributed to the slow erasure of Los Angeles's historically Black beach from the map. In contrast to the bloody riots that erupted when Chicagoans desegregated their beaches, Bay Street Beach's slow disappearance from Angelenos' consciousness was remarkably uneventful. Yet it was effective. By the 1960s, African Americans had stopped going to the Inkwell.[46]

By the end of 1958, Ocean Park could be reborn. The marginalized, alternative beach cultures of Muscle Beach, Crystal Beach, and Bay Street Beach had no place in a new coastal regime that was clean, orderly, and homogeneous. Of course, the decline of these cultures was also linked to the repression of all forms of social and sexual nonconformity that marked 1950s America. The imposition of restrictive rules governing how beachgoers comported themselves contributed to the development of a moral geography of the beach that underpinned the economic exploitation of the coast. The Ocean Park clean-up was the price to be paid to attract the key demographic in the age of coastal capitalism. Over the next few years, city leaders, working together with private interests, used federal funds to reinvent Ocean Park as the preserve of the white nuclear family.

Figure 6.2. The building where the Ebony Beach Club was set to open, photographed by Lolita Lowell. Santa Monica History Museum, Gilmore Family Collection.

REBUILDING OCEAN PARK

On December 30, 1964, almost a decade after Rex Minter announced his intention to clean up Ocean Park and turn it into a "resort city," as the city's mayor he presided over the groundbreaking ceremony for Santa Monica Shores.[47] Facing Pacific Ocean Park, the two seventeen-story towers were the first step of an ambitious redevelopment program in which city officials and their partners in the private sector envisioned a beachscape of elegant high-rises with ocean views where once there had been cheap apartments and dilapidated concession stands. Santa Monica Shores thus symbolized the victory for the new urban elites who advocated for a growth strategy for the city. The towers were part of a national trend in which developers transformed fragile coastlines into "vacationlands" using federal subsidies and work programs.[48]

The first concrete step toward construction of the towers was the 1957 creation of the Santa Monica Redevelopment Agency (SMRA), a public body in charge of drafting urban renewal plans for the city.[49] The passage of the Federal Housing Act in 1949 gave a boost to large-scale redevelopment projects in "blighted" urban areas by providing federal funding for parcel acquisition. In 1954, a new law expanded the types of projects that the funds could address. Across the country, local elites jumped on this opportunity to redevelop old neighborhoods at low costs, often setting their sights on working-class and multiracial areas. Santa Monica was no different. Composed of five members appointed by the mayor, the SMRA was to be advised by the Santa Monica Citizens' Progress Committee (SMCPC), a group of fifty "community leaders" appointed by the city council and mayor. The composition of the two bodies reflected the entanglements of local business elites—particularly from the real estate industry—and city officials. Among the five members of the SMRA were two former or current members of the city council and several members of the city's Chamber of Commerce, including a prominent real estate agent. The SMCPC included many lawyers and bankers, several of whom would later join the city council.[50] At the Santa Monica Shores' groundbreaking ceremony, ten shovels were handed symbolically to representatives of the city, the SMCPC, the two companies involved in the project, and the local business community.[51] The photograph of the men and one woman—Audrey Carver, chair of the SMCPC—posing with their shovels was a striking image of the common vision that animated the city's political and business elite.

In 1958, the SMRA designated a 45-acre beach strip in Ocean Park as its first redevelopment project. With 78 percent of the neighborhood's structures deemed "substandard," the area had reached "a point of no return," noted the SMRA. Its objective was thus to "return this prime urban land to its highest and best use."[52] By demolishing the area's blighted apartments and replacing them with upscale high-rises, the SMRA estimated the real estate value increase at forty million dollars. The first part of the project, called Project I(a), was to be essentially residential in nature and would provide eighteen hundred units, while Project I(b) would be developed later for commercial purposes. In 1961, thanks to a two-and-a-half-million-dollar loan approved by the Federal Housing and Home Finance Agency, the SMRA started purchasing land designated as "blighted."[53] Later that year, the Kern-Webb consortium—a joint venture between the Del E. Webb Building Company and the Kern County Land Company—was selected out of eleven private redevelopers to build eight high-rise apartment buildings, a shopping center, and a motel on the 26.3 acres encompassed by Project I(a). Over the next two years, the SMRA bought the land parcel by parcel and cleared it of all existing structures and streets. In 1965, the Kern-Webb partnership bought the title to a 20-acre segment on which Santa Monica Shores would be built.

As a Phoenix-based company with experience in building suburban developments, campuses, hospitals, and high-rises in the Southwest, Webb played a significant role in defining the architectural characteristics of the built environment in the emerging Sunbelt. Influenced by modernist and functionalist aesthetics, Webb favored the use of concrete slabs and luxury features. Commercial and recreational spaces were systematically integrated in Webb's residential projects so that inhabitants would not have to leave the building for their daily needs.[54] Santa Monica Shores followed these principles. Although architect Walton Becket claimed to have included "the traditional informality of the oceanfront within the framework of bold contemporary architecture," it was hard to tell exactly where this "informality" lay. With their "wall-to-wall carpeting, built-in kitchen, private balcony, and unobstructed view of the ocean," the apartment units catered to middle- and upper-class professionals. The towers also included a post office, delicatessen–snack bar, liquor store, beauty parlor, and a three-level underground parking garage, to provide "a total environment that solved [the residents'] daily requirements."[55] The towers provided all the benefits of living by the ocean without any of the drawbacks of life in a "substandard" neighborhood. At the Shores' private pool, residents could also perfect their tans and enjoy the ocean view without ever having to set foot on the sand. Finally, a nine-hole golf course fronting the towers served as a buffer zone between the private world of the Shores and the public world of the beach.

Figure 6.3. The Santa Monica Shores, circa 1983, photographed by Dean Musgrove. *Herald Examiner* Collection / Los Angeles Public Library.

The towers were initially deemed a success. In November 1967, even though construction was not yet finished, 70 percent of the 532 apartment units were already leased by people from across Los Angeles and Orange Counties. The following year, Webb received a prize for its "creative use of concrete" at the Santa Monica Shores.[56] This complex was only the beginning. On the remaining parcels of land, the developers that took over from the Kern Company planned on building eight twenty-nine-story towers with 522 apartments and eight hundred parking spaces, a high-rise hotel, and a twenty-story condominium.[57]

In subsequent years, the redevelopment project's popularity diminished. For many locals, the prospect of seeing Santa Monica transformed into the "Miami of the Pacific," a concrete playground for the elite, was not a happy one. At the same time, the displacement and relocation of residents forced to leave their Ocean Park dwellings was widely denounced. By the late 1960s, the beach modernization project was being radically challenged on a variety of fronts: by the emerging modern environmentalist movement, by coastal property owners in revolt against beach acquisition, and by a growing contingent of city-dwellers appalled by the destruction and heartache left in the wake of renewal projects.

Be that as it may, the mood in Ocean Park had changed. Oceanview properties were increasingly the preserve of the upper classes. The construction of the two Santa Monica Shores towers effectively excluded many low-income residents from the neighborhood. Moreover, the alternative beach cultures that gave this section of the coast its vibrant atmosphere had been moved or had disappeared altogether. Muscle Beach bodybuilders, for instance, found the weightlifting area in the more tolerant Venice, a few miles farther south, to their liking. In fact, Venice, home to "the rebellious, the nonconformist, the bohemian, the deviant among the youth," welcomed many of the "undesirables" Santa Monica no longer wanted on its beaches.[58] Everywhere else, surveillance increased and took on new forms.

LAW AND ORDER ON THE POSTWAR BEACH

Too large to be properly policed, beaches had long benefited from a more tolerant legal regime than the rest of the city's public spaces. But the postwar obsession with juvenile delinquency, the emergence of a conservative discourse on law and order, rising crime rates, and the city's growing demographic diversity combined to transform local officials' relationship to the coast. At the local level, urban renewal policies brought an increasing number of affluent residents to the shores, which had a knock-on effect on beach policing. Against the backdrop of a ballooning coastal real estate market, any beachgoer who threatened the sensibilities of local property owners was vulnerable to being stopped and questioned by the police.

From the early 1950s on, the presence of young people on the sands was the central concern of coastal officials and residents. With the surfing craze and the growing popularity of Spring Break, new laws were passed to rein in beach bums and to limit the extent of the lawless areas that formed on the sands. Paradoxically, this period of strict surveillance coincided with the height of the beach movie craze. While the rest of America was imagining Gidget and Frankie and Annette—the famous heroes of the *Beach Party* movies—dancing around a nighttime bonfire, Southern California officials were doing everything in their power to limit just that sort of activity.

By 1950, a number of laws were already in place restricting beachgoers' behavior. Alcohol was generally prohibited in parks as well as on beaches. Similarly, with exception of Zuma Beach and Playa Del Rey, building a fire on the beach was strictly forbidden. Some beaches were closed at night, but this was not an absolute rule. The bongo-drumming beatniks were likely relieved to learn that Venice Beach was exempt from a countywide night curfew passed in 1960. On balance, prohibitions and penalties varied greatly depending on the location; urban beaches such as Venice, where local residents included renters and low-income homeowners, were not as strictly regulated as those situated in upscale neighborhoods. Yet between the early 1950s and the late 1960s, the trend was toward standardization. Moreover, the growing presence of young people on the coast led local officials to systematically strengthen regulations concerning alcohol, fire bans, surfing, and nighttime beach closings.

At Zuma Beach, for instance, the county adopted a string of strict regulations targeting surfers in 1960. The beach fire ban was intended to put an end to their wild parties, which left the beach in such a state that "the crews couldn't get it cleaned up in time for the Sunday crowds." That same year, the county decided to ban access to the beach between midnight and 6 a.m. Yet the ordinance, which initially made it illegal for people to "come into and remain" on the beach, could potentially affect the activities of early risers and fishermen, "individuals who engaged in legitimate recreational pursuits." County lawmakers quickly fixed this initial wording and made it illegal to "loiter" on the shore.[59] In doing so, they defined the beach as the exclusive territory of the nuclear family and banned what they considered to be illegitimate forms of recreation.

It is difficult to evaluate whether the passage of these new laws reflected an increase in juvenile vandalism on the shore. Certainly, postwar youth were more numerous, more visible to adult society, and more mobile than ever. Although crime rates were also increasing elsewhere in the city, the popularity of rock 'n' roll appeared to provide a ready-made explanation for rising crime on the beaches.[60] The best example of this blame game took place in 1961, when a "grunion derby and beach ball" publicized by local radio station KRLA devolved into chaos. Held on Zuma Beach, the event attracted more than ten thousand young people and resulted in what the press called a "near-riot."[61] According to police officers and lifeguards, fights broke out toward the end of concert. At 11:30 p.m., with the crowd not clearing and officers beginning to fear a riot, the sheriff decided to call for backups. When fifty police cars arrived, the crowd dispersed, and fourteen young people were arrested.[62] County Parks and Recreation Department director Norman Johnson believed the radio station acted recklessly by heavily promoting the concert but giving no thought to how many people might show up. He also accused the concert promoters of deliberately ignoring existing regulations: how could it organize a grunion run (grunion are sardinelike fish that rush to the sandy shores at night during spawning season) "when the beach, by law, must close at 12 midnight and the grunion were scheduled to run at 2:30 am"? As a result, the county introduced stronger measures regulating beach gatherings. Thereafter, organizers would have to file a written application with the county and sheriff to obtain a permit, as well as provide a certain number of monitors, including possible private security. County officials made clear that their intent was not to "penalize groups or organizations such as church societies or boy scouts who may want to use our beaches in an orderly manner." The sheriff would be free to decide how much security was needed based on the type of event. Here, too, enacted measures were intended to exempt "respectable" leisure practices.[63]

Other measures reflected a different strategy: confining the troublemakers to a specific part of the beach. The establishment of surfers-only beaches in the early 1960s flowed from this logic. Although officially set up to avoid accidents, officials also saw them as an opportunity to control the surfers more closely and to cut down on the "excessive noise, vandalism, and various crimes" attributed to them.[64] These schemes were not always considered sufficient. In 1966, Newport Beach began to require surfers to buy annual stickers to affix to their boards if they wanted to surf on the city's beaches.[65] Surfing groups came out against the law, which they considered unfair and discriminatory. According to Vince Moorehouse, city director of Harbors and Beaches, Newport Beach's true intention was not to fight against surfboard theft, as the municipality claimed, but to "control . . . the antisocial activities of a small number of beach attendants."[66]

A surfer had to give his name and address when buying a sticker, which allowed the city to put together a list of potential delinquents. Requiring stickers also kept the number of surfers on the beach to a minimum. Many surfers only visited Newport Beach once or twice a year; for them, the (admittedly modest) price of three dollars was not worth the expense. In this way, the municipality defined its beaches as a family-friendly space rather than as a surfers' hangout.

Newport Beach had a long history of regulating beachgoers. The city had been a popular Spring Break destination since the 1930s, attracting students from across the region. Throughout the 1940s, when year-round residents were few and absentee homeowners collected high rents from students, residents had tolerated Spring Break. By the 1950s, the situation had changed as the number of year-round residents increased and working-class youths joined the students in the festivities. In 1958, the Newport Beach homeowners' association was formed with the explicit goal of limiting the number of young people who came to party on the beach during Easter break. Under pressure from local homeowners, the police started systematically enforcing curfew laws, fire bans, and nighttime closures.[67]

At the same time, Newport Beach officials developed innovative measures for controlling rowdy spring-breakers that spread rapidly throughout the region. In order to crack down on alcohol consumption, for example, the city created a motorized police patrol in 1958 to supervise the beach; it also developed one of the first "plain clothes"—or in its case, swimsuit—patrols to monitor the sands.[68] Their casual attire—some wore T-shirts, while others sported swim shorts or rode bicycles—allowed them to catch violators by surprise without worrying other beachgoers. Equipped with binoculars and high-performance video cameras, they were nicknamed the "mole patrol" by locals.[69] Soon, Hermosa Beach followed suit; the "disguised" patrol of ten officers wearing sports clothes was first deployed during the 1958 Spring Break season, before becoming fully integrated into the departments' day-to-day operations two years later. By the mid-1960s, most of the region's beaches boasted similar "invisible" patrols.[70]

Newport Beach also led the way in crowd control by modifying traffic patterns and street furniture to reduce congestion. During Easter Week, for instance, city officials removed the benches that normally lined the avenues to limit crowds.[71] Starting in 1958, the city decided to block all drivers without a special permit from crossing the only bridge to Balboa Island. The permit was only issued to members of the homeowners' association and to local businesses.[72] While the measure was originally conceived only to address traffic problems that arose each year during Easter Week, it was eventually extended to cover all peak periods, proof that the successful measures implemented for Bal Week led to a tightening of city regulations overall. In another Easter Week innovation, in 1965 the Balboa homeowners' association hired two private security guards to patrol the seaside boardwalk equipped with walkie-talkies. While the association claimed that the guards would only "supplement, not replace" police patrols, the decision was a harbinger of the use of private police by wealthy communities, a phenomenon that became ubiquitous throughout the region in the 1980s and 1990s.[73] In other words, Spring Break became a kind of laboratory for developing new crowd control measures, which were then adopted year-round and disseminated more widely.

The year 1960 was a turning point in the history of Spring Break in Newport Beach and in the neighboring communities of San Clemente, Huntington Beach, and Laguna Beach, which also received their fair share of spring-breakers. That year, Los Angeles County and Orange County high schools had the same vacation dates, so the residents of the beach resorts found their communities overridden with teenagers. Following this particularly tense Bal Week, ordinances multiplied, and the Newport Beach City Council began to crack down not only on young people but also on businesses that profited from Spring Break and landlords who rented their properties to them.[74] Landlords had to undertake an onerous application process to obtain a permit to rent their properties and were forbidden to rent them to more than five people who were not relatives.[75] Families, then, not partying students, were given priority. The new ordinances had teeth. In 1964, the owner of a Balboa apartment was arrested for renting her four-room apartment to sixteen young people.[76] At the same time, juvenile curfews were systematically applied, which led to mass arrests. In 1957, 334 youths were arrested during Bal Week; seven years later, that figure had more than doubled to 725.[77] This rise in arrests did not reflect an increase in juvenile delinquency. As one of the city's police officers bluntly put it at the end of the 1965 event, "We arrested the troublemakers before they had a chance to cause real trouble."[78] In fact, most offenses were minor: the vast majority of youth were arrested for violating the 10 p.m. curfew or on vague charges such as "lack of parental control."[79] Still others were arrested for alcohol possession, speeding, or trying to sleep in their cars.

The renewed vigor in applying existing decrees and the multiplication of new regulations eventually tempered young people's enthusiasm for spending their vacation in Balboa. From 1967 on, the number of university and high school students who traveled to the region's beach resorts during Easter vacations dramatically declined.[80] Some locals attributed the drop in spring-breakers to the political climate on American campuses. In the words of one business owner, "The kids were more fun-minded then [the

1930s and 1940s], less concerned with civil rights and demonstrations."[81] Others pointed to the lure of beach resorts that were more tolerant of youthful excess, particularly those of Baja California, Mexico, where the legal drinking age was eighteen. The few young people interviewed in the press blamed the increased police presence in Newport Beach. During Bal Week 1967, three young girls in bikinis recounted how they were stopped three times by the police on their way back from a party.[82] In fact, several factors came together to explain Bal Week's declining popularity. The steep drop in the number of seasonal rentals and the emergence of competing vacation destinations certainly played an important role. But Newport Beach's transformation from a small coastal town into an upscale residential suburb was the deciding factor. Wealthy, year-round residents simply did not want late-night parties or underage drinking in their midst. Their influence over local policing spelled the end of Bal Week.

"JUST ANOTHER VERSION OF CITY LIFE"

In the late 1960s and early 1970s, young people and surfers continued to attract the attention of the police, but not to the same degree. With soaring numbers of visitors coming to the beach, law enforcement had its hands full. In 1948, 2.8 million people visited Santa Monica Beach annually. Between 1960 and 1965, that figure increased to 15 million. On a summer day, over three hundred thousand visitors could be found enjoying the ocean there.[83] Many new bathers were African American and Latino. Indeed, the number of Black Angelenos increased rapidly during and after the Second World War, but in the immediate postwar years, Black bathers remained few and far between. Due to decades of residential segregation, most Black neighborhoods were located on the Eastside and Southside, far from the coast. Even when Black Angelenos did come to the beach, they usually stuck to Bay Street Beach, at least until the 1950s.[84] Similarly, most Mexican Americans lived on the Eastside and thus only occasionally came to the beach. Young Chicano men could also become the target of racial slurs and violence perpetrated by white bathers.[85] In the 1960s, coastal development challenged the status quo. Bay Street Beach gradually lost its identity as the historic Black beach of Los Angeles. With the 1966 opening of the Santa Monica Freeway, which connected the ocean to Downtown, it became much easier for residents of the Eastside and Southside to get to the beach.[86] Finally, immigration reform in 1965 led to an influx of immigrants from Latin America and Asia settling in the Los Angeles region.[87] By the early 1970s, the beach public was more diverse than ever.

These changes occurred at a time when soaring crime rates in US cities became a "national dilemma." Southern California had some of the highest rates in the country.[88] On the beach, local authorities also claimed that delinquency and crime were on the rise. The topic interested UCLA anthropologist Robert Edgerton, who decided to study public order on Santa Monica Beach, a remarkably quiet and serene public space compared to the violence reported in the rest of the city. Edgerton wanted to find out the reason for this discrepancy. In 1975, he sent some of his students to interview local lifeguards and beachgoers. While the book that he eventually wrote based on his investigation must be analyzed critically—he tends to show more empathy toward the (mostly) white lifeguards than toward Black and Latino bathers—it is an exceptional primary source that gives a voice to all the participants in the seaside order.[89] The book opens with the observation, largely shared by all lifeguards, that the beach was "less and less pleasant." All spoke of the "increasing intrusion of the 'city atmosphere'" since the inauguration of the freeway. The beach, they felt, was "becoming just another version of city life."[90] While rising crime rates could partially explain this impression, it was also inextricably linked to the increasing visibility of ethnic and racial minorities. Lifeguards systematically made a distinction between those bathers they called "the beach people" and "people from the inner cities." Such expressions, at a time when urban areas were becoming more starkly divided between "vanilla suburbs" and "chocolate cities," had obvious racial connotations.[91] While the "beach people," to whom the lifeguards felt closest, were white, the "people from the inner cities" were either Latino or Black. Using this coded language, lifeguards made distinctions between the behaviors of these different groups. "Beach people" "truly love[d] and respect[ed]" the beach, but there were fewer of them each year. Conversely, lifeguards felt that the number of Black and Latino beachgoers was increasing. The beach, they thought, was turning into "a melting-pot at the end of a freeway, a playground for people from the inner city."[92]

While this binary opposition was based on perceptions, it had a real impact on how lifeguards policed the beach. According to Edgerton, "Lifeguards who work[ed] in areas where there [were] large numbers of Chicano or Black beachgoers admit[ted] that they [were] often tense and uncomfortable."[93] Some of the immigrants who had recently settled in the region were not familiar with local rules and drank beer in front of lifeguards, who then interpreted such cavalier attitudes as a provocation. Moreover, lifeguards scrutinized nonwhite bathers more intensely and thus policed their behaviors more systematically. One of them explained: "We've been taught that you got to watch blacks and Mexican

Americans because of their poor swimming ability. So automatically when a group comes to the beach you just go, 'Oh,' and a mental image goes into your brain to keep an eye on those people."[94] This lifeguard thus candidly acknowledged the existence of differential treatments based on race and ethnicity on the beach. While paying more attention to nonwhite bathers did not matter so much when it came to lifesaving issues, it could have serious consequences for behaviors outside of the water. In paying closer attention to nonwhite beachgoers, lifeguards took part in the broader process of criminalizing urban space by more tightly regulating bodies and behaviors of minorities.[95]

Starting in the mid-1960s, the increasing visibility of ethnic and racial minorities on the beach, rising crime rates, and fear of gang violence led to a notable increase in the number of lifeguards and officers on the beat. Coastal cities also tried new policing techniques such as "camouflaged" units, mounted police, and beach uniforms of sneakers and shorts in the early 1970s.[96] These measures were meant to simultaneously make bathers feel safe and not frighten them since the presence of a police officer in a blue uniform or on a motorcycle was associated with city problems. A policeman in shorts or on a horse seemed calming and trustworthy. In the same spirit, in 1970, the county granted lifeguards—who benefited from a positive public image—the power to issue misdemeanor citations along the coast.[97] Most lifeguards, however, acknowledged that they lacked proper police training. In 1974, the City of Santa Monica responded to this common complaint by introducing motorized mixed units, including lifeguards and police officers, on the beach.[98]

These innovative measures responded to the contradictory demands of the beachgoing public. Most bathers interviewed by Robert Edgerton and his students claimed they felt safe on the beach, even women who came unaccompanied. Many beachgoers were not aware of beach regulations, and even when they were, they routinely violated them. In 1980, for instance, county lifeguards claimed that half of beachgoers brought alcohol with them.[99] Moreover, while bathers did see lifeguards in a positive light, they were often unaware of their citation powers. Interestingly, some interviewed in Edgerton's study went so far as to pronounce themselves against police presence on the beach because, the author claimed, "the sight of a police officer would make them think that there was something to fear, and would change the beach from a relaxing place to a tense one."[100] At the same time, many residents and beach homeowners fought for more police protection with a more visible presence on the beach. They wrote to their local city councils and newspapers asking for the strict enforcement of beach ordinances regarding dog leashes, brawls, and homeless people.[101]

Local authorities thus faced the impossible task of responding to such demands while making their activities and presence as discreet as possible.

The flexible approach adopted by local authorities reflected the selective application of written law to situations on the ground, which critically enabled police officers to make decisions based on the local context.[102] In Edgerton's study, many police officers claimed that they did not systematically enforce beach regulations. According to a female officer, enforcing laws against alcohol and marijuana use "would create more problems than it would solve."[103] Others talked of the right of visitors to enjoy themselves at the beach. Even the director of the Los Angeles County Department of Beaches freely admitted to a journalist that "[he himself] had drunk beer on the beach in the past." As for the lifeguards Edgerton interviewed, they all agreed that they would not be able to do their job—ensuring bathers' safety—if they had to enforce all municipal ordinances. The county officially condoned this attitude by encouraging lifeguards to "cope with problems in a 'low-key' manner [so as not to] alienate themselves from the citizens."[104]

By the 1970s, beach policing was intense but not necessarily as aggressive as it had been two decades earlier when the police chased gay men and surfers off the coast. The history of urban order cannot be understood as a linear narrative of increasing police surveillance. Rather, the period from the 1960s until the 1980s appears to be one of compromises, with the emergence of a "security contract" between bathers and the police, according to which minor violations were tolerated as long as security and good morals were preserved. While this flexible approach to law enforcement echoed the attitude adopted by the police in the 1930s, it actually responded to different "selection processes." It was not a choice made by default due to a shortage of staff. Santa Monica in the 1970s, for example, had eighty-seven lifeguards equipped with twenty lifeguard towers and four vehicles, including a dune buggy.[105] Coastal homeowners in the postwar period were wealthier and had more influence over the police's actions than they did in the 1930s. Finally, coastal municipalities did not depend on tourists' dollars anymore. On the contrary, many residents dreaded the arrival of summer crowds and the security problems that accompanied them. Policing the beach had become a balancing act, which consisted of preventing serious offenses—in particular thefts and sexual crimes—while tolerating minor violations. By turning a blind eye to visitors drinking alcohol on the beach, policemen and lifeguards sought to avoid needless confrontations and preserve the peace and quiet so many beachgoers loved. At the very least, that is how the authorities justified their flexible approach to law enforcement on the seashore. Tolerance toward violators was not evenly applied, however. Latino and Black beachgoers, groups of young males in particular, rarely benefited from such lenience.

—————

By the early 1960s, a few years after the Ocean Park clean-up, the mile-long beach was no longer the alternative space it had been, but neither had it met all the expectations of the anti–Muscle Beach crowd. Although the gay bars and bathhouses had disappeared from the landscape, gay men had returned, more visible than ever. In his 1963 semiautobiographical novel *City of Night*, author John Rechy described the "queens in extravagant bathing suits often candy-striped, molded to the bodies . . . , the masculine-acting, -looking homosexuals with tapered bodies and brown skins . . . , the older men [and] the male-hustlers," who peopled Crystal Beach. His portrayal reflected gay men's growing assertiveness in public space, a development connected to the emergence of a more aggressive gay rights movement.[106] The bodybuilders also returned, but they chose to settle in the more tolerant Venice, where their pit developed its own following. African Americans, however, never found another Bay Street Beach. In the late 1960s and 1970s, the number of Black and Latino beachgoers increased with the city's growing demographic diversity and the construction of the Santa Monica Freeway connecting the beach to the Eastside. By 1972, 15 percent of the people present on Santa Monica's beaches on a summer afternoon were nonwhite.[107] Increasing racial diversity on the beaches negated the need for an exclusive space. Yet, the end of Jim Crow beaches was not the logical and sole result of the end of segregation alone. It was also brought about by the systematic dispossession of Black coastal landowners. The story of Ebony Beach Club is a reminder of the necessity of challenging easy explanations for the disappearance of Jim Crow spaces.[108]

In parallel with the Ocean Park clean-up, increased police surveillance further restricted the type of activities in which beachgoers could engage. Depending on the period, surfers, students, homosexuals, and Black and Latino beachgoers were all subjected to varying degrees of police surveillance. Only Venice, which a journalist deemed "the last poor beach," remained a safe haven for marginal groups and bohemian types.[109] Everywhere else was a sanctuary for the middle-class nuclear family.

While the beach lobby was relatively successful in cleaning up the coast, the results were more mixed when it came to shoreline development. Resistance to the "Miamization" of the coastline was growing just as the modern environmental movement and demands for human-scale urbanism were on the rise. At the same time, the fates of other large-scale coastal development projects were called into question while the campaign to purchase beaches for the public experienced its first setbacks. The strong consensus behind beach modernization and acquisition that had reigned supreme for nearly two decades was falling apart.

CHAPTER 7

⚬⚬⚬

Ebbing Tides

Between the 1930s and the 1960s, a wide consensus animated the coalition behind the Southern California beach modernization movement. There were several interrelated components to this road map: acquiring beaches for the public, improving road infrastructure, curbing ocean pollution, enlarging beaches while fortifying the coast against erosion, cleaning up the shore of its decaying facilities and "undesirable" elements, and finally, building modern accommodations for the deserving beach public. Spurred on by the powerful beach lobby, the State of California worked in partnership with Los Angeles County and coastal cities to finance these projects. Coastal development and beach acquisition tapped into a deep reservoir of public support: after decades of hearing the beach associations' mantra that "beaches belong to everybody," Californians saw the shore as a democratic investment that had to be freed from the grip of private interests. Together they profoundly transformed the Los Angeles shoreline. Artificially widened, cleared of sewage pollution, accessible to the public, and dotted with modern restrooms and attractive athletic centers, the beaches were finally equal to the city's ambitions as a major metropolis. At the same time, large-scale development projects were underway along the Pacific.

Yet by the mid-1960s, the consensus behind beach modernization was itself eroding, in the process reshaping coastal residents' and homeowners' hopes and dreams for the shoreline and their communities. The rise of the modern environmentalist movement in the 1960s and 1970s profoundly challenged the development-friendly attitude of the traditional beach preservation associations. For the new crop of environmental activists inspired by the counterculture and the New Left, combining beach development with a preservation agenda was no longer self-evident. As the region's population exploded and beach resorts turned into exclusive residential suburbs, homeowners up and down the coast began to question the state's rationale for beach acquisition, asserting their right to enjoy what they thought of as their beaches. In the very cradle of the "New Right," the shore became a hot-button issue. Finally, urban renewal projects met with resistance from those who opposed the "Miamization" of the coastline, which, they believed, risked turning the shores into playgrounds for the rich. Just as thousands of residents were displaced in the wake of the Ocean Park urban renewal project, a progressive movement emerged vowing to protect the right of all Santa Monicans to enjoy seaside living. A new day was dawning in the history of the Los Angeles coastline.

"WHO IN FACT WANTS A FREEWAY?": THE RISE OF MODERN BEACH ENVIRONMENTALISM

By the early 1950s, members of the Shoreline Planning Association (SPA) could rejoice in their success. Not only had the association achieved its initial goals of acquiring beaches for the public, restoring eroded shores, and building modern accommodations on the coastline, but thanks to its tenacious lobbying, the bitter dispute pitting California (as well as Louisiana and Texas) against the federal government over ownership of the oil-rich tidelands had been resolved in favor of the states in 1953. With 70 percent of the oil royalties earmarked for future park, beach, and recreation projects, the SPA sent self-congratulatory letters to legislators who had supported their campaign, emphasizing that their activities had "been more effective than all other efforts combined."[1] Yet the SPA was already showing signs of a loss of momentum. In December 1950, the SPA's president declared small boat harbors to be the organization's new priority, but the issue evidently failed to energize its members.[2] That same year, the County of Los Angeles, rather than automatically renew its membership as it usually did, asked for a report on the SPA's activities. After failing to obtain the document, the county's chief administrative officer turned to an expert who claimed that "that the Shoreline Planning Association had done nothing since 1947."[3] With an annual budget of twelve thousand dollars the SPA did not need much to survive, but the membership fees of institutions such as LA County were essential. In the end, the county forked out the required twenty-five hundred dollars , but the board of supervisors' initial reaction

did not bode well.[4] In 1952, *California Coast*, the association's richly illustrated magazine, was reduced to a cheap leaflet with no pictures. In August
1953, the SPA published the last edition of its official bulletin. According
to one source, the SPA eventually merged with the California Marine Parks
and Harbor Association.[5]

While financial troubles certainly weakened the association, its death
resulted from its inability to renew its own ranks. In April 1952, the SPA
grieved the loss of its president and passionate leader, Geoffrey F. Morgan.
Active in the association since its beginnings, Morgan had served as its
president throughout most of the 1940s and up until 1952. To replace him,
the association's members elected seventy-one-year-old Carl P. Staal, who
had contributed to the association's foundation in 1935.[6] The SPA's aging
membership reflected the transformation of the environmentalist movement at the national scale. From the beginning of the conservation movement in the late nineteenth century, conservation groups had recruited
economic and business elites and the growing field of experts employed by
public agencies. They had pushed for policies that preserved nature so as
to ultimately benefit economic growth. In that same vein, elite members
of the SPA had campaigned for the preservation and development of the
California coastline, conceiving the two projects as compatible and even
necessary to boost tourism and real estate prices. While this approach
had long prevailed, it clashed with the new environmental sensibilities
of the 1960s. Other conservation groups, such as the National Wildlife
Federation, the Sierra Club, and the National Audubon Society, managed
to adapt their goals and methods of membership recruitment to a new era.
By refusing to question its commitment to unchecked development and
keeping a mostly institutional roster of members, the SPA failed to inspire
a new generation.[7]

SPA leaders were apparently oblivious to the beginnings of a national
reckoning with the costs and benefits of progress. This shift in attitudes
was triggered by several trends and forces that would eventually fuel the
modern environmental movement in the 1970s. As the summer road trip
to regional and national parks became a beloved family ritual in the affluent postwar decades, many Americans became more alert to the loss of
wilderness areas. This sentiment was reinforced by the high-profile battle
led by the Sierra Club and the Wilderness Society in the late 1950s to save
Dinosaur National Monument from being flooded by the construction of
Echo Park Dam on the Colorado River. Americans were also more aware of
the destruction of open space closer to home. As forests, meadows, and
fields gave way to sprawl, some suburbanites started to question the pace
of development. In the words of Interior Secretary Stewart Udall, American

cities had "grown too fast to grow well." The deterioration of nature could also be more insidious and invisible, such as in the form of radioactive fallout or chemicals. Rachel Carson's bestselling *Silent Spring* (1962), in particular, shone a light on the dangers of pesticides. By creating a "chemically sterile, insect-free world," she wrote, humans were contaminating every living being on earth, from "fish in remote mountain lakes" to "the unborn child." Spraying dust laced with chlordane on their lawns, as many suburban readers discovered in her book, had not only poisoned their grass but their own bodies. City-dwellers also reacted to changes in their environment. Overcrowded cities, pocket parks strewn with litter, and polluted streams left little space for children to play and enjoy nature, especially in deprived neighborhoods. Meanwhile, the construction of high-rise apartment buildings and gleaming office towers in "blighted" downtown areas, thanks to urban renewal subsidies, reinforced the sense that cities were becoming less inclusive and more privatized.[8]

In Los Angeles, these feelings surfaced in the 1960s, as projects such as Marina Del Rey came to completion. In 1957, when ground was broken on the Marina Del Rey yacht harbor, near the mouth of Ballona Creek, the press hailed the project as a long-awaited step toward Los Angeles becoming a major recreational boating destination.[9] By the time the marina's channels were opened to boating enthusiasts in 1965, the mood had changed. Beset by financial difficulties in the early 1960s, the marina was amended to maximize revenue-producing facilities, becoming in the process "an intensely developed residential-commercial-recreational complex."[10] To be sure, the new marina was appreciated by many. For its new residents, who moved into modern apartment units around the harbor, the marina was "like a party . . . in a vacation-type atmosphere."[11] Yet in the eyes of some observers, the luxurious mini-city with its six yacht clubs, restaurants, and high-priced apartment complexes was akin to public space privatization. In 1961, *Los Angeles Herald-Examiner* reporter Jack Keating criticized the fact that vast expanses of land were being "turned over to promoters" while the marina only provided "for general public use some 35 acres for parking, two tiny park sites . . . and one beach of less than 7 acres."[12] In his 1972 BBC documentary dedicated to his beloved Los Angeles, architectural historian Reyner Banham dismissed the area as "another executive ghetto," or "plastic people in plastic boats."[13] While it was too late to stop Marina Del Rey, other shoreline development projects began to face unprecedented resistance.

Among these projects, the plan to build a freeway, beaches, and commercial space on a series of artificial islands off the Santa Monica coast was certainly the most audacious and expensive. The idea for the Santa

Monica Causeway came about in the late 1950s, as congestion on coastal highways, especially the four-lane Pacific Coast Highway (PCH) that ran along Santa Monica Beach, worsened. At the time, many American cities were building new urban freeways to reduce congestion and ease the flow of commuters from downtown business districts to the suburbs. While Los Angeles was at the forefront of this movement, projects sometimes faced opposition. Santa Monica residents were concerned that their city would be divided in two by I-10, the new freeway linking Downtown Los Angeles to the ocean (completed in 1965). There was also concern that the narrow PCH would not be able to handle the added traffic—thirty-five hundred vehicles an hour during the evening rush—once this route was opened to the public. City and county officials agreed that a new coastal road should be built. Yet they also knew that residents were likely to reject a second inland highway that would cause more disruption. By relocating traffic to a two-thousand-feet offshore highway supported by a string of islands, the city council hoped to avoid such thorny issues while opening up new development possibilities. In 1958, the council commissioned a U.S. Army Corps of Engineers (USACE) report on the feasibility of the project.[14] Over the next few years, the project took on unprecedented scope, eventually calling for a six-mile, eight-lane causeway to be built on an artificial island parallel to the coast, with space enough for new beaches on the ocean side of the causeway, shops, park areas, a harbor accommodating seventeen hundred boats, and an eighteen-hole golf course. More than a simple freeway, a whole new city, it was hoped, would sprout up along the coast. According to the Santa Monica engineer and member of the Chamber of Commerce who came up with the plan, 206 million cubic yards of rock excavated from the Santa Monica Mountains would provide the material to construct the offshore island. By leveling the mountainside, the project would also create a wide plateau ideal for residential development. In 1963, the USACE gave the green light to the project. Despite the misgivings voiced by some engineers about the project's impact on littoral currents and the precarious funding situation, the city council decided to move forward with the causeway and selected the engineering firm Moffatt & Nichol to turn the plan into a reality.[15]

As with many other past beach development projects, the city council, the mayor, the Chamber of Commerce, and several engineers supported the two-hundred-million-dollar project. For supporters of this "city on the water," the aim was to create from scratch new coastal land that could be bought and leased at a premium. Yet their support proved insufficient. Starting in the mid-1960s, the project faced strong opposition from a growing number of residents and organizations. The Los Angeles chapter of the Sierra Club, the conservation group undergoing rapid growth under the leadership of David Brower, took the lead. At a hearing organized at the state capitol on the future of the shoreline, the group's chairman criticized the project's environmental impact on the bay, its "scenic effect," and the fact that it entailed destroying a portion of the Santa Monica Mountains.[16] Eager not to see their mountains dynamited, the Santa Monica Canyon Civic Association (SMCCA), the community organization devoted to preserving the area, also joined the fray opposing both the causeway and the alternative route proposed on Will Rogers Beach. Finally, in 1967, the Santa Monica Save the Beach Association was created expressly to fight the project. With the help of movie stars who lived in the area, such as James Arness, the group put together a short film denouncing the causeway and circulated a petition that quickly gathered fifteen thousand signatures. The grassroots opposition movement was victorious: in 1968, the project was officially abandoned. To be sure, the project was also beset by financial uncertainties. But Santa Monicans' staunch opposition also played a key role. Even in car-loving Los Angeles, new freeway infrastructure could be rejected if the coastline was at stake.[17]

Over the next few years, similar projects faced opposition all along the coastline—from Venice, where a beach freeway was also considered and abandoned, to South LA, where local social worker Pat Herrera founded the Citizens' Committee to Save Cabrillo Beach in 1967. This grassroots organization protested the construction of a yacht marina that was slated to destroy a large section of Cabrillo Beach in San Pedro Bay, one of the rare beaches in the region frequented predominantly by Black and Latino beachgoers. In the Cabrillo case, multiple motivations were at play, including environmental concerns and racial and social justice issues. Overall, the Cabrillo activists framed their battle as one about coastal access. In the wake of the 1965 Watts riots, members of Save Cabrillo Beach insisted that young people from Watts and surrounding neighborhoods, where places of recreation were few and far between, needed a place to enjoy the sun. Moreover, with its thirty-one hundred boat slips, apartments, hotels, and retail areas, the marina, they claimed, would transform the area into a playground for a privileged white population disconnected from the economic and social realities of South LA. By sending letters to the media and city council, collecting signatures, and voicing its opposition at public hearings, Save Cabrillo Beach played a crucial role in the city's decision to significantly reduce the size of the marina. Their victory also galvanized the growing number of groups working on coastal access issues.[18]

The new beach activists who emerged in the 1960s differed from the traditional defenders of the California coastline. Perhaps most obviously, they represented a more diverse range of the population, with low-income workers and students, women, and ethnic and racial minorities heavily involved in campaigning. When she founded Save Cabrillo Beach, Pat Herrera, who identified "as a chicano," was living on a modest stipend thanks to a UCLA fellowship for minority students.[19] Unlike the SPA and CBA members, activists such as Herrera considered beach development incompatible with a preservation agenda. Their commitment to public beaches also included a systematic opposition to marinas and harbors—projects that were seen as a form of privatization of the shores. Finally, unlike the SPA members who proudly called themselves "shoreliners," they did not identify as beach activists but rather viewed their actions to protect the coastline as part of a larger fight for social and racial equality.

These new activists could rely on broad public support for their actions. By the late 1960s, the priorities of beachgoers and local residents had radically shifted. They cared less about facilities and more about fundamentals: preserving the beach for public use. At a 1968 state hearing on the public interest in the shoreline held in Sacramento, the Santa Monica Save the Beach Association detailed its 1967 campaign against plans to build a highway on Will Rogers State Beach and the causeway project. As explained by member George Wagner, the association's volunteers hunted for signatures on street and shore. Wagner was careful to point out that signatories were not limited to "surfers, or volley ball players or Santa Monica residents," but involved "people throughout the county." When volunteers mentioned congestion on coastal roads and the possibility of building a new highway on the beach or offshore, interviewees acknowledged the problem, but still preferred "the inconvenience of waiting for a traffic light" if it meant "keeping the beach." "We wonder," Wagner insisted, "who in fact wants a freeway." Building new facilities and roads was regarded as a secondary, even unnecessary issue: "The majority of the people expressed the view that the beach should remain in its natural state providing opportunities for them to look at the ocean, lie on the sand, walk along the shore, swim and surf, and do whatever they please while visiting the beach." The interviewees' simple wishes contrasted sharply with the dream of a six-mile artificial island supporting a highway. In the span of a decade, the beach had come from being seen as a work in progress, something to be molded into a better version of itself thanks to technology and ambition, to a piece of nature that should remain untouched, unspoiled. As Wagner concluded his report, "A sincere concern for the environment seemed to outweigh all consideration of benefits gained by 'progress.'"[20]

A few months after the hearing was held, a major coastal event would forever change Californians' relationship to their beaches. On January 28,

1969, a blowout on a Union Oil platform six miles off the Santa Barbara coast released three million gallons of crude oil into the ocean. As the first environmental disaster captured in technicolor, the Santa Barbara oil spill profoundly shook the American public. Images of blackened beaches and dead seabirds, seals, and dolphins covered in sticky oil gave credence to what many early environment activists and scientists had been saying for several years: human "progress" and development had gone too far. At the national level, the event played an important role in the emergence of the modern environmental movement. According to an often-recounted anecdote, Wisconsin senator Gaylor Nelson was flying home from California after having toured the oil-scarred beaches when he came up with the idea of a nationwide environmental teach-in. On April 22, 1970, twenty million Americans across the nation attended Earth Day events, making it the second-largest protest in US history after the 2020 Black Lives Matter demonstrations. The Santa Barbara oil spill—together with other well-publicized environmental catastrophes of the 1960s, including the Cuyahoga River fires—gave impetus to a "green generation."[21]

At the local level, the Santa Barbara oil spill invigorated an already strong opposition to large-scale coastal projects. Whether in the shape of oil platforms, marinas, highways, nuclear power reactors, or artificial islands, many Southern Californians had had enough of beach development. The disaster also provided a major impetus to the passage of Proposition 20 in 1972, which allowed for the creation of the California Coastal Commission (CCC). According to some accounts, the establishment of a state agency in charge of reviewing permits for construction projects along the entire California shoreline and ensuring public access to the coast was nothing short of a miracle. From the land developers' lobbies to Governor Ronald Reagan himself, many powerful groups and personalities opposed a coastal agency with regulatory powers. Prior to the proposition being added on the ballot, several coastal bills had failed in the state legislature between 1967 and 1972. To some extent, the CCC was the result of fortunate timing. Yet beachfront homeowners and land developers had also become more aggressive in their attempts to seal off the shores from outsiders. High-profile coastal battles up and down the state, including the late 1960s "Save Salt Creek" movement in Orange County and the Sea Ranch development controversy in Sonoma County, engaged the public and raised awareness about the pressing need to preserve the state's coastal ecology and public accessibility.[22] In fact, large-scale citizen participation was instrumental to the passage of Proposition 20. A coalition involving over one hundred groups—including unions, students' clubs, surfers' associations, and women's coalitions—led a resourceful grassroots campaign to obtain enough signatures to put Proposition 20 on the ballot and then to garner public support for its passage. Over a hundred cyclists went on a 550-mile coastal ride between San Francisco and San Diego to build public support; Hollywood actors and cartoonists gave their time and talents to speak in favor of the measure; students went out with white paint and brushes to cover up billboards erected by the opposing side. In other words, the new beach activists were joined by thousands of ordinary Californians who also felt compelled to protect the state's most cherished natural resource.[23]

Most accounts of the agency's creation emphasize the work of Northern California–based environmental groups, in particular the San Francisco activists who founded "Save the Bay" in 1961 to protect the Bay Area's shores from pollution and overdevelopment. When this effort led to the founding of the San Francisco Bay Conservation and Development Commission in 1965, they did provide a useful template of a coastal regulatory agency for the future CCC. But the new beach activists who emerged in Southern California in the 1960s, whether protesting the Santa Monica Causeway or the Cabrillo yacht harbor, also played a major role. The LA beach lobby had successfully instilled in Californians a sense of entitlement to beaches among Californians. For over thirty years, the Los Angeles–based beach associations had hammered home the idea that the state's shoreline should belong to the public. To some extent, then, the coastal agency was the heir to that public beach tradition and reaped the benefits of decades of lobbying efforts led by the CBA and the SPA.

In 1976, the California Coastal Act turned the commission into a permanent fixture in the state's regulatory landscape. Although enshrining one of the nation's strongest coastal land-use policies in law was a major victory, coastal advocates had many opponents. Among them were wealthy beachfront homeowners who wished to keep their small seaside enclaves to themselves and resented having to provide public beach access along or across their properties. This was especially true in Southern California, where the postwar surf boom and rapid population growth and development turned the coast into a hot real estate market. From the late 1950s, homeowners had grown increasingly hostile toward the state's attempt to acquire beaches for the public. In the 1960s, hostility turned into action as some coastal municipalities in Los Angeles and Orange Counties sought to exclude out-of-town visitors from going to what they conceived as their beaches. As coastal municipalities and residents turned inward, they distanced themselves from the public beach acquisition consensus that had presided over postwar coastal development.

THE REVOLT OF THE HOMEOWNERS

In the 1940s and 1950s, few coastal private owners objected to the state purchasing beach lots to create new public parks. Considering the high cost of erosion control projects and the hefty property taxes on coastal land, owning a beach was not necessarily a good financial investment, especially if it did not produce any income. Officials were also careful to leave out private beach clubs from acquisition plans, which limited friction with this privileged set. When homeowners did object to the state's actions, they usually approached state officials individually to make their case. For instance, in 1956, Joseph L. Szekely, who owned part of Westward Beach in Malibu, wrote to LA County supervisor John Anson Ford asking for his land to be excluded from the proposed Point Dume State Park. In his letter, he argued that "the county already own[ed] a long strip of beach in that vicinity, Zuma Beach," which he felt was sufficient to meet the public's needs. Indeed, he continued, the state buying his land would only worsen congestion on the road leading to the beach. During surf season, he explained, "the road is jammed far beyond any reasonable limits," which, ironically, also revealed the need for additional public beaches along the coast. Worried about being perceived as selfish, he also insisted that the acquisition price was unjustifiable, especially since Westward Beach was already well used by its owners: "Why should the taxpayer be called upon to pay for achieving the same ends already assured?" Ford was unmoved by Szekely's letter. The extension of Zuma Beach, he wrote, was "both practical and necessary." By reaffirming the original goals for the acquisitions in a context of rapid population growth—"we must act now in acquiring property suitable for recreational uses"—Ford provided a strong rebuttal. Yet Szekely's call to protect the taxpayers' dollars was a telling sign that homeowners were ready to take strong stands in order to keep the public off their beaches.[24]

By the late 1950s, homeowners like Szekely had abandoned personal letter-writing campaigns and addressed the issue collectively. In 1957, Szekely was likely part of the Malibu–Riviera Beach Homeowners Association that opposed the state's purchase of eighty acres of coastal land at Point Dume. According to the group, "Widespread use of private swimming pools and other factors such as television and heavy traffic congestion" led to fewer and fewer people visiting the beach. In fact, their representative insisted, "statistics indicate that public beaches' needs are likely to decline in the future."[25] Yet official figures showed the opposite. In Santa Monica, for instance, ten million visitors had enjoyed the beach in 1958–1959, a 30 percent increase from the previous year. For the South Bay cities, this was precisely the problem. A 1961 article reported on the lack of seasonal rentals available for the ever-increasing number of tourists.[26] The cities of Newport Beach, Seal Beach, and Huntington Beach in Orange County were experiencing such an increase in the number of beachgoers that they demanded that the state contribute to "the financial burden of beach visitors." According to the mayor of Newport Beach, 98 percent of them came from outside city limits. And the beach crowds did not necessarily equate to corresponding profits for local businesses. The Hermosa Beach mayor denounced the "crowds of outsiders" who did not spend a single penny on the beach, having bought their beers, sandwiches, and gas in their hometowns: "What does Hermosa get out of the deal? Nothing . . . except the job of cleaning up the litter."[27] Even when visitors wanted to spend their money at the beach, they were not always welcome. Part of the reason for the shortage of vacation rentals in Redondo Beach was that landlords preferred renting to year-round residents "because they are more dependable and take better care of property."[28]

Quarrels about who should pay for beach maintenance were nothing new, but beach cities in the late 1950s and early 1960s instead began trying to keep more outsiders from coming onto their beaches in the first place. The main factor fueling this change was the demographic and economic boom experienced by South Bay cities and Orange County beach communities in relation to federal investment in the defense and technology sectors.[29] As they started attracting affluent residents who commuted to Los Angeles, beach resorts like Newport Beach turned into prosperous suburban communities that no longer depended on tourism for their revenues and instead wanted to protect their splendid surroundings from new development. Southern California "homeowner politics," as Mike Davis explains in *City of Quartz*, had entered a new phase. While homeowners had striven to establish "homogeneous residential enclaves" in the 1920–1960 period, they were now turning to the "*defense* of this suburban dream against unwanted development . . . as well as against unwanted persons." The beach, as the main attraction for visitors from throughout the region, was central to this project.[30]

In 1961, the opposition of coastal homeowners became apparent during public hearings held by Los Angeles County to update the shoreline Master Plan, in particular with regards to the beach acquisition program.[31] Some Manhattan Beach homeowners demanded that their land not be included in the plan. Tom Stevens of Hermosa Beach, who said he represented the "Citizens Committee for Private Domain," asked simply, "How can we get out of this Master Plan?" As for the Palos Verdes homeowners, they were happy not to be included in the program but protested against new recreational improvements in the South Bay area as it risked worsening road congestion.[32] Yet for all their influence, the homeowners were unable to sway county officials who were determined "to give sea-room not only for the millions who live here now but for the millions yet to settle here."[33] For the director of the State Department of Natural Resources, the plan's ultimate objective was the same as it had always been: "The majority of the coastline should be in public ownership."[34]

Over the opposition of homeowners, beach acquisition continued, if at a slower pace. Amid pressure from the state to open new beaches to the public, some cities took more radical measures to ward off the beachgoing crowds. In 1961, for instance, Laguna Beach in Orange County considered restricting use of all but a two-block-long beach in the city center to residents and hotel guests during summer weekends and spring and summer holidays. In addition, the ordinance would have imposed an admission fee for out-of-towners seeking "beach privileges."[35] According to the city council, the measure was intended to help with the cost of maintaining the beach. While it enjoyed wide local support, the measure was blocked at the state level. In 1963, the California Legislature passed a law invalidating the proposed measure and guaranteeing that all persons, "regardless of color, race, religion, national origin or residence," could access public beaches.[36]

The state's strong rebuff did not prevent other coastal cities from considering other measures restricting beach access. In 1969, the San Clemente City Council proposed charging an annual user fee for beach access. As long as the fee was applied to both residents and nonresidents, city officials assured, it would be legal. Although the fee in question was modest—a symbolic dollar—some argued that it had the potential to discourage large families from Los Angeles who only came once or twice a year to San Clemente. The measure would also set a precedent (what if all beach cities in the region started levying a similar charge?) and involve some tricky practical questions. As the Los Angeles Times asked, "Would the beaches be fenced off with turnstile gates?" Even the city manager of Newport Beach, where similar measures were being discussed, agreed that fences would be an aesthetic concern. Yet many residents in Laguna Beach, Newport Beach, Huntington Beach, and Seal Beach supported the initiative. According to the Times reporter, Orange County residents too questioned, "Why do we pay for other people's use of the beaches?"[37] While the measure was eventually abandoned, debates over beach access continued to rage throughout the 1970s. As Democrat assemblyman and coastal advocate Alan Sieroty told a crowd in 1970, "Nowhere in this state is the demand for space so great, the competition for use so intense, as it is along the shoreline."[38]

Part of the reason why beach access became such a hot-button issue locally was linked to the emergence of a conservative, individualistic political

culture in Southern California in the 1960s and the intensification of social
and racial segregation in the burgeoning suburbs of Orange County. These
new political sensibilities led to a profound shift in perceptions of the natural environment. The coastline was no longer being seen as the property
of all Californians but rather as belonging to residents of the municipality
who paid for its maintenance. The stark economic and racial homogeneity
of the new Orange County suburbs, combined with a built environment
that "reinforced privacy, individual property rights, home ownership, and
isolation at the expense of public space" fueled a latent hostility toward
nonresidents drawn to the ocean. In the eyes of many citizens of these
coastal cities, the beaches belonged to those who paid local taxes.[39]

This was hardly a uniquely Southern California debate. Nationwide,
similar beach access battles were also taking place, most strikingly
along Connecticut's Gold Coast, where private clubs, municipalities, and
homeowners' associations had managed to hang "sand curtains" along
the shoreline, effectively preventing the general public from accessing the
state's most coveted beaches.[40] Unlike in the Northeast, however, coastal
homeowners in California had to contend with a strong sense of the beach
as a public common, thanks to decades of lobbying by Southern California
beaches associations. Of course, members of these associations had in mind
a vision of the public as white middle-class families when they advocated
for beach acquisition. But in the 1960s and 1970s, the new beach activists
appropriated the California public beach tradition while expanding the notion of the "public." The progressive coalition that emerged in Santa Monica
in reaction to the demolition of the Ocean Park neighborhood and its replacement with luxury apartments illustrates this phenomenon. For this
new generation of activists, the "Miamization" of the coastline was a form
of appropriation of public space by the wealthy. Building on the state's rich
public beach tradition, they campaigned to make sure that all Californians
would have access to the shoreline.

RESISTING THE MIAMIZATION OF THE COASTLINE

If supporters of shoreline development viewed the inauguration of the
Santa Monica Shores project in 1964 as heralding the rebirth of Ocean Park
as the "Miami of the Pacific," they were quickly disappointed. On December
30, 1964, as Santa Monica mayor Rex Minter and other members of the
Santa Monica Citizens' Progress Committee (SMCPC) posed with their
shovels at the building site, criticism of urban renewal was already well
underway across the country. Conservative circles denounced the cost,

slowness, and inefficiency of urban renewal projects and instead wanted to let the free market take care of inner-city slums. And the 1961 publication of *The Death and Life of Great American Cities* (1961), Jane Jacobs's book denouncing the systematic destruction of mixed-use neighborhoods, had a significant impact on perceptions of urban aesthetics and the need to conserve traditional buildings.[41] Major projects like the Santa Monica Shores, imposed from on high onto the urban fabric, were the exact opposite of Jacobs's vision of the city as a "living organism."[42]

In addition, urban renewal was widely denounced by conservatives and progressives alike for leading to the expulsion of hundreds of thousands of low-income residents from their homes. This criticism was particularly effective when it focused not on ethnic or racial minorities, who were disproportionately affected, but on the elderly.[43] At Ocean Park, particular attention was paid to the 150 people over the age of sixty-two who lost their homes between 1962 and 1964. The displacement of the 1,216 people from their Ocean Park homes was carefully monitored by the city council, which wanted to avoid controversy. In the face of growing criticism, the city circulated a brochure in 1968 explaining the relocation process. According to the brochure, the operation had been a success for everybody involved, having "improved the lives of these residents" who used to "live in daily conflict with substandard conditions."[44]

While several programs were put in place to find housing for displaced residents, for many of the older Jewish residents who used to sit and chat on the oceanfront benches, nothing could replace the community and view they had enjoyed in Ocean Park.[45] Unfortunately, staying in the area was financially impossible for many. Most had paid very low rents, between $30 and $35 a month. By comparison, rent on an apartment in the Santa Monica Shore towers ran between $150 and $330.[46] With no public housing available in Santa Monica, the vast majority of residents were relocated far from the beach. A number of families of modest means headed to the Mar Vista Gardens, a public housing complex in Culver City, a few miles to the east.[47] Others were relocated to privately owned apartments, with the SMRA committed to paying the difference in rent. Finally, another alternative was implemented: buildings deemed structurally sound were moved in their entirety from the urban renewal zone and reinstalled in the immediate vicinity. In other words, poor residents and their dwellings were literally moved out of the target area and relocated away from the coastline. The strategy is a particularly concrete illustration of postwar urban renewal: not so much acting to "alleviate urban blight and poverty," as effectively "shift[ing] it from one city area to another."[48]

Judging by the efforts of Venice residents to fight against the specter of urban renewal in the 1960s, the SMRA's relocation policy was far from satisfactory. Indeed, the demolition of the Ocean Park neighborhood and the construction of the towers troubled Venice homeowners and renters, many of whom were elderly. Fearing their neighborhood would be next in line for the wrecking ball, the local homeowners' association formed the Venice Citizens' Planning Committee and, taking a proactive approach, conducted targeted demolitions of dilapidated buildings.[49] As a representative explained, they wanted better housing, "not a bulldozer to come through and replace everything with high-priced high-rises."[50] The construction of the "two high-rise things" in Santa Monica—as a journalist mockingly nicknamed the Santa Monica Shores towers in 1967—offered an unappealing vision of the future for coastal residents. From the end of the 1960s, avoiding becoming "an intolerable version of Miami Beach" became the watchword in Venice and what remained of the Ocean Park neighborhood.[51]

The movement against the overdevelopment of the coastline and a backlash against the two towers eventually spread within Santa Monica, putting an end to urban renewal projects in Ocean Park and laying the groundwork for the 1970s Santa Monica renters' rights movement. The radical revolt carried out by the renters was the paradoxical product of the urban growth strategy supported by the city council.[52] The 1966 opening of the Interstate 10 Freeway, which positioned the city just twenty minutes from Downtown offices, had a tremendous impact on Santa Monica. Rapid demographic growth was supported by a real estate boom, with fourteen thousand new apartments being built between 1960 and 1972. Many newcomers chose to settle in what was left of Ocean Park, attracted to the neighborhood's rich history and its social and racial diversity. Like David Schulman, a thirty-one-year-old "part-time teacher, part-time graduate student and full-time foe of development in Ocean Park" interviewed by the *Los Angeles Times*, they were young, educated, and politically engaged. In their eyes, the Santa Monica Shores represented an abomination. Moreover, financing issues blocked the construction of additional towers. By 1972, only five of the twenty-six acres of cleared-out property had been redeveloped, leaving the towers isolated amid empty lots. The visible eyesore, for which thousands of residents had been displaced, catalyzed resentment and fueled the controversy.[53]

In 1971, a new private company was selected by the city council to build nine twenty-nine-story towers and a hotel on the oceanfront. Headed by Ruth Galanter, a young urban planner, an opposition movement was immediately formed and took advantage of the recently passed Proposition

20 authorizing the creation of the California Coastal Commission. The CCC sided with the activists, organized as the "Save Santa Monica Bay" association, and cancelled the developer's permits, thus ending the project. In subsequent years, Ocean Park activists sued the city to negotiate the inclusion of a residential building for retired people of modest means, a public park along the shoreline, and a public pathway to the beach.[54] Having reached their objectives, the Ocean Park activists turned to new targets. In 1972, they joined forces with a socially diverse group of Santa Monica residents opposed to a project to build an island off the Santa Monica coast for the creation of a convention center and conference hotels. The following year, they successfully campaigned with local preservationists to prevent demolition of the run-down Santa Monica Pier, one of the last standing structures of its era. This victory further galvanized the movement. Originally aiming to give "every income group [the chance] to enjoy living in the beach," they expanded their goals to making the entire city affordable.[55] In 1979, after a relentless grassroots campaign, the activists obtained passage of one of the most restrictive rent control measures in the country. In 1981, four leaders from the Renters' Rights coalition won seats on the city council. In a complete reversal of local politics, the city council, led for decades by the city's economic and political elite, was in the hands of a majority opposed to large-scale development projects.[56]

The emergence of new players in the debate over shoreline development marked the end of a period of consensus during which the Santa Monica City Council, in partnership with the federal government and private interests, determined the future direction of the city's urban and economic development. After the construction of the Santa Monica Shores, a new chapter in the history of the Los Angeles coastline was being written that reflected a changing economic, legal, and cultural landscape. The economic crisis of the 1970s, the arrival of new residents with progressive ideals, the creation of the Coastal Commission, the emerging desire for an "authentic urban experience," and the preservation of historic buildings—including the old amusement piers—represented many residents' hopes and desires for the shoreline.[57]

The postwar beach consensus suffered a mortal blow when, over a matter of months, Santa Barbara turned from a wealthy, conservative seaside community to ground zero for the nascent environmentalist movement. As the 1969 Santa Barbara oil spill transformed "tide pools . . . once brimming with marine life" into "silent puddles of petroleum," Californians took stock of what truly mattered for the future of the shoreline.[58] Preserving the beach in its natural state trumped promises of cheap oil, faster commutes, ocean-view high-rises, and new jobs created by beach tourism and the real estate economy. In fact, even before the Union Oil slick reached the Santa Barbara shores, signs abounded that an environmental consciousness was transforming how people conceived of the beach. As one journalist commented just a few months before the blowout, you didn't have "to be a nut to be an ocean conservationist," you only needed to look at "how beautiful, water-washed and wind-scrubbed these beaches [were] despite what man has already done to them with his greed and his garbage."[59]

Widespread popular support for ocean and beach conservation played a major role in the passage of Proposition 20 and the creation of the Coastal Commission. Paradoxically, the agency, so derided in conservative circles as the epitome of government overreach, was the heir to the beach lobby, the elite group that instilled a sense of entitlement to beaches among Californians. After all, even Frankie, the protagonist of the AIP *Beach Party* cycle, did not cower when confronted by developers. As he told Harvey Huntington Honeywagon III, when he tried to dislodge the beach gang in *Bikini Beach* (1964) in order to build a resort for senior citizens, "Look, this is a public beach, and just what do you think you're going to do something about?" In the 1960s, a new generation of activists built on the California public beach tradition, changing its meaning in the process. Beaches should not only be open to the white, middle-class public, but should also serve the needs of racial and ethnic minorities and low-income residents. The continuities between the "shoreliners" and the new generation of activists may seem paradoxical given everything that separated them, but the achievements of the latter would not have been possible without the groundwork laid by the former. By making the public beach a core tenet of California's political culture, the beach lobby had opened up the possibility, however tenuous, of truly inclusive shores.

Epilogue

The View from the Santa Monica Pier

At 1 a.m. on January 24, 1973, following a tense five-hour hearing attended by one thousand concerned citizens, the Santa Monica City Council voted 4 to 3 to tear down the "monstrosity" lying on the city's oceanfront. Erected in the early twentieth century when the beach resort sought to attract well-heeled eastern tourists and weekend visitors from Los Angeles, the fifteen-hundred-foot Santa Monica Pier was in bad condition. For the councilmen who voted in favor of its demolition, the pier's "sagging pilings" were only one of the many issues they had with the aging structure; the site was known for "its high level of criminal incidence" and came at a high cost to the city's taxpayers. According to City Manager Perry Scott, who was determined to see it demolished, the pier attracted "those who do not spend money. . . . I'm talking about kids and the elderly who come out to dangle hooks." Instead, Scott supported the construction of a thirty-five-acre island off the coast, complete with an artificial lagoon and waterfall, a high-rise hotel, a convention center, gourmet restaurants, and tourist shops. The island project was another attempt at turning the oceanfront into a real estate opportunity after the Santa Monica Causeway project was abandoned in 1968. For Scott and his supporters, the pier, with its dilapidated shops selling shell necklaces, its outdated arcade, and its turbaned psychics, belonged to the past. As Scott explained, the pier "may be charming to some folks. . . . But I wonder how much the general public should pay for that charm."[1]

As it turned out, Santa Monicans were ready to spend quite a lot on the "creaky anachronism" jutting out into the ocean. Days after the council's decision, a grassroots movement took shape to fight for the preservation and renovation of the pier. An organization called the Friends of the Santa Monica Pier gathered over forty thousand signatures to protest the demolition order. Supporters of the pier came from across the political spectrum and included "doctors, lawyers, shaggy hippies, [and] anyone who doesn't want to see this city turned into instant Miami Beach." In their eyes, the pier was a piece of history, a place to enjoy nature and "forget your problems," and "one of the last places in the Los Angeles area that is not made out of plastic." By April 1973, not only had the city council rescinded its January decision, but three out of the four councilmen who had voted in favor of demolition were voted out of office and replaced by pro-pier candidates. In subsequent years, the city spent millions of dollars in repairs and new attractions to give the structure a new lease on life and preserve its quaint, low-cost atmosphere.[2] Santa Monicans had made their voices heard.

The campaign to save the Santa Monica Pier marked the end of an era. For decades, a consensus had animated the forces behind coastal development: starting in the early 1930s, local business elites, supported by a regional network of engineers, scientists, and urban planners, promoted a vision of the modern beach as a vast, clean, and safe playground for the white middle class devoid of any "honky-tonk" and other undesirable elements and groups. Throughout the 1940s and 1950s, the beach lobby put those principles in practice and erected modern infrastructure along the coastline, while purchasing, cleaning, and expanding the beaches. Hotdog stands, rotting piers, dilapidated bathhouses, and bodybuilding spectacles had to go. By the early 1960s, as the beach modernization campaign strayed from its popular goals of buying beaches for the public and restoring them, many residents found themselves more and more at odds with local officials. Rejecting plans for artificial islands, high-rises, marinas, and elevated highways, they made it clear they wanted to keep the beaches as they were, warts and all. As it turned out, dilapidated piers were nostalgic reminders of the region's seaside past and the sites of treasured childhood memories. According to a protester shouting from the back of the room during a council meeting, the pier was "the very heart of Santa Monica."[3]

More than this, coastal residents demanded to have a voice in the future of their communities and surroundings. Growth should not come at all costs, especially when it came to the beach, the one place that seemed to embody the nation's democratic ideals. In 1973, the Santa Monica City Council responded to these demands by appointing a citizens' committee to make recommendations for the future of the waterfront area and agreeing to submit to a popular vote any major project set to be built on the coastline. This decision echoed the creation of an interim Coastal Commission just a year earlier whose mission was to protect public access to the California shoreline and preserve it from development. The Coastal Act of 1976, which made the commission a permanent body, explicitly called out the public's right "to fully participate in decisions affecting coastal planning, conservation, and development."[4] This was not just a California phenomenon. Inspired by the social movements of the Sixties, activists and legislators across the country were agitating to open beaches to the public and ward off developers. Coastal development, once a topic reserved for a small elite, had become a matter of public debate.[5]

The 1973 Save the Pier campaign crystallized the widening gap between two models of shoreline development that continue to dominate debates about the future of beaches in the region and, more generally, in the industrialized world. Partisans of the pier defended its status as a free public space open to all. The pier was a place worth saving precisely because it attracted "a deliciously rich cross section of people," from local characters to tourists.[6] In that sense, the campaign supported a vision of the beach as a democratic space, where all visitors stood on the same footing and enjoyed the same view of the ocean. Pier lovers were also nature lovers. Most had successfully opposed the island project and, more generally, rejected any development that threatened coastal ecology. To this day, many Angelenos defend this vision, persistently fighting for a truly public and sustainable beach.

Advocates of beach development, in contrast, conceive of the shoreline as a revenue-making area where the public is welcome insofar as it is spending money. With its high-rise hotels and residential buildings ribboning the beach, Miami Beach has served as the poster child for this type of development since the 1960s. Beyond the signature aesthetics of skyscrapers towering above the aqua blue ocean and sparkling white sand, Miami Beach (and Florida writ large) represents a carelessness toward the environment in the face of developers' ambitions. Since the 1940s, developers have wantonly destroyed Florida's coastal ecology, turning submerged lands, mangroves, estuaries, and bays into new subdivisions.[7] Once home to mangrove forests and swamps on its lagoon side and majestic dunes on the oceanfront, Miami Beach is now devoid of these protective features and has to regularly replenish its beaches with offshore sand. By rejecting extravagant coastal development plans from the late 1960s onward and by voting yes on Proposition 20 in 1972, Californians refused to continue on this path of development.

Since 1973, many other battles have been fought on the Los Angeles shoreline (and elsewhere) where opposing factions roughly align themselves along these two models of development. In California, the public beach ideal remains alive and strong, despite multiple attempts, including some successful ones, by wealthy homeowners and developers to erode the Coastal Commission's mandate to protect and preserve the shoreline. The most tangible legacy of the decades of campaigns over the shore is no doubt the public beaches themselves, totaling over thirty-five miles in Los Angeles County. This vast playground has remained an important site for Angelenos to enjoy nature, sustain a sense of community, exercise, and show off their bodies. The beaches have continued to play a central role in innovating new body trends and beauty standards. More recently, they have also served as pioneering grounds for the pursuit of reparative justice. Today's beaches are cleaner, more accessible, and more inclusive than they have been in over a century. And yet they are more fragile than ever due to the multipronged effects of climate change. As Californians come to terms with the fact that they cannot fully control a dynamic natural world, they might also need to accept the possibility of a future without beaches.

"BEACHES ARE PUBLIC IN CALIFORNIA": THE RIGHT TO THE BEACH (AND CLEAN OCEAN WATER) IN THE COASTAL COMMISSION ERA

Passed during a brief window in the 1970s when a bipartisan consensus undergirded the environmental movement, the 1976 California Coastal Act represented a significant roadblock to development and attempts at closing access to the shoreline. This legislative landmark determined the legal framework in which future battles over coastal development would play out.[8]

In the immediate years following its confirmation, the young agency's reputation suffered as the bipartisan commitment to environmental regulation was tested nationally and California politics increasingly took a right-wing turn. Moreover, as soon as the agency started imposing easements (public paths) on private land in exchange for building permits, it made powerful enemies. Most notably, Governor Jerry Brown, once supportive of the CCC, turned against the commission's "bureaucratic thugs" following the 1978 Malibu-Agura fire controversy. Although the commission had only banned three homeowners from building back closer to the sea, the decision was distorted in the press, and Brown's comment fueled Republicans' critiques of bureaucratic overreach. But even environmentalists were disappointed with the agency's results when it came to improving coastal access and taking a resolute stand against developers. Out of the more than one thousand public access paths negotiated by the commission with property owners, only thirty-nine were effectively opened in 1981, due to lack of funds to pay for maintenance and liability insurance, a legal prerequisite before a path could official open. As historian Jared Orsi explains, the young commission "faced a nearly impossible task" of trying to manage a vast and diverse coastline without a proper budget. Political pressure, bad press, and eroding public participation further undermined the agency and the movement for coastal conservation at large.[9]

In the early 1980s, the agency entered a very challenging period as Republican George Deukmejian won the California governorship and Ronald Reagan, one of the CCC's longtime adversaries, occupied the White House. Although Deukmejian never quite managed to act on his campaign promise to abolish the commission, he did impose drastic budget cuts and filled the commission's empty seats with pro-development appointees. The 1980s also saw the commission implicated in major legal battles, some of which eroded its powers to guarantee public access. Most significantly, in the 1987 case of *Nollan v. California Coastal Commission*, the US Supreme Court ruled in favor of the plaintiff, a Ventura beachfront homeowner who contested the commission's imposition of a lateral easement across his property in exchange for a building permit. According to the court majority, opening a public path on the plaintiff's land without financial compensation was akin to a violation of property rights. The decision reverberated far beyond California, giving reassurance to beach homeowners that the highest court in the land was on their side.[10] After the surge of victories in favor of shoreline preservation and public access in the early 1970s, the tide had definitely turned for beach activists.

Providing access was particularly tricky along Malibu's twenty-seven-mile coastline, where the public was "treated to a claustrophobic vista . . . of the ass-ends of private beach homes," as art critic Peter Plagens put it.[11] Even purchasing beaches was no guarantee of making them available for the public. In the late 1970s, the state purchased several pocket beaches in Malibu where houses had been destroyed by brush fires. Starting in 1980, Malibu residents, supported by their elected representatives, denounced plans to open these sands up to the public, arguing that these were sensitive coastal areas that could not withstand crowds and that, paradoxically, their secluded nature risked turning them into a magnet for "drug dealers, rapists, thieves, and gangs." The residents' lawsuit was declared void in 1982, and three of the four beaches were eventually opened to the public in 1984 (today's El Matador, El Pescador, and La Piedra beaches). In subsequent years, signs directing the public to them were regularly painted over or destroyed. The commission's signs indicating the location of coastal access pathways (stairways or walkways allowing beachgoers to access the sands from the Pacific Coast Highway) met the same fate. More than twenty were reported missing from the Malibu shoreline in 1984. Improving the situation was not just a case of fighting homeowners' guerilla tactics; local residents with powerful connections, such as Disney's then-CEO Michael Eisner, found receptive ears among county officials, who favored improving access at the two big public beaches in the area (Surfrider and Zuma) to spending money on maintaining the coastal paths to small, isolated coves. To this day, whether due to lack of political will or lack of funds, El Sol County Beach (the fourth beach bought in the 1970s) remains inaccessible except by foot at low tide.[12]

In addition to limiting choices for improving public access, budget woes weighed heavily on California officials in charge of maintaining public beaches in the 1980s. The tax revolt, which paved the way for Ronald Reagan's economic policies, started in California with the passage of Proposition 13 in 1978 before spreading to more than twenty states. By slashing property taxes, the initiative forced brutal budget cuts on all public services, from schools and libraries to beaches, leaving the low-income, mostly nonwhite population who relied on them in the lurch.[13] To avoid closing the beaches, which came dangerously close to being a reality in 1981, Los Angeles County officials turned to "marketing" them. Coppertone trash cans, branded lifeguard swimsuits, and Seven Up litter patrols did not necessarily bring revenues, but it allowed the county (which has been in charge of all beach cleaning and lifeguard crews since 1975) to save on maintenance and uniforms. The move angered partisans of the public beach ideal for whom "beaches belong[ed] to the people, not to private commercial interests." Yet, as one official remarked, "You're never going to get two-thirds of the voters to give money to the beaches." Rather than pay for a public resource open to all, white suburban homeowners, who had overwhelmingly supported Proposition 13, preferred saving for a backyard pool or, even better, a beachfront home.[14]

Budget cuts also affected beach cleanliness. With fewer staff members on the county payrolls to pick up trash, volunteers and county jail inmates filled the gap starting in the 1980s.[15] But beach clean-up drives could only do so much when the City of Los Angeles pumped up to twenty-five million pounds of toxic-laden sludge a month into Santa Monica Bay. What was public access worth if beaches were routinely too polluted for use? By the mid-1980s, the City of Los Angeles was still not complying with the Clean Water Act (1972), which regulated the removal of solid wastes, as well as bacterial and viral pathogens from sewage poured into bodies of water (known as "secondary treatment"). As a result, pollution had turned the seafloor at the end of the Hyperion outfall into a dead zone. Even more concerning, evidence showed that hundreds of tons of DDT, a highly toxic pesticide, had been discharged into the ocean for years prior to the 1972 national ban of the substance.[16] In 1985, a small group of Westside residents formed Heal the Bay to pressure the city to clean up its act. Two years later, the fledgling organization joined an Environmental Protection Agency (EPA) lawsuit challenging the city's use of waivers that exempted it from Clean Water Act standards. Not only did Los Angeles lose the lawsuit, but Heal the Bay was also invited by the court to monitor the city's cleanup efforts for the next twelve years. By 1990, all sewage received at least primary treatment before entering the ocean, and Heal the Bay, with its seventy-five hundred members, had become a major player in regional politics.[17] In 1998, the City of Los Angeles proudly announced that all the sewage discharged into the bay received secondary treatment, just in time to fulfill the 1987 court settlement. According to scientists who analyzed samples of the bay's seafloor near the Hyperion outfall twenty years later, the return of species such as the brittle star, which thrives in clean water, was a sign that biodiversity was improving.[18] The sewage success story may have emboldened the EPA, which sued the Montrose Chemical Corporation and other chemical companies in 1990 for dumping DDT and PCBs, another toxic substance, through sewers off the Palos Verdes Peninsula. Before the parties agreed to a settlement in 2000, the EPA declared the area a Superfund site, hoping to clean up the worst of the pollution, which was harming birds, marine life, and even people eating the contaminated fish. At the time, it was the worst pollution case ever handled at such depths.

Was the bay finally "healed"? Urban runoff has remained a thorny issue, with all sorts of chemicals, debris, and trash—from shopping carts to car batteries—finding their way into the ocean, especially after a big rainstorm when storm drains overflow. "Every time it rains," commented a Heal the Bay staff scientist in 1992, "our beaches look like a landfill."[19] Throughout the 1990s and 2000s, Heal the Bay focused its efforts on pressuring the city to improve storm drain filtering and educating people about gutters and the role they play in ocean pollution. This work is paying off. Starting in 1990, Heal the Bay started releasing annual report cards that translate statistics about public bacteria levels from different beaches across the region into simple letters (from A for the cleanest beaches to F for the most polluted), a scale the general public can comprehend. In 2002, for instance, 83 percent of tested beaches had received As or Bs, and 7% received Fs. Twenty years later, the annual report card indicated that 94 percent of California's beaches scored high in water quality. Yet, according to the *Los Angeles Times*, "Urban runoff from storm drains remains the largest source of pollution for California's beaches."[20] For that reason, Heal the Bay advises people to wait seventy-two hours after a rainstorm before swimming in the ocean. In addition, deteriorating pipes across the wastewater system, as well as occasional failures at Hyperion, continue to cause sewage spills and beach closures. Updating the city's aging equipment will come at a high cost, but the alternative is a return to the fetid conditions of the 1980s, when the bay's seafloor was left "rotting out."[21] More worryingly, recent seafloor explorations have provided irrefutable proof that chemical companies not only dumped DDT through the sewers but also routinely unloaded leaking barrels of DDT off barges near the shoreline up until the 1970s. Some of the DDT was offloaded directly into the water, without even being contained in barrels. The EPA, with matching funds from the state, is currently looking into the problem, but the scale of contamination is hard to fathom; the area that would need cleaning up is larger than the City of San Francisco. Uncovering the toxic legacy of deep-ocean dumping in LA will take determination and significant financial commitment from federal and local officials.[22]

Just as the beaches were getting somewhat cleaner in the mid-1990s, battles over coastal access became fiercer. As the rate of urbanization accelerated along the coast, the number of wealthy homeowners buying several parcels and applying for building permits to remodel and extend their houses steadily increased, creating more obstacles for beachgoers to access the sand. At the same time, many of the public easements negotiated in the late 1970s and early 1980s by the Coastal Commission in exchange for building permits were slated to expire. Indeed, these "Offers to Dedicate" (OTDs) were only valid for twenty-one years, and if not turned into public coastal paths, they would simply lapse. One option was for the CCC to find a public agency or a nonprofit group that would agree to pay for maintenance and accept legal liability for the so-called sidewalks to the ocean. In 1995, only one in five of the 1,269 potential access ways in California had been opened to the public. As the *Los Angeles Times* warned, "The clock [was] running out for the state to claim many of the easements."[23] Another problem, as the Coastal Commission's staff quickly discovered, was that property owners in wealthy enclaves simply refused to keep their promises. Lateral pathways rarely caused problems, but perpendicular ones, which allowed the public to access the beach from the road, were controversial. Malibu, again, provided a perfect example of a few owners' selfishness overriding the public's legal right to coastal access. By 2001, as more OTDs were set to expire, one coastal activist compared Malibu to "Normandy in 1944."

The Coastal Commission found itself repeatedly clashing with Malibu homeowners, including high-profile music and film industry figures. New coastal activists also joined the cause. For example, Steve Hoyt, former head of the Malibu Democratic Club, founded Access for All, a nonprofit dedicated to making Malibu's shores accessible to the public. In 2002, the commission won an important victory when the California Supreme Court confirmed the legality of OTDs negotiated before the 1987 *Nollan* decision (which strictly limited the agency's authority to impose new OTDs).[24] The decision gave more weight to the commission's case against record producer David Geffen, who refused to open three easements (negotiated in 1983, 1990, and 2000) on Malibu's Carbon Beach. The legal battle was widely covered in the local and national press, including stories describing hired "goons on ATVs" chasing beachgoers from the beach and portraying Geffen and his ilk as selfish billionaires. The affair also gave coastal activists a platform to communicate to the wider public about their rights. In a 2005 interview, Hoyt, billed as the "comandante of the beach liberation front," explained in accessible language the legal foundation for his quest.[25] Whether the coverage of the story played a role in the lawsuit's outcome is hard to know, but it certainly did not help the homeowners' cause. In April 2005, Geffen agreed to open the gates to Carbon Beach and negotiated a settlement with the commission, which involved reimbursing $300,000 in attorneys' fees to the state and Access for All. As CCC executive director Peter Douglas claimed, the victory sent "a signal to other holdouts." Soon the commission would be "going after them with equal vigor."[26]

Next in line was Broad Beach, where homeowners had similarly refused to honor the negotiated easements. In 2003, Sara Wan, a Coastal Commission member, tested public access by spreading her towel on a public part of the beach, only to be immediately asked to leave by a security guard. In the spring of 2005, Access for All printed maps of the "checkerboard" of public easements on Broad Beach (made available on the Coastal Commission's website) and organized a "beach brigade" to encourage beachgoers to enjoy their rights.[27] In subsequent years, a collective of artists, writers, and social scientists called the Los Angeles Urban Rangers also started organizing "Beach Safaris" on Broad Beach and other similar enclaves with humorous activities ranging from "a lateral easement hike" to "sign-watching" (a reference to the fake "no trespassing" and "no parking" signs used by homeowners to ward off the public).[28] Building upon this work, Urban Ranger and author Jenny Price co-created in 2013 the smartphone app Our Malibu Beaches to help the public identify public coastal accessways and public easements. Five years later, the Coastal Commission launched its own app, YourCoast, which provides users information on coastal access and amenities, but this time for the entire state's shoreline. Ironically, the app was funded by a fine imposed by the commission on a tech mogul who had held his wedding in Big Sur without applying for a permit.[29]

Taken together, beach activism and the determined work of Coastal Commission staff have made a difference. As explained in the Our Malibu Beaches app Q&A, it is rare these days to be chased off Malibu's public sands by private guards.[30] Yet high-profile battles continue to be fought on the California shoreline. A recent "beach villain" is Vinod Khosla, a tech billionaire who closed off Martin's Beach in San Mateo County in 2010. After an almost decadelong legal fight between Khosla (who has yet to spend one night at his beach property) and the commission, along with the nonprofit Surfrider Foundation, the Supreme Court declined in 2018 to review the homeowner's appeal. Coastal activists across the nation had feared that the conservative-leaning body would side with Khosla and potentially alter decades of land-use regulations. Two years later, the state, on behalf of the Coastal Commission, sued Khosla to reopen the beach. As of 2023, the lawsuit was ongoing, but the Khosla affair ensured that the public good stays in the news. As attorney Joseph Cotchett put it in the *Washington Post* in 2020, "Beaches are public in California, and the immensely wealthy must comply with the Coastal Act just like everyone else."[31]

ARNOLD AND PAMELA: THE PERSISTENT ALLURE OF LOS ANGELES'S BEACH BODIES

Even after the closing of Muscle Beach, the region's beaches continued to attract athletes and inspire Hollywood directors and writers. In the late 1960s and 1970s, Muscle Beach found a second life in Venice where Arnold Schwarzenegger's fame contributed to the wider acceptance of the male muscular body in mainstream culture. A decade later, the worldwide success of *Baywatch*, a TV show revolving around the lives of Los Angeles lifeguards, made the California beach body a fixture in global imaginaries. By then, bleached air, toned muscles, and a deep tan were not enough; surgically enhanced breasts and hyper-thin bodies were de rigueur for women, as were sculpted six-pack abs for men. In addition, the show perpetuated the Hollywood tradition of erasing nonwhite Angelenos' contribution to the local beach and body culture while also reinforcing damaging stereotypes about Latinos.

In the 1940s and 1950s, Santa Monica's Muscle Beach had brought muscles and bodybuilders out of sweaty, dimly lit gyms and associated muscularity with West Coast fitness and Hollywood glamour. After Muscle Beach moved to Venice, its weightlifting platform, which had been in existence since 1950, rapidly gained a reputation as a refuge for local bodybuilders and weightlifters. In a 1965 local TV show, host Ralph Story explained that most of the Muscle Beach athletes had indeed "packed up their muscles" and headed to Venice, "where weightlifting was not thought incompatible with civic image."[32] As Los Angeles's "last poor beach," Venice gave these athletes a safe space away from conservative politicians and urban renewal projects.[33]

By the mid-1970s, the "Pit," as regulars called it, was home to famous champions, including the reigning Mr. Olympia (bodybuilding's most prestigious competition), Arnold Schwarzenegger. The young Austrian, like many other local bodybuilders, did most of his training at Joe Gold's Gym in Venice, but he also spent afternoons perfecting his tan at the Pit. The publication of Charles Gaines's book *Pumping Iron* (1974), an exploration of the bodybuilding culture, followed by the release of a documentary of the same name in 1977, brought considerable attention to the Venice weightlifting scene. The book included photographs of the bodybuilders lounging in small briefs near the weightlifting platform, while the film featured a scene at the Pit in which Arnold Schwarzenegger coached Franco Columbu through a series of bench press lifts.[34] Although Gaines had clearly distinguished between the old Muscle Beach and Venice in the book, confusion between the two sites spread in the mainstream press.[35] Following *Pumping Iron*'s box office success, bodybuilding films such as *The Hustler of Muscle Beach* (1980), which was set in Venice, contributed to this confusion. By the early 1980s, bodybuilders and non-bodybuilders alike called the Pit "Muscle Beach Venice."[36]

The Muscle Beach of the 1960s and 1970s differed in important ways from its predecessor. For one, women bodybuilders completely disappeared from view. According to Ralph Story, women were not even allowed inside the weightlifting area. Whether women were ever banned from the Pit or not, evidence points to their second-class-citizen status. In architectural historian Reyner Banham's 1972 documentary on Los Angeles, for instance, only one woman was filmed exercising in the Pit.[37] In *Pumping Iron*, both the book and the film, women were confined to roles as girlfriends, wives, and groupies. Sexist attitudes, pervasive in the sport, compounded this trend. In the 1970s, Gold's Gym, the famous weightlifting facility in Venice, was said to pride itself on being "ovary free."[38] Throughout the 1960s and 1970s, women were represented in the press and popular culture as the intended audience for men's visible muscularity rather than as muscular athletes themselves.

This evolution reflected the focus on the hyper-heterosexual muscleman at the new Muscle Beach. While Muscle Beach bodybuilders of the past had emphasized their heterosexuality by posing next to pretty actresses and recounting their military experiences, their 1960s and 1970s counterparts openly made sexual references. In one of *Pumping Iron*'s most iconic scenes, Arnold Schwarzenegger hinted at bodybuilders' extraordinary libido by comparing the action of pumping (the process through which muscles fill up with blood during a workout) with having orgasmic sex with a woman. The intense focus on women's obsession with the male athletes' bodies further guaranteed that no suspicion would arise regarding the musclemen's sexuality. According to Ralph Story, Muscle Beach Venice was closed to the ladies for fear they "touch some monumental bicep and fall away in a dead swoon." Interviewed by *Cosmopolitan* in 1977, a young woman who "spen[t] much of her free time at 'Muscle Beach,'" described with rapture her pleasure at watching musclemen work out "*especially* when they're covered with suntan oil." Another one specifically praised their "sexual stamina."[39]

By the 1980s, as historian of fitness Shelly McKenzie argues, "sculpted muscles were the goal." Exercise in general experienced something of a boom during the decade. In Southern California, where fitness had always been a way of life, the trend fueled the already established fitness industry. Angelenos flocked to yoga studios, took up mountain biking, and sweated in their living rooms while working out with Jane Fonda's aerobic videos. Even the busiest executives could work out thanks to "gyms on wheels"— trucks fitted with aerobic and weightlifting equipment.[40]

Did the beach remain a space where new forms of exercise and body trends originated and gained popularity? To some extent, yes. Joggers and cyclists flocked to the beach bike path built in the 1970s from Santa Monica to Palos Verdes. In the late 1980s, following on the heels of the skateboard boom, the rollerblade frenzy took off on the Venice boardwalk, where several shops rented the trendy in-line skates to visitors.[41] In addition, Muscle Beach continued to inspire copycats, with Long Beach's first outdoor gym opening near Belmont Pier in 1990.[42] Even tony Santa Monica wanted to claim its role as the "birthplace of the physical fitness boom." In 1989, the city accepted the Muscle Beach Alumni Association's offer to set up a discreet sign at "the original location of Muscle Beach," honoring the legacy of the famous athletes who trained on the sands.[43]

The same year, NBC aired the first season of an hourlong drama centered on the lives of Los Angeles County lifeguards. Mediocre ratings and scathing criticism led NBC to cancel *Baywatch* after only one season.[44] However, after its revival in syndication in 1992, *Baywatch* set records for ratings in both domestic and international markets. Aired in 72 countries (later expanding to 145), the show was, according to a British TV journalist, "incredibly bad but compulsively watchable."[45] The compulsion not only buoyed the show for eleven seasons; it eventually gave rise to a global franchise, complete with a spin-off series and countless branded products, from Barbie dolls to air fresheners. By 1995, the *New York Times* claimed that "*Baywatch* had a wider audience on the planet Earth than any other entertainment show in history." "Apparently," the journalist noted somewhat sarcastically, "nothing c[ould] match the magnetic pull of wet California girls—and guys—on a beach."[46]

As tempting as it is to dismiss *Baywatch* as a vapid TV show, its success reveals the continuing appeal in global imaginaries of the Southern California beaches and their associated lifestyle. In fact, there would have been no *Baywatch* phenomenon were it not for the European market. For the first time in television history, reported *Variety*, "foreign sales to overseas broadcasters [drove] the production of a US series in syndication."[47] Europeans' enthusiasm took even the show's publicists by surprise. One explanation offered in the United Kingdom, where 10.5 million viewers tuned in to ITV for the Saturday "teatime show," was that watching *Baywatch* "was like having a holiday in Florida." No matter that the series was actually shot on Will Rogers State Beach in California. "The real stars of the show" were "the sun and the sea," and regional nuances escaped most British viewers anyway.[48]

While pristine beaches were certainly appealing from the vantage point of rainy Britain, beautiful bodies mattered as much as the background. Take the case of *Eldorado* (1992–1993), a BBC series launched around the same time that revolved around the lives of British expatriates living in a Spanish coastal resort. According to *Guardian* journalist Judy Rumbold, *Eldorado* was canceled after only one year because it involved "pale, ordinary plebs like you and me," whereas *Baywatch* featured "sexy youngsters who were clearly born with sand between their toes" and for whom "unwanted body hair and melanoma were foreign concepts."[49] The show's close-up shots of women's almost-bare backsides and men's ripped abs rapidly became its most iconic features. Renamed "Bumwatch" by UK critics, the show tapped into a growing interest in fitness videos, plastic surgery, and indoor tanning abroad. For those who wanted visual inspiration rather than a workout, *Baywatch* provided the highest number of square inches of skin per minute. It also felt authentic: *Daily Mail* critic Jeannette Kupfermann had no doubt that "if you go on the beach in California that is what it is like."[50] *Baywatch*'s appeal in Europe was thus partly based on the fascination with the latest Hollywood beauty and body trends—from fake tanning to silicone implants.

Of course, there were national nuances. According to a British reporter in 1996, Italian and Spanish men were flocking to the cosmetic surgeon to get rid of their paunches, while in "stolid Britain, the 'Baywatch mentality' ha[d] not yet taken root and the beer gut still enjoy[ed] a certain prestige." In India, men were not quite ready to go under the knife, but they were willing to exercise for a chance at *"Baywatch* abs." Whatever the locale, it was widely agreed that "Baywatch's biggest strength [wa]s its unabashed eagerness to objectify the human body." To be more specific, the show's "slight soft-porn quality" offered sexual titillation without stigma. By the mid-1990s, the show was so popular that its name became part of the everyday vocabulary used to designate a certain type of body: huge, high-pointed breasts and skinny thighs for women, and six-pack abs on a tanned chest for men. Magazines and newspapers regularly referenced *"Baywatch* breasts" and the *"Baywatch* look."[51] In that sense, not much had changed since the time when Mack Sennett launched his bathing beauties on the screens: the shores of Los Angeles remained central to global imaginaries of beauty.

While it is hard to say whether *Baywatch* played a direct role in the rise of eating disorders and the rapid increase in breast augmentation procedures (182,378 American women underwent augmentation in 1998, which represented a 306 percent increase from 1992), the show was widely seen as damaging to women's body image and self-esteem. In many psychological studies published in the 1990s, *Baywatch* was mentioned or used to conduct experiments measuring the impact of "thin shows" on young women's perception of themselves.[52] Pamela Anderson, who played lifeguard C. J. Parker and became famous for her silicone-enhanced cleavage, was singled out for having done "at least as much as any other figure in history to promote an unhealthy obsession with breast size."[53]

This was far from the only criticism directed at the show. Commentators often remarked on the wide gap between the "silicone-implanted fantasy" and the reality of Los Angeles's polluted and crime-ridden beaches where the homeless camped at night.[54] Yet the fantasy elements were key to the show's success. It also tapped into nostalgia among baby boomers who had spent their youth hanging out at the beach. The yearning for a return to the beach of the 1960s was already evident when Paramount released an umpteenth sequel to *Beach Party* titled *Back to the Beach* (1987), in which Annette and Frankie, the main characters in the AIP movies, now a middle-aged, permed-haired couple, returned to California for some fun in the sun. As a *Los Angeles Times* journalist remarked, the pair "represent[ed] a final pre-Vietnam era of innocence," a breath of fresh air "in the AIDS era of sexual conservatism."[55] Just as beach movies had assuaged the fears of a generation confronting Cold War threats and racial tensions, *Baywatch* may well have been, at least for its American viewers, an opportunity to escape the drumbeat of unemployment, crime, race riots, and pollution in the 1990s news cycle. Some critics agreed. As one put it, as a "titillating yet innocent" show, *Baywatch* was "almost a piece of nostalgia, with its bevy of voluptuous beauties in bathing suits, set in a dorm-like LA beach culture that never really existed."[56]

If nostalgia was the draw, at least for American viewers, it played heavily on racial anxieties, which increased among Angelenos as new waves of Asian and Latin American immigrants arrived in the city in the 1980s and 1990s. In sharp contrast to this demographic trend, the TV show featured a lily-white team of lifeguards until its seventh season (1996), when African American actress Traci Bingham and Latino actor José Solano joined the cast as regulars. Before that, the sole Black character was Sgt. Garner Ellerbee, the police officer assigned to the beach, whose dislike for swimming and wearing shorts set him apart from the ocean gods and goddesses. The centrality of whiteness to the show's brand was also evident in the short lifespan of *Baywatch Nights* (1995–1997), a spin-off that featured Mitch Buchannon and Garner Ellerbee working together as private detectives. Characterized as "taking a more multiethnic, multicultural approach" by the *Los Angeles Times*, the show failed to attract viewers and was axed after two seasons.[57]

The unbearable whiteness of *Baywatch*, however jarring when set against an increasingly multiethnic city, bore some resemblance to reality: the vast majority of lifeguards were still white in the 1990s.[58] The crowds and victims of drowning depicted on the show did include a more diverse cast, but more often than not, they played into racial stereotypes, with Latino youths portrayed as inner-city gang bangers.[59] In that sense, the *Baywatch* beach represented a white refuge, just as it had in the 1960s beach movies, but one to be preserved from an incoming tide of racial others whose presence on the sands proved disruptive.

Building upon Hollywood's century-old tradition of beach-centric movies, *Baywatch* continued to spread the idea that, in Los Angeles, the beach was "the preserve of the young, the lean and the tanned."[60] By the late 1990s, however, *Baywatch* had packed its bags and moved to Hawaii for its final two seasons. By then, the allure of the shapely lifeguards had to compete, on the small screen, with the popularity of *Friends*, with its New York coffee shops and apartment settings. Even Pamela Anderson could sense a cultural shift. Around this time, she had her breast implants removed, saying she wanted her body to look more natural.[61]

Figure E.1. The unbearable whiteness of the *Baywatch* cast in its third season, 1992–1993. © The Baywatch Production Company / Fremantle.

Yet this was far from the end of Hollywood's incursions at the beach. In 2017 Paramount released *Baywatch*, a much-anticipated film adaptation of the now legendary TV show. Although set in Florida, the film tapped into audiences' nostalgia for the show's iconic red one-piece bathing suit and infamous slow-motion running scenes. A movie based on nostalgic yearnings for a TV show, which itself had based its appeal on nostalgia for the beach scene of the 1960s, was always going to be tricky business. Critics were scathing. Unresolved subplots, cringy penis jokes, and lackluster digital effects conspired to make for a spectacularly bad movie. Domestic box office figures were disappointing too. Once again, the movie was rescued by its international audience. The *Baywatch* combination of sandy beaches and shapely bodies still proved powerfully magnetic for viewers abroad. The movie "collared more than 63% of its total box office from offshore turnstiles," turning it into a profitable enterprise.[62] Geographically speaking, Florida's reputation as home to chic resorts and vast beaches worked well for the brand. Athletic, tanned, and thin beach bodies were now part of a global culture, detached from their local history and original landscapes. As if anticipating a beachless future for the region, *Baywatch* had severed its ties with the Southern California shores.

FROM BEACH REPARATIONS TO BEACH SUBMERSION: THE UNCERTAIN FUTURE OF LOS ANGELES'S BEACHES

Today, the Santa Monica Pier is the pride of the city, and no city councilor would ever dream of suggesting its demolition. But the pier has new enemies, more difficult to combat than its 1970s detractors. According to visual projections released by the nonprofit environmental organization Climate Central in 2021, the Santa Monica Pier will be entirely submerged in water by 2100, apart from its famous Ferris wheel and the tops of buildings, if carbon dioxide emissions continue unabated and human-caused global warming exceeds 3 degrees Celsius (5.4 degrees Fahrenheit). The rest of the region's beaches will not fare much better. According to scientific estimates, "31% to 67% of Southern California beaches may become completely eroded by 2100" due to sea-level rise (using projections of a 3- to 6.6-foot rise).[63]

Even if greenhouse gas emissions ceased entirely tomorrow, the beaches would still be in trouble. Ever since the 1970s, scientists have been warning

Figure E.2. Visual projections of the effects of sea-level rise on the Santa Monica Pier if global warming reaches 3 degrees Celsius above preindustrial temperatures. © climatecentral.org.

officials and the public about the damage caused by coastal development and flood control and reservoir projects. The vast majority of beach sand in Southern California comes from riverine sediments deposited on the coast during periods of heavy flooding. By building flood control and water supply dams and channelizing coastal rivers, engineers have protected people and buildings from flooding, but they have also cut off the beaches from their main sediment supply. During the three decades that followed World War II, the sand deficit was compensated for by the seemingly endless amount of sand dredged on the coast for the construction of marinas, small boat harbors, the sewage treatment plant at Hyperion, and other major coastal projects. Yet beginning in the early 1970s, when coastal construction came to a halt due to environmental concerns, the sand spigot was shut off and beaches began to starve. Other regional sources of sediment—coastal dunes and cliff erosion—were also affected by development, which limited their ability to protect and feed the beaches. Faced with erosion, municipalities turned to armoring the beach by building seawalls, jetties, and groins. This provided some relief in the short term, but often worsened beach erosion or simply displaced it. Sand nourishment from offshore or inland supplies was another option, but it came at a high cost. When the disastrous El Niño storms of 1982–1983 battered Southern California, thousands of homes and businesses were damaged, and beaches lost on average 150 feet of their width.[64] While the following winters were mild, allowing the beaches to re-plenish themselves, erosion problems eventually returned.

Starting in the early 1990s, scientists began sounding the alarm about sea-level rise and its impact on beaches. As warmer temperatures caused glaciers to melt and ocean water to expand, the sea was advancing, aggravating existing erosion problems. At that point, the threat was seem-ingly far off in the future, and coastal retreat, an adaptation strategy involving pushing homes and buildings away from the shoreline, was out of question. As the twenty-first century dawned, the threat became re-ality. Up until the 2010s, scientists explained, the West Coast had been relatively spared from sea-level rise compared to other coastlines due to a climate cycle creating cold surface waters. This cycle, however, was ending. In the Los Angeles region, the Malibu and Venice areas are particularly threatened. Projections in 2022 estimated that sea level will rise at least eight inches by 2050 on the West Coast (compared to a national average of ten to twelve inches).[65] By 2050, all but the largest Malibu beaches are expected to be below annual flood level.[66]

Such projections have yet to deter wealthy Malibu beachfront homeowners from trying to save their small patch of paradise. After "sandbagging" and the controversial construction of a berm using sand from a nearby public beach failed to save their beach, Broad Beach homeowners started an unprecedented privately funded battle against rising seas. In 2010, they hired the best experts on the subject and set up a public agency to collect funds and restore the beach to its former glory. Using some of their twenty-million-dollar war chest, they built an emergency eight-foot-high rock seawall. With septic tanks at risk of submersion, the Coastal Commission had no choice but to authorize the construction.[67] Five years later, the Broad Beach homeowners enacted the second part of their plan: using offshore sand to build protective dunes on the beach. The costly replenishment is only temporary, however. Every five to ten years, more sand will be needed as the waves swallow the precious load. Appropriately for a beach frequented by Hollywood stars, some critics call this "Botox for the beach." Homeowners who oppose the costly nourishment plan have proposed an alternative: building an artificial reef offshore to keep the sand in place. A third option, managed retreat, is the most viable strategy in the long term. It's also the only one that would not impact nearby beaches. Even so, it's an option nobody at Broad Beach wants since it would involve moving back $180 billion worth of premium real estate. Meanwhile, beach homes in the area continue to be sold in multimillion-dollar deals, with some real estate agents actively trying to spread disinformation about the effects of climate change. The commission watches the Broad Beach situation from a distance. With all that money and expertise invested, will the residents save their beach?[68]

Clashes between the public and private homeowners have become rare now on Broad Beach as it has just a sliver of sand at low tide. There simply is no public beach left to fight over. This does not mean that the commission and activists should relax their vigilance. As past experience has shown, Malibu homeowners are so desperate to save their homes that the solutions they propose could threaten nearby public beaches. Rising sea levels and rampant beach privatization could work in concert to deprive Angelenos of what will become even more precious as climate chaos delivers more frequent heat waves: a free space where one can enjoy cooling breezes and a dip in the ocean.

Public beaches have a key role to play in fostering climate justice. Not all Angelenos have access to air conditioning, and coastal access has the potential to become a key public health issue. The beach closures during the spring 2020 COVID-19 lockdown provoked passionate debates in Southern California precisely because they coincided with an early heat wave. With millions of Angelenos cooped up in stuffy homes, the thought of forgoing a trip to the beach was too much to bear for some. "Going to the beach," journalist George Skelton protested, "is our birthright as native

Californians—and our promise to newcomers."[69] Whether this promise can be kept for future generations is uncertain.

In some places along the California coast, bringing about justice means re-privatizing the beach. Seized from its African American owners by the Manhattan Beach City Council in the 1920s, Bruce's Beach was eventually turned into a public park in the late 1950s. By the early 2000s, calls for renaming the park brought the city's shameful history of racism to light. After lengthy debates and some pushback from those on the council who preferred to bury divisive stories, the beach was officially renamed Bruce's Beach in 2006. A plaque, placed at the site, controversially praised city founder George Peck (who did not oppose the Bruces' eviction) for his help in establishing a resort "for all people."[70] In the summer of 2020, the murder of George Floyd and the ensuing Black Lives Matter protests revived calls for racial justice. In Manhattan Beach, the "Justice for Bruce's Beach" group demanded a new plaque, financial reparations, and the return of the land to the Bruce descendants. While the city council refused to issue a formal apology, Los Angeles County (which has owned the beach since the 1990s) had supportive officials at the helm. In an unprecedented move, county officials transferred the property, estimated at twenty million dollars, to Willa and Charles Bruce's descendants in July 2022.[71] The fact that the first major example of land reparation in the United States happened to be a piece of a Southern California beach is no coincidence. No other piece of land in the United States, except perhaps in downtown Manhattan, has increased so much in value over the twentieth and twenty-first centuries. People thus immediately grasp the immense financial loss suffered by the Bruces and their descendants. At the same time, the beach represents the ultimate California dream, the promise of a better life at the edge of the continent.

With the transfer of Bruce's Beach, the California dream has regained some of its luster. Yet the transfer ironically arrives at a time when there is no guarantee that this beach will continue to exist by the end of the century. Returning Bruce's Beach to its rightful owners is not enough. To guarantee its existence and that of other ocean sands for future generations, to achieve racial and climate justice, will demand an end to armoring the coast and implementing a plan for selective managed retreat, allowing beaches to wax and wane seasonally, as they used to do before coastal engineering became ubiquitous. It means continuing to fight for public access to the shores. Finally, and most urgently, it means ending our dependence on fossil fuels. These are no small tasks, but continuing business as usual will only deliver a future with narrower and less accessible beaches, if not a beachless future altogether.

In his 2020 novel *The Wall*, science fiction author John Lanchester imagined a dystopian world where sea-level rise and climate chaos have turned Britain into an island-fortress protected from hordes of refugees by an immense, concrete wall. Young people who have never known any other world, he writes, "have a thing about beaches."

> They watch movies and TV programmes about beaches, they look at pictures of beaches, they ask the old what it was like to go to a beach, what it felt like to lie on sand all day, and what was it like to build a sandcastle and watch the water come in and see the sandcastle fight off the water and then succumb to it, a castle which once looked so big and invulnerable, just melting away, so that when the tide goes out you can't see that there was anything there.[72]

The history of Los Angeles's beaches, and Lanchester's prose, remind us of what is at stake when it comes to the shores. Beaches are places of joy, wonder, and play. It's on to us to make sure they don't just melt away.

NOTES

ABBREVIATIONS

ASBPA	American Shore and Beach Preservation Association
BEB	Beach Erosion Board
CBA	California Beaches Association
CCC	California Coastal Commission
CSULB	California State University–Long Beach
CSUN	California State University–Northridge
LACA	Los Angeles City Archives
LAT	Los Angeles Times
LAPL	Los Angeles Public Library
LMU	Loyola Marymount University
MHL	Margaret Herrick Library
NYT	New York Times
SCWH	Seaver Center for Western History
SMEO	*Santa Monica Evening Outlook* (note that the name of the newspaper varied over the twentieth century)
SMHM	Santa Monica History Museum
SPA	Shoreline Planning Association
UCLA	University of California–Los Angeles
USC	University of Southern California
WRCA	Water Resources Collection & Archives
YRL UCLA	Charles E. Young Research Library, University of California–Los Angeles

INTRODUCTION

1. LA County beaches account for about 1,400 acres of sand, which is about two square miles, while Central Park covers 843 acres (1.317 square miles). LA figures found in "Beachgoers Still Like to Make Own Waves," *LAT*, September 6, 1982, D1; beach attendance figures come from the Los Angeles County Fire Department Lifeguard Division, http://www.laalmanac.com/fire/fi20.php, accessed January 29, 2020.

2. Mike Davis, *City of Quartz: Excavating the Future in Los Angeles* (New York: Vintage Books, 1990), 230.

3. Deike Peters, "Density Wars in Silicon Beach: The Struggle to Mix New Space for Toil, Stay and Play in Santa Monica, California," in *Protest and Resistance in the Tourist City*, ed. Claire Colomb and Johannes Novy (London: Routledge, 2017), 93.

4. Hillel Aron, "How Venice Became the Most Expensive Neighborhood in Los Angeles," *LA Weekly*, January 18, 2017, http://www.laweekly.com/news/how-ven ice-became-the-most-expensive-neighborhood-in-los-angeles-7831779.

5. Reyner Banham, *Los Angeles: The Architecture of Four Ecologies* (1971; repr. Berkeley: University of California Press, 2009), 37.

6. Roy Rosenzweig and Elizabeth Blackmar, *The Park and the People: A History of Central Park* (Ithaca, NY: Cornell University Press, 1998), 3.

7. The San Pedro Bay, which is located just south of the Santa Monica Bay, has a very different history, having been chosen in the late nineteenth century as the site for the industrial and commercial port of Los Angeles and, eventually, the port of Long Beach. It deserves its own history and, in fact, has been the subject of a recent monograph that unpacks the entanglement of sociotechnical systems and ecological relations in the port complex and its surrounding area. See Christina Dunbar-Hester, *Oil Beach: How Toxic Infrastructure Threatens Life in the Ports of Los Angeles and Beyond* (Chicago: University of Chicago Press, 2023).

8. Cornelia Dean, *Against the Tide: The Battle for the American Coast* (New York: Columbia University Press, 1999), 27–29.

9. Gary Griggs, *Living with the Changing California Coast* (Berkeley: University of California Press, 2005), 433.

10. Alain Corbin, *The Lure of the Sea: The Discovery of the Seaside in the Western World, 1750–1840* (Berkeley: University of California Press, 1994); Peter Borsay and John K. Walton, *Resorts and Ports: European Seaside Towns since 1700* (Bristol, UK: Channel View Publications, 2011); Yves Perret-Gentil, Alain Lottin, and Jean-Pierre Poussou, eds., *Les villes balnéaires d'Europe Occidentale du XVIIIe siècle à nos jours* (Paris: PUPS, 2008).

11. Gabriel Désert, *La vie quotidienne sur les plages normandes du Second Empire aux années folles* (Paris: Hachette, 1983); Jon Sterngass, *First Resorts: Pursuing Pleasure at Saratoga Springs, Newport, and Coney Island* (Baltimore: Johns Hopkins University Press, 2001); Johan Vincent, *L'intrusion balnéaire. Les populations littorales bretonnes et vendéennes face au tourisme (1800–1945)* (Rennes: Presses Universitaires de Rennes, 2007); Alice Garner, *A Shifting Shore: Locals, Outsiders, and the Transformation of a French Fishing Town, 1823–2000* (Ithaca, NY: Cornell University Press, 2005).

12. Marc Boyer, *L'hiver dans le Midi: L'invention de la Côte d'Azur XVIIIe–XXIe siècle* (Paris: Editions L'Harmattan, 2010); Mercedes Tatjer, "En los orígenes del turismo litoral: Los banos del mar y los balnearios marítimos en Cataluna," *Scripta Nova* 13, no. 296 (August 2009).

13. John K. Walton and Gary Cross, *The Playful Crowd: Pleasure Places in the Twentieth Century* (New York: Columbia University Press, 2005); John F. Kasson, *Amusing the Million: Coney Island at the Turn of the Century* (New York: Hill & Wang, 1978); Kathy Peiss, *Cheap Amusements: Working Women and Leisure in Turn-of-the-Century New York* (Philadelphia: Temple University Press, 1987).

14. Scholars have not yet fully engaged with the history of the beach in the twentieth century, especially for its second half. It is almost as if, after what Alain Corbin termed the "invention of the beach" in the late nineteenth century and the golden age of Coney Island shortly thereafter, the shores stopped evolving, remaining in a state of arrested development ever since. Corbin, *The Lure of the Sea*, 70; Kasson, *Amusing the Million*, 109–12. There are some exceptions, in particular on the history of Australian beaches. See Douglas Booth, *Australian Beach Cultures: The*

History of Sun, Sand and Surf (London: Routledge, 2012), and Caroline M. Ford, *Sydney Beaches: A History* (Sydney: New South Wales University Press, 2014).

15. Mark Fiege, *The Republic of Nature: An Environmental History of the United States* (Seattle: University of Washington Press, 2013), 12; on ocean and marine environmental history, see Jeffrey W. Bolster, "Opportunities in Marine Environmental History," *Environmental History* 11, no. 3 (July 2006): 567–597, and Helen M. Rozwadowski, "The Promise of Ocean History for Environmental History," *Journal of American History* 100, no. 1 (June 2013): 136–139.

16. Isaac Land, "The Urban Amphibious," in *The New Coastal History: Cultural and Environmental Perspectives from Scotland and Beyond*, ed. David Worthington (London: Palgrave Macmillan, 2017), 33–34; John R. Gillis, *The Human Shore: Seacoasts in History* (Chicago: University of Chicago Press, 2012), 161. David Worthington pinpointed the mid-2000s as the moment when, independent of each other, several scholars turned their attention to coastal communities. David Worthington, "Introducing the New Coastal History: Cultural and Environmental Perspectives from Scotland and Beyond," in *The New Coastal History: Cultural and Environmental Perspectives from Scotland and Beyond* (London: Palgrave Macmillan, 2017), 4. On coastal history, see also Joana Gaspar de Freitas, Robert James, and Isaac Land, "Coastal Studies and Society: The Tipping Point," *Coastal Studies & Society*, 1, no. 1 (2022): 3–9; Land has kept a blog on coastal history for many years, which provides important theoretical insights on the subfield: http://porttowns. port.ac.uk/coastal-history-blog/. A recent example of a monograph that shifts the historical narrative by focusing on coastal spaces is Kara Murphy Schlichting, *New York Recentered: Building the Metropolis from the Shore* (Chicago: University of Chicago Press, 2019).

17. See Andrew A. Kahrl, *The Land Was Ours: African American Beaches from Jim Crow to the Sunbelt South* (Cambridge, MA: Harvard University Press, 2012); Connie Y. Chiang, *Shaping the Shoreline: Fisheries and Tourism on the Monterey Coast* (Seattle: University of Washington Press, 2008); Andrew A. Kahrl, *Free the Beaches: The Story of Ned Coll and the Battle for America's Most Exclusive Shoreline* (New Haven, CT: Yale University Press, 2018); Sara Fingal, "Turning the Tide: The Politics of Land and Leisure on the California and Mexican Coastlines in the Age of Environmentalism" (PhD dissertation, Brown University, 2012).

18. On Brazilian beaches, see Bruno Carvalho, "Mapping the Urbanized Beaches of Rio de Janeiro: Modernization, Modernity and Everyday Life," *Journal of Latin American Cultural Studies* 16, no. 3 (2007): 325–339; on Australian beach cultures, see Booth, *Australian Beach Cultures*; Leone Huntsman, *Sand in Our Souls: The Beach in Australian History* (Melbourne: Melbourne University Press, 2001).

19. On Disneyland, see Eric Avila, *Popular Culture in the Age of White Flight: Fear and Fantasy in Suburban Los Angeles* (Berkeley: University of California Press, 2004); Sharon Zukin, *Landscapes of Power: From Detroit to Disneyworld* (Berkeley: University of California Press, 1991); George Lipsitz, "The Making of Disneyland," in *True Stories from the American Past*, vol. 2 (New York: McGraw-Hill, 1993), 179–196; Timothy J. Gilfoyle, "White Cities, Linguistic Turns, and Disneylands: The New Paradigms of Urban History," *Reviews in American History* 26, no. 1 (1998): 175–204.

20. In *The Frontier of Leisure*, historian Lawrence Culver does acknowledge the centrality of Southern California beaches and resorts "in shaping urban recreation—and struggles for civil rights—in twentieth-century America." Yet he lumps together Disneyland and the beaches as part of the regional promotion of leisure

as a way of life. Lawrence Culver, *The Frontier of Leisure: Southern California and the Shaping of Modern America* (New York: Oxford University Press, 2010), 9.

21. Kasson, *Amusing the Million*; Peiss, *Cheap Amusements*; David Nasaw, *Going Out: The Rise and Fall of Public Amusements* (Cambridge, MA: Harvard University Press, 1999); Jeff Wiltse, *Contested Waters: A Social History of Swimming Pools in America* (Chapel Hill: University of North Carolina Press, 2007).

22. Nasaw, *Going Out*, 1.

23. Bryant Simon, *Boardwalk of Dreams: Atlantic City and the Fate of Urban America* (New York: Oxford University Press, 2006), 13; Alison Isenberg, *Downtown America: A History of the Place and the People Who Made It* (Chicago: University of Chicago Press, 2004), 6; Victoria W. Wolcott, *Race, Riots, and Roller Coasters: The Struggle over Segregated Recreation in America* (Philadelphia: University of Pennsylvania Press, 2012), 4.

24. For a history of urban renewal that focuses on the West Coast, see Alison Isenberg, *Designing San Francisco: Art, Land and Urban Renewal in the City by the Bay* (Princeton, NJ: Princeton University Press, 2017).

25. Among Kevin Starr's multivolume history of California, see in particular *Inventing the Dream: California through the Progressive Era* (New York: Oxford University Press, 1985); *Material Dreams: Southern California through the 1920s* (New York: Oxford University Press, 1990); *The Dream Endures: California Enters the 1940s* (New York: Oxford University Press, 1997); and *Golden Dreams: California in an Age of Abundance, 1950–1963* (New York: Oxford University Press, 2009).

26. Davis, *City of Quartz*, 196–198; 160–185. For another key essay by Davis on the Los Angeles beaches, see "The Case for Letting Malibu Burn," *Environmental History Review* 19, no. 2 (1995): 1–36.

27. Mike Davis, "How Eden Lost Its Garden: A Political History of the Los Angeles Landscape," in *The City: Los Angeles and Urban Theory at the End of the Twentieth Century* (Berkeley: University of California Press, 1996), 164.

28. On the California Coastal Commission, see Fingal, "Turning the Tide"; Richard A. Walker, *The Country in the City: The Greening of the San Francisco Bay Area* (Seattle: University of Washington Press, 2007), 110–129; Jared Orsi, "Restoring the Common to the Goose: Citizen Activism and the Protection of the California Coastline, 1969–1982," *Southern California Quarterly* 78, no. 3 (1996): 257–284; Thomas J. Osborne, *Coastal Sage: Peter Douglas and the Fight to Save California's Shore* (Berkeley: University of California Press, 2018).

29. Walker, *The Country in the City*, 4.

30. Clark Davis, "From Oasis to Metropolis: Southern California and the Changing Context of American Leisure," *Pacific Historical Review* 61, no. 3 (May 1992): 363.

31. Giacomo Parrinello et al., "Shifting Shores of the Anthropocene: The Settlement and (Unstable) Stabilisation of the North-Western Mediterranean Littoral over the Nineteenth and Twentieth Centuries," *Environment and History*, January 2019 [online first], 25.

32. Sean Vitousek et al., "A Model Integrating Longshore and Cross-Shore Processes for Predicting Long-Term Shoreline Response to Climate Change," *Journal of Geophysical Research: Earth Surface* 122, no. 4 (2017): 782.

CHAPTER 1

1. According to some accounts, the full name of the pueblo was actually "El Pueblo de Nuestra Señora La Reina de Los Angeles de Porciùncula." Pueblos were agricultural

communities created during the Spanish colonial period. Federal Writers' Project, *California in the 1930s: The WPA Guide to the Golden State* (Berkeley: University of California Press), 210.

2. A search for "Westside" in the *Los Angeles Times* database shows that the term experienced a sudden surge in popularity beginning in the early 1960s. It is used more and more frequently from this period on; Reyner Banham, *Los Angeles: The Architecture of Four Ecologies* (Berkeley: University of California Press, 2001), 37.

3. Bruno Carvalho explains how a similar cartographic shift turned the wealthy Zonal Sul into Rio de Janeiro's new center in his article, "Mapping the Urbanized Beaches of Rio de Janeiro: Modernization, Modernity and Everyday Life," *Journal of Latin American Cultural Studies* 16, no. 3 (December 2007): 325. For a 1930 map of Los Angeles foregrounding the beaches, see for instance "Special Sightseeing Map: Los Angeles and Vicinity," Tanner Motor Tours, 1930 (private collection of the author). For historical maps of Los Angeles, see "Los Angeles Mapped," online exhibition, Library of Congress, accessed November 12, 2021, https://www.loc.gov/exhibits/lamapped/lamapped-exhibit.html.

4. Alain Corbin, *The Lure of the Sea: The Discovery of the Seaside in the Western World, 1750–1840* (Berkeley: University of California Press, 1994), 70.

5. Robert M. Fogelson, *The Fragmented Metropolis: Los Angeles, 1850–1930* (Berkeley: University of California Press, 1993); Greg Hise, *Magnetic Los Angeles: Planning the Twentieth-Century Metropolis* (Baltimore: Johns Hopkins University Press, 1999); Jeremiah B. C. Axelrod, *Inventing Autopia: Dreams and Visions of the Modern Metropolis in Jazz Age Los Angeles* (Berkeley: University of California Press, 2009).

6. Kevin Starr, *Inventing the Dream: California through the Progressive Era* (New York: Oxford University Press, 1985), 3; Gary Griggs, Kiki Patsch, and Lauret Savoy, *Living with the Changing California Coast* (Berkeley: University of California Press, 2005), 428. On Native Californians of the Los Angeles Basin during the colonial era, see, for instance, John G. Douglass, Kathleen L. Hull, and Seetha N. Reddy, "The Creation of Community in the Colonial-Era Los Angeles Basin," in *Forging Communities in Colonial Alta California*, ed. Kathleen L. Hull and John G. Douglass (Tucson: University of Arizona Press, 2018), 35–61; Paula A. Scott, *Santa Monica: A History on the Edge* (Mount Pleasant, SC: Arcadia Publishing, 2004), 33.

7. Fogelson, *Fragmented Metropolis*, 66–67; John E. Baur, *The Health Seekers of Southern California, 1870–1900* (San Marino, CA: Huntington Library, 2010); Lawrence Culver, *The Frontier of Leisure: Southern California and the Shaping of Modern America* (New York: Oxford University Press, 2010), 15–51.

8. Catherine Cocks, *Tropical Whites: The Rise of the Tourist South in the Americas* (Philadelphia: University of Pennsylvania Press, 2013), 100; Kate Cowick, *The Outlook's Story of Santa Monica* (Santa Monica, CA: Evening Outlook, 1932), 17; Louise B. Gabriel, *Early Santa Monica* (Charleston, SC: Arcardia Publishing, 2006), 25; Ronald A. Davidson, "Before 'Surfurbia': The Development of the South Bay Beach Cities through the 1930s," *APCG Yearbook* 66 (2004): 84.

9. Scott, *Santa Monica*, 57; Davidson, "Before 'Surfurbia'" 83; Fred W. Viehe, "Black Gold Suburbs: The Influence of the Extractive Industry on the Suburbanization of Los Angeles, 1890–1930," *Journal of Urban History* 8, no. 1 (November 1981): 8.

10. Jennifer Krintz, *Redondo Beach Pier* (Charleston, SC: Arcadia Publishing, 2011), 2; William F. Deverell, "The Los Angeles 'Free Harbor Fight,'" *California History* 70, no. 1 (March 1991): 16.

11. See, for instance, the case of France's Brittany coast in Johan Vincent, *L'intrusion balnéaire: Les populations littorales bretonnes et vendéennes face au tourisme (1800-1945)* (Rennes: Presses universitaires de Rennes, 2007).

12. Culver, *Frontier of Leisure*; Thomas S. Wadsworth, *El Pizmo Beach for Pleasure and Profit* (Los Angeles: Renfrew Adv., 1908), 11; "Coronado Tent City, Coronado Beach, California," publicity brochure, 1908, 12, Rare Books Collection, Huntington Library; Lyra Kilston, *Sun Seekers: The Cure of California* (Los Angeles: Ateliers Editions, 2019), 45.

13. Cocks, *Tropical Whites*, 103.

14. John Higham, "The Reorientation of American Culture in the 1890s," in *The Origins of Modern Consciousness*, ed. John Weiss (Detroit: Wayne State University Press, 1965), 42–47; John F. Kasson, *Amusing the Million: Coney Island at the Turn of the Century* (New York: Hill & Wang, 1978).

15. On the invention of the "Mediterranean Summer," see Christophe Granger, *Les corps d'été: naissance d'une variation saisonnière, XXe siècle* (Paris: Autrement, 2009), 44; on the transition to summer as the high season in Southern California, see Carey McWilliams, *Southern California: An Island on the Land* (1946; repr. Santa Barbara, CA: Peregrine Smith, 1973), 137.

16. Corbin, *Lure of the Sea*; Charles R. Stapleton, "Recreation and Its Problems on the Santa Monica-Venice Shoreline, Southern California" (MA thesis, UCLA, 1952), 34.

17. Charles S. Warren, *History of the Santa Monica Bay Region: In Two Parts, Narrative and Biographical* (Santa Monica, CA: A. H. Cawston, 1934), 34; Patricia Adler, *A History of the Venice Area* (Los Angeles: Department of City Planning, October 1969), 9–12; Starr, *Inventing the Dream*, 80–81.

18. *SMEO* (note that the name of the newspaper varied over the twentieth century), February 22, 1900, 2; *SMEO*, July 13, 1901, 1.

19. Fogelson, *The Fragmented Metropolis*, 78.

20. McWilliams, *Southern California*, 276–277; Fogelson, *The Fragmented Metropolis*, 132; Becky M. Nicolaides, *My Blue Heaven: Life and Politics in the Working-Class Suburbs of Los Angeles, 1920–1965* (Chicago: University of Chicago Press, 2002), 48.

21. Fogelson, *The Fragmented Metropolis*; Hise, *Magnetic Los Angeles*.

22. Axelrod, *Inventing Autopia*, 16; Dana Webster Bartlett, *The Better City: A Sociological Study of a Modern City* (Los Angeles: Neuner Company Press, 1907).

23. The first zoning ordinances in Los Angeles date from 1904. Mansel G. Blackford, *The Lost Dream: Businessmen and City Planning on the Pacific Coast, 1890–1920* (Columbus: Ohio State University Press, 1993), 92.

24. Axelrod, *Inventing Autopia*, 210–16; Fogelson, *The Fragmented Metropolis*, 261.

25. Blackford, *The Lost Dream*, 91; *LAT*, February 18, 1917, II1; Andrew Deener, *Venice: A Contested Bohemia in Los Angeles* (Chicago: University of Chicago Press, 2012), 23–24.

26. Blackford, *The Lost Dream*, 91. The Pacific Electric streetcars owed their nickname to their red color; by comparison, automobile ownership was at one for thirteen inhabitants nationally, and one for thirty in Chicago.

27. Annual financial report of the Board of Playground and Recreation, 1938, box A 2060, LACA.

28. Most of Mack Sennett's short films cannot be seen today as they have been lost or destroyed, but the scripts are still available. Box 71, folder 696, and box 75, folder 839, Production Files, Mack Sennett Collection, Margaret Herrick Library.

29. Viehe, "Black Gold Suburbs"; Banham, *Los Angeles*, 38.

30. Newspaper clipping, *Los Angeles Examiner*, June 26, 1927. Box 1, file 5, Fritz Burns Papers, LMU; *SMEO*, July 11, 1936, 9.

31. Clara Byrd, telephone interview with author, March 29, 2012; Jonathan Booth, interview, August 23, 1982, transcript, Virtual Oral/Aural History Archive, CSULB, https://csulb-dspace.calstate.edu/handle/10211.3/224406?show=full.

32. Corbin, *Lure of the Sea*; Advertisement in the *Los Angeles Examiner*. Box 7 ov, Fritz Burns Papers, LMU; *Palisades Del Rey Press*, April 10, 1926, 1.

33. Advertising brochure "Rancho Malibu," 1938, box 58, folder "Malibu," Ephemera Collection-1299, SCWH; *Palisades Del Rey Press*, January 1, 1926, 1, Fritz Burns Papers, LMU.

34. Malibu remained virtually untouched up until 1929, when the Roosevelt Highway was inaugurated. Before that, the owner of the vast rancho, businessman Frederick Rindge and, following his death in 1905, his widow, May K. Ridge, doggedly refused to open up their piece of paradise to development. In 1923, the State of California obtained a right-of-way to construct the Roosevelt State Highway. Ridge spent a fortune defending her piece of land in the courts, but she was eventually forced to declare bankruptcy in 1935. By then, the movie colony was already settling in the area. See David K. Randall, *The King and Queen of Malibu: The True Story of the Battle for Paradise* (New York: W. W. Norton & Company, 2017).

35. Advertising brochures, box 1, 5. Fritz Burns Papers, LMU.

36. Ibid.

37. John Steven McGroarty, *Hollywood Riviera* (Los Angeles: Clifford R. Reid Company, 1921).

38. Douglas Flamming, *Bound for Freedom: Black Los Angeles in Jim Crow America* (Berkeley: University of California Press, 2006), 272–275; Alison Rose Jefferson, "African-American Leisure Space in Santa Monica," *Southern California Quarterly* 91, no. 2 (2009): 155–189.

39. *California Eagle*, September 25, 1925, 5; *California Eagle*, October 8, 1925, 6; *California Eagle*, October 16, 1925, 6.

40. *Souvenir of Long Beach California*, Long Beach Heritage Museum, 1984 [1932], 10; box 1, 13, Fritz Burns Papers, LMU.

41. "Rancho Malibu," 1938; see the photographs in boxes 4 ov and 5:12, Fritz Burns Papers, LMU; Heather Addison, *Hollywood and the Rise of Physical Culture* (London: Routledge, 2003), 143–151.

42. *Palisades Del Rey Press*, February 1, 1926, 1; *Palisades Del Rey Press*, November 10, 1928, 5.

43. Advertising brochures, Box 1, 5. Fritz Burns Papers, LMU.

44. In 1919, the California Supreme Court struck down racial restrictions on who could *purchase* property but upheld them on who could *occupy* property. This allowed real estate companies to continue to enforce the color line. See Flamming, *Bound for Freedom*, 156.

45. Federal Writers Project, *Los Angeles*, 266; *Souvenir of Long Beach California*, 1932.

46. *SMEO*, June 1, 1930, section 3, 8; *Souvenir of Long Beach California*, 5; Eric Avila, *Popular Culture in the Age of White Flight: Fear and Fantasy in Suburban Los Angeles* (Berkeley: University of California Press, 2004), 111; Sterngass, *First Resorts*, 95.

47. Bryant Simon, *Boardwalk of Dreams: Atlantic City and the Fate of Urban America* (New York: Oxford University Press, 2006).

48. *LAT*, April 13, 1914, II6.

49. "Long Beach, California Today. Fastest Growing City in the World," 1913.

50. Kasson, *Amusing the Million*, 34.
51. Late 1920s advertising brochure, box 58, folder "Manhattan Beach." Ephemera Collection-1299, SCWH; Federal Writers' Project of the Works Progress Administration of Northern California, *California: A Guide to the Golden State*, American Guide Series (New York: Hastings House, 1939), 419.
52. On the Mediterranean metaphor, see Starr, *Inventing the Dream*, 45–46; William F. Deverell, *Whitewashed Adobe: The Rise of Los Angeles and the Remaking of Its Mexican Past* (Berkeley: University of California Press, 2004), 76–77.
53. Federal Writers Project, *Los Angeles*, 354.
54. *SMEO*, July 8, 1950, 10A.
55. *LAT*, February 18, 1917, II1; August 1, 1934, A4.
56. Nancy Mowll Mathews, *Moving Pictures: American Art and Film, 1880–1910* (Manchester, VT: Hudson Hills Press, 2005), 92–93; Starr, *Inventing the Dream*, 292; Gabriel Solomons, *World Film Locations: Los Angeles* (Chicago: University of Chicago Press, 2011), 27; *Palisades Del Rey Press*, August 15, 1927, 8, Fritz Burns Papers, LMU.
57. *Palisades Del Rey Press*, August 1, 1927, 3, Fritz Burns Papers, LMU.
58. Randall, *The King and Queen of Malibu*; Scott, *Santa Monica*, 95.
59. Richard DeCordova, *Picture Personalities: The Emergence of the Star System in America* (Champaign: University of Illinois Press, 2001).
60. Box 28, folder "tours." Ephemera Collection-1299, SCWH.
61. Federal Writers' Project, *California*, 415.
62. See, for instance, "Redondo Beach," Los Angeles and Redondo Railway brochure, 1900, and "Redondo Beach and the Pleasures You May Have There," 1920, both held by the Huntington Library, San Marino, California.
63. Hilde D'Haeyere, "Splashes of Fun and Beauty. Mack Sennett's Bathing Beauties," in *Slapstick Comedy*, ed. Tom Paulus and Rob King (London: Taylor & Francis, 2009), 207.
64. Addison, *Hollywood*, 38.
65. See, for instance, "Feminine Football on the Beach at Del Rey," *Palisades Del Rey Press*, August 15, 1927, 8.
66. *SMEO*, May 24, 1919, 4.
67. King, *The Fun Factory*, 244; D'Haeyere, "Splashes of Fun and Beauty," 213.
68. *LAT*, May 4, 1916, III2; *SMEO*, June 22, 1936, 1; May 31, 1928, 6; May 23, 1928, 2.
69. Transcript of Verna Williams's 1991 interview, https://exhibits.lapl.org/shadeso fla/wp-content/uploads/2022/07/Verna_Williams-ada.pdf.
70. *California Eagle*, August 28, 1925, 1; September 11, 1925, 7; September 18, 1925, 1; Alison Rose Jefferson, *Living the California Dream: African American Leisure Sites during the Jim Crow Era* (Lincoln: University of Nebraska Press, 2020), 200; photographs of the event are printed in Deborah Willis, *Posing Beauty: African American Images from the 1890s to the Present* (New York: W. W. Norton & Co., 2009), 122–123.
71. On the early twentieth-century history of fitness, see Harvey Green, *Fit for America: Health, Fitness, Sport, and American Society* (New York: Pantheon Books, 1986), and Natalia Mehlman Petrzela, *Fit Nation: The Gains and Pains of America's Exercise Obsession* (Chicago: University of Chicago Press, 2023).
72. See chapter 1 in Addison, *Hollywood*.
73. Culver, *The Frontier of Leisure*, 63; McWilliams, *Southern California*, 110.
74. *LAT*, August 25, 1904, 7.
75. See, for instance, *California Eagle*, July 23, 1921, 2.

76. *LAT*, July 2, 1926, B4; *LAT*, July 16, 1926, B4; *SMEO*, June 2, 1929, 14.
77. Michel Rainis, "French Beach Sports Culture in the Twentieth Century," *International Journal of the History of Sport* 17, no. 1 (2000): 148.
78. *LAT*, July 31, 1904, C11.
79. The Benevolent and Protective Order of Elks is a fraternal organization that organizes social and charitable activities. A lodge has existed in Santa Monica since 1904. *SMEO*, May 30, 1928, 2.
80. "Marion Davies and Her Colonial Beach Home, Santa Monica," Werner Von Boltenstern Postcard Collection, LMU.
81. *SMEO*, September 4, 1935, 2; September 8, 1936, 10.
82. *Life*, August 5, 1946, 14. In my research I found no date for the installation of the rings and bars, either in newspaper references or in Santa Monica city archives, but they are mentioned in oral interviews and a posteriori testimonies. Harold Zinkin and Bonnie Hearn, *Remembering Muscle Beach: Where Hard Bodies Began: Photographs and Memories* (Santa Monica, CA: Angel City Press, 1999), 25. On the history of Muscle Beach, see Marla Matzer Rose, *Muscle Beach* (New York: St. Martin's Griffin, 2001), and Elsa Devienne, "The Life, Death, and Rebirth of Muscle Beach: Reassessing the Muscular Physique in Postwar America, 1940s–1980s," *Southern California Quarterly* 100, no. 3 (August 2018): 324–367.
83. *SMEO*, July 16, 1940, 5.
84. Arthur C. Verge, "George Freeth: King of the Surfers and California's Forgotten Hero," *California History* 80, no. 2/3 (2001): 82–105.
85. Tom Blake, *Hawaiian Surfriders* (Redondo Beach, CA: Mountain and Sea, 1998), 61.
86. Matt Warshaw, *The History of Surfing* (San Francisco: Chronicle Books, 2010), 55.
87. Gary Y. Okihiro, *Island World: A History of Hawai'i and the United States* (Berkeley: University of California Press, 2008), 149.
88. Lorrin A. Thurston, "What Hawaii Really Means to Southern California," *LAT*, January 1, 1925, E2.
89. Arthur C. Verge, *Santa Monica Lifeguards* (Charleston, SC: Arcadia Publishing, 2007), and *Los Angeles County Lifeguards* (Charleston, SC: Arcadia Publishing, 2005).
90. See, for instance, *LAT*, April 13, 1924, H1.
91. Tom Blake, "Waves and Thrills at Waikiki," *National Geographic* 67 (May 1935): 597–604.
92. Kristin Lawler, *The American Surfer: Radical Culture and Capitalism* (London: Routledge, 2011), 74.
93. Verge, *Los Angeles County Lifeguards*, 52.
94. *LAT*, April 14, 1941, A3.
95. Margaret DePond, "Southland Surf: Hawaiians, Surfing, and Race in Los Angeles, 1907–1928," *Southern California Quarterly* 101, no. 1 (February 1, 2019): 45–78.
96. Culver, *Frontier of Leisure*, 3.

CHAPTER 2

1. *LAT*, July 5, 1936, 15.
2. George J. Sánchez, *Becoming Mexican American: Ethnicity, Culture, and Identity in Chicano Los Angeles, 1900–1945* (New York: Oxford University Press, 1993), 90.
3. For accounts of the incident, see Victoria Wolcott, *Race, Riots, and Roller Coasters: The Struggle over Segregated Recreation in America* (Philadelphia: University of Pennsylvania Press, 2012), 24–28; Colin Fisher, "Outdoor Recreation and the Chicago Race Riot," in *To Love the Wind and the Rain: Essays in African American*

Environmental History ed. Dianne D. Glave and Mark R. Stoll (Pittsburgh: University of Pittsburgh Press, 2005), 63–76.

4. See Andrew J. Diamond, *Mean Streets: Chicago Youths and the Everyday Struggle for Empowerment in the Multiracial City, 1908–1969* (Berkeley: University of California Press, 2009); Jeffrey Wiltse, *Contested Waters: A Social History of Swimming Pools in America* (Chapel Hill: University of North Carolina Press, 2007); Wolcott, *Race, Riots, and Roller Coasters*; Andrew Kahrl, *The Land Was Ours: How Black Beaches Became White Wealth in the Coastal South* (Chapel Hill: University of North Carolina Press, 2016).

5. John K. Walton, *The British Seaside: Holidays and Resorts in the Twentieth Century* (Manchester: Manchester University Press, 2000), 3.

6. John F. Kasson, *Amusing the Million: Coney Island at the Turn of the Century* (New York: Hill & Wang, 1978); Gary S. Cross and John K. Walton, *The Playful Crowd: Pleasure Places in the Twentieth Century* (New York: Columbia University Press, 2005).

7. Alison Rose Jefferson, *Living the California Dream: African American Leisure Sites during the Jim Crow Era* (Lincoln: University of Nebraska Press, 2020).

8. Flamming, Douglas, *Bound for Freedom: Black Los Angeles in Jim Crow America* (Berkeley: University of California Press, 2006), 8.

9. Ibid., 25.

10. Ibid., 81.

11. Jefferson, *Living the California Dream*, 35.

12. Interview with Verna Williams, tape 1, side A, Shades of L.A. Oral History Project, LAPL, accessed January 17, 2022, transcript at https://www.lapl.org/sites/defa ult/files/shades/transcripts/Verna_Williams.pdf.

13. Jefferson, *Living the California Dream*, 82–85.

14. *California Eagle*, July 11, 1930, 2.

15. On interracial encounters on the streets and corners of Chicago, see Diamond, *Mean Streets*, 47–50.

16. See Ronald A. Davidson, "Before 'Surfurbia': The Development of the South Bay Beach Cities through the 1930s," *APCG Yearbook* 66 (2004): 81–94.

17. "Souvenir of Long Beach California," Long Beach Historical Society, 5.

18. *SMEO*, June 27, 1917, 1.

19. *LAT*, August 1, 1911, III1.

20. Los Angeles counted one police officer per 1,300 inhabitants in 1900 (by comparison with 1 per 430 in New York City, for example). Albert J. Reiss Jr., "Police Organization in the Twentieth Century," *Crime and Justice: An Annual Review of Research* (1992): 56–57; Arthur C. Verge, *Los Angeles County Lifeguards* (Charleston, SC: Arcadia, 2005), 24, and *Santa Monica Lifeguards* (Charleston, SC: Arcadia, 2007).

21. Roy Rosenzweig and Elizabeth Blackmar, *The Park and the People: A History of Central Park* (Ithaca, NY: Cornell University Press, 1998), 313.

22. *SMEO*, August 19, 1916, 1.

23. *American City*, June 28, 1923, 569.

24. *LAT*, March 11, 1930, A2.

25. See Wiltse, *Contested Waters*, 111–112; cited in Catherine Cocks, *Tropical Whites: The Rise of the Tourist South in the Americas* (Philadelphia: University of Pennsylvania Press, 2013), 107.

26. *SMEO*, June 27, 1912.

27. *SMEO*, August 22, 1916, 8; *SMEO*, July 18, 1919, 1; *SMEO*, August 2, 1919, 1. For more details on this controversy, see Elsa Devienne, "City Limits: Bather Arrests in Early-20th-Century Los Angeles," *Modes pratiques. Journal of Clothes and Fashion History*, Special Issue (January 2018): 48–65.

28. Wiltse, *Contested Waters*, 121.

29. Emory Stephen Bogardus, *The City Boy and His Problems: A Survey of Boy Life in Los Angeles* (Los Angeles: House of Ralston, printers, 1926), 126.

30. Joy Elliott, interviewed by Kaye Briegel on December 13, 1989. Interview 1c, Segment 7 (18:58–27:31), Segkey: ab3453. Long Beach Area History, Signal Hill. The Virtual Oral/Aural History Archive, California State University, Long Beach.

31. Ads in *SMEO*, September 30, 1928, 20, and *SMEO*, August 21, 1924, 2. These clubs were the Edgewater and Casa Del Mar, the Breakers, the Deauville, the Santa Monica Athletic Club, the Club Chateau, the Sea Breeze, the Gables, the Miramar, the Santa Monica Swimming Club, and the Santa Monica Beach Club.

32. *LAT*, February 27, 1927, B1.

33. The 1935 figure is mentioned in A. G. Johnson, "Beach Protection and Development around Los Angeles," *Shore & Beach* 3, no. 4 (October 1935): 110; *LAT*, July 28, 1923, V7.

34. *SMEO*, September 30, 1928, 20.

35. *Splashes*, newsletter of the Bel Air Bay Club, September 1939, 2.

36. *Los Angeles Examiner*, January 15, 1939. Los Angeles Examiner Clippings collection, Special Collections, USC.

37. A 1939 photograph of the Waverly Beach Club shows one of these signs. See photograph no. 00044128, Herald Examiner Collection, LAPL; on thefts, see *LAT*, October 14, 1930, A3, and *LAT*, July 8, 1935, A1.

38. Rupert Hughes, *City of Angels* (New York: Scribner's, 1941), 3–5.

39. *LAT*, August 9, 1925, C1; *LAT*, August 15, 1926, B1; *SMEO*, July 16, 1936, 1.

40. On white society's perceptions of Black leisure in that period, see Andrew W. Kahrl, "'The Slightest Semblance of Unruliness': Steamboat Excursions, Pleasure Resorts, and the Emergence of Segregation Culture on the Potomac River," *Journal of American History* 94, no. 4 (2008): 1108–1136.

41. The Jonathan Beach Club in Santa Monica was still facing accusations of racial discrimination in the late 1980s. Al Martinez, "I Have a Feeling That the Jonathan Club Is Going to Do All It Can to Remain Exactly What It Is," *LAT*, August 8, 1985 at https://www.latimes.com/archives/la-xpm-1985-08-08-we-3664-story.html.

42. On the myth of a "Golden Age" for early twentieth-century Afro-Angelenos, see Flamming, *Bound for Freedom*, 2.

43. On the Valentine affair, see ibid., 183–184, 202–204.

44. "Caucasians Organize Protective League," *LAT*, June 9, 1922, 14.

45. Jefferson, *Living the California Dream*, 41–42.

46. Ibid., 4–-44.

47. *California Eagle*, January 22, 1926, 1.

48. Jefferson, *Living the California Dream*, 41.

49. *California Eagle*, May 13, 1927, 2.

50. *California Eagle*, August 5, 1927, 1.

51. *California Eagle*, June 10, 1927, 1; *California Eagle*, July 8, 1927, 1; *California Eagle*, August 5, 1927, 1; *California Eagle*, August 19, 1927, 1.

52. *LAT*, August 16, 1927, A4.

53. *California Eagle*, July 8, 1927, 1, 5 (for cartoon).

54. At the time, some foreign-born Japanese (called Issei) who lived in the United States were allowed to naturalize, but most were prevented from doing so due to the Nationality Acts of 1790 and 1870, which restricted naturalization to white immigrants and African Americans. Asian-Americans' ineligibility was confirmed by *Ozawa vs. United States* (1922). Racial restrictions to naturalization were eventually removed in 1952. American-born Japanese (Nisei) were citizens by birth.

55. Valerie J. Matsumoto, *City Girls: The Nisei Social World in Los Angeles, 1920–1950* (New York: Oxford University Press 2014), 33; "Fourth of July at Venice Beach," photograph no. 00003629, LAPL Photo Collection.

56. Louise Leung Larson, *Sweet Bamboo: A Memoir of a Chinese American Family* (Berkeley: University of California Press, 1990), 61, 105, 123–124, 133.

57. Matsumoto, *City Girls*, 24–25.

58. Interview with Chuck Furutani, May 14, 1973, 1a, Segment 4 (9:04–10:51), Segkey: g175. The Virtual Oral/Aural History Archive, CSULB. Audio files at https://csulb-dspace.calstate.edu/handle/10211.3/215352.

59. Minutes of the BPRC, June 17, 1926, box C0368, LACA.

60. *Palisades Del Rey Press*, November 11, 1927, 2.

61. *Los Angeles Times*, July 5, 1936, 15.

62. See, for instance, the petition by Venice residents sent on September 19, 1951, to the LA City Council, box A1106, file 50 103, CCC, LACA.

63. Ordinance no. 90 738, April 23, 1946, box A893, file 23172, CCC, LACA; *LAT*, September 15, 1930, A1.

64. Letter, box A1513, file 89691, CCC, LACA; *SMEO* July 1, 1940, 1.

65. *LAT*, December 30, 1940, A1.

66. August 18, 1927, Minutes of the BPRC, box C0368, LACA; August 2, 1928, Minutes of the BPRC, box C0368, LACA.

67. Los Angeles Police Department Annual Report, 1936–1937, 4.

68. *LAT*, July 5, 1936, 15.

69. Letter from Mrs. H. Frederickson, July 7, 1930, Minutes of the BPRC, box C0368, LACA; *Manhattan Beach Pilot*, September 19, 1940, 4.

70. Mach 1942, council communications, box A803, file 11077, LACA.

71. *LAT*, July 5, 1936, 15.

72. Ibid.

73. *California Eagle*, October 28, 1927, 1.

74. *Los Angeles Examiner*, January 8, 1939, January 13, 1939, Los Angeles Examiner Clippings Collection, Special Collections, USC.

75. Andrew Kahrl, "New Negroes at the Beach: At Work and Play outside the Black Metropolis," in *The New Negro Renaissance beyond Harlem*, ed. Davarian L. Baldwin and Minkah Makalani (Minneapolis: University of Minnesota Press, 2013), 339.

76. *Los Angeles Sentinel*, August 29, 1940, 1; *SMEO*, August 26, 1940, 7; *LAT*, August 26, 1940, 1.

77. On the zoot-suit riots, see Robin Kelley, *Race Rebels: Culture, Politics, and the Black Working Class* (New York: Free Press, 1994), 161–181; Maurizio Mazón, *The Zoot Suit Riots: The Psychology of Symbolic Annihilation* (Austin: University of Texas Press, 1984); Luiz Alvarez, *The Power of the Zoot: Youth Culture and Resistance during World War II* (Berkeley: University of California Press, 2008); Kathy Peiss, *Zoot Suit: The Enigmatic Career of an Extreme Style* (Philadelphia: University of Pennsylvania Press, 2011).

78. Eduardo Obregón Pagán, *Murder at the Sleepy Lagoon: Zoot Suits, Race, and Riot in Wartime L.A.* (Chapel Hill: University of North Carolina Press, 2003), 8–9;

Eduardo Obregón Pagán, "Los Angeles Geopolitics and the Zoot Suit Riot," *Social Science History* 24, no. 1 (Spring 2000): 223–256.

79. *SMEO*, May 10, 1943, 7; *SMEO*, May 17, 1943, 7; *SMEO*, June 26, 1943, 1.

80. Alfred Barela, Mexican American teenager. Letter to the Honorable Arthur S. Guerin, May 21, 1943. Julian Nava collection, Urban Archives Center, CSUN. Quoted in Sánchez, *Becoming Mexican American*, 207.

81. Ibid., 259; Vesta Penrod, "Civil Rights Problems of Mexican-Americans in Southern California" (MA thesis, Claremont College, 1948), 27.

82. Pagán, *Murder at the Sleepy Lagoon*, 49.

83. Interview with Ramona Frias and Della Ortega, Shades of L.A., LAPL, part 2 (013), accessed August 17, 2022, https://www.lapl.org/sites/default/files/shades/tran scripts/Della_Ortega_and_Ramona_Frias.pdf, ; Eric Avila, *Popular Culture in the Age of White Flight: Fear and Fantasy in Suburban Los Angeles* (Berkeley: University of California Press, 2004), 112.

84. *LAT*, July 5, 1936, 15.

CHAPTER 3

1. William F. Deverell and Greg Hise, *Eden by Design: The 1930 Olmsted-Bartholomew Plan for the Los Angeles Region* (Berkeley: University of California Press, 2000), 3.

2. On beaches and oil, see Paul Sabin, "Beaches versus Oil in Greater Los Angeles," in *Land of Sunshine: An Environmental History of Metropolitan Los Angeles*, ed. William Deverell and Greg Hise (Pittsburgh: University of Pittsburgh Press, 2005), 95–114; Sarah S. Elkind, "Oil in the City: The Fall and Rise of Oil Drilling in Los Angeles," *Journal of American History* 99, no. 1 (June 2012): 82–90; Sarah S. Elkind, *How Local Politics Shape Federal Policy: Business, Power, and the Environment in Twentieth-Century Los Angeles* (Chapel Hill: University of North Carolina Press, 2011), 20–30. On the transformation of nature in LA, see Jared Orsi, *Hazardous Metropolis: Flooding and Urban Ecology in Los Angeles* (Berkeley: University of California Press, 2004); William F. Deverell and Greg Hise, *Land of Sunshine: An Environmental History of Metropolitan Los Angeles* (Pittsburgh: University of Pittsburgh Press, 2005); Douglas Cazaux Sackman, *Orange Empire: California and the Fruits of Eden* (Berkeley: University of California Press, 2005).

3. Annual Report of the Department of Playground and Recreation, 1927–1928, box A2060, LACA.

4. "Clean Beach Is Major Hermosa Asset," *Western City*, October 1939, 48; *Life*, June 28, 1937, 31.

5. Hise and Deverell, *Eden by Design*, 83, 85.

6. Ibid., 78, 98.

7. Ibid., 7.

8. Mike Davis, "How Eden Lost Its Garden: A Political History of the Los Angeles Landscape," in *The City: Los Angeles and Urban Theory at the End of the Twentieth Century*, ed. Allen J. Scott and Edward W. Soja (Berkeley: University of California Press, 1996), 164.

9. *California Beaches Association Bulletin* 1, no. 1 (January 1936): 1.

10. US Congress, *Congressional Record*, vol. 28, part 6 (1896): 5026; A. G. Johnson, "Beach Protection and Development around Los Angeles," *Shore & Beach* 3, no. 4 (October 1935): 111

11. Wallace Kaufman and Orrin H. Pilkey, *The Beaches Are Moving: The Drowning of America's Shoreline* (Durham, NC: Duke University Press, 1983), 12.

12. A. G. Johnson, "A Report on Erosion of the Beaches in the Venice District" (Los Angeles, 1940), 13–14; Johnson, "Beach Protection," 111.

13. Harry Leypoldt, "Shoreline Formation by Currents," *Shore & Beach* 9, no. 1 (January 1941): 17.

14. "Million-Dollar Beach Ruined by Erosion," *California Beaches Association Bulletin* 1, no. 5 (May 1936): 7; O. F. McEwen, "Harbor and Beach Problems of Santa Barbara, California," *Shore & Beach* 3, no. 4 (October 1935): 122.

15. *SMEO*, March 27, 1933, 1; Charles T. Leeds, "California's Beach Erosion and Development Problems," *Shore & Beach* 4, no. 4 (October 1936): 167.

16. BPRC commissioners' minutes, 1939, volume 20, p. 421, LACA.

17. Letter by John Anson Ford to R. R. Kilroy, January 3, 1938, box 43, folder B III, 10d, John Anson Ford Papers, Huntington Library; Master Plan of Shoreline Development, 1941, 9.

18. *LAT*, September 5, 1925, 5.

19. Thomas Parke Hughes, *American Genesis: A Century of Invention and Technological Enthusiasm, 1870–1970* (Chicago: University of Chicago Press, 2004).

20. Stéphane Durand, "L'apprentissage des lois de la nature. L'impact environnemental des aménagements portuaires en Languedoc aux XVIIe et XVIIIe siècles," in *Aménagement et environnement. Perspectives historiques,* ed. Geneviève Massard-Guilbaud and Patrick Fournier (Rennes: Presses universitaires de Rennes, 2016), 219–230.

21. Alain Corbin, *The Lure of the Sea: The Discovery of the Seaside in the Western World, 1750–1840* (Berkeley: University of California Press, 1994).

22. Transcript of the mayor of Santa Barbara's welcoming address at the May 16, 1936, conference organized by the California Beaches Association, M1, box 14, folder 99, Morrough P. O'Brien Papers, WRCA.

23. *LAT*, March 13, 1938, E1.

24. Sabin, "Beaches versus Oil," 96.

25. *SMEO*, June 12, 1930, 1.

26. Elkind, "Oil in the City," 82–83.

27. *SMEO*, June 12, 1930, 1.

28. *SMEO*, July 21, 1931, 1; March 1, 1939, 1, 6.

29. *California Beaches Association Bulletin* 1, no. 8 (August 1936): 2.

30. Elkind, "Oil in the City," 88.

31. "Report on a Pollution Survey of Santa Monica Bay Beaches in 1942," Sacramento, State of California, Department of Public Health, 1943, 6; *California Beaches Association Bulletin* 1, no. 10 (October 1936): 5.

32. Joel A. Tarr, *The Search for the Ultimate Sink: Urban Pollution in Historical Perspective* (Akron, OH: University of Akron Press, 1996), 121; John Hassan, "Were Health Resorts Bad for Your Health? Coastal Pollution Control Policy in England, 1945–76," *Environment and History* 5 (February 1999): 53–74.

33. "Report on a Pollution Survey," 6, 15–16.

34. Ibid.

35. Letter from Harry A. Scott to the State Department of Public Health, January 17, 1940; letter from Frances H. Thomsen to C. G. Gillespie of the State Bureau of Sanitary Engineering, September 1, 1936; letter from the Venice South Beach Improvement Association to C. G. Gillespie, November 29, 1939; letter from Dixie Dunnigan to the State Department of Public Health, July 25, 1941, box 30, folder 135.14, California Bureau of Sanitary Engineering Papers, WRCA; "Report on a Pollution Survey of Santa Monica Bay Beaches in 1942," 37, 63.

36. Letter from the State Board of Public Health to the City Council of Los Angeles, May 6, 1941, box A772, folder 7258, CCC, LACA.
37. Letter from Bertram P. Brown, director of the Public Health and Welfare Committee, to the City Council, June 3, 1941, box A772, folder 7258, CCC, LACA.
38. "Report on a Pollution Survey of Santa Monica Bay Beaches in 1942," 6–7.
39. Ibid., 34.
40. *Los Angeles Sentinel*, June 27, 1935, 2.
41. On urban summers before the advent of air conditioning, see Kara Murphy Schlichting, "Hot Town: Sensing Heat in Summertime Manhattan," *Environmental History* 27, no. 2 (April 2022): 354–368; *SMEO*, June 28, 1928, 2.
42. Hise and Deverell, *Eden by Design*, 153.
43. Transcript of a contribution by Major William J. Fox, "Proceedings of Meeting of Representatives of Governmental and Private Agencies, Called by the Board of Supervisors of the County of LA to Consider Beach and Shoreline Problems," April 12, 1940, WRCA, 35.
44. May 14, 1931, BPRC minutes, vol. 12, 1931, box C0368, LACA.
45. Transcript of the March 28, 1936, CBA Conference, M16, box 14, folder 99, O'Brien Papers, WRCA.
46. Andrew Kahrl, *Free the Beaches: The Story of Ned Coll and the Battle for America's Most Exclusive Shoreline* (New Haven, CT: Yale University Press, 2018), 16; "Courts Must Settle Line Controversy," *SMEO*, July 23, 1924, 1.
47. *LAT*, August 15, 1926, B1; Hise and Deverell, *Eden by Design*, 98; George W. Braden, "Progress in Conserving the Pacific Coast Beaches for the Public," *American City*, February 1929, 128; "Beach Playgrounds Are Threatened," *LAT*, August 9, 1925, C1.
48. *SMEO*, June 1, 1922, 1; *LAT*, June 7, 1922, II12; May 3, 1925, 8: July 25, 1925, A4.
49. Newton B. Drury, "California's Part in Preserving Shore and Beach," *Shore & Beach* 3, no. 3 (July 1936): 80. The vote also provided for the creation of a "Division of Parks" within the Natural Resources Department.
50. "California's State Parks," *LAT*, August 2, 1931, K12; "Appeal Made on Park Fund," *LAT*, May 22, 1933, A2.
51. Hugh R. Pomeroy, "Planning in Relation to the Beaches," *Shore & Beach* 4, no. 4 (October 1936): 115.
52. Contribution of Mr. Cheney, town planner of Palos Verdes Estates, transcript of proceedings at the American Shore and Beach Preservation Association Conference, Los Angeles, September 24, 1936, *Shore & Beach* 4, no. 4 (October 1936): 119; Hugh R. Pomeroy, "Scale and Balance Needed in Beach Planning," *California Beaches Association Bulletin* 1, no. 12 (December 1936): 8.
53. Editorial, *SMEO*, August 7, 1924, 1.
54. March 22, 1934, BPRC Minutes, box C0368, LACA.
55. "Report on a Pollution Survey," 34.
56. Lee Franklin Hanmer, *Public Recreation: A Study of Parks, Playgrounds and Other Outdoor Recreation Facilities* (New York: Regional Plan of New York and Its Environs, 1928).
57. Jamin Wells, *Shipwrecked: Coastal Disasters and the Making of the American Beach* (Chapel Hill: University of North Carolina Press, 2020), 73–84.
58. Cornelia Dean, *Against the Tide: The Battle for America's Beaches* (New York: Columbia University Press, 1999), 158; Robert L. Wiegel and Thorndike Saville Jr., "History of Coastal Engineering in the USA," in *History and Heritage of Coastal Engineering: A Collection of Papers on the History of Coastal Engineering in Countries*

Hosting the International Coastal Engineering Conference 1950–1996, ed. Nicholas C. Kraus (New York: American Society of Civil Engineers, 1996), 519, 567; R. S. Patton, Excerpt from a Paper Presented in Washington, DC, December 8, 1926, in *Shore & Beach* 2, no. 4 (October 1934): 132.

59. Wells, *Shipwrecked*, 13.
60. Patton, Excerpt, 132.
61. American Shore and Beach Preservation Association, "A Story of Cooperation: A Message to Coastal Communities," 1940, Doheny Library, USC.
62. Editorial, *Shore & Beach* 2, no. 4 (October 1934): 131.
63. The first took place at La Jolla on March 28, 1936, and the second at Santa Barbara on May 16, 1936.
64. "A Much-Needed Program," *California Beaches Association Bulletin* 1, no. 1 (January 1936): 1.
65. "Conference Show Shoreline Perils," *California Beaches Association Bulletin* 1, no. 5 (May 1936): 1.
66. "To Save the Beaches," *LAT*, February 3, 1936, A4; Transcript of President Beckwith's opening remarks at the May 16, 1936, CBA Conference in Santa Barbara, M3, box 14, folder 99, O'Brien Papers, WRCA; "Entering our Second Year," *California Beaches Association Bulletin* 1, no. 12 (December 1936): 2.
67. Transcript of President Beckwith's opening remarks, M3-4, box 14, folder 99, O'Brien Papers, WRCA; "A Much Needed Program," 1.
68. Samuel P. Hays, *Conservation and the Gospel of Efficiency: The Progressive Conservation Movement, 1890-1920* (Pittsburgh: University of Pittsburgh Press, 1999), 2.–
69. "A Much Needed Program," 1; transcript of President Beckwith's opening remarks.
70. "Program Lauded in Letters to Association: Hotel Man Tells Need," *California Beaches Association Bulletin* 1, no. 3 (March 1936): 11.
71. Transcript of President Beckwith's opening remarks.
72. The classic (but much-debated) study on wilderness is Roderick Nash, *Wilderness and the American Mind* (New Haven, CT: Yale University Press, 2001).
73. Colonel Marcel Garsaud, "The Need for Beach Attendance Statistic in Order to Promote Cooperative Effort," *Shore & Beach* 1, no. 1 (April 1933): 17; George F. McEwen, "Planning Needed to Solve Beach Problems," *California Beaches Bulletin Association* 1, no. 5 (May 1936): 11.
74. "Los Angeles's Projects," *California Beaches Bulletin Association* 1, no. 3 (March 1936): 6; Transcript of the "Beach and Shoreline Problems" Conference, Los Angeles, April 12, 1940, County of Los Angeles Board of Supervisors, 27, WRCA.
75. Communication of John C. Porter, September 24, 1936, *Shore & Beach* 4, no. 4 (October 1936): 103.
76. Garsaud, "The Need for Beach Attendance Statistic," 17.
77. "Methods to Protect Ocean Beaches Discussed," *California Beaches Bulletin Association* 1, no. 3 (March 1936): 6.
78. The diversity of rhetorical repertoires mobilized by the beach lobby confirms Robert Gottlieb's claim that the history of environmentalism has too often been told in a schematic manner, pitting the "romantic, unyielding, Scottish mountaineer John Muir" against the "German-trained, management-oriented forested Gifford Pinchot," to the exclusion of less well-known figures and groups who defended environments that could neither be classified as "wilderness" nor quite labeled as "resources." Robert Gottlieb, *Forcing the Spring: The Transformation of the American Environmental Movement* (Washington, DC: Island Press, 2005), 35–36.

79. "Discuss Association's Program for 1937," *California Beaches Association Bulletin* 2, no. 1 (January–February 1937): 8.

80. Editorial, *California Beaches Association Bulletin* 1, no. 10 (October 1936): 2; "Why No Aid for California?" *California Beaches Association Bulletin* 2, no. 1 (January–February 1937): 2.

81. "Proceedings of Meeting of Representatives of Governmental and Private Agencies, Called by the Board of Supervisors of the County of Los Angeles to Consider Beach and Shoreline Problems," April 12, 1940, 46, WRCA.

82. A. G. Johnson, "The Relation of Engineering to the Beaches," *California Beaches Association Bulletin* 1, no. 12 (December 1936): 3; Wiegel and Saville, "History of Coastal Engineering in the USA," 516–518.

83. Dean, *Against the* Tide, 8, 11.

84. Wiegel and Saville, "History of Coastal Engineering in the USA," 519.

85. "Morrough P. O'Brien: Dean of the College of Engineering, Pioneer in Coastal Engineering, and Consultant to General Electric," An Oral History Conducted 1986–88 by Marilyn Ziebarth, University of California–Berkeley, Regional Oral History Office, 1988, 19.

86. Bruce Seely, "Research, Engineering, and Science in American Engineering Colleges: 1900–1960," *Technology and Culture* 34, no. 2 (April 1993): 364; see also "Morrough P. O'Brien: Dean of the College of Engineering."

87. Morrough P. O'Brien, "How Models Help in Study of Beach Problems," *California Beaches Association Bulletin* 1, no. 4 (April 1936): 8; Morrough P. O'Brien, "The Coast of California as Beach Erosion Laboratory," *Shore & Beach* 4, no. 3 (July 1936): 74–79; and Morrough P. O'Brien, "Shoreline Phenomena and Research," *Shore & Beach* 4, no. 4 (October 1936): 120–125. In February 1939, he had lunch with the president of the SPA and George Hjelte, BPRC minutes, February 17, 1939, box C0370, LACA.

88. William Herron, *Oral History of Coastal Engineering Activities in Southern California, 1930–1981* (Fort Belvoir, VA: Defense Technical Information Center, 1986), 2–3.

89. A. G. Johnson, "Beach Protection and Development around Los Angeles," *Shore & Beach* 3, no. 4 (October 1935): 111.

90. Wiegel and Saville, "History of Coastal Engineering in the USA," 514.

91. Ibid., 520.

92. O'Brien, "How Models Help in Study of Beach Problems," 6.

93. Seely, "Research, Engineering, and Science in American Engineering Colleges."

94. Herron, *Oral History of Coastal Engineering*, foreword.

95. Transcript of the March 28, 1936, CBA Conference, M33–M35, box 14, folder 99, O'Brien Papers, WRCA.

96. Johnson, "A Report on Erosion of the Beaches in the Venice District," 12.

97. Morrough P. O'Brien, "The Coast of California as Beach Erosion Laboratory," *Shore & Beach* 4, no. 3 (July 1936): 79; Wiegel and Saville, "History of Coastal Engineering in the USA," 523.

98. Douglas Johnson, *Shore Processes and Shoreline Development* (New York: John Wiley & Sons, 1919), ix; Klaus J. Meyer Arendt, "Historical Coastal Environmental Changes: Human Responses to Shoreline Erosion," in *The American Environment: Interpretations of Past Geographies* ed. Craig E. Colten and Lary M. Dilsaver (Lanham, MD: Rowman and Littlefield, 1992), 222.

99. Editorial, *California Beaches Association Bulletin* 1, no. 2 (February 1936): 1; "Santa Barbara Beach Ruined," *California Beaches Association Bulletin* 1, no. 3 (March 1936): 9.

100. Transcript of a contribution by Morrough P. O'Brien at the Beach and Shoreline Problems Conference, April 12, 1940, 18, WRCA.
101. May 27, 1929, BPRC Minutes, box C0368, LACA.
102. O'Brien, "The Coast of California as Beach Erosion Laboratory," 79.
103. Douglas L. Inman, "Littoral Cells," UC–San Diego, Scripps Institution of Oceanography, 2003, 1, https://escholarship.org/uc/item/61p812hc.
104. O'Brien, "The Coast of California as Beach Erosion Laboratory," 79.
105. *SMEO*, August 5, 1940, 1; "Samuel L. Carpenter Jr., etc. (plaintiff) vs. City of Santa Monica (defendant), Pacific Mutual Life Insurance, a Corporation (Intervener)," 3, box 25, folder 148, O'Brien Papers, WRCA.
106. "Samuel L. Carpenter Jr., etc. (plaintiff) vs. City of Santa Monica (defendant), Pacific Mutual Life Insurance, a Corporation (Intervener)," 6, box 25, folder 148, O'Brien Papers, WRCA.
107. Press clipping, *Los Angeles Daily Journal*, 1939, box 25, folder 148, O'Brien Papers, WRCA.
108. Francis Price, "Legal Problems of California's Shoreline," *California Beaches Association Bulletin* 1, no. 11 (November 1936): 3.
109. Robert A. Caro, *The Power Broker: Robert Moses and the Fall of New York* (New York: Vintage Books, 1975), 308.
110. Ibid., 8.
111. Ibid., 310; "Development Plan for the Santa Monica Bay Shoreline, Topanga Canyon to El Segundo," Los Angeles City Planning Commission, 1945, 8.
112. Caro, *The Power Broker*, 318.
113. Thomas J. Campanella, "Robert Moses and His Racist Parkways, Explained," Bloomberg CityLab, July 9, 2017, https://www.bloomberg.com/news/articles/2017-07-09/robert-moses-and-his-racist-parkway-explained; "Super Public Beach of East Puts Southland to Shame with Its Mediocre Facilities," *Los Angeles Daily News*, July 28, 1941, 3.
114. Los Angeles County, "The Master Plan of Shoreline Development for the Los Angeles County Regional Planning District," 1940, 10; *LA Daily News*, July 28, 1941, 3.
115. George P. Larsen, "The Beaches Must Belong to the People: California's Statewide Program," *Shore & Beach* 14, no. 2 (October 1946): 67.
116. George P. Larsen, "Real Progress Continues in California," *Shore & Beach*, 10, no. 2 (October 1942): 53.
117. "Notes from California Beach Communities," *California Beaches Association Bulletin* 1, no. 8 (August 1936): 11.
118. *SMEO*, June 30, 1936, 16.
119. "Reclaimed Land Forms Beach," *California Beaches Association Bulletin* 1, no. 6 (June 1936): 7; transcription of A. G. Johnson's intervention at the March 28, 1936, CBA conference organized at La Jolla, A38, box 14, folder 99, O'Brien Papers, WRCA.
120. "Statement on the Major Problems Affecting the Venice–Santa Monica Beach Area," December 15, 1937, 2, box 25, folder 148, O'Brien Papers, WRCA.
121. "Beach Will Be Built out into the Ocean," *California Beaches Association Bulletin* 1, no. 11 (November 1936): 1; Johnson, "A Report on Erosion of the Beaches in the Venice District," April 1940, WRCA.
122. Letter from John Anson Ford to R. R. Kilgore, December 6, 1937, box 43, John Anson Ford Papers, Huntington Library.

123. Letter from John Anson Ford to R. R. Kilgore, January 3, 1938, box 43, John Anson Ford Papers, Huntington Library.
124. L. Deming Tilton, "Master Plan Needed for Coastal Areas," *California Beaches Association Bulletin* 1, no. 7 (July 1936): 3.
125. Editorial, *Shore & Beach* 9, no. 1 (January 1941): 2.
126. "The Master Plan of Shoreline Development for Orange County," Orange County Planning Commission, 1941.
127. Editorial, *Shore & Beach* 10, no. 2 (October 1941): 34.
128. Herron, *Oral History*, 11-3.
129. One exception in historical scholarship is Sarah S. Elkind's account of the Shoreline Planning Association's role in postwar beach planning, Elkind, *How Local Politics Shape Federal Policy*, 37–46. In terms of public memory, there is a little-known memorial plaque on Santa Monica Beach that honors the legacy of Geoffrey F. Morgan, who presided over the SPA in the 1940s. For a photograph of the memorial plaque, see Joe Oliva, "Geoffrey Francis Morgan: Orator, Civic Leader, Writer," May 6, 2010, http://bix1951.blogspot.com/2010/05/geoffrey-francis-morgan-orator-civic.html.
130. Elkind, *How Local Politics Shape Federal Policy*, 2.
131. Corbin, *Lure of the Sea*, 283.

CHAPTER 4

1. "Los Angeles Plans Model Facility," *California Coast* 4, no. 2 (March 1950): 3.
2. "Recreational Development of the Los Angeles Area Shoreline: An Engineering and Economic Report to the Mayor and the City Council, City of Los Angeles," New York, 1949, 148, box B1380, LACA.
3. *LAT*, September 25, 1948, 14.
4. Clark Davis, "From Oasis to Metropolis: Southern California and the Changing Context of American Leisure," *Pacific Historical Review* 61, no. 3 (May 1992): 375.
5. On white flight and urban decline, see Eric Avila, *Popular Culture in the Age of White Flight: Fear and Fantasy in Suburban Los Angeles* (Berkeley: University of California Press, 2004); Kevin M. Kruse, *White Flight: Atlanta and the Making of Modern Conservatism* (Princeton, NY: Princeton University Press, 2007); Robert O. Self, *American Babylon: Race and the Struggle for Postwar Oakland* (Princeton, NJ: Princeton University Press, 2003); Thomas Sugrue, *The Origins of the Urban Crisis: Race and Inequality in Postwar Detroit* (Princeton, NJ: Princeton University Press, 1996); Alison Isenberg, *Downtown America: A History of the Place and the People Who Made It* (Chicago: University of Chicago Press, 2004).
6. Arthur C. Verge, *Paradise Transformed: Los Angeles during the Second World War* (Dubuque, IA: Kendall/Hunt, 1993); Roger W. Lotchin, *The Bad City in the Good War: San Francisco, Los Angeles, Oakland and San Diego* (Bloomington: Indiana University Press, 2008); Kevin Starr, *Embattled Dreams: California in War and Peace, 1940–1950* (New York: Oxford University Press, 2002); Tom Sitton, *Los Angeles Transformed: Fletcher Bowron's Urban Reform Revival, 1938–1953* (Albuquerque: University of New Mexico Press, 2005).
7. The expression is journalist Miton Silverman's. Paul Rhode, "California in the Second World War: An Analysis of Defense Spending," in *The Way We Really Were: The Golden State in the Second Great War*, ed. Roger W. Lotchin (Urbana: University of Illinois Press, 2000), 93.
8. Arthur C. Verge, "Daily Life in Wartime California," in *The Way We Really Were: The Golden State in the Second Great War*, ed. Roger W. Lotchin (Urbana: University of

Illinois Press, 2000), 13; Arthur C. Verge, "The Impact of the Second World War on Los Angeles," *Pacific Historical Review* 63, no. 3 (August 1994): 297.

9. Connie Chiang, *Nature behind Barbed Wire: An Environmental History of the Japanese American Incarceration* (New York: Oxford University Press, 2018), 15–16.

10. George Fukasawa interview, August 12, 1974, California State University, Fullerton, Japanese American Oral History Project, https://oac.cdlib.org/view?docId=ft18700334;NAAN=13030&chunk.id=d0e17004&toc.id=&toc.depth=1&brand=calisphere&anchor.id=p226.

11. Report, August 9, 1943, box A826, file 14669, CCC, LACA.

12. *SMEO*, July 27, 1942, 1.

13. *LAT*, May 27, 1942, 1.

14. *SMEO*, March 28, 1942, 3; June 1, 1942, 1; Resolution of March 31, 1942, box A803, folder 11077, CCC, LACA.

15. *Splashes*, October 1942, 1 (available at the Bel Air Bay Club); *LAT*, May 27, 1942, 1.

16. *SMEO*, June 5, 1943, 4.

17. *SMEO*, July 6, 1942, 4; *LAT*, August 31, 1942, A3.

18. *SMEO*, June 8, 1942, 8; Letter from Rosalyn Rankin to the City Council, April 12, 1943, box A826, folder 14717, CCC, LACA.

19. *SMEO*, July 6, 1942, 1; June 21, 1943, 1.

20. *Splashes*, April 1944, 1.

21. *SMEO*, July 3, 1942, 5.

22. Salka Viertel, *The Kindness of Strangers* (New York: Holt, Rinehart, and Winston, 1969), 239. Cited in Verge, *Paradise Transformed*, 70.

23. Andrew Diamond, *Chicago on the Make: Power and Inequality in a Modern City* (Berkeley: University of California Press, 2017, 94.

24. April 12, 1944, Minutes of the Santa Monica City Council, Santa Monica Clerk Office; *SMEO*, July 12, 1943, 3.

25. *SMEO*, August 18, 1944, 10; June 6, 1944, 9; July 10, 1943, 11.

26. James K. Kimble, *Mobilizing the Home Front: War Bonds and Domestic Propaganda* (College Station: Texas A&M University Press, 2006); George H. Roeder, *The Censored War: American Visual Experience during World War Two* (New Haven, CT: Yale University Press, 1993).

27. "Life Goes to a Party at Santa Monica Beach," *Life*, April 27, 1942, 94–95; "Here Is a Girl's Guide for Entertaining Soldiers," *Life*, July 6, 1942, 8.

28. Clayton R. Koppes and Gregory D. Black, *Hollywood Goes to War: Patriotism, Movies and the Second World War* (New York: Free Press, 1987).

29. Gary Gerstle, "The Working Class Goes to War," in *The War in American Culture: Society and Consciousness during World War II*, ed. Lewis A. Erenberg and Susan E. Hirsch (Chicago: University of Chicago Press, 1996), 105.

30. Parks and Recreation Annual Report, 1944, box C2012, LACA.

31. *SMEO*, July 1, 1943, 11.

32. Letter from Rosalyn Rankin, April 12, 1943, box A826, folder 14717, CCC, LACA.

33. Letter, January 19, 1942, box A798, folder 10201, CCC, LACA.

34. George P. Larsen, "Real Progress Continues in California," *Shore & Beach* 10, no. 2 (October 1942): 47.

35. Letter, July 7, 1943, box 43, folder B III, 10d, John Anson Ford Papers, Huntington Library.

36. George P. Larsen, "New Laws Reinforce California Progress," *Shore & Beach* 11, no. 2 (October 1943): 42.

37. Letter from the SPA Inc. to all California newspapers, August 25, 1944, box 43, folder B III, 10d, John Anson Ford Papers, Huntington Library.

38. George P. Larsen, "The Public Beach Program in California," *Shore & Beach* 12, no. 2 (October 1944): 60.

39. See Andrew M. Shanken, "Planning Memory: Living Memorials in the United States during World War II," *Art Bulletin* 84, no. 1 (2002): 130–147.

40. George P. Larsen, "The Beaches Must Belong to the People," *Shore & Beach* 14, no. 2 (October 1946): 67.

41. "Midsummer," *Life*, August 12, 1946, 32–33.

42. Letter from Lloyd Aldrich, Minutes of the Santa Monica City Council, Santa Monica Clerk Office; Los Angeles County, *Shoreline Development, County of Los Angeles, 1944; Report on the Revised Master Plan of Shoreline Development*, Los Angeles, 1946; Letter, January 19, 1942, box A798, folder 10201, CCC, LACA.

43. Resolution of the City Council, August 17, 1944, box A748, folder 4145, CCC, LACA.

44. "A General Description of the 1945 Survey from June 13 to September 19," October 8, 1945, box A876, folder 21197, CCC, LACA.

45. "Quarantine Order," October 13, 1945, box A 876, folder 21 197, CCC, LACA.

46. Elmer Belt and California Sewage Works Association, "A Sanitary Survey of Sewage Pollution of the Surf and Beaches of Santa Monica Bay," 1942, 13, available at YRL UCLA; *SMEO*, June 2, 1943, 8.

47. *SMEO*, May 2, 1943, 8.

48. Letter from the Finance Committee on October 20, 1943, box A826, folder 14669, CCC, LACA.

49. Letter from George M. Uhl on August 27, 1943, box A826, folder 14669, CCC, LACA.

50. *SMEO*, May 1, 1943, 10; report, August 9, 1943, box A826, folder 14669, CCC, LACA.

51. *LAT*, April 5, 1945, 6; *Western City* 22 (February 1946): 16–17.

52. Greater Los Angeles Citizens Committee, *Shoreline Development Study, Playa Del Rey to Palos Verdes, a Portion of a Proposed Master Recreation Plan for the Greater Los Angeles Region*, Los Angeles, 1944, 7–8.

53. Donald F. Griffin, *Coastline Plans and Action for the Development of the Los Angeles Metropolitan Coastline*, Haynes Foundation, Los Angeles, 1944, 12, Special Collections, UCLA.

54. Robert Moses, "Post-war Beach Problems," *Shore & Beach* 11, no. 2 (October 1943): 35.

55. Editorial, *Shore & Beach* 11, no. 2 (October 1943): 34.

56. Greater Los Angeles Citizens Committee, *Shoreline Development Study, Playa Del Rey to Palos Verdes*; City Planning Commission, *Development Plan for the Santa Monica Bay Shoreline, Topanga Canyon to El Segundo* (Los Angeles: City Planning Commission, 1945). Los Angeles County (Calif.), *Shoreline Development, County of Los Angeles, 1944; Report on the Revised Master Plan of Shoreline Development*.

57. California State Park Commission, *Preliminary Master Plan of Shoreline Development for the State of California and Status Report on County Master Plans of Acquisition*, Sacramento, 1946.

58. General Warren T. Hannum, "Future Beach Planning for California," *Shore & Beach* 12, no. 2 (October 1944): 35.

59. *LAT*, August 23, 1945, A1.

60. Greater Los Angeles Citizens Committee, *Shoreline Development Study*, 22.

61. Ibid., 32.
62. George P. Larsen, "The Beaches Must Belong to the People," *Shore & Beach* 14, no. 2 (October 1946): 67.
63. The ceded shoreline included Castle Rock Beach (north of Pacific Palisades), Colorado Avenue Beach in Santa Monica, El Porto Beach, and Redondo Beach County Park.
64. *SMEO*, August 26, 1946, 1.
65. Letter, August 8, 1947, box 43, folder B III, 10d, John Anson Ford Papers, Huntington Library.
66. For the 1944 figure, see Griffin, *Coastline Plans and Action*; for 1946, see California State Park Commission, *Preliminary Master Plan of Shoreline Development for the State of California*.
67. Report of Special Commission, "State Beaches for Massachusetts," *Shore & Beach* 18, no. 1 (April 1950): 4; Allen T. Edmunds, "The Seashore Recreation Area Survey, 1945–1955," *Shore & Beach* 23, no. 2 (October 1955): 14.
68. *LAT*, April 16, 1949, A5.
69. "Public Gets Break at Santa Monica's 'Gold Coast,'" *California Coast* 3, no. 2 (May 1949): 1; *SMEO*, July 10, 1952, 19.
70. *Property Acquisition for the Period of July 1, 1945 to June 30, 1958*, Office of the Auditor General, Division of Beaches and Parks of the Department of Natural Resources, Special Collections, UCLA.
71. The report mentions 36.7 miles of "publicly owned beaches and upland parks" and 1.5 miles of "other publicly owned shoreline." Division of Beaches and Parks, *Los Angeles County Beach Study*, 1965, 6.
72. Charles A. DeTurk, "The Problem of California's Public Beaches," *Shore & Beach* 28, no. 2 (October 1960): 8.
73. Division of Beaches and Parks, "Too Few for So Many," brochure, Special Collections, UCLA.
74. George P. Larsen, "The Beaches Must Belong to the People," *Shore & Beach* 14, no. 2 (October 1946): 67.
75. "Shoreline Development, County of Los Angeles," Los Angeles, 1944, 7; *Los Angeles Examiner*, April 26, 1957, Examiner Clippings Collection, USC; on hostility against outsiders in Malibu's beach communities, see, for instance, Paul Lovas, *Topanga Beach Experience 1960s–70s* (Los Angeles: Brass Tacks Press, 2011), 2–4.
76. *California Beach Restoration Study*, Department of Boating and Waterways and State Coastal Conservancy, Sacramento, January 2002, 6–16.
77. R. O. Eaton, "Some Examples of Large-Scale Shore Protection Processes," *Shore & Beach* 27, no. 1 (June 1959): 10.
78. A. G. Johnson, "History of Santa Monica Bay Shoreline Development Plans," Los Angeles, Bureau of Engineering, 1950, 7.
79. "Six-Mile Los Angeles Beach Now Four Times as Wide," *California Coast* 2, no. 5 (July 1948): 3.
80. "Million Cubic Yards of Sand Dredged from Santa Monica Harbor," *California Coast* 4, no. 1 (January 1950): 3.
81. "Historical Changes in the Beaches of Los Angeles County: Malaga Cove to Topanga Canyon: 1935–1990," County of Los Angeles, 1992, 16, WRCA.
82. Ibid.
83. James Ingle, *The Movement of Beach Sand: An Analysis Using Fluorescent Grains* (New York: Elsevier, 1966); see, for example, Andrew A. Kahrl, *The Land Was*

Ours: African American Beaches from Jim Crow to the Sunbelt South (Cambridge, MA: Harvard University Press, 2012), 82–83; Lyall A. Pardee, "Beach Development and Pollution Control by City of Los Angeles in Hyperion-Venice Area," *Shore & Beach* 28, no. 2 (October 1960): 17–18; cover of *Shore & Beach* 27, no. 2 (December 1959).

84. William Herron, *Oral History of Coastal Engineering Activities in Southern California, 1930–1981* (Fort Belvoir, VA: Defense Technical Information Center, 1986), 2–3; J. W. Johnson (ed.), *Proceedings of First Conference on Coastal Engineering, Long Beach, October 1950*, Council on Wave Research, Engineering Foundation, 1951.

85. James A. Purpura, "Coastal Engineering Research and Administration in Florida," *Shore & Beach* 27, no. 2 (December 1959): 24; Robert L. Wiegel and Thorndike Saville Jr., "History of Coastal Engineering in the USA," in *History and Heritage of Coastal Engineering: A Collection of Papers on the History of Coastal Engineering in Countries Hosting the International Coastal Engineering Conference 1950–1996*, ed. Nicholas C. Kraus (New York: American Society of Civil Engineers, 1996), 547.

86. See, for example, "Annual Report. Assessment of Offshore Sand Resources for Potential Use in Restoration of Beaches in California," California Geological Survey, 2005, 58.

87. S. Vitousek, P. L. Barnard, P. Limber, L. Erikson, and B. Cole, "A Model Integrating Longshore and Cross-Shore Processes for Predicting Long-Term Shoreline Response to Climate Change," *Journal of Geophysical Research: Earth Surface* 122, no. 4 (2017): 782–806.

88. "Los Angeles New 245 M. G. D. Hyperion Treatment Plan Nears Completion," *Western City*, April 1950, 28.

89. Anna Sklar, *Brown Acres: An Intimate History of the Los Angeles Sewers* (Santa Monica, CA: Angel City Press, 2008), 115.

90. *SMEO*, June 16, 1950, 14; *Los Angeles Sentinel*, June 7, 1951, B1; Communication from the State Board of Public Health, July 23, 1951, box A110, folder 49372, CCC, LACA.

91. See letters exchanged in box A1241, folder 63864, CCC, LACA; *Los Angeles Examiner*, April 14, 1956, Examiner Clippings Collection, USC; *Los Angeles Examiner*, August 14, 1956, Examiner Clippings Collection, USC; "Enlargement of the Hyperion Treatment Plant," *Municipal Construction* 4, no. 8 (October 1959): 115–116.

92. Editorial, *LA Examiner*, November 6, 1956, Examiner Clippings Collection, USC.

93. Suellen Hoy, *Chasing Dirt: The American Pursuit of Cleanliness* (New York: Oxford University Press, 1995), 173.

94. *Life*, August 29, 1949, 104.

95. Morgan used the same joke on several occasions, including in *California Coast* 4, no. 2 (May 1950): 2.

96. *SMEO*, June 30, 1954, 15.

97. *Newport Balboa News*, April 9, 1946, 1.

98. M. Mark Allan Herlihy, "Leisure, Space, and Collective Memory in the 'Athens of America': A History of Boston's Revere Beach" (PhD dissertation, Brown University, 2000), 110.

99. C. P. L. Nicholls, "Los Angeles Beach Operations," *Shore & Beach* 18, no. 2 (October 1950): 22; "A Message from the President," *California Coast* 2, no. 7 (November 1948): 2.

100. "Southlanders Limited in Choice of Beaches," *LAT*, July 28, 1961, B1; William Curtis Kinder Jr., "An Investigation of the Administration of California Tidelands" (PhD dissertation, University of Southern California, 1955), 36–38; "Senate Group in Accord on Tideland Funds," *LAT*, April 4, 1956, 6.

101. *California Coast* 3, no. 3 (August 1949): 3; "Recreational Development of the Los Angeles Area Shoreline," 148.

102. "Recreational Development of the Los Angeles Area Shoreline," 74, 147–148.

103. Charles R. Stapleton, "Recreation and Its Problems on the Santa Monica–Venice Shoreline" (master's thesis, UCLA, 1952), 64.

104. Raymond Chandler, *Farewell My Lovely* (1940; repr. New York: Vintage Books, 1998), 143–144.

105. Robert Caro, *The Power Broker: Robert Moses and the Fall of New York* (New York: Vintage, 1975), 224; "Recreational Development of the Los Angeles Area Shoreline," 48–49.

106. Maritta Wolff, *The Big Nickelodeon* (New York: Random House, 1956), 6–7.

107. Avila, *Popular Culture in the Age of White Flight*, 71.

108. Francesca Russello Ammon, *Bulldozer: Demolition and Clearance in the Postwar Landscape* (New Haven, CT: Yale University Press, 2016), 1.

109. *Manhattan Beach Pilot*, February 14, 1941, 1; *Los Angeles Examiner*, November 29, 1946, Examiner Clippings Collection, USC; *SMEO*, July 10, 1952, 19; *Los Angeles Examiner*, Examiner Clippings Collection, USC.

110. *SMEO*, December 14, 1955, 23.

111. Department of Recreation and Parks Progress Report, 1946–1950, box B1371, LACA.

112. George P. Larsen, "Real Progress Continues in California," *Shore & Beach* 10, no. 2 (October 1942): 53; "Los Angeles Plans Model Facility at North Beach," *California Coast* 4, no. 2 (May 1950): 2.

113. Avila, *Popular Culture in the Age of White Flight*, 106, 118–119.

114. "Recreational Development of the Los Angeles Area Shoreline," 74; *Los Angeles Examiner*, January 10, 1957; *Los Angeles Examiner*, January 31, 1957; *Los Angeles Examiner*, May 20, 1958; all from the LA Examiner Clippings Collection, USC. Autopia is described in Avila, *Popular Culture in the Age of White Flight*, 121–122; *LAT*, April 3, 1960, J3.

115. *The Billboard*, February 17, 1958, 65; publicity brochure, 1961, box 3, California Ephemera Collection, Special Collections, YRL UCLA.

116. "100 Yeas of Yachting," *Life*, August 30, 1954, 58; "Recreational Development of the Los Angeles Area Shoreline," 84.

117. Geoffrey Morgan, "Message from the President," *California Coast* 4, no. 4 (December 1950): 1–2.

118. James W. Dunham, "The California Small Craft Harbors Program," *Shore & Beach* 28, no. 2 (October 1960): 27–28; *Marina Del Rey Area: General Plan Study*, Los Angeles, City of Los Angeles Planning Commission, 1965, 53–54; Marsha V. Rood and Robert Warren, *The Urban Marina: Managing and Developing Marina del Rey*, Center for Urban Affairs / Sea Grant Program, University of Southern California, 1974, v–vi, 64–66.

119. Andrew J. Diamond and Thomas J. Sugrue, *Neoliberal Cities: The Remaking of Postwar Urban America* (New York: New York University Press, 2020); Diamond, *Chicago on the Make*, 229.

120. *LAT*, November 17, 1978, H1; Donald F. Griffin and Charles W. Eliot, "Coastline: Plans and Action for the Development of the Los Angeles Metropolitan Coastline," Haynes Foundation, Los Angeles, 1944, 22.

121. On the decline of East Coast seaside resorts and amusement parks in the 1960s, see Francesca Russello Ammon, "Postindustrialization and the City of Consumption: Attempted Revitalization in Asbury Park, New Jersey," *Journal of Urban History* 41, no. 2 (2015): 159; Simon, *Boardwalk of Dreams*, 85–119; David Nasaw, *Going Out: The Rise and Fall of Public Amusements* (Cambridge, MA: Harvard University Press, 1999), 253.

CHAPTER 5

1. *LAT*, August 20, 1962, 1; *Life*, August 31, 1962, 3.

2. Kirse Granat May, *Golden State, Golden Youth: The California Image in Popular Culture, 1955–1966* (Chapel Hill: University of North Carolina Press, 2002), 4–5; Gary Morris, "Beyond the Beach: Social & Formal Aspects of AIP's Beach Party Movies," *Journal of Popular Film and Television* 21, no. 1 (1993): 2–12.

3. These figures are mentioned respectively in *SMEO*, July 5, 1950, 13; *Life*, September 1961, 48; *Newport Harbor (CA) Daily Pilot*, April 3, 1961, 1.

4. Granat May, *Golden State*; Bill Osgerby, *Playboys in Paradise: Masculinity, Youth and Leisure-Style in Modern America* (Oxford: Berg, 2001); Shelly McKenzie, *Getting Physical: The Rise of Fitness Culture in America* (Lawrence: University Press of Kansas, 2013), 65.

5. Gary R. Mormino, *Land of Sunshine, State of Dreams: A Social History of Modern Florida* (Gainesville: University Press of Florida, 2008), 320.

6. *LAT*, May 8, 1950, 27; February 3, 1958, 7.

7. *Life*, January 1, 1951, 45.

8. Remi A. Nadeau, *The New Society* (Philadelphia: D. McKay, 1963), 138–139.

9. Tom Wolfe, *The Pump House Gang* (New York: Farrar, Straus & Giroux, 1964), 22.

10. *Balboa (CA) Times*, March 29, 1928, 1; April 28, 1927, 1; Paula Fass, *The Damned and the Beautiful: American Youth in the 1920s* (New York: Oxford University Press, 1977), 8.

11. Grace Palladino, *Teen-agers: An American History* (New York: Basic Books, 1996), 54.

12. *Life*, April 1, 1940, 27; Letters to the Editors, *Life*, April 22, 1940, 8.

13. Skip Gillett interview by author, April 1, 2012; Ann Winfield, interview by author, May 5, 2013.

14. *LA Mirror*, June 18, 1958; the quotation is by Christopher Isherwood.

15. *SMEO*, August 11, 1950, 11; June 22, 1950, 26.

16. *SMEO*, July 18, 1952, 15.

17. Sandra Odor, interview by author, March 27, 2012.

18. Lois Warner, telephone interview by author, June 16, 2013.

19. *Los Angeles Examiner*, March 20, 1961, Examiner Clippings Collection, USC.

20. *Life*, October 22, 1945, 113.

21. "California Vacation," *Ebony*, May 1948, 22.

22. In 1959, Joe Johnson, a thirty-two-year-old Black engineer and surf and skin-diving enthusiast, threatened to sue the Los Angeles Athletic Club for discrimination when he was told he could not lease a house on the club's estate. The LAAC eventually recanted its position. "Athletic Club Denies Negro Bar at Malibu," *Los Angeles Tribune*, January 9, 1959, 2.

23. See, e.g., the social life section of the *Los Angeles Tribune*.
24. In 1951, for instance, a young man named Albert Ruiz won the title of Mr. Muscle Beach Junior. *SMEO*, July 5, 1951, 15.
25. *California Eagle*, July 17, 1947.
26. *California Eagle*, June 8, 1961, 1.
27. "Surfing," *Ebony*, April 1965, 111.
28. May, *Golden State*, 4; Thomas Doherty, *Teenagers and Teenpics: The Juvenilization of American Movies in the 1950s* (Philadelphia: Temple University Press, 2002), 159.
29. May, *Golden State*, 125–126.
30. Peter Westwick and Peter Neushul, *The World in the Curl: An Unconventional History of Surfing* (New York: Crown Publishers, 2013), 112–113.
31. *LAT*, April 20, 1958, K34; May, *Golden State*, 119.
32. The best description of the 1960s Southern California beach mania in the music and film industries can be found in May, *Golden State*.
33. John Stenger, "Mapping the Beach: Beach Movies, Exploitation Film and Geographies of Whiteness," in *The Persistence of Whiteness: Race and Contemporary Hollywood Cinema* (New York: Routledge, 2008), 33. See also R. L. Rutsky, "Surfing the Other: Ideology on the Beach," *Film Quarterly* 52, no. 4 (Summer 1999): 12–23.
34. James Patterson Smith, "Local Leadership, the Biloxi Beach Riot, and the Origins of the Civil Rights Movement on the Mississippi Gulf Coast, 1959–1964," in *Sunbelt Revolution. The Historical Progression of the Civil Rights Struggle in the Gulf South, 1866–2000*, ed. Samuel C. Hyde Jr. (Gainesville: University Press of Florida, 2003), 210–230.
35. *Life*, January 1, 1951, 45.
36. McKenzie, *Getting Physical*, 3–4; "California Youth Best in Tests," *LAT*, March 27, 1961, C1; Nadeau, *The New Society*, 128, 139.
37. *The World in the Curl*, 1; *LAT*, April 23, 1961, cs1.
38. *LAT*, August 9, 1959, WS1.
39. *LAT*, Sept 20, 1959, WS1.
40. *LAT*, May 12, 1963, WSA16.
41. Figures found in the *Wall Street Journal*, July 22, 1963, 1, and *NYT*, August 10, 1965, 31; *LAT*, May 29, 1960, J1.
42. *Life*, September 9, 1966, 37; *LAT*, May 29, 1960, J1.
43. *LAT*, August 4, 1957, E8; *Life*, August 26, 1940, 50–52.
44. *Life*, May 24, 1963, 70.
45. McKenzie, *Getting Physical*, 55; *LAT*, August 26, 1962, WS1.
46. *Life*, October 19, 1962, 119.
47. *LAT*, September 11, 1966, W58; June 23, 1963, GB1.
48. On women's exercise in the 1960s, see chapter 2 in McKenzie, *Getting Physical*, 54–81; on female surfers' knobs, see *LAT*, September 11, 1966, W58; July 25, 1965, SF-A1.
49. *LAT*, August 5, 1962, GB1.
50. On student activism in high schools, see Gael Graham, "Flaunting the Freak Flag: *Karr v. Schmidt* and the Great Hair Debate in American High Schools, 1965–1975," *Journal of American History* 91, no. 2 (September 2004): 522–543.
51. *LAT*, April 23, 1961, CS1; "The Long, Strange Tale of California's Surf Nazis," *NYT*, September 28, 2019, https://www.nytimes.com/2019/09/28/opinion/sunday/surf-racism.html.
52. *Newport Balboa (CA) News Times*, April 23, 1946, 1; March 25, 1948, 1; *LAT*, April 4, 1955, 2; *Newport Harbor (CA) Daily Pilot*, April 3, 1961, 1.

53. *LAT*, April 7, 1966, OC1.
54. See coverage in the *Newport Balboa (CA) News Times* and *LA Times*; for national magazines, see, for instance, "Life Goes on a Beach Vacation," *Life*, April 26, 1947, 136–141, and "The Rites of Spring," *Newsweek*, April 26, 1954, 67–68.
55. *Newport Balboa (CA) News Times*, March 25, 1948, 1.
56. *LAT*, April 7, 1966, OC1; *Los Angeles Examiner*, March 28, 1961, Examiner Clippings Collection, USC.
57. Winifred Wise Palmer, "The Teen-Agers of Balboa," *American Mercury* (March 1957): 83–88; *LAT*, March 27, 1961, 2.
58. Thomas Frank, *The Conquest of Cool: Business Culture, Counterculture, and the Rise of Hip Consumerism* (Chicago: University of Chicago Press, 1997), 169.
59. On the "third" Beat scene, see John Arthur Maynard, *Venice West: The Beat Generation in Southern California* (New Brunswick, NJ: Rutgers University Press, 1991); on the relationship between surfers and the Beats, see Osgerby, *Playboys in Paradise*, 103; Lawrence Lipton, *The Holy Barbarians* (New York: Julian Messner, 1959); "Squareville USA vs Beatsville," *Life*, September 21, 1959, 31–36.
60. *NYT*, April 26, 1964, SMA90.
61. Nadeau, *The New Society*, 143; *NYT*, August 10, 1965, 31.
62. *LAT*, August 20, 1962, 1.
63. *LAT*, January 10, 1971, 1.
64. *LAT*, August 10, 1969, N2; the photo op is briefly described in David Gergen, *Eyewitness to Power: The Essence of Leadership, Nixon to Clinton* (New York: Simon and Schuster, 2000), 29.
65. Frederick Kohner, *Gidget* (New York: Berkley Books, 2001); Allison Lurie, *The Nowhere City* (New York: Coward-McCann, 1966), 107, 116.
66. Jean-Claude Kaufmann, *Corps de femmes, regards d'hommes. Sociologie des seins nus* (Paris: Nathan, 1995), 129.
67. *Life*, January 1, 1951, 45–50; January 22, 1951, 8.
68. Elsa Devienne, "The Life, Death, and Rebirth of Muscle Beach: Reassessing Muscularity in Postwar America," *Southern California Quarterly* 100, no. 3 (2018): 324–367.
69. Nadeau, *California: The New Society*, 52, 56–57.
70. Merry Ovnick, interview by author, May 13, 2011; Sandra Odor, interview by author, March 27, 2012; Clara Byrd, telephone interview with author, March 29, 2012.
71. Nadeau, *California: The New Society*, 144; "Peekaboo Sex, or How to Fill a Drive-in," *Life*, July 16, 1965, 87.
72. Lurie, *The Nowhere City*, 30, 51, 53, 275, 276.
73. Catherine Cocks, *Tropical Whites: The Rise of the Tourist South in the Americas* (Philadelphia: University of Pennsylvania Press, 2013), 110.
74. *LA Sentinel*, September 5, 1957, C4.
75. *LAT*, August 12, 1962, WS1.
76. For instance, visitors at L Street Beach in Boston could use high and low bars for their gymnastic exercises. William Howard King, "A Survey of the Public Bathing Areas in Boston, Massachusetts" (PhD dissertation, Boston University, 1949), 56.
77. Jonathan Black, *Making the American Body: The Remarkable Saga of the Men and Women Whose Feats, Feuds, and Passions Shaped Fitness History* (Lincoln: University of Nebraska Press, 2013), 32; *SMEO*, July 24, 1940, 5; July 29, 1940, 3.

78. Harold Zinkin and Bonnie Hearn, *Remembering Muscle Beach: Where Hard Bodies Began: Photographs and Memories* (Santa Monica, CA: Angel City Press, 1999), 33; see also *LAT*, August 9, 1942, F16.

79. Seymour Koenig, interview by author, May 14, 2009, Venice, CA; Zinkin and Hearn, *Remembering Muscle Beach*, 50; Joel Sayre, "The Body Worshipers of Muscle Beach," *Saturday Evening Post*, May 25, 1957, 140.

80. "Ralph Story," KNXT Channel 2, Los Angeles, September 12, 1965, 7, 9, Ralph Story's LA Scripts Collection, Special Collections, YRL UCLA.

81. *SMEO*, July 5, 1950, 13; July 5, 1951, 15; August 11, 1950, 11.

82. *Strength and Health*, December 1957, 10; Sayre, "The Body Worshipers of Muscle Beach," 34.

83. Sayre, "The Body Worshipers," 35, 136, 138.

84. *LAT*, February 9, 1953, 2.

85. *Strength & Health*, November 1950, 9.

86. See chapters 1 and 2 of McKenzie, *Getting Physical*.

87. Natalia Mehlman Petrzela, "From Performance to Participation: The Origins of the Fit Nation," *Transatlantica* [Online], 2 | 2020, March 1, 2021, http://journals.openedition.org/transatlantica/16318; Brochure of the Santa Monica Department of Recreation, 1953–1954, box 97, folder 3, California Ephemera Collection, YRL UCLA.

88. *SMEO*, July 2, 1951, 9.

89. *LAT*, May 16, 1957, A12; Ira Wallach, *Muscle Beach* (Boston: Little, Brown, 1959), 102.

90. Lynne Luciano, *Looking Good: Male Body in Modern America* (New York: Hill & Wang, 2002), 57; McKenzie, *Getting Physical*, 2.

91. Whitney Strub, "The Clearly Obscene and the Queerly Obscene: Heteronormativity and Obscenity in Cold War Los Angeles," *American Quarterly* 60, no. 8 (June 2008): 373–398.

92. *Life*, January 1, 1951, 49.

93. *SMEO*, June 23, 1954, 15.

94. *Strength & Health*, December 1957, 13.

95. *LAT*, June 10, 1951, 16.

96. *NYT*, October 5, 1958, S9.

97. *LAT*, March 14, 1954, B11.

98. Hearst newsreel footage, Santa Monica, Muscle Queen, tape 1, CS1701, July 1954, Film & Television Archive, UCLA; *LAT*, September 2, 1947, 2.

99. Devienne, "The Life, Death, and Rebirth of Muscle Beach."

100. *Life*, July 3, 1939, 49.

101. Steve Reeves worked out in the gym opened by Vic Tanny, a Muscle Beach regular, in Santa Monica. Jan Todd and Terry Todd, "The Last Interview," *Iron Game History* 6, no. 4 (2000): 5.

102. Terry Todd, "Armand Tanny Remembers Steve Reeves," *Iron Game History* 6, no. 4 (1999): 24.

103. Ibid., 58.

104. Cecil Whiting, *Pop L.A.: Art and the City in the 1960s* (Berkeley: University of California Press, 2006), 49.

105. *LAT*, September 5, 1952, 16; February 8, 1953, B2.

106. *SMEO*, August 25, 1954, 15; August 4, 1954, 15.

107. *SMEO*, June 13, 1950, 15.

108. *SMEO*, September 5, 1951, 13.

109. *Saturday Evening Post*, May 5, 1957, 136; *LAT*, July 28, 1954, 13.
110. *LAT*, September 11, 1966, W58.
111. "Peekaboo Sex, or How to Fill a Drive-in," *Life*, July 16, 1965, 87.

CHAPTER 6

1. Elaine Tyler May, *Homeward Bound: American Families in the Cold War Era* (New York: Basic Books, 1988).
2. Andrew A. Kahrl, *The Land Was Ours: African American Beaches from Jim Crow to the Sunbelt South* (Cambridge, MA: Harvard University Press, 2012), 4–5, 10–11.
3. Charles S. Warren, *Santa Monica Community Book* (Santa Monica: A. H. Cawston and Publisher, 1944), 37.
4. Charles R. Stapleton, "Recreation and Its Problems on the Santa Monica–Venice Shoreline" (master's thesis, UCLA, 1952), 74.
5. Santa Monica Redevelopment Agency, "Redevelopment Relocation in Santa Monica," 1968, 4, Santa Monica Public Library.
6. See, for instance, *Los Angeles Examiner*, March 24, 1929; July 10, 1931; February 8, 1934. "Gambling" folder, Examiner Clippings Collection, USC.
7. On gambling boats, see Ernest Marquez, *Tony Cornero and the Notorious Gambling Ships of Southern California* (Los Angeles: Angel City Press, 2011).
8. *SMEO*, September 20, 1928, 20.
9. Raymond Chandler, *The Lady on the Lake* (1943; repr. New York: Vintage Books, 1988), 103; Scott, *Santa Monica*, 122, 127.
10. *LAT*, June 19, 1945, 12.
11. See Simon Eisner and Associates, "Master Plan for the City of Santa Monica," 1957, https://www.smgov.net/uploadedFiles/Departments/PCD/Plans/General-Plan/1957-Master-Plan.pdf. For an overview of the projects set in motion by Santa Monica's civic leaders in the 1950s and 1960s, see Scott, *Santa Monica*, 125–139. Robert E. McClure, as member of the Santa Monica Chamber of Commerce and of the California Highway Commission, campaigned forcefully for Santa Monica to become the western terminal of the Interstate 10 freeway starting in 1950. See *LAT*, April 14, 1950, A11, and Scott, *Santa Monica*, 134.
12. *Los Angeles Examiner*, May 20, 1954; March 25, 1955, Examiner Clippings Collection, USC.
13. Daniel Hurewitz, *Bohemian Los Angeles and the Making of Modern Politics* (Berkeley: University of California Press, 2006), 54; Lillian Faderman and Stuart Timmons, *Gay L.A.: A History of Sexual Outlaws, Power Politics, and Lipstick Lesbians* (Berkeley: University of California Press, 2009), 73–74; see photographs in "Los Angeles County Beaches Survey," 1947, Special Collections, USC.
14. *SMEO*, December 3, 1956, 1.
15. On anti-homosexuality during the Cold War, see George Chauncey, "The Postwar Sex Crime Panic," in *True Stories from the American Past*, ed. William Graebner (New York: McGraw-Hill, 1993); John D'Emilio, *Sexual Politics, Sexual Communities: The Making of a Homosexual Minority in the United States, 1940–1970* (Chicago: University of Chicago Press, 1998); David K. Johnson, *The Lavender Scare: The Cold War Persecution of Gays and Lesbians in the Federal Government* (Chicago: University of Chicago Press, 2004). On police harassment of gays and lesbians under Parker, see Faderman and Timmons, *Gay L.A.*, 75–77.
16. *SMEO*, April 2, 1955, 1; April 6 1955, 1.
17. *Los Angeles Examiner*, March 25, 1955, Examiner Clippings Collection, USC.

18. *SMEO*, April 13, 1955, 1; December 5, 1955, 1; December 6, 1955, 1; December 14, 1955, 1, 23.
19. *People v. Nash*, 52 Cal. 2d 36 (1959), 4; *LAT*, December 2, 1956, A.
20. Chauncey, "The Postwar Sex Crime Panic"; Estelle B. Freedman, "'Uncontrolled Desires': The Response to the Sexual Psychopath, 1920–1960," *Journal of American History* 74, no. 1 (1987): 83–106.
21. *SMEO*, December 3, 1956, 1.
22. *SMEO*, December 1, 1956, 1; December 3, 1956, 1; December 4, 1956, 1.
23. *SMEO*, December 10, 1956, 4.
24. *LAT*, February 17, 1957, F1.
25. Press releases sent to *Los Angeles Examiner*, January 18, 1958, May 20, 1958, January 31, 1957; October 24, 1959, Examiner Clippings Collection, USC; Brochure, 1961, box 3, California Ephemera Collection, YRL UCLA.
26. *SMEO*, December 10, 1956, 1; Letter to the editor, *SMEO*, December 4, 1956, 1; *SMEO*, July 31, 1959, 1.
27. "Amendment to the City Master Plan concerning Shoreline Development," 1956, Legislative Files 308 006, Santa Monica Clerk Office.
28. Interestingly enough, the location proposed, between Bay and Bicknell Streets, corresponded to Bay Street Beach, the city's historically Black beach. Minutes of the Santa Monica City Council, Vol. 22, October 14, 1958, Santa Monica Office of the City Clerk; *SMEO*, December 11, 1958, 1; *LAT*, February 2, 1958, WS1; *Strength & Health*, December 1957, 12–13; Tolga Ozyurtcu, "Flex Marks the Spot: Histories of Muscle Beach," (PhD dissertation, University of Texas–Austin, 2014), 47–50.
29. *SMEO*, December 10, 1958, 1.
30. *LAT*, March 8, 1959, WS1; *SMEO*, March 16, 1959, 1; April 15, 1959, 23.
31. *SMEO*, December 11, 1958, 1.
32. *SMEO*, December 10, 1958, 1; December 11, 1958, 1.
33. *SMEO*, December 11, 1958, 1; December 16, 1958, 4.
34. *SMEO*, March 5, 1959, 2; June 12, 1959, 1.
35. *LAT*, December 17, 1958, 21.
36. Ibid.
37. See, for instance, Steve Reeves's interview in *Iron Games History* 6, no. 4 (December 2000): 13.
38. *SMEO*, December 15, 1958, 13; December 17, 1958, 1.
39. *SMEO*, December 17, 1958, 1.
40. *LAT*, August 9, 1959, WS1; *SMEO*, August 10, 1959, 11.
41. *LAT*, August 17, 1958, WS1. Historian Alison Rose Jefferson explains that some African Americans referred to the beach as Bay Street Beach while others used the term "Inkwell." Considering the derogatory connotations of the latter term, I use mostly Bay Street Beach here. See Alison Rose Jefferson, *Living the California Dream: African American Leisure Sites during the Jim Crow Era* (Lincoln: University of Nebraska Press, 2020), 87.
42. Douglas Flamming, *Bound for Freedom: Black Los Angeles in Jim Crow America* (Berkeley: University of California Press, 2006), 271–275.
43. In the early 1950s, a geography MA student noted it was still "the one area on the shore where Negroes congregate in relatively large numbers." Stapleton, "Recreation and Its Problems," 67.

44. *LAT*, August 17, 1958, WS1; August 27, 1958, WS1; *SMEO*, August 29, 1958, 1; January 7, 1959, 1; *SMEO*, November 27, 1959, 1. Photograph, Gilmore family collection, Santa Monica History Museum.
45. *LAT*, May 5, 1957, I10.
46. For pictures of Black children on the Santa Monica beach in official leaflets, see, for instance, "A New Oceanfront Community to Be Built in Beautiful Santa Monica," 1958, Santa Monica Public Library; on the declining use of Bay Street Beach, see Alison Rose Jefferson, "African-American Leisure Space in Santa Monica," *Southern California Quarterly* 91, no. 2 (2009): 184.
47. *LA Examiner*, March 25, 1955, LAE USC; *SMEO*, April 2, 1955, 1; *Webb Spinner* 19, no. 1–2 (January–February 1965): 1.
48. Kahrl, *The Land Was Ours*, 10.
49. *SMEO*, May 30, 1958, 1; *LAT*, March 16, 1958, WS2. The creation of the SMRA was made possible by passing of the 1945 California Community Redevelopment Act. John C. Teaford, *The Metropolitan Revolution: The Rise of Post-Urban America* (New York: Columbia University Press, 2006), 43.
50. Among the SMRA members were J. Lee Schimmer Jr., its president and a former councilman; Martin Goodfriend, then a councilman; Russell F. Priebe, city manager; Mortimer T. Richey, real estate agent; and Lawrence Wayne Harding, manager of the Santa Monica Ford dealership and member of the Santa Monica Chamber of Commerce. James Reidy, member of the Citizens' Progress Committee, went on to serve as councilman in 1965.
51. Don McQuade was present both as president of the Santa Monica Chamber of Commerce and as the Santa Monica Shores project manager. *Webb Spinner* 19, no. 1–2 (January–February 1965): 1.
52. "Redevelopment Relocation in Santa Monica," 1968 brochure, Santa Monica Public Library.
53. "A New Oceanfront Community to Be Built in Beautiful Santa Monica," 1958 prospectus, Santa Monica Public Library.
54. An example of these principles was the Pacific Plaza, another Santa Monica tower, which included 289 senior-citizen residential units and a garden area, arts and crafts center, game room, library, and a "sidewalk café." *Webb Spinner* 17, no. 3 (August 1964): 1 and 3.
55. *Webb Spinner* 19, no. 1–2 (January–February 1965): 1; *Webb Spinner* 21, no. 9–10 (September–October 1967): 3; *Independent Star News*, November 5, 1967, 11.
56. *Independent Star News*, November 5, 1967, 11; *Webb Spinner* 23, no. 4 (April 1969): 2.
57. *LAT*, October 7, 1971, WS1.
58. Lawrence Lipton, *The Holy Barbarians* (New York: Julian Messner, 1959), 16.
59. *SMEO*, June 16, 1954, 17; *Los Angeles Examiner*, June 9, 1960, 8; June 17, 1960; July 26, 1960, Examiner Clippings Collection, USC.
60. *LAT*, November 13, 1965, B4.
61. *Los Angeles Examiner*, June 7, 1961, Examiner Clippings Collection, USC.
62. See press clippings of this event, box 7, "violence," Remi Nadeau Papers, YRL UCLA.
63. *Los Angeles Examiner*, June 7, 1961; July 10, 1961, Examiner Clippings Collection, USC.
64. *SMEO*, January 20, 1960, 1; *LAT*, May 14, 1966, OC8.
65. City Ordinance no. 1163, September 5, 1966, Newport Beach Archives; *LAT*, May 15, 1966, OC2.

66. *LAT*, May 25, 1967, OC1.
67. *LAT*, May 11, 1958, OC2; ordinance no. 1079, January 27, 1964, Newport Beach City Council online archives. On Bal Week, see Jerry Nikas, *Would You Believe This Was Bal Week '66; The Swinging Easter Week at Balboa in Photos* (Newport Beach, CA: G. N. Nikas Publications, 1966).
68. Three jeeps patrolled the beach on weekends. *LAT*, July 6, 1958, OC1;July 24, 1960, OC1; March 23, 1961, D1.
69. *Newport (CA) Daily Pilot*, April 1, 1966, 1.
70. *LAT*, August 21, 1960, CS1.
71. *Newport (CA) Daily Pilot*, March 24, 1961, 1.
72. *Newport Harbor (CA) News Press*, April 2, 1958, 3; *Los Angeles Examiner*, August 14, 1957, Examiner Clippings Collection, USC.
73. *Newport (CA) Daily Pilot*, March 12, 1965, 1. Mike Davis, *City of Quartz: Excavating the Future in Los Angeles* (New York: Vintage Books, 1992), 250–253.
74. Businesses had to close by 10 p.m. and needed a permit to organize a dance. Ordinance no. 1053, August 12, 1963, Newport Beach City Council online archives, http://ecms.newportbeachca.gov/Web/Browse.aspx?startid=33498&cnb=CouncilOrdinances.
75. Ordinance no. 741, January 10, 1955, Newport Beach City Council online archives.
76. *Newport (CA) Daily Pilot*, March 25, 1964, 1.
77. Ordinance no. 1079, January 27, 1964, Newport Beach City Council online archives; *Los Angeles Examiner*, August 10, 1957, Examiner Clippings Collection, USC; *LAT*, April 19, 1965, OC8.
78. *LAT*, April 19, 1965, OC8.
79. *Newport (CA) Daily Pilot*, March 23, 1964, 1.
80. *Newport (CA) Daily Pilot*, March 20, 1967, 1.
81. *LAT*, April 11, 1968, OC A1.
82. *Newport (CA) Daily Pilot*, March 24, 1967, 1.
83. Madigan-Hyland, "Recreational Development of the Los Angeles Area Shoreline," New York, 1949, 26; Los Angeles County Beach Study, 1965, 14–15.
84. Stapleton, "Recreation and Its Problems," 67.
85. See the letter of a young Mexican American man sent to a court judge in 1943, quoted in George J. Sanchez, *Becoming Mexican-American: Ethnicity, Culture, and Identity in Chicano Los Angeles, 1900–1945* (New York: Oxford University Press, 1993), 207.
86. Woodrow Nichols, "A Spatio-Perspective Analysis of the Effect of the Santa Monica and Simi Valley Freeways on Two Selected Black Residential Areas in Los Angeles County" (PhD dissertation, UCLA, 1973), 73.
87. David Grant, "A Demographic Portrait of Los Angeles County, 1970 to 1990," in *Prismatic Metropolis: Inequality in Los Angeles*, ed. Lawrence D. Bobo, Melvin L. Oliver, James H. Johnson, and Abel Valenzuela (New York: Russell Sage Foundation, 1999), 51–52.
88. *LAT*, November 13, 1965, B4.
89. Robert B. *Edgerton, Alone Together: Social Order on an Urban Beach* (Berkeley: University of California Press, 1979).
90. Ibid., 51.
91. See Eric Avila, *Popular Culture in the Age of White Flight: Fear and Fantasy in Suburban Los Angeles* (Berkeley: University of California Press, 2004), 5–6.
92. Edgerton, *Alone Together*, 51.

93. Ibid., 44.
94. Ibid., 45.
95. Heather Ann Thompson, "Why Mass Incarceration Matters: Rethinking Crisis, Decline, and Transformation in Postwar American History," *Journal of American History* 97, no. 3 (2010): 703–734.
96. *LAT*, July 24, 1960, OC1;November 13, 1966, WS1; Edgerton, *Alone Together*, 55.
97. *LAT*, May 24, 1970, SF A9.
98. Edgerton, *Alone Together*, 50–55.
99. *LAT*, October 13, 1980, F1.
100. Edgerton, *Alone Together*, 124.
101. Letter, January 11, 1963, council communications, box A1513, file 89691, CALA; Motion taken on June 23, 1965, council communications, box A1914, file 124633, LACA; *LAT*, January 5, 1969, CS1.
102. Dominique Monjardet, *Ce que fait la police. Sociologie de la force publique* (Paris: La Découverte, 1996).
103. Edgerton, *Alone Together*, 59.
104. *LAT*, October 13, 1980, F1; Edgerton, *Alone Together*, 48.
105. Edgerton, *Alone Together*, 34.
106. John Rechy, *City of Night* (New York: Grove Press, 1963), 212. On the emergence of the gay rights movement in the mid- and late 1960s, see Robert O. Self, "Sex in the City: The Politics of Sexual Liberalism in Los Angeles, 1963–79," *Gender & History* 20, no. 2 (August 2008): 301–303.
107. Edgerton, *Alone Together*, 140.
108. Kahrl, *The Land Was Ours*.
109. *LAT*, November 5, 1967, B20.

CHAPTER 7

1. Letter dated November 18, 1954, box 43, folder B III, 10d, John Anson Ford Papers, Huntington Library.
2. *California Coast* 4, no. 4 (December 1950): 2.
3. Letter dated June 9, 1950, box 43, folder B III, 10d, John Anson Ford Papers, Huntington Library.
4. Letter dated May 15, 1950, box 43, folder B III, 10d, John Anson Ford Papers, Huntington Library.
5. Linda Chilton McCallister, *The Waterfront of Manhattan Beach* (Manhattan Beach, CA: Manhattan Beach Historical Series no. 6, n.d.), 42.
6. *Bulletin of the Shoreline Planning Association*, April 1952, no. 1.
7. Adam Rome, *The Genius of Earth Day: How a 1970 Teach-In Unexpectedly Made the First Green Generation* (New York: Hill and Wang, 2013), 47–56.
8. Rachel Carson, *Silent Spring* (1962; repr. New York: Mariner Books, 2002), 13–14; Stewart Udall is quoted in Adam Rome, *The Bulldozer in the Countryside: Suburban Sprawl and the Rise of American Environmentalism* (Cambridge: Cambridge University Press, 2001), 139; on the rise of the modern environmentalist movement, see Rome, *The Genius of Earth Day*, and Robert Gottlieb, *Forcing the Spring: The Transformation of the American Environmental Movement* (Washington, DC: Island Press, 2005).
9. *LAT*, December 12, 1957, 4.
10. Marsha V. Rood and Robert Warren, *The Urban Marina: Managing and Developing Marina del Rey*, Center for Urban Affairs / Sea Grant Program, University of Southern California, 1974, 110.

11. *LAT*, August 16, 1970, I12; September 3, 1967, CS1.

12. Quoted in Rood and Warren, *The Urban Marina*, 53.

13. Reyner Banham, *Reyner Banham Loves Los Angeles*, BBC documentary, 1972 (51 min.).

14. Paula A. Scott, *Santa Monica: A History on the Edge* (Mount Pleasant, SC: Arcadia Publishing, 2004), 137–138; *LAT*, August 3, 1958, WS7; July 26, 1959, WS7; February 19, 1961, WS1.

15. *LAT*, August 2, 1959, WS8; February 19, 1961, WS1; June 24, 1965, WS1; James W. Dunham, "The Santa Monica Causeway Project," *Shore & Beach*, vol. 33, no. 1 (April 1, 1965): 5; Moffatt & Nichol, Engineers, "The Santa Monica Causeway Project Feasibility Study," City of Santa Monica, 1964, available at the Santa Monica Public Library.

16. Committee on Natural Resources, Planning, and Public Works, "Hearing of Conservation and Beaches Subcommittee on the Public Interest in the Shoreline, October 11, 1968, Santa Monica, Calif. Transcript of Proceedings," California Legislature, 1969, 196.

17. *LAT*, September 7, 1967, WS1; September 18, 1966, WS1; December 22, 1968, K6.

18. See chapter 1 in Sara Fingal, "Turning the Tide: The Politics of Land and Leisure on the California and Mexican Coastlines in the Age of Environmentalism" (PhD, Brown University, 2012).

19. *LAT*, September 26, 1969, G1.

20. California Legislature Assembly Committee on Natural Resources, Planning, and Public Works, "Hearing of Conservation and Beaches Subcommittee on the Public Interest in the Shoreline," Sacramento, October 11, 1968, 103–108.

21. Rome, *The Genius of Earth Day*, 67; Teresa Sabol Spezio, *Slick Policy: Environmental and Science Policy in the Aftermath of the Santa Barbara Oil Spill* (Pittsburgh: University of Pittsburgh Press, 2018).

22. Thomas J. Osborne, *Coastal Sage: Peter Douglas and the Fight to Save California's Shore* (Berkeley: University of California Press, 2018), 38–39, 47–48; see also Fingal, "Turning the Tide," chapter 2.

23. On the creation of the CCC, see Richard A. Walker, *The Country in the City: The Greening of the San Francisco Bay Area* (Seattle: University of Washington Press, 2007), 126–127; Jared Orsi, "Restoring the Common to the Goose: Citizen Activism and the Protection of the California Coastline, 1969–1982," *Southern California Quarterly* 78, no. 3 (1996): 257–284; Osbone, *Coastal Sage*; Fingal, "Turning the Tide," chapter 3.

24. Letters, December 14, 1956, and January 21, 1957, box 43, folder B III, 10d, John Anson Ford Papers, Huntington Library.

25. *Los Angeles Examiner*, April 26, 1957, Examiner Clippings Collection, USC.

26. *LAT*, June 11, 1961, CS1.

27. *Los Angeles Examiner*, November 5, 1957, Examiner Clippings Collection, USC; "Hermosa Takes a Look at Itself," newspaper clipping, box 8, "Beach Life," Remi Nadeau Collection.

28. *LAT*, June 11, 1961, CS1.

29. Lisa McGirr, *Suburban Warriors: The Origins of the New American Right* (Princeton, NJ: Princeton University Press, 2001), 20–53.

30. Mike Davis, *City of Quartz: Excavating the Future in Los Angeles* (New York: Vintage Books, 1992), 169–170.

31. *LAT*, February 26, 1961, E1; *Los Angeles Examiner* , March 30, 1961, Examiner Clippings Collection, USC.

32. *Los Angeles Examiner*, July 14, 1961, Examiner Clippings Collection, USC.
33. Ibid.
34. *Los Angeles Examiner* , July 28, 1961, 1, Examiner Clippings Collection, USC.
35. *LAT*, December 14, 1961, D1; February 15, 1962, E1.
36. *LAT*, June 16, 1963, OC9.
37. *LAT*, November 9, 1969, B1; January 9, 1970, OC-A10.
38. *LAT*, February 1, 1970, K1.
39. McGirr, *Warriors*, 39.
40. Andrew Kahrl, *Free the Beaches: The Story of Ned Coll and the Battle for America's Most Exclusive Shoreline* (New Haven, CT: Yale University Press, 2018).
41. John C. Teaford, "Urban Renewal and Its Aftermath," *Housing Policy Debate* 11, no. 2 (2000): 454.
42. Jane Jacobs, *The Death and Life of Great American Cities* (New York: Vintage Books, 1961).
43. See, for instance, the debates on this issue in Congress in 1962. US Senate, "Relocation of Elderly People. Hearings before the Subcommittee on Involuntary Relocation of the Elderly of the Special Committee on Aging," Washington, DC, 1962.
44. Redevelopment Agency of Santa Monica, "A New Oceanfront Community to Be Built in Beautiful Santa Monica," 5–6, Santa Monica Public Library.
45. Charles Stapleton, "Recreation and Its Problems on the Santa Monica–Venice Shoreline," (master's thesis, UCLA, 1952), 79.
46. *LAT*, October 22, 1967, J8.
47. "A New Oceanfront Community to Be Built in Beautiful Santa Monica," 12.
48. Derek S. Hyra, "Conceptualizing the New Urban Renewal: Comparing the Past to the Present," *Urban Affairs Review* 48, no. 4 (2012): 504.
49. *LAT*, October 26, 1961, G1.
50. *LAT*, March 19, 1967, WS1.
51. *LAT*, November 5, 1967, B20; September 16, 1973, WS1.
52. On the Santa Monica renters' rights movement, see William B. Fulton, *The Reluctant Metropolis: The Politics of Urban Growth in Los Angeles* (Baltimore: Johns Hopkins University Press, 2001), 23–41, and Stella M. Capek and John I. Gilderbloom, *Community versus Commodity: Tenants and the American City* (Albany: State University of New York Press, 1992), 58–87.
53. In 1974, more than 60 percent of Ocean Park residents were under thirty-five years old. *LAT*, June 23, 1974, WS1.
54. *LAT*, October 31, 1971, WS9; May 13, 1973, WS1; June 19, 1973, 3; July 11, 1976, SW1; September 8, 1977, WS1; October 23, 1977, WS2.
55. *LAT*, June 23, 1974, WS1.
56. Fulton, *The Reluctant Metropolis*, 30–33.
57. Sharon Zukin, *Naked City: The Death and Life of Authentic Urban Places* (New York: Oxford University Press, 2010), 4.
58. *Life*, February 21, 1969, 58.
59. *Life*, June 13, 1969, 23; *LAT*, May 19, 1968, B22.

EPILOGUE: THE VIEW FROM THE SANTA MONICA PIER

1. *LAT*, January 28, 1973, F1.
2. *LAT*, January 29, 1976, WS1; January 28, 1973, F1; see also Jeffrey Stanton, *Santa Monica Pier: A History from 1875 to 1990* (Los Angeles: Donahue Publishing, 1990), 138.

3. Stanton, *Santa Monica Pier,* 138.
4. The Coastal Act of 1976, section 30006.
5. Andrew Kahrl, *Free the Beaches: The Story of Ned Coll and the Battle for America's Most Exclusive Shoreline* (New Haven, CT: Yale University Press, 2018), 175.
6. *LAT,* January 28, 1973, F1.
7. Gary R. Mormino, *Land of Sunshine, State of Dreams: A Social History of Modern Florida* (Gainesville: University Press of Florida, 2008), 341–343.
8. Thomas J. Osborne, *Coastal Sage: Peter Douglas and the Fight to Save California's Shore* (Oakland: University of California Press, 2018), 82–88.
9. Jared Orsi, "Restoring the Common to the Goose: Citizen Activism and the Protection of the California Coastline, 1969–1982," *Southern California Quarterly* 78, no. 3 (1996): 272, 274; *LAT,* May 12, 1981, B3.
10. Kahrl, *Free the Beaches,* 263–264.
11. Peter Plagens, "Los Angeles: The Ecology of Evil," *Artforum* 11, no. 4 (December 1972): 67–76, http://www.art-agenda.com/reviews/los-angeles-the-architecture-of-four-ecologies/.
12. *LAT,* December 13, 1980, A24; June 3, 1984, WS1; August 2, 1987, WS1; September 2, 2007, https://www.latimes.com/archives/la-xpm-2007-sep-02-me-elsol2-story.html.
13. Robert O. Self, *American Babylon: Race and the Struggle for Postwar Oakland* (Princeton, NJ: Princeton University Press, 2003), 326.
14. *LAT,* October 11, 1981, I1.
15. *LAT,* August 18, 1985, WS4.
16. *LAT,* December 17, 1985, B1; Bill Sharpsteen, *Dirty Water: One Man's Fight to Clean Up One of the World's Most Polluted Bays* (Berkeley: University of California Press, 2010), 39.
17. *LAT,* February 8, 1990, B3.
18. Sharpsteen, *Dirty Water,* 210, 216.
19. *LAT,* July 9, 1992, SBB8.
20. *LAT,* June 23, 2022, B1.
21. Sharpsteen, *Dirty Water,* 17.
22. Rosanna Xia, "History of DDT Ocean Dumping off L.A. Coast Even Worse Than Expected, EPA Finds," *LAT,* August 4, 2022, https://www.latimes.com/environment/story/2022-08-04/ddt-ocean-dumping-in-l-a-even-worse-than-expected.
23. *LAT,* September 21, 1995, OCA3.
24. *LAT,* December 30, 2001, B1; January 22, 2002, A5; October 22, 2002, A1.
25. *LAT,* July 14, 2004, B12; May 15, 2005, MAG6.
26. *LAT,* April 16, 2005, B1; on the Geffen affair, see Osborne, *Coastal Sage,* 102–105.
27. *Washington Post,* March 20, 2005, A12.
28. *LAT,* August 2, 2007, E14.
29. *The Guardian,* June 4, 2013, https://www.theguardian.com/technology/2013/jun/04/apps-beaches-public-access-california; *LAT,* December 13, 2018, https://www.latimes.com/business/technology/la-me-coastal-commission-parker-app-20181213-htmlstory.html.
30. See screenshots available at https://play.google.com/store/apps/details?id = com.ourmalibubeaches.app.ourmalibubeaches&hl = en_GB&gl = US, accessed July 19, 2022.
31. *NYT,* August 30, 2018, https://www.nytimes.com/2018/08/30/technology/vinod-khosla-beach.html; *Washington Post,* January 8, 2020, https://www.washingtonpost.com/technology/2020/01/08/california-sues-vinod-khosla-beach/.

32. "Ralph Story's Los Angeles" Scripts Collection, RS 74, September 12, 1965, Ralph Story Papers, Special Collections, YRL UCLA.
33. *LAT*, November 5, 1967, B20.
34. Charles Gaines and George Butler, *Pumping Iron: The Art and Sport of Bodybuilding* (New York: Simon and Schuster, 1974), 93–94, 97.
35. Ibid., 91, 131.
36. *LAT*, July 25, 1976, I4; July 11, 1981, OC-C1; March 30, 1986, B1.
37. *Reyner Banham Loves Los Angeles* (BBC, 1972).
38. Sarah Grogan et al., "Femininity and Muscularity: Accounts of Seven Women Body Builders," *Journal of Gender Studies* 13, no. 1 (2004): 50.
39. *Cosmopolitan*, August 1977, 191, 208.
40. Shelly McKenzie, *Getting Physical: The Rise of Fitness Culture in America* (Lawrence: University Press of Kansas, 2013), 145; *LAT*, December 5, 1991, OCD5.
41. *LAT*, March 9, 1990, E14.
42. *LAT*, June 21, 1990, SE-AJ1.
43. *LAT,* September 2, 1989, 16.
44. *LA Times*, December 25, 1990, https://www.latimes.com/archives/la-xpm-1990-12-25-ca-7120-story.html.
45. *Daily Mail*, April 7, 1990, 21.
46. *NYT*, July 3, 1995, 41.
47. *Variety*, December 24, 1990, 17.
48. *Daily Mail*, April 7, 1990, 21.
49. Judy Rumbold, "The Bottom Line on *Baywatch*," *The Guardian*, April 10, 1993, 25.
50. *Daily Mail*, February 14, 1992, 19.
51. *The Observer*, September 8, 1996, 24; *Times of India*, November 17, 1996, A5; "It's a Baywatch World," *Edmonton Journal*, November 17, 1996, C1; *LAT*, February 22, 2002, E1; June 13, 2005.
52. Estimates of breast augmentation procedures were found in *LAT*, April 30, 1999, OCE1; Renée A. Botta, "Body Image Disturbance in Adolescent Girls: A Test of Thoughtful Processing as an Intervening Variable on the Effects of TV Exposure," (PhD dissertation, University of Wisconsin, 1998), 29.
53. *NYT*, May 2, 1999, SM34.
54. Ibid.
55. Kevin Thomas, "Annette, Frankie Hang 20 in 'Beach,'" *LAT*, August 10, 1987, E5.
56. Chris Willman, "'Tarzan,' 'Baywatch' Stand Corrected" *LAT*, September 27, 1991, OCF30.
57. "Club Baywatch," *LAT*, August 13, 1995, I4.
58. Kathleen Kelleher, "First Black Lifeguard Working to Blaze Trail," *LAT*, March 28, 1993, https://www.latimes.com/archives/la-xpm-1993-03-28-we-16355-story.html.
59. See for instance season 2, episode 8, "Point of Attack," and season 4, episode 10, "Tower of Power."
60. *The Observer*, January 2, 1994, C16-C17.
61. *LAT*, April 30, 1999, D1A.
62. "Why 'Baywatch' Is Catching a $100M+ Wave," *Deadline*, July 7, 2017, https://deadline.com/2017/07/baywatch-box-office-success-overseas-despite-flop-in-america-1202123612/.
63. See Climate Central's visual projections at https://picturing.climatecentral.org/location/34.008562,-118.497358, accessed July 7, 2022); Sean Vitousek et al., "A Model Integrating Longshore and Cross-Shore Processes for Predicting Long-Term

Shoreline Response to Climate Change," *Journal of Geophysical Research: Earth Surface* 122, no. 4 (2017): 782.

64. *LAT*, May 25, 1986, B1.
65. *LAT*, September 14, 2011, AA1; February 16, 2022. https://www.latimes.com/california/story/2022-02-16/rising-sea-levels-pose-perilous-threat-to-california-coast-study-raises-new-alarms.
66. This means that the beaches will be completely submerged at least once a year due to coastal floods.
67. *LAT*, February 2, 2010, AA1.
68. Michaela Haas, "The Fight to Save Broad Beach," *Curbed*, April 23, 2020, https://la.curbed.com/2020/4/22/21230250/sea-level-rise-malibu-california.
69. George Skelton, "Newsom Could Use Some Beach Time," *LAT*, April 30, 2020, https://www.latimes.com/california/story/2020-04-30/skelton-california-beaches-coronavirus-gavin-newsom.
70. See Alison Rose Jefferson, *Living the California Dream: African American Leisure Sites during the Jim Crow Era* (Lincoln: University of Nebraska Press, 2020), 51–69.
71. Michael Scott Moore, "California's Novel Attempt at Land Reparations," *New Yorker*, May 27, 2021, https://www.newyorker.com/news/us-journal/californias-novel-attempt-at-land-reparations; the Bruce descendants decided to sell the property back to Los Angeles County in 2023, which has opened up a new debate about what land reparations are supposed to accomplish. See Soumya Karlamangla, "The Debate around Bruce's Beach," *NYT*, March 9, 2023, https://www.nytimes.com/2023/03/09/us/california-bruces-beach.html.
72. John Lanchester, *The Wall* (London: Faber & Faber), 56.

BIBLIOGRAPHY

PRIMARY SOURCES
ARCHIVES AND COLLECTIONS

Bel Air Bay Club, Los Angeles.
   Splashes, Bulletin of the Bel Air Bay Club

Del Webb Sun Cities Museum (online collections).
   The Webb Spinner, https://scdwm.com/web-spinners/

Film & Television Archive, University of California–Los Angeles, Los Angeles.
   Hearst newsreel footage. Santa Monica, Muscle Queen, tape 1, CS1701

Steve Ford Muscle Beach Oral History Collection, http://www.musclebeach.net.

Huntington Library, San Marino, California.
   John Anson Ford Collection

Japanese American Oral History Project, California State University–Fullerton.

Los Angeles City Archives, Records Management Division, Office of the Los Angeles
   City Clerk.
   Annual reports of the Department of Playground & Recreation
   Board of Playground and Recreation Commissioners Minutes
   Council Communications
   Fiscal Year of the Department of Playground & Recreation

Los Angeles Public Library, Los Angeles.
   Photograph Collection, https://tessa.lapl.org/photocol
   "Shades of L.A." Oral History Project, http://www.lapl.org/collections-resources/
   photo-collection/shades-la

Long Beach Historical Society, Long Beach.
   Ephemera Collection

Loyola Marymount University, Los Angeles.
   Fritz Burns Papers
   Werner von Boltenstern Postcard Collection

Margaret Herrick Library, Los Angeles.
   Production Code Administration Records
   Mack Sennett Papers, Production Files
   Thematic folders "beach movies" and "Malibu"

Newport Beach City Archives (online), Newport Beach.
    Council ordinances, http://ecms.newportbeachca.gov/Web/Browse.aspx?star
    tid=33498&cnb=CouncilOrdinances

Santa Monica City Archives, Office of the Santa Monica City Clerk, Santa Monica.
    Proceedings of the City Council
    Thematic folders ("beach" and "breakwater")

Santa Monica History Museum, Santa Monica.
    Photograph Collection
    Scrapbooks Collection

Santa Monica Public Library, Santa Monica.
    California History Collection
    Photograph Collection

Seaver Center for Western History Research, Natural History Museum of Los Angeles
    County, Los Angeles.
    Ephemera Collection

Special Collections, Charles E. Young Research Library, University of California–Los
    Angeles.
    California Ephemera Collection
    Haynes Collection
    Irving Lerner Papers
    Los Angeles Daily News Photograph Collection
    Los Angeles Times Photograph Collection
    Remi Nadeau Papers
    Stuart Z. Perkoff Papers
    Ralph Story's LA Scripts Collection
    UCLA Oral History Archives

Special Collections, Delmar T. Oviatt Library, California State University–Northridge,
    Los Angeles.
    California Tourism and Promotional Literature Collection, 1880–1939, Los
    Angeles County
    Greater Los Angeles Visitors and Convention Bureau Archives

Special Collections, Doheny Library, University of Southern California–Los Angeles.
    Los Angeles Chamber of Commerce Collection
    Los Angeles County Beach Survey of 1947
    Los Angeles Examiner Clippings Collection

University of Southern California Digital Library
    Los Angeles Examiner Photograph Collection, http://digitallibrary.usc.edu/cdm/
    landingpage/collection/p15799coll44

Virtual Oral Archive, California State University–Long Beach.

Water Resources Collections & Archives (WRCA), University of California–Riverside.
    California Bureau of Sanitary Engineering Papers
    Omar Lillevang Papers
    Morrough P. O'Brien Papers

FILMS

The Circus (1928)
The Beach Club, Mack Sennett Comedies (1928)
Double Indemnity, Paramount Pictures (1944)
Mildred Pierce, Warner Bros. (1945)
T-Men, Edward Small Productions (1948)
Quicksand, Samuel H. Stiefel Productions (1950)
Rebel without a Cause, Warner Bros. (1955)
Juvenile Jungle, Coronado Pictures (1958)
Gidget, Columbia Pictures (1959)
Where the Boys Are, MGM (1960)
Gidget Goes Hawaiian, Columbia Pictures (1961)
Beach Party, AIP (1963)
Beach Blanket Bingo, AIP (1964)
Bikini Beach, AIP (1964)
For Those Who Think Young, Aubrey Schenck Productions (1964)
The Horror of Party Beach, Iselin-Tenney Productions (1964)
Muscle Beach Party, AIP (1964)
Pajama Party, AIP (1964)
Surf Party, 20th Century Fox (1964)
Beach Ball, La Honda Services (1965)
The Girls on the Beach, Paramount Pictures (1965)
How to Stuff a Wild Bikini, AIP (1965)
The Endless Summer, Bruce Brown Films (1966)
Baywatch, Paramount Pictures (2017)

INTERVIEWS BY AUTHOR

Byrd, Clara. Phone interview. March 29, 2012.
Connelly, Michael. Phone interview. June 14, 2013.
Gillett, Skip. Personal interview in Los Angeles. April 1, 2012.
Johnson, Merritt. Personal interview in Santa Monica. August 2, 2012.
Koenig, Seymour. Personal interview in Santa Monica. May 14, 2009.
Nagy, Ken. Phone interview. April 18, 2013.
Odor, Sandra. Personal interview in Los Angeles. March 27, 2012.
Ovnick, Merry. Personal interview in Los Angeles. May 13, 2011.
Salter, Jeanette. Personal interview in Beverly Hills. August 17, 2012.
Saylors, Bruce. Personal interview in Santa Monica. August 1, 2012.
Warner, Lois. Phone interview. June 16, 2013.
Windfield, Ann. Personal interview in Paris. May 5, 2013.

NEWSPAPERS

California Eagle
Daily Mail (UK)
Los Angeles Daily News
Los Angeles Examiner
Los Angeles Herald
The Los Angeles Mirror
Los Angeles Sentinel
Los Angeles Times
Los Angeles Tribune

Manhattan Beach (CA) Pilot
Newport News (CA)
The New York Times
Santa Monica (CA) Evening Outlook (other names over the years include *Santa Monica Daily Outlook* and *The Daily Outlook*)
Wall Street Journal
The Washington Post

PERIODICALS

American City
Ebony
Independent Star-News
Life
Look
Newsweek
Saturday Evening Post
Shore & Beach
Strength and Health
The Webb Spinner
Variety
Western City

PUBLISHED SOURCES

Adler, Patricia. *A History of the Venice Area*. Los Angeles: Department of City Planning, 1969.

Ames Taylor, Katherine. *The Los Angeles Tripbook*. New York: Putnam, 1928.

Bartlett, Dana Webster. *The Better City: A Sociological Study of a Modern City*. Los Angeles: Neuner Company Press, 1907.

Blake, Tom, *Hawaiian Surfriders*. Redondo Beach, CA: Mountain & Sea, 1998.

Bogardus, Emory Stephen. *The City Boy and His Problems: A Survey of Boy Life in Los Angeles*. Los Angeles: House of Ralston Printers, 1926.

Brinig, Myron. *The Flutter of an Eyelid*. New York: Farrar & Rinehart, 1933.

Chandler, Raymond. *Farewell, My Lovely*. New York: Vintage Books, 1988 [1940].

Chandler, Raymond. *The Lady in the Lake*. New York: Vintage Books, 1988 [1943].

Cowick, Kate. *The Outlook's Story of Santa Monica*. Santa Monica, CA: The Evening Outlook, 1932.

Edgerton, Robert B. *Alone Together: Social Order on an Urban Beach*. Berkeley: University of California Press, 1979.

Gaines, Charles, and George Butler. *Pumping Iron: The Art and Sport of Bodybuilding*. New York: Simon and Schuster, 1974.

Fante, John, *Ask the Dust*. New York: HarperCollins, 1980.

Federal Writers Project. *Los Angeles: A Guide to the City and Its Environs*. New York: Hastings House, 1941.

Federal Writers Project of the Works Progress Administration of Northern California. *California: A Guide to the Golden State*. New York: Hastings House, 1939.

Feuling, Jim, and Doc Ball. *Early California Surfriders*. Seattle, WA: Pacific Publishing, 1995.

Fray, Al. *Built for Trouble*. New York: Dell, 1958.

Herron, William. *Oral History of Coastal Engineering Activities in Southern California, 1930–1981*. Fort Belvoir, VA: Defense Technical Information Center, 1986.

Hjelte, George. *The Administration of Public Recreation*. New York: Macmillan, 1940.

Hughes, Rupert, *City of Angels*. New York: Scribner's, 1941.

Ingersoll, Luther, A. *Ingersoll's Century History, Santa Monica Bay Cities*. Los Angeles: Ingersoll, 1908.

Ingle, James. *The Movement of Beach Sand: An Analysis Using Fluorescent Grain*. New York: Elsevier, 1966.

Jacobs, Jane. *The Death and Life of Great American Cities*. New York: Vintage Books, 1961.

Johnson, Douglass. *Shore Processes and Shoreline Development*. New York: John Wiley & Sons, 1919.

Johnson, J. W (ed.). *Proceedings of First Conference on Coastal Engineering, Long Beach, October 1950*. Council on Wave Research, Engineering Foundation, 1951.

Kohner, Frederick. *Gidget*. New York: Berkley, 2001 [1957].

Lanchester, John. *The Wall*. London: Faber & Faber, 2019.

Larson, Louise Leung. *Sweet Bamboo: A Memoir of a Chinese American Family*. Berkeley: University of California Press, 1990.

Lipton, Lawrence. *The Holy Barbarians*. New York: Julian Messner, 1959.

Los Angeles & Redondo Railway. *Redondo Beach*. Los Angeles: Los Angeles & Redondo Railway, 1900.

Lurie, Alison. *The Nowhere City*. London: Heinemann, 1965.

McGroarty, John Steven. *Hollywood Riviera*. Los Angeles: Clifford R. Reid Company, 1921.

Nadeau, Remi A. *The New Society*. Philadelphia: D. McKay, 1963.

Nikas, Jerry. *Would You Believe This Was Bal Week '66; The Swinging Easter Week at Balboa in Photos*. Newport Beach, CA: G. N. Nikas Publications, 1966.

Olmsted & Bartholomew. *Parks, Playgrounds and Beaches for the Los Angeles Region*, Los Angeles, 1930. Reprinted in Greg Hise and William F. Deverell, *Eden by Design: The 1930 Olmsted-Bartholomew Plan for the Los Angeles Region*. Berkeley: University of California Press, 2000.

Rechy, John. *City of Night*. New York: Grove Press, 1963.

Redondo Beach Railway Co. *Redondo Beach and the Pleasures You May Have There*. Los Angeles, 1910.

US Congress, *Congressional Record*, volume 28, part 6 (Washington, D.C.: US Government Printing Office, 1896).

Wadsworth, Thomas S. *El Pizmo Beach for Pleasure and Profit*. Los Angeles: Renfrew Adv., 1908.

Wallach, Ira Jan. *Muscle Beach*. Boston: Little, Brown, 1959.

Warren, Charles S. *Santa Monica Community Book*. Santa Monica, CA: A. H. Cawston and Publisher, 1944.

West, Nathanael. *The Day of the Locust*. New York: Random House, 1939.

Wolfe, Tom. *The Pump House Gang*. New York: Farrar, Straus & Giroux, 1964.

Wolff, Maritta. *The Big Nickelodeon*. New York: Random House, 1956.

UNPUBLISHED SOURCES

Botta, Renée A. "Body Image Disturbance in Adolescent Girls: A Test of Thoughtful Processing as an Intervening Variable on the Effects of TV Exposure." PhD dissertation, University of Wisconsin, 1998.

California Department of Boating and Waterways. *California Beach Restoration Study*. Sacramento, January 2002.

California Department of Public Health. *Report on a Pollution Survey of Santa Monica Bay Beaches in 1942*. Sacramento, State of California, 1943.

California Division of Beaches and Parks. *Los Angeles County Beach Study*, 1965.

California Division of Beaches and Parks. *Property Acquisition for the Period of July 1, 1945, to June 30, 1958*. Office of the Auditor General.

California Division of Beaches and Parks. "Too Few for So Many." Brochure, n.d.

California Sewage Works Association. *A Sanitary Survey of Sewage Pollution of the Surf and Beaches of Santa Monica Bay*, 1942.

California State Park Commission. *Preliminary Master Plan of Shoreline Development for the State of California and Status Report on County Master Plans of Acquisition*. Sacramento, 1946.

California Water Conference. *Proceedings of California Water Conference*. Sacramento, California State Printing Office, 1946.

City of Santa Monica. *Annual Report*. 1948.

Committee on Natural Resources, Planning, and Public Works. *Hearing of Conservation and Beaches Subcommittee on the Public Interest in the Shoreline, October 11, 1968, Santa Monica, California. Transcript of Proceedings*, California Legislature, 1969.

Coronado Tent City. *Coronado Tent City, Coronado Beach*. California, 1908.

Greater Los Angeles Citizens Committee. *Shoreline Development Study, Playa Del Rey to Palos Verdes, a Portion of a Proposed Master Recreation Plan for the Greater Los Angeles Region*. Los Angeles, 1944.

Griffin, Donald, and Charles W. Eliot. *Coastline Plans and Action for the Development of the Los Angeles Metropolitan Coastline*. Haynes Foundation, Los Angeles, 1944.

Hanmer, Lee Franklin, *Public Recreation: A Study of Parks, Playgrounds and Other Outdoor Recreation Facilities*. Regional Plan of New York and Its Environs, New York, 1928.

Haynes Foundation. *Parks, Beaches, and Recreational Facilities for Los Angeles County; Report of County Citizens Committee and Experience of Other Metropolitan Counties*. Los Angeles, 1945.

Johnson A. G. *History of Santa Monica Bay Shoreline Development Plans, Los Angeles, California*. Los Angeles, Bureau of Engineering, 1950.

Johnson A. G. *A Report on Erosion of the Beaches in the Venice District*. Los Angeles, The City, 1940.

Joint Legislative Committee on Water Problems. *Report to Legislature on Water Problems of the State of California*. Sacramento, 1943.

Kinder, William Curtis, Jr. "An Investigation of the Administration of California Tidelands." PhD dissertation, University of Southern California–Los Angeles, 1955.

King, William Howard. "A Survey of the Public Bathing Areas in Boston, Massachusetts." PhD dissertation, Boston University, 1949.

Long Beach California Today, Fastest-Growing City in the World. Southern California Publicity Bureau, 1913.

Los Angeles City Planning Commission. *Development Plan for the Santa Monica Bay Shoreline, Topanga Canyon to El Segundo*. Los Angeles, 1945.

Los Angeles City Planning Commission. *Marina Del Rey Area: General Plan Study*. Los Angeles, 1965.

Los Angeles County. *Shoreline Development, County of Los Angeles, 1944; Report on the Revised Master Plan of Shoreline Development, as Amended by the Regional Planning Commission, Los Angeles County Regional Planning District, August 30, 1945, the Regional Planning Commission, County of Los Angeles, August 30, 1945, the Board of Supervisors, County of Los Angeles, September 4, 1945*. Los Angeles, 1946.

Los Angeles County Board of Supervisors. *Proceedings of Meeting of Representatives of Governmental and Private Agencies, Called by the Board of Supervisors of the County of Los Angeles to Consider Beach and Shoreline Problems,* 1940.

Los Angeles Department of Beaches and Harbors. *Historical Changes in the Beaches of Los Angeles County: Malaga Cove to Topanga Canyon: 1935–1990.* Los Angeles, County of Los Angeles, 1992.

Los Angeles Department of City Planning. *Master Plan of Shoreline Development.* Los Angeles, 1941.

Los Angeles Recreation and Youth Services Planning Council. *The Operation of Public Beaches in the Los Angeles Region; Report and Recommendations Submitted to the County of Los Angeles Park and Recreation Commission and Department of Parks and Recreation, and the City of Los Angeles Recreation and Park Commission and Department of Recreation and Parks,* 1964.

Los Angeles Regional Planning Commission. *The Master Plan of Shoreline Development for the Los Angeles County Regional Planning District.* Los Angeles, 1940.

Madigan-Hyland. *Recreational Development of the Los Angeles Area Shoreline: An Engineering and Economic Report to the Mayor and the City Council, City of Los Angeles.* New York, 1949.

Moffatt & Nichol, Engineers. *The Santa Monica Causeway Project Feasibility Study.* Santa Monica, City of Santa Monica, 1964.

Nichols, Woodrow W. "A Spatio-perspective Analysis of the Effect of the Santa Monica and Simi Valley Freeways on Two Selected Black Residential Areas in Los Angeles County." PhD dissertation, University of California–Los Angeles, 1973.

Orange County. *The Master Plan of Shoreline Development for Orange County,* 1941.

Penrod, Vesta. "Civil Rights Problems of Mexican-Americans in Southern California." MA dissertation, Claremont University, 1948.

Redevelopment Agency of the City of Santa Monica. *A New Oceanfront Community to Be Built in Beautiful Santa Monica.* Santa Monica, 1960.

Redevelopment Agency of the City of Santa Monica. *An Appraisal of Neighborhood Environment in the Ocean Park Redevelopment Area.* Santa Monica, 1958.

The Regents of the University of California. "Morrough P. O'Brien: Dean of the College of Engineering, Pioneer in Coastal Engineering, and Consultant to General Electric." College of Engineering Oral History Series, Bancroft Library, 1988.

Rood, Marsha V., and Warren Robert. *The Urban Marina: Managing and Developing Marina del Rey.* Center for Urban Affairs / Sea Grant Program, University of Southern California, 1974.

Souvenir of Long Beach California. Long Beach Heritage Museum, 1984 [1932].

Stapleton, Charles R. "Recreation and Its Problems on the Santa Monica–Venice Shoreline, Southern California." MA dissertation, University of California–Los Angeles, 1952.

United States Army Corps of Engineers, Los Angeles District. *Santa Monica Breakwater, Santa Monica, California: Feasibility Report,* 1995.

United States Senate. *Relocation of Elderly People. Hearings before the Subcommittee on Involuntary Relocation of the Elderly of the Special Committee on Aging.* Washington, DC, 1962.

SOURCES

Addison, Heather. *Hollywood and the Rise of Physical Culture.* London: Routledge, 2003.

Alvarez, Luiz. *The Power of the Zoot: Youth Culture and Resistance during World War II.* Berkeley: University of California Press, 2008.

Avila, Eric. *Popular Culture in the Age of White Flight: Fear and Fantasy in Suburban Los Angeles*. Berkeley: University of California Press, 2004.

Axelrod, Jeremiah B. C. *Inventing Autopia: Dreams and Visions of the Modern Metropolis in Jazz Age Los Angeles*. Berkeley: University of California Press, 2009.

Banham, Reyner. *Los Angeles: The Architecture of Four Ecologies*. Berkeley: University of California Press, 2001 [1971].

Baur, John E. *The Health Seekers of Southern California, 1870–1900*. San Marino, CA: Huntington Library, 2010.

Black, Jonathan. *Making the American Body: The Remarkable Saga of the Men and Women Whose Feats, Feuds, and Passions Shaped Fitness History*. Lincoln: University of Nebraska Press, 2013.

Blackford, Mansel G. *The Lost Dream: Businessmen and City Planning on the Pacific Coast, 1890–1920*. Columbus: Ohio State University Press, 1993.

Bolster, Jeffrey W. "Opportunities in Marine Environmental History." *Environmental History* 11, no. 3 (July 2006): 567–597.

Booth, Douglas. *Australian Beach Cultures: The History of Sun, Sand and Surf*. London: Routledge, 2012.

Borsay, Peter, and John K. Walton. *Resorts and Ports: European Seaside Towns since 1700*. Bristol, UK: Channel View Publications, 2011.

Boyer, Marc. *L'hiver dans le Midi: L'invention de la Côte d'Azur XVIIIe–XXIe siècle*. Paris: Éditions L'Harmattan, 2010.

Campanella, Thomas J. "Robert Moses and His Racist Parkways, Explained." Bloomberg CityLab, July 9, 2017. https://www.bloomberg.com/news/articles/2017-07-09/robert-moses-and-his-racist-parkway-explained.

Capek, Stella M., and John I. Gilderbloom. *Community versus Commodity: Tenants and the American City*. Albany: State University of New York Press, 1992.

Caro, Robert A. *The Power Broker: Robert Moses and the Fall of New York*. New York: Vintage, 1975.

Carvalho, Bruno. "Mapping the Urbanized Beaches of Rio de Janeiro: Modernization, Modernity and Everyday Life." *Journal of Latin American Cultural Studies* 16, no. 3 (2007): 325–339.

Chauncey, George. "The Postwar Sex Crime Panic." In *True Stories from the American Past*, edited by William Graebner, 160–178. New York: McGraw-Hill, 1993.

Chiang, Connie Y. *Nature behind Barbed Wire: An Environmental History of the Japanese American Incarceration*. New York: Oxford University Press, 2018.

Chiang, Connie Y. *Shaping the Shoreline: Fisheries and Tourism on the Monterey Coast*. Seattle: University of Washington Press, 2008.

Chilton McCallister, Linda. *The Waterfront of Manhattan Beach*. Manhattan Beach, CA: Manhattan Beach historical series no. 6, 1978.

Cocks, Catherine. *Tropical Whites: The Rise of the Tourist South in the Americas*. Philadelphia: University of Pennsylvania Press, 2013.

Corbin, Alain. *The Lure of the Sea: The Discovery of the Seaside in the Western World, 1750–1840*. Berkeley: University of California Press, 1994.

Culver, Lawrence. *The Frontier of Leisure: Southern California and the Shaping of Modern America*. New York: Oxford University Press, 2010.

Davidson, Ronald A. "Before 'Surfurbia': The Development of the South Bay Beach Cities through the 1930s." *APCG Yearbook* 66 (2004): 81–94.

Davis, Clark. "From Oasis to Metropolis: Southern California and the Changing Context of American Leisure." *Pacific Historical Review* 61, no. 3 (May 1992): 357–386.

Davis, Mike. "The Case for Letting Malibu Burn." *Environmental History Review* 19, no. 2 (1995): 1–36.

Davis, Mike. *City of Quartz: Excavating the Future in Los Angeles*. New York: Vintage Books, 1990.

Davis, Mike. "How Eden Lost Its Garden: A Political History of the Los Angeles Landscape." In *The City: Los Angeles and Urban Theory at the End of the Twentieth Century*, edited by Allen J. Scott and Edward W. Soja, 160–185. Berkeley: University of California Press, 1996.

Dean, Cornelia. *Against the Tide: The Battle for the American Coast*. New York: Columbia University Press, 1999.

DeCordova, Richard. *Picture Personalities: The Emergence of the Star System in America*. Champaign: University of Illinois Press, 2001.

Deener, Andrew. *Venice: A Contested Bohemia in Los Angeles*. Chicago: University of Chicago Press, 2012.

D'Emilio, John. *Sexual Politics, Sexual Communities: The Making of a Homosexual Minority in the United States, 1940–1970*. Chicago: University of Chicago Press, 1998.

Dennis, Jan. *A Walk beside the Sea: A History of Manhattan Beach*. Manhattan Beach, CA: Janstan Studio, 1987.

DePond, Margaret. "Southland Surf: Hawaiians, Surfing, and Race in Los Angeles, 1907–1928." *Southern California Quarterly* 101, no. 1 (February 1, 2019): 45–78.

Deverell, William F. "The Los Angeles 'Free Harbor Fight.'" *California History* 70, no. 1 (March 1991): 12–29.

Deverell, William F. *Whitewashed Adobe: The Rise of Los Angeles and the Remaking of Its Mexican Past*. Berkeley: University of California Press, 2004.

Deverell, William F., and Greg Hise. *Eden by Design: The 1930 Olmsted-Bartholomew Plan for the Los Angeles Region*. Berkeley: University of California Press, 2000.

Deverell, William F., and Greg Hise, eds. *Land of Sunshine: An Environmental History of Metropolitan Los Angeles*. Pittsburgh: University of Pittsburgh Press, 2005.

Deverell, William F., and Tom Sitton, eds. *California Progressivism Revisited*. Berkeley: University of California Press, 1994.

Devienne, Elsa. "City Limits: Bather Arrests in Early 20th-Century Los Angeles." *Modes pratiques. Journal of Clothes and Fashion History*, Special issue (January 2018): 48–65.

Devienne, Elsa. "The Life, Death, and Rebirth of Muscle Beach: Reassessing Muscularity in Postwar America." *Southern California Quarterly* 100, no. 3 (2018): 324–367.

D'Haeyere, Hilde. "Splashes of Fun and Beauty: Mack Sennett's Bathing Beauties." In *Slapstick Comedy*, edited by Tom Paulus and Rob King, 207–255. London: Taylor & Francis, 2009.

Diamond, Andrew J. *Chicago on the Make: Power and Inequality in a Modern City*. Berkeley: University of California Press, 2017.

Diamond, Andrew J. *Mean Streets: Chicago Youths and the Everyday Struggle for Empowerment in the Multiracial City, 1908–1969*. Berkeley: University of California Press, 2009.

Diamond, Andrew J., and Thomas J. Sugrue, eds. *Neoliberal Cities: The Remaking of Postwar Urban America*. New York: New York University Press, 2020.

Doherty, Thomas. *Teenagers and Teenpics: The Juvenilization of American Movies in the 1950s*. Philadelphia: Temple University Press, 2002.

Douglass, John G., Kathleen L. Hull, and Seetha N. Reddy. "The Creation of Community in the Colonial Era Los Angeles Basin." In *Forging Communities in*

Colonial Alta California, edited by Kathleen L. Hull and John G. Douglass, 35–61. Tucson: University of Arizona Press, 2018.

Dunbar-Hester, Christina. *Oil Beach: How Toxic Infrastructure Threatens Life in the Ports of Los Angeles and Beyond*. Chicago: University of Chicago Press, 2023.

Durand, Stéphane, "L'apprentissage des lois de la nature. L'impact environnemental des aménagements portuaires en Languedoc aux XVIIe et XVIIIe siècle." In *Aménagement et environnement. Perspectives historiques*, edited by Geneviève Massard-Guilbaud and Patrick Fournier, 219–230. Rennes: Presses universitaires de Rennes, 2016.

Elkind, Sarah S. *How Local Politics Shape Federal Policy: Business, Power, and the Environment in Twentieth-Century Los Angeles*. Chapel Hill: University of North Carolina Press, 2011.

Elkind, Sarah S. "Oil in the City: The Fall and Rise of Oil Drilling in Los Angeles." *Journal of American History* 99, no. 1 (June 2012): 82–90.

Faderman, Lillian, and Stuart Timmons. *Gay L.A.: A History of Sexual Outlaws, Power Politics, and Lipstick Lesbians*. Berkeley: University of California Press, 2009.

Fass, Paula S. *The Damned and the Beautiful: American Youth in the 1920s*. New York: Oxford University Press, 1977.

Federal Writers' Project. *California in the 1930s: The WPA Guide to the Golden State*. Berkeley: University of California Press, 2013.

Fiege, Mark. *The Republic of Nature: An Environmental History of the United States*. Seattle: University of Washington Press, 2013.

Fingal, Sara. "Turning the Tide: The Politics of Land and Leisure on the California and Mexican Coastlines in the Age of Environmentalism." PhD dissertation, Brown University, 2012.

Fisher, Colin. "Outdoor Recreation and the Chicago Race Riot." In *To Love the Wind and the Rain: Essays in African American Environmental History*, edited by Dianne Glave and Mark Stoll, 63–76. Pittsburgh, University of Pittsburgh Press, 2005.

Flamming, Douglas. *Bound for Freedom: Black Los Angeles in Jim Crow America*. Berkeley: University of California Press, 2006.

Fogelson, Robert M. *The Fragmented Metropolis: Los Angeles, 1850–1930*. Berkeley: University of California Press, 1993.

Ford, Caroline M. *Sydney Beaches: A History*. Sydney: New South Wales University Press, 2014.

Frank, Thomas. *The Conquest of Cool: Business Culture, Counterculture, and the Rise of Hip Consumerism*. Chicago: University of Chicago Press, 1997.

Freedman, Estelle B. "'Uncontrolled Desires': The Response to the Sexual Psychopath, 1920–1960." *Journal of American History* 74, no. 1 (June 1987): 83–106.

Freitas, Joana Gaspar de, Robert James, and Isaac Land. "Coastal Studies and Society: The Tipping Point." *Coastal Studies & Society* 1, no. 1 (2022): 3–9.

Fulton, William B. *The Reluctant Metropolis: The Politics of Urban Growth in Los Angeles*. Baltimore: Johns Hopkins University Press, 2001.

Gabriel, Louise B. *Santa Monica: 1950–2010*. Mount Pleasant, SC: Arcadia Publishing, 2011.

Garner, Alice. *A Shifting Shore: Locals, Outsiders, and the Transformation of a French Fishing Town, 1823–2000*. Ithaca, NY: Cornell University Press, 2005.

Gergen, David. *Eyewitness to Power: The Essence of Leadership: Nixon to Clinton*. New York: Simon and Schuster, 2000.

Gerstle, Gary. "The Working Class Goes to War." In *The War in American Culture: Society and Consciousness during World War II*, edited by Lewis A. Erenberg and Susan E. Hirsch, 105–127. Chicago: University of Chicago Press, 1996.

Gilfoyle, Timothy J. "White Cities, Linguistic Turns, and Disneylands: The New Paradigms of Urban History." *Reviews in American History* 26, no. 1 (1998): 175–204.

Gillis, John R. *The Human Shore: Seacoasts in History*. Chicago: University of Chicago Press, 2012.

Gottlieb, Robert. *Forcing the Spring: The Transformation of the American Environmental Movement*. Washington, DC: Island Press, 2005.

Graham, Gael. "Flaunting the Freak Flag: *Karr v. Schmidt* and the Great Hair Debate in American High Schools, 1965–1975." *Journal of American History* 91, no. 2 (September 2004): 522–543.

Granger, Christophe. *Les corps d'été: naissance d'une variation saisonnière, XXe siècle*. Paris: Autrement, 2009.

Green, Harvey. *Fit for America: Health, Fitness, Sport, and American Society*. New York: Pantheon Books, 1986.

Griggs, Gary. *Living with the Changing California Coast*. Berkeley: University of California Press, 2005.

Grogan, Sarah, et al. "Femininity and Muscularity: Accounts of Seven Women Body Builders." *Journal of Gender Studies* 13, no. 1 (2004): 49–61.

Hassan, John. "Were Health Resorts Bad for Your Health? Coastal Pollution Control Policy in England, 1945–76." *Environment and History* 5 (February 1999): 53–74.

Hays, Samuel P. *Conservation and the Gospel of Efficiency: The Progressive Conservation Movement, 1890–1920*. Pittsburgh: University of Pittsburgh Press, 1999.

Herlihy, Mark Allan. "Leisure, Space, and Collective Memory in the 'Athens of America': A History of Boston's Revere Beach." PhD dissertation, Brown University, 2000.

Higham, John. "The Reorientation of American Culture in the 1890s." In *The Origins of Modern Consciousness*, edited by Carl Guarneri, 42–47. Detroit: Wayne State University Press, 1965.

Hise, Greg. *Magnetic Los Angeles: Planning the Twentieth-Century Metropolis*. Baltimore: Johns Hopkins University Press, 1999.

Hoy, Suellen. *Chasing Dirt: The American Pursuit of Cleanliness*. New York: Oxford University Press, 1995.

Hughes, Thomas. *American Genesis: A Century of Invention and Technological Enthusiasm*. New York: Penguin, 1990.

Huntsman, Leone. *Sand in Our Souls: The Beach in Australian History*. Melbourne: Melbourne University Press, 2001.

Hurewitz, Daniel. *Bohemian Los Angeles and the Making of Modern Politics*. Berkeley: University of California Press, 2007.

Hyra, Derek S. "Conceptualizing the New Urban Renewal: Comparing the Past to the Present." *Urban Affairs Review* 48, no. 4 (July 2012): 498–527.

Isenberg, Alison. *Designing San Francisco: Art, Land and Urban Renewal in the City by the Bay*. Princeton, NJ: Princeton University Press, 2017.

Isenberg, Alison. *Downtown America: A History of the Place and the People Who Made It*. Chicago: University of Chicago Press, 2004.

Jefferson, Alison Rose. "African-American Leisure Space in Santa Monica: The Beach Sometimes Known as the 'Inkwell,' 1900s–1960s." *Southern California Quarterly* 91, no. 2 (Summer 2009): 155–189.

Jefferson, Alison Rose. *Living the California Dream: African American Leisure Sites during the Jim Crow Era*. Lincoln: University of Nebraska Press, 2020.

Kahrl, Andrew W. *Free the Beaches: The Story of Ned Coll and the Battle for America's Most Exclusive Shoreline*. New Haven, CT: Yale University Press, 2018.

Kahrl, Andrew W. *The Land Was Ours: African American Beaches from Jim Crow to the Sunbelt South*. Cambridge, MA: Harvard University Press, 2012.

Kahrl, Andrew W. "New Negroes at the Beach: At Work and Play outside the Black Metropolis." In *The New Negro Renaissance beyond Harlem*, edited by Davarian L. Baldwin and Minkah Makalani, 335–358. Minneapolis: University of Minnesota Press, 2013.

Kahrl, Andrew W. "'The Slightest Semblance of Unruliness': Steamboat Excursions, Pleasure Resorts, and the Emergence of Segregation Culture on the Potomac River." *Journal of American History* 94, no. 4 (2008): 1108–1136.

Kasson, John F. *Amusing the Million: Coney Island at the Turn of the Century*. New York: Hill & Wang, 1978.

Kasson, John F. *Houdini, Tarzan, and the Perfect Man: The White Male Body and the Challenge of Modernity in America*. New York: Hill & Wang, 2001.

Kaufman, Wallace, and Orrin H. Pilkey. *The Beaches Are Moving: The Drowning of America's Shoreline*. Durham, NC: Duke University Press, 1983.

Kaufmann, Jean-Claude. *Corps de femmes, regards d'hommes. Sociologie des seins nus*. Paris: Nathan, 1995.

Kelley, Robin D. G. *Race Rebels: Culture, Politics, and the Black Working Class*. New York: Free Press, 1994.

Kilston, Lyra. *Sun Seekers: The Cure of California*. Los Angeles: Ateliers Editions, 2019.

Kimble, James K. *Mobilizing the Home Front: War Bonds and Domestic Propaganda*. College Station: Texas A&M University Press, 2006.

Koppes, Clayton R., and Gregory D. Black. *Hollywood Goes to War: Patriotism, Movies and the Second World War*. New York: Free Press, 1987.

Kraus, Nicholas C., ed. *History and Heritage of Coastal Engineering: A Collection of Papers on the History of Coastal Engineering in Countries Hosting the International Coastal Engineering Conference 1950–1996: Prepared under the Auspices of the Coastal Engineering Research Council of the American Society of Civil Engineers*. New York: American Society of Civil Engineers, 1996.

Krintz, Jennifer. *Redondo Beach Pier*. Charleston, SC: Arcadia Publishing, 2011.

Kruse, Kevin M. *White Flight: Atlanta and the Making of Modern Conservatism*. Princeton, NJ: Princeton University Press, 2007.

Ladd, Tony, and James A. Mathison, eds. *Muscular Christianity: Evangelical Protestants and the Development of American Sport*. Grand Rapids: Baker Books, 1999.

Land, Isaac. "Tidal Waves: The New Coastal History." *Journal of Social History* 40, no. 3 (Spring 2007): 731–743.

Land, Isaac. "The Urban Amphibious." In *The New Coastal History: Cultural and Environmental Perspectives from Scotland and Beyond*, edited by David Worthington, 31–48. London: Palgrave Macmillan, 2017.

Lawler, Kristin. *The American Surfer: Radical Culture and Capitalism*. London: Taylor & Francis, 2011.

Lipsitz, George. "The Making of Disneyland." In *True Stories from the American Past*, edited by William Graebner, 179–196. New York: McGraw-Hill, 1993.

Lotchin, Roger W. *The Bad City in the Good War: San Francisco, Los Angeles, Oakland and San Diego*. Bloomington: Indiana University Press, 2008.

Lovas, Paul. *Topanga Beach Experience 1960s–70s*. Los Angeles: Brass Tacks Press, 2011.

Luciano, Lynne. *Looking Good: Male Body in Modern America*. New York: Hill & Wang, 2002.

Marquez, Ernest. *Tony Cornero and the Notorious Gambling Ships of Southern California*. Los Angeles: Angel City Press, 2011.

Matsumoto, Valerie J. *City Girls: The Nisei Social World in Los Angeles, 1920–1950*. New York: Oxford University Press 2014.

May, Kirse Granat. *Golden State, Golden Youth: The California Image in Popular Culture, 1955–1966*. Chapel Hill: University of North Carolina Press, 2002.

Maynard, John Arthur. *Venice West: The Beat Generation in Southern California*. New Brunswick, NJ: Rutgers University Press, 1991.

Mazón, Maurizio. *The Zoot-Suit Riots: The Psychology of Symbolic Annihilation*. Austin: University of Texas Press, 1984.

McGirr, Lisa. *Suburban Warriors: The Origins of the New American Right*. Princeton, NJ: Princeton University Press, 2001.

McKenzie, Shelly. *Getting Physical: The Rise of Fitness Culture in America*. Lawrence: University Press of Kansas, 2013.

McWilliams, Carey. *Southern California: An Island on the Land*. Santa Barbara, CA: Peregrine Smith, 1973 [1946].

Mehlman Petrzela, Natalia. *Fit Nation: The Gains and Pains of America's Exercise Obsession*. Chicago: University of Chicago Press, 2023.

Mehlman Petrzela, Natalia. "From Performance to Participation: The Origins of the Fit Nation." *Transatlantica* [Online], 2 | 2020, Online since March1, 2021; connection on May 11, 2022. http://journals.openedition.org/transatlantica/16318.

Meyer Arendt, Klaus J. "Historical Coastal Environmental Changes: Human Responses to Shoreline Erosion." In *The American Environment: Interpretations of Past Geographies*, edited by Craig E. Colten and Lary M. Dilsaver, 217–234. Lanham, MD: Rowman and Littlefield, 1992.

Monjardet, Dominique. *Ce que fait la police. Sociologie de la force publique*. Paris: La Découverte, 1996.

Mormino, Gary R. *Land of Sunshine, State of Dreams: A Social History of Modern Florida*. Gainesville: University Press of Florida, 2008.

Morris, Gary. "Beyond the Beach. Social & Formal Aspects of AIP's Beach Party Movies." *Journal of Popular Film and Television* 21, no. 1 (Spring 1993): 2–12.

Mowll Mathews, Nancy. *Moving Pictures: American Art and Film, 1880–1910*. Manchester, VT: Hudson Hills Press, 2005.

Nasaw, David. *Going Out: The Rise and Fall of Public Amusements*. Cambridge, MA: Harvard University Press, 1999.

Nash, Roderick. *Wilderness and the American Mind*. New Haven, CT: Yale University Press, 2001 [1967].

Nicolaides, Becky M. *My Blue Heaven: Life and Politics in the Working-Class Suburbs of Los Angeles, 1920–1965*. Chicago: University of Chicago Press, 2002.

Okihiro, Gary Y. *Island World: A History of Hawai'i and the United States*. Berkeley: University of California Press, 2008.

Orsi, Jared. *Hazardous Metropolis: Flooding and Urban Ecology in Los Angeles*. Berkeley: University of California Press, 2004.

Orsi, Jared. "Restoring the Common to the Goose: Citizen Activism and the Protection of the California Coastline, 1969–1982." *Southern California Quarterly* 78, no. 3 (Fall 1996): 257–284.

Osborne, Thomas J. *Coastal Sage: Peter Douglas and the Fight to Save California's Shore*. Oakland: University of California Press, 2018.

Osgerby, Bill. *Playboys in Paradise: Masculinity, Youth and Leisure-Style in Modern America*. Oxford: Berg, 2001.

Obregón Pagán, Eduardo. "Los Angeles Geopolitics and the Zoot Suit Riot, 1943." *Social Science History* 24, no. 1 (Spring 2000): 223–256.

Obregón Pagán, Eduardo. *Murder at the Sleepy Lagoon: Zoot Suits, Race & Riot in Wartime L.A.* Chapel Hill: University of North Carolina Press, 2003.

Palladino, Grace. *Teenagers: An American History*. New York: Basic Books, 1996.

Parrinello, Giacomo, et al. "Shifting Shores of the Anthropocene: The Settlement and (Unstable) Stabilisation of the North-Western Mediterranean Littoral over the Nineteenth and Twentieth Centuries." *Environment and History* 28, no. 1 (February 2022): 129–154.

Patterson Smith, James. "Local Leadership, the Biloxi Beach Riot, and the Origins of the Civil Rights Movement on the Mississippi Gulf Coast, 1959–1964." In *Sunbelt Revolution. The Historical Progression of the Civil Rights Struggle in the Gulf South, 1866–2000*, edited by Samuel C. Hyde Jr., 210–230. Gainesville: University Press of Florida, 2003.

Peiss, Kathy. *Cheap Amusements: Working Women and Leisure in Turn-of-the-Century New York*. Philadelphia: Temple University Press, 1987.

Peiss, Kathy. *Zoot Suit: The Enigmatic Career of an Extreme Style*. Philadelphia: University of Pennsylvania Press, 2011.

Perret-Gentil, Yves, Alain Lottin, and Jean-Pierre Poussou, eds. *Les villes balnéaires d'Europe occidentale du XVIIIe siècle à nos jours*. Paris: PUPS, 2008.

Peters, Deike. "Density Wars in Silicon Beach: The Struggle to Mix New Space for Toil, Stay and Play in Santa Monica, California." In *Protest and Resistance in the Tourist City*, edited by Claire Colomb and Johannes Novy, 90–106. London: Routledge, 2017.

Pilkey, Orrin H., and Katharine L. Dixon. *The Corps and the Shore*. Washington, DC: Island Press, 1996.

Rainis, Michel. "French Beach Sports Culture in the Twentieth Century." *International Journal of the History of Sport* 17, no. 1 (March 2000): 144–158.

Randall, David K. *The King and Queen of Malibu: The True Story of the Battle for Paradise*. New York: W. W. Norton & Company, 2017.

Rhode, Paul. "California in the Second World War: An Analysis of Defense Spending." In *The Way We Really Were: The Golden State in the Second Great War*, edited by Robert Lotchin, 93–119. Urbana: University of Illinois Press, 2000.

Roeder, George H. *The Censored War: American Visual Experience during World War Two*, New Haven, CT: Yale University Press, 1993.

Rome, Adam W. *The Bulldozer in the Countryside: Suburban Sprawl and the Rise of American Environmentalism*. Cambridge, MA: Cambridge University Press, 2001.

Rome, Adam W. *The Genius of Earth Day: How a 1970 Teach-In Unexpectedly Made the First Green Generation*. New York: Hill and Wang, 2013.

Rose, Marla Matzer. *Muscle Beach*. New York: St. Martin's Griffin, 2001.

Rosenzweig, Roy, and Elizabeth Blackmar. *The Park and the People: A History of Central Park*. Ithaca, NY: Cornell University Press, 1998.

Rozwadowski, Helen M. "The Promise of Ocean History for Environmental History." *Journal of American History* 100, no. 1 (June 2013): 136–139.

Russello Ammon, Francesca. *Bulldozer: Demolition and Clearance of the Postwar Landscape*. New Haven: Yale University Press, 2016.

Russello Ammon, Francesca. "Postindustrialization and the City of Consumption: Attempted Revitalization in Asbury Park, New Jersey." *Journal of Urban History* 41, no. 2 (2015): 158–174.

Rutsky, R. L. "Surfing the Other: Ideology on the Beach." *Film Quarterly* 52, no. 4 (Summer 1999): 12–23.

Sabin, Paul. "Beaches versus Oil in Greater Los Angeles." In *Land of Sunshine: An Environmental History of Metropolitan Los Angeles*, edited by William F. Deverell and Greg Hise, 95–114. Pittsburgh: University of Pittsburgh Press, 2005.

Sabol Spezio, Teresa. *Slick Policy: Environmental and Science Policy in the Aftermath of the Santa Barbara Oil Spill*. Pittsburgh: University of Pittsburgh Press, 2018.

Sánchez, George J. *Becoming Mexican-American: Ethnicity, Culture, and Identity in Chicano Los Angeles, 1900–1945*. New York: Oxford University Press, 1993.

Sandoval-Strausz, Andrew K. "Latino Landscapes: Postwar Cities and the Transnational Origins of a New Urban America." *Journal of American History* 101, no. 3 (December 2014): 804–831.

Schlichting, Kara Murphy. "Hot Town: Sensing Heat in Summertime Manhattan." *Environmental History* 27, no. 2 (April 2022): 354–368.

Schlichting, Kara Murphy. *New York Recentered: Building the Metropolis from the Shore*. Chicago: University of Chicago Press, 2019.

Scott, Paula A. *Santa Monica: A History on the Edge*. Mount Pleasant, SC: Arcadia Publishing, 2004.

Seely, Bruce. "Research, Engineering, and Science in American Engineering Colleges: 1900–1960." *Technology and Culture* 34, no 2 (April 1993): 344–386.

Self, Robert O. *American Babylon: Race and the Struggle for Postwar Oakland*. Princeton, NJ: Princeton University Press, 2003.

Shanken, Andrew M. "Planning Memory: Living Memorials in the United States during World War II." *Art Bulletin* 84, no. 1 (2002): 130–147.

Sharpsteen, Bill. *Dirty Water: One Man's Fight to Clean Up One of the World's Most Polluted Bays*. Berkeley: University of California Press, 2010.

Sides, Josh. *L.A. City Limits: African American Los Angeles from the Great Depression to the Present*. Berkeley: University of California Press, 2003.

simon, Bryant. *Boardwalk of Dreams: Atlantic City and the Fate of Urban America*. New York: Oxford University Press, 2006.

Sitton, Tom. *Los Angeles Transformed: Fletcher Bowron's Urban Reform Revival, 1938–1953*. Albuquerque: University of New Mexico Press, 2005.

Sklar, Anna. *Brown Acres: An Intimate History of the Los Angeles Sewers*. Santa Monica, CA: Angel City Press, 2008.

Solomons, Gabriel. *World Film Locations: Los Angeles*. Chicago: University of Chicago Press, 2011.

Stanton, Jeffrey. *Santa Monica Pier: A History from 1875 to 1990*. Los Angeles: Donahue Publishing, 1990.

Starr, Kevin. *The Dream Endures: California Enters the 1940s*. New York: Oxford University Press, 1997.

Starr, Kevin. *Embattled Dreams: California in War and Peace, 1940–1950*. New York: Oxford University Press, 2002.

Starr, Kevin. *Endangered Dreams: The Great Depression in California*. New York: Oxford University Press, 1996.

Starr, Kevin. *Golden Dreams: California in an Age of Abundance, 1950–1963*. New York: Oxford University Press, 2009.

Starr, Kevin. *Inventing the Dream: California through the Progressive Era*. New York: Oxford University Press, 1985.

Starr, Kevin. *Material Dreams: Southern California through the 1920s*. New York: Oxford University Press, 1990.

Stenger, John. "Mapping the Beach: Beach Movies, Exploitation Film, and Geographies of Whiteness." In *The Persistence of Whiteness: Race and Contemporary Hollywood Cinema*, edited by Daniel Bernardi, 28–50. London: Routledge, 2008.

Sterngass, Jon. *First Resorts: Pursuing Pleasure at Saratoga Springs, Newport, and Coney Island*. Baltimore: Johns Hopkins University Press, 2001.

Strub, Whitney. "The Clearly Obscene and the Queerly Obscene: Heteronormativity and Obscenity in Cold War Los Angeles." *American Quarterly* 60, no. 8 (June 2008): 373–398.

Sugrue, Thomas J. *The Origins of the Urban Crisis: Race and Inequality in Postwar Detroit*. Princeton, NJ: Princeton University Press, 2005 [1996].

Tarr, Joel A. *The Search for the Ultimate Sink: Urban Pollution in Historical Perspective*. Akron, OH: University of Akron Press, 1996.

Tatjer, Mercedes. "En los orígenes del turismo litoral: Los banos del mar y los balnearios marítimos en Cataluna." *Scripta Nova* 13 no. 296 (5) (August 2009): http://www.ub.edu/geocrit/sn/sn-296/sn-296-5.htm.

Teaford, John C. *The Metropolitan Revolution: The Rise of Post-Urban America*. New York: Columbia University Press, 2006.

Teaford, John C. "Urban Renewal and Its Aftermath." *Housing Policy Debate* 11, no. 2 (2000): 443–465.

Thompson, Heather Ann. "Why Mass Incarceration Matters: Rethinking Crisis, Decline, and Transformation in Postwar American History." *Journal of American History* 97, no. 3 (December 2010): 703–734.

Todd, Jan, and Terry Todd. "The Last Interview." *Iron Game History* 6, no. 4 (December 2000): 1–14.

Todd, Terry. "Armand Tanny Remembers Steve Reeves." *Iron Game History* 6, no. 4 (December 2000): 24–26.

Tyler May, Elaine. *Homeward Bound: American Families in the Cold War Era*. New York: Basic Books, 1988.

Verge, Arthur C. "Daily Life in Wartime California." In *The Way We Really Were: The Golden State in the Second Great War*, edited by Roger W. Lotchin, 289–314. Urbana: University of Illinois Press, 2000.

Verge, Arthur C. "George Freeth: King of the Surfers and California's Forgotten Hero." *California History* 80, no. 2/3 (Summer–Fall 2001): 82–105.

Verge, Arthur C. "The Impact of the Second World War on Los Angeles." *Pacific Historical Review*. 63, no. 3 (August 1994): 289–314.

Verge, Arthur C. *Los Angeles County Lifeguards*. Charleston, SC: Arcadia Publishing, 2005.

Verge, Arthur C. *Paradise Transformed: Los Angeles during the Second World War*. Dubuque, IA: Kendall/Hunt, 1993.

Verge, Arthur C. *Santa Monica Lifeguards*. Charleston, SC: Arcadia Publishing, 2007.

Viehe, Fred W. "Black Gold Suburbs: The Influence of the Extractive Industry on the Suburbanization of Los Angeles, 1890–1930." *Journal of Urban History* 8, no. 1 (November 1981): 3–26.

Vincent, Johan. *L'intrusion balnéaire. Les populations littorales bretonnes et vendéennes face au tourisme (1800–1945)*. Rennes: Presses Universitaires de Rennes, 2007.

Vitousek, Sean, et al. "A Model Integrating Longshore and Cross-Shore Processes for Predicting Long-Term Shoreline Response to Climate Change." *Journal of Geophysical Research: Earth Surface* 122, no. 4 (2017): 782–806.

Walker, Richard A. *The Country in the City: The Greening of the San Francisco Bay Area*. Seattle: University of Washington Press, 2007.

Walton, John K. *Resorts and Ports: European Seaside Towns since 1700*. Bristol, UK: Channel View Publications, 2011.

Walton, John K., and Gary Cross. *The Playful Crowd: Pleasure Places in the Twentieth Century*. New York: Columbia University Press, 2005.

Warshaw, Matt. *The History of Surfing*. San Francisco: Chronicle Books, 2010.

Wells, Jamin. *Shipwrecked: Coastal Disasters and the Making of the American Beach*. Chapel Hill: University of North Carolina Press, 2020.

Westwick, Peter, and Peter Neushul. *The World in the Curl: An Unconventional History of Surfing*. New York: Crown Publishers, 2013.

Whiting, Cecil. *Pop LA: Art and the City in the 1960s*. Berkeley: University of California Press, 2006.

Wiegel, Robert, and Thorndike Saville Jr. "History of Coastal Engineering in the USA." In *History and Heritage of Coastal Engineering*, edited by Nicolas C. Kraus, 513–600. New York: American Society of Civil Engineers, 1996.

Willis, Deborah. *Posing Beauty: African American Images from the 1890s to the Present*. New York: W. W. Norton & Co., 2009.

Wiltse, Jeff. *Contested Waters: A Social History of Swimming Pools in America*. Chapel Hill: University of North Carolina Press, 2007.

wolcott, Victoria W. *Race, Riots, and Roller Coasters: The Struggle over Segregated Recreation in America*. Philadelphia: University of Pennsylvania Press, 2012.

Worthington, David. "Introducing the New Coastal History: Cultural and Environmental Perspectives from Scotland and Beyond." In *The New Coastal History: Cultural and Environmental Perspectives from Scotland and Beyond*, edited by David Worthington, 3–30. London: Palgrave Macmillan, 2017.

Zinkin, Harold, and Bonnie Hearn. *Remembering Muscle Beach: Where Hard Bodies Began: Photographs and Memories*. Santa Monica, CA: Angel City Press, 1999.

Zukin, Sharon. *Landscapes of Power: From Detroit to Disneyworld*. Berkeley: University of California Press, 1991.

Zukin, Sharon. *Naked City: The Death and Life of Authentic Urban Places*. New York: Oxford University Press, 2010.

INDEX

For the benefit of digital users, indexed terms that span two pages (e.g., 52–53) may, on occasion, appear on only one of those pages.

Figures indicated by an italic *f* following the page number.